*The Sociology
of Social Conflicts*

The Sociology
of Social Conflicts

LOUIS KRIESBERG
Syracuse University

Prentice-Hall, Inc., *Englewood Cliffs, New Jersey*

Library of Congress Cataloging in Publication Data

KRIESBERG, LOUIS.
    The sociology of social conflicts.

    Includes bibliographies.
    1. Social conflict.   2. Social problems.
I. Title.   [DNLM: 1. Conflict (Psychology)
2. Social conditions.   3. Social problems.   HM 136
K92s   1973]
HM136. K77   301.6'3   72–7491
ISBN   0–13–821546–4

PRINTED IN THE UNITED STATES OF AMERICA

10 9 8 7 6 5 4 3 2 1

Prentice-Hall International, Inc., *London*
Prentice-Hall of Australia, Pty. Ltd., *Sydney*
Prentice-Hall of Canada, Ltd., *Toronto*
Prentice-Hall of India Private Limited, *New Delhi*
Prentice-Hall of Japan, Inc., *Tokyo*

For *DANIEL* and *JOSEPH*
and their generation

Contents

Preface

As a teacher of social conflicts and as a partisan and observer of them, I have long felt the need for a comprehensive study of conflicts. I felt it was necessary to bring together the main ideas pertaining to each aspect of a struggle or, better yet, to consistently relate these ideas. This might mean disproving some, reinterpreting others, and specifying and synthesizing still others.

I have tried to meet these needs in this book by presenting a comprehensive analysis of all kinds of group conflicts. Instead of describing certain kinds of conflicts or particular aspects of struggles, this book provides a framework for analyzing all kinds of disputes, struggles, fights, and contentions. The framework is relevant for conflicts between groups in organizations, communities, societies, and even between national governments. For illustrative purposes, the discussion focuses upon some recent struggles: women's liberation, the cold war, the Arab–Israeli conflict, collective bargaining, student protests, and the fight for racial equality.

In presenting a comprehensive framework, I hope to raise important and neglected questions. We shall ask about de-escalation as well as escalation, outcomes as well as bases, and noncoercive as well as coercive means of conducting struggles. We will ask why fights differ in consequences, in origins, and in violence.

In answering these questions I have tried to be systematic and specific. Nevertheless, competing ideas and interpretations have not been excluded. I have sought to counterpose plausible ideas and to assess them. I have tried to be honest and open about the theoretical and evidential difficulties with the positions taken. Rather than gloss over the problems, I have directly discussed them and given my best current judgment.

The general orientation of this work is sociological, but I have not hesitated to draw upon theoretical and empirical work from political science, anthropology, economics, psychology, and history. I have also examined and analyzed sample surveys, newspaper accounts, census, and other kinds of data to probe some of the ideas examined in the illustrative cases.

The comprehensive scope of this effort necessarily leaves out many details. More significantly, many issues are inadequately resolved. I hope that my efforts will stimulate and facilitate the work of others to overcome those failures. I hope to continue in that endeavor myself.

Acknowledgments

This kind of book requires the author (and the reader) to draw upon personal experiences. I have drawn much from my own engagement in a variety of social conflicts and the several roles I have played in them. I owe a debt to those with whom I have fought as allies and adversaries and to the discussions with them about the struggles.

I have necessarily taken ideas and evidence from a wide range of sources, for conflicts pervade all social relations and every kind of social interaction is important to particular struggles. I am indebted especially to my teachers and fellow students at the University of Chicago, and to my colleagues at Columbia University's Department of Sociology and Bureau of Applied Social Research; at the University of Cologne; at the University of Chicago's Law School, Sociology Department, and National Opinion Research Center; and at Syracuse University's Youth Development Center and Sociology Department.

I have learned much about particular conflicts and the social processes implicated in them from casual comments and heated discussions with many persons. It is difficult to cite all of them but I wish to acknowledge some who have so informed me, particularly, Seymour S. Bellin, Irwin Deutscher, Blanche Geer, Warren C. Haggstrom, Everett C. Hughes, Lois Ablin Kriesberg, Martin Kriesberg, S. M. Lipset, S. M. Miller, Lee K-Thorpe, Charles V. Willie, and George Wiley.

This book emerged from the seminar on social conflict I gave over several years and I learned much from the reactions and comments of the participants. For aid in gathering, preparing, and analyzing data for this book I wish to express gratitude to Syracuse University's Educational Policy Research Center and the Computing Center; to The Roper Public Opinion Research Center; and to colleagues at Tel Aviv University, Hebrew University, and The Israel Institute of Applied Social Research. I want to thank Mary Belle-Isle for her conscientious typing of much of the manuscript. Several persons have read one or more chapters of this book; for the observations made, I thank Mark Abrahamson, Irving Kriesberg, Allan Mazur, David Nachmias, Manfred Stanley, and Sidney Sufrin. Since I have persisted in what others have sometimes regarded as errors, they are not responsible for what I say in this book—I am.

*The Sociology
of Social Conflicts*

chapter one

Variations
Among Social Conflicts

All about us are social conflicts. They are inherent in human relations. But this does not mean that every social relationship is entirely or even partly conflicting *all* the time. Nor does it mean that every underlying conflicting relationship will be expressed with the same degree and kind of hostility or violence. Conflicts vary in their bases, their duration, their mode of settlement, their outcomes, and their consequences. This book is about such variations. The focus of concern is upon the development of specific social conflicts, of fights and struggles, rather than upon the role of conflict in social life. It is about contentions between groups of people, and not within specific groups or between individuals acting alone. Finally, we are more concerned with struggles in which coercion and violence are likely or possible, than with ones which are so highly regulated that coercion and violence do not occur.

The major questions we seek to answer are within these realms. We are inquiring about the conditions that produce violent fights. We want to know what makes groups believe that they have incompatible goals. We want to know how aggrieved groups seek justice. We ask why some groups do, and others do not, attain what they seek. We want to learn the consequences of conflict for the contending parties and for the larger system of which they are a part, even if those consequences are not desired or anticipated by any of the parties.

In trying to answer these and related questions we will assume that all conflicts have some things in common. We assume it possible and even useful to consider the similarities as well as the differences among class, community, international, and industrial struggles. Having said that, it is also necessary to point out that there is a wide variety of social conflicts. In order to begin to answer the questions we have raised, it is necessary to distinguish among the different types of conflict and the several aspects or stages in the course of a struggle. In this chapter we will discuss the several types of conflicts and general orientations toward contentions. This discussion will provide the basis for characterizing social conflicts and for the analysis in the rest of the book.

EVALUATIONS OF SOCIAL CONFLICTS

Conflicts are exciting. People certainly are drawn to their study because of that stimulation as well as from intellectual curiosity. Other persons may be drawn to study social conflicts because they want help in deciding what stand to take on an issue. Many others, to a greater or lesser extent, are partisans in a social conflict. Whatever the stimulus or incentive to study conflicts, two major evaluative orientations may be discerned among students of social strife.

Some persons are concerned about the disruptiveness or violence of fights. They see a larger collectivity or system which is threatened or injured by conflict and wish to discover ways of mitigating its disruptive character. Thus, some people may be troubled by the prospects of international wars or interracial violence. For them conflict tends to be evaluated negatively. On the other hand, some persons are concerned about the injustice or repression of some category of persons and, siding with that collectivity, they are interested in learning how such people may form conflict groups and successfully end or reduce their oppression. These persons would tend to view such conflicts as necessary and even desirable.

I have suggested two positions a student of social conflict may take: that of the larger system to which the partisans belong or that of one of the partisans (Gamson, 1968). I have also suggested that the latter students would consider conflict necessary or even admirable while the former would consider it regrettable or even evil. A strong evaluative position may be a powerful motivation for study and analysis, but it also may distort the analysis. The dangers of evaluations corrupting the analysis can be lessened if one keeps in mind alternative viewpoints and a wide range of conflicts.

Even if one takes a partisan perspective it is possible to regard conflict as undesirable. It depends upon who is causing the trouble. Consider the shifting evaluations of community strife. During the early 1950s in the U.S. many persons concerned with community conflict felt it to be unhealthy and dangerous. The prototypical conflict seemed to be attacks from the political right upon the good liberal establishment which was being innovative in the schools or was trying to introduce flouridation into the cities' water systems (Coleman, 1957). In the 1960s community conflicts more often referred to the attempts of the poor and the blacks to gain greater influence in decision making (Haggstrom, 1964). People who were sympathetic to the community controversies of the 1950s are likely to have been unsympathetic to those of the 1960s. Or consider international conflict. Partisans of countries relatively satisfied with the status quo are likely to view international war as reprehensible: they would not accept the legitimacy of a "just war" or a "war of national liberation."

Even taking a system perspective does not mean that one must regard conflict as harmful and evil (Coser, 1956; Simmel, 1955; Sumner, 1952). Thus many persons believe that conflict, properly institutionalized, is an effective vehicle for discovering truth, for attaining justice, and for the long-run benefit of a society as a whole. For example, the American judicial system is based upon the adversary principle. The struggle between the lawyer for the prosecution and the lawyer for the defense, conducted within the court, is considered to be the best way of obtaining justice. Similarly, both management and trade unions in the U.S. now generally feel that the struggle between them, conducted through collective bargaining, serves the interests of the entire society, as well as their own.

Evaluations of conflict in general or of specific struggles depend upon many considerations: for example, upon the unit with which one identifies, upon the issue in contention, and upon the means used in attaining a given outcome. To unconsciously accept a particular evaluation toward a struggle handicaps its analysis and understanding. One safeguard against such implicit assumptions is to keep in mind the many grounds of evaluation and consequently the alternative judgements of the conflict. We cannot simply put aside our own evaluations, but we can avoid ignoring alternative assessments. Another way to avoid some of the risks of examining conflicts from too narrow a point of view is to use a comparable framework of analysis. One of the tasks of this book is to provide such a framework.

DIMENSIONS OF SOCIAL CONFLICTS
AND CONFLICT BEHAVIOR

This analysis of aspects of social conflicts and conflict behavior should serve several purposes. It will indicate disagreement among students of social conflict; this will facilitate the comparison and reading of different writers on the subject. It will provide the basis for distinguishing different kinds of conflicts and the stages in the course of a struggle. It will also underlie the definition of social conflict used in this book and indicate how that definition is related to other definitions in the field and to the framework presented within this book (Fink, 1968; Angell, 1965).

Awareness. A fundamental aspect of social conflicts is the awareness of the parties that an incompatibility exists. Most writers about social conflict regard consciousness by the parties that they are in contention as an essential element in the definition of a conflict. (Coser, 1956, p. 8; Weber, 1947, pp. 132–133). Thus Park and Burgess state:

> Conflict is always conscious. Indeed it evokes the deepest emotions and strongest passions and enlists the greatest concentration of attention and of effort. Both competition and conflict are forms of struggle. Competition, however, is continuous and impersonal. Conflict is intermittent and personal (Park and Burgess, 1921, p. 574).

This kind of formulation is also followed by Boulding who defines conflict as a form of competition in which the competing parties recognize that they have mutually incompatible goals (Boulding, 1962).

Even formulations of social conflict which emphasize its subjective character often assume that there is an underlying, objective, conflict situation. Presumably, mutually incompatible interests exist whether or not the parties are aware of them. Some writers broaden the definition of conflict to include such objective conditions (Dahrendorf, 1959). Thus, a conflict may be latent and unrecognized by partisans but still exist. Recognizing the distinction between the objective and subjective conflict, some writers have elaborated the various combinations of their relationship (Bernard, 1957). Thus, if one assumes two parties who may or may not be in objectively in a conflict situation; both may *believe* they are, or one may, or neither side may. As shown in Table 1.1, this yields six possibilities. For example, the first possibility includes cases in which both parties correctly perceive that they are in an objective conflict situation. In cell three are instances in which neither party believes they are in conflict, although they are. Instances in which one party but not the other believes they are in conflict and they actually are not are in cell five; this is one kind of "unrealistic conflict."

The relative frequency of instances in each cell is an empirical matter. Some persons argue that "conflicts" often or usually are "unrealistic" in the sense that the parties are not in an objective conflict situation. Such disputes, it might be argued, are the result of agitators creating the belief in a conflict situation. It might also be argued that unrealistic conflicts

TABLE 1.1

Objective Situation	Parties' Belief about Conflict Situation		
	Both believe conflict exists	One believes and other does not	Neither believes conflict exists
Conflicting	1	2	3
Not Conflicting	4	5	6

arise from inadequate or improper communication and presumably could be quickly resolved if the parties better understood each other. This is illustrated by appeals made by political leaders to opponents for understanding and attempting to reassure dissidents by telling them that they are being listened to and heard.

On the other hand, many observers argue that conflicts arise from incompatibility of interests and that parties generally are aware of such incompatibility (Madison, 1937). However, even persons who believe that objective conflict relations underlie awareness may argue that people sometimes falsely believe that there is no conflict. In such cases they might speak of "false consciousness" or charge that the people are being duped and manipulated. Such persons might then go on to argue that leadership and organization are necessary to make the potential partisans aware of their conflicting relations. The success of such leaders in mobilizing the partisans and bringing the conflict to the desired outcome, however, still depends upon the leaders' correctness in interpreting the objective situation. As Lenin said in *"Left-Wing" Communism, an Infantile Disorder*:

> ... in order that actually the whole class, that actually the broad masses of toilers and those oppressed by capital may take up such a position [in support of or neutrality toward the vanguard], propaganda and agitation are not enough. For this the masses must have their own political experience. (Lenin, 1940, p. 74).

The disagreements about the relationship between objective conditions and awareness of incompatible interests is partly a factual matter. Research might resolve the issue. But the differences are also conceptual and theoretical and until these matters are further clarified empirical evidence cannot be clearly relevant. In the next two chapters of this book, we will return to this issue.

Intensity. Another fundamental dimension of social conflict is its degree of intensity. Intensity may vary in terms of the feelings or the behavior of the partisans in the conflict. Feelings may be more or less intense depending upon how strongly committed the partisans are about the goals they wish to reach, how hostile they feel toward each other, and how much they want to harm and injure each other. The intensity of behavior depends upon the means the parties use to attain their aims. They may try to coerce each other and they may use more or less severe forms of coercion. Some observers restrict the term social conflict to disputes in which parties kill or physically harm their adversaries or threaten to do so.

It might seem reasonable to assume that feelings and behavior vary together in intensity. One might expect that if one party wants to injure its adversary, it will; that as the emotional desire to hurt another party increases, so does its use of coercion in expressing that desire. Conversely, great violence is not usually employed without great anger. A little reflection, however, should reveal the inadequacy of such assumptions. There are times when one or both parties to a conflict feel intense hostility and yet do not try to injure the other. They may be deterred by the fear of counter-coercion or by the belief that coercion will not be effective in getting what they want from the adversary. On the other hand, in some circumstances great injury may be inflicted upon an adversary with little or no hostile feeling accompanying the violence. This is most likely when large collectivities are engaged in the conflict; the violence is committed via complex technologies and there is great division of labor in the conduct of the struggle and the use of violence. Such circumstances are especially apparent in international wars where high altitude bombing is employed. Even among infantry combat soldiers, however, "hatred of the enemy, personal and impersonal, was not a major element in combat motivation," the authors of the study of American soldiers in World War II concluded (Stouffer, *et al.*, 1949, p. 166). Dispassionate killing may seem particularly repugnant, but intense hate can be the cause of that personally conducted indiscriminate violence which we call atrocities.

Although behavioral and attitudinal aspects of conflicts can be independent of each other, each may be determined by similar conditions and hence be associated with each other. Feelings and behavior also affect each other. Consequently, as a matter of fact, we do expect some association between these two aspects of conflict intensity.

Regulation. The third dimension of conflict which requires attention is the degree to which it is regulated and institutionalized. Regulations vary in comprehensiveness and precision. Regulations usually include rules about the means used in pursuing incompatible goals to reach a joint decision. They certainly include rules about the kinds and degree of coercion which can be exercised. Established procedures may also delimit the conditions under which force is legitimately exercised and also prescribe what degrees and forms of coercion are legitimate. Thus, in collective bargaining in the United States, rules are agreed upon which define legitimate and illegitimate force.

Regulation is institutionalized insofar as the rules (1) have been internalized by the participants, (2) are expressed in tradition, formal writing, or some other embodiment external to the participants, and (3) are enforced by sanctions (Blau, 1964, pp. 273–76). That is, rules may have more or less effect in prescribing and proscribing conduct. The control of conduct is greater insofar as the participants so believe in the rules that violating them makes the violators feel guilty. The existence of rules in a form which is external to the participants constrains the actors since they are less able to modify the rules by reinterpretation. Finally, the rules are more likely to be followed when violators are known to be punished. Thus, Tittle (1969) found that crime rates are lower when the certainty of punishment is higher.

Certain kinds of conflicts may be so highly regulated and institutionalized that the participants do not even regard themselves as in conflict. Thus, participants in a legal proceeding, partisans in a legislative body, or parties in established electoral races are seeking mutually incompatible goals by procedures which may be so well accepted by all the participants that violence is eschewed and hostility is minimal. The partisans are then in a contest which may even take on some of the spirit of a game being played for the fun of it. The rules which regulate conflict, then, differ in content, specification, and degree of institutionalization. The bases and consequences of conflict regulation and institutionalization are analyzed in chapter 4.

Purity. The fourth dimension of conflict which must be considered is the degree to which the relationship between two parties is purely one of conflict. Two parties with some bases for conflict between them also have some common and complementary interests and therefore could engage in cooperation or exchange, as well as conflict (Kriesberg, 1968). In a larger time or relational context, some nonconflicting relations always can be found. Parties to a dispute, therefore, have varying *proportions* of conflicting relations as well as nonconflicting ones. In a given dispute the conflict is more or less pure or mixed. This can be illustrated in the language of game theory (Von Neuman and Morgenstern, 1944).

In pure conflict, we speak of a zero-sum game. That is, what one side loses, the other side wins. Suppose two persons, Dan and Joe, agree to play a game of matching pennies; if the pennies match, either both heads or both tails, Joe gives Dan a penny; if the pennies do not match, Dan gives Joe a penny. The payoff matrix of this game is shown in

Figure 1.1. We will follow the convention that the actor identified on top of the figure has his payoff written first in each box. In this payoff matrix, you can see that the sum within each box is constant: they add up to zero: it is indeed a zero-sum game.

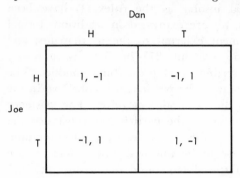

FIGURE 1.1

The other major kind of matrix is nonconstant sum; one interesting variety of this is the mixed motive game. A frequently used example is that of the prisoners' dilemma (Rappaport, 1960). In this case, suppose two persons have been arrested upon suspicion of committing a serious crime. They are guilty, but there is insufficient evidence for conviction of the serious offense but enough for a lesser one. They are not allowed to communicate with each other. They have the following possibilities. If they both confess, they will be convicted of the serious offense, but their sentence will be reduced slightly for their cooperation. If one confesses, he gets off without punishment and his confederate gets the maximum sentence of twelve years. If they both hold out and do not confess, they can be convicted only for the lesser offense and sentenced for one year. The payoff matrix based on years in prison is diagrammed below in Figure 1.2.

This payoff matrix poses a dilemma for the prisoners because if each tries to maximize his own gain, he will confess and implicate his confederate. If they both do that they will be worse off than if they both

| | A | |
	Confess	Not confess
B Confess	-9, -9	-12, 0
Not confess	0, -12	-1, -1

FIGURE 1.2

held out and did not confess. Yet, if each one considers what he should do, regardless of what the other does, he should confess. Thus, if *B* confesses, *A* is better off if he too confesses; and if *B* does not confess, *A* is again better off if he confesses. The dilemma can be resolved only if the prisoners trust each other, or follow a criminal code of never co-operating with the police, or so identify with each other that the confederate's payoff in some degree is his own.

Some conflicts embody such dilemmas. Consider two countries in an arms race; each fears the other. If one nation does not increase its arms expenditures, it is at a military disadvantage and becomes subject to domination by the other side. Each side sees only the alternatives of submission or increasing its arms. It is as if they see cells (b) and (c) in Figure 1.3 as the only alternatives. But let us also assume that if both sides continue to increase their expenditures, both suffer some loss in that they cannot use their resources for other purposes and yet neither gains relatively from their arms. Finally, assume that if both halt their arms expenditures, they will both have some gains. The payoff matrix is presented in Figure 1.3. Again, if each side pursues its own interest they will both be worse off than if they acted cooperatively.

Obviously, real-life conflict situations are much more complex than such simple payoff matrices, but the matrices reveal how individual, reasonable calculations can result in aggregate losses. We will consider various aspects of this dilemma and some of its dynamics in later chapters. At this time, I want to discuss the extent to which conflicts are actually zero sum.

In one sense pure zero-sum conflicts can be readily transformed. Consider even standard games with rules such as chess, poker, or tic-tac-toe. The players of one of these games have many social relations with each other which transcend the game. Within that larger social context, *how* each player wins or loses and whether or not each pursues a set of games until the players all agree the series is concluded is important to all the players. In other words, the players have an interest in playing the game through and doing so properly and honestly. They all would suffer some

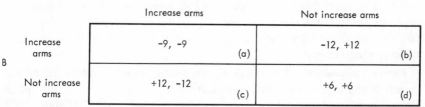

	A	
	Increase arms	Not increase arms
B Increase arms	-9, -9 $\quad$ (a)	-12, +12 $\quad$ (b)
Not increase arms	+12, -12 $\quad$ (c)	+6, +6 $\quad$ (d)

FIGURE 1.3

loss if the game were not played to a conclusion correctly. In that sense, playing the game is part of a larger payoff matrix which has the quality of a mixed motive game. The counterpart of all this in natural conflicts is that the parties to a conflict have greater or fewer common ties and may be more or less integrated with each other. If the parties are highly integrated or have many common interests, the issue in contention will not be viewed as a pure zero-sum situation.

What seems like pure conflict may also be transformed when the issue in contention is fractionated (Fisher, 1964). That is, the issue which is in contention may be broken up into many components. Some may be traded off against each other. Instead of one side winning and the other side losing the entire game, the game is thought to include many components and one party may lose one and not another part. For example, think of the payoff in a game of poker not just in the winning or losing of money but also in the winning or losing of prestige and honor. These can be gained without necessarily winning money, depending upon the skills used in handling a poor hand of cards, in interpreting the events of the game, and in reacting to the others winning and losing money.

This point can also be illustrated by considering what should be a simple zero-sum international dispute: contention over a boundary. The conflict may be considered zero sum if each party regards control over the disputed territory as total and one side or the other has absolute control. It is possible, however, to consider the variety of specific referents of possible control. One government may have the right to have the people pay taxes to it, the other to ensure that the people study in schools in which their language is used. Both governments may agree that the people in the disputed territory have complete freedom of movement across any borders they draw. They may agree that one side will have sovereign rights over the territory, but neither will station any military forces there.

In short, the purity of a conflict depends upon the whole set of relations between the parties in conflict. It also depends upon the degree to which the issue in dispute may be broken down into smaller issues. These characteristics of a struggle in part depend upon the way the parties to the conflict view it—to what extent is it isolated from common interests or embedded in a wide range of common interests. These perceptions are likely to change in the course of a struggle. The purity of the conflict, in turn, affects its intensity and the choice of ways to reach collective agreement.

Power Inequality. The final dimension of social conflicts to be discussed is the degree to which one party has power relative to the other. Power is a fundamental concept and is variously used (Weber, 1947, pp. 324–29; Goldhammer and Shils, 1939; Bierstedt, 1950); we should be explicit about its meaning here. Within the context of our concern with social conflicts we will use the term power to refer to the relative coercive strength of the conflicting parties. That is, we are concerned here with the force which one side can exert against another aside from the other side's evaluation of the legitimacy of that force. We might think of force or strength as the resources available to be directed at an adversary (Aron, 1966, pp. 48–50). Power depends upon the strength one side has relative to the other side. Power is specific to a given relationship. Great force applied against a much greater force turns out to be little power.

Since power is relative, it can be assessed only in terms of the specific relationship and issue in contention. This relativity has several components. First, there is the matter of the cost to each side of exercising coercion against the other side. In exercising force against another party or even organizing to do so, some costs are incurred. The magnitude of such costs relative to the resources remaining for other purposes for each party affects their power relative to each other. Secondly, the costs to each side of enduring the other's coercion varies for each. The costs depend upon the nature of the coercion and the total resources of the side subject to the coercion. Furthermore, the costs and the willingness to exercise coercion and to absorb the coercion of the adversary depends in good measure upon the importance of the issue at stake. The costs are meaningful only in relation to what is being sought by each side.

All this should indicate why it is so difficult for partisans in a conflict to assess their power. Consequently, a direct test or confrontation is often necessary for the parties to assess their relative power and how valuable the matter in contention is to each of them. Noting these components of power should also make explicable how it is possible for one party with an apparently small force to withstand or even defeat a much larger force. This may be seen in international affairs especially in the breaking of colonial bonds. For the people in a colony, their national independence may appear so important that they are willing to suffer great losses while the colonial power is unwilling to endure much discomfiture for an objective which is not central to it.

The degree of power differences can affect the awareness of the conflict by both parties, how the parties will try to reach an agreement to terminate the conflict, what that outcome is likely to be, and even whether an underlying conflict exists. These effects will be examined in the course of the book. At this point it is appropriate simply to note that the implications of power differences are not the same for all aspects of social conflicts and indeed can appear to be contradictory. Thus, large power differences can be a source of grievance to the less powerful but deter overt expression of the grievance. Thus, too, the less powerful may yield to threats of coercion and so coercion will be exercised infrequently but the more powerful may tend to seek further gains because of the tempting weakness of the less powerful.

If the power differences are small a different set of contradictory implications can be suggested. If the parties are equally powerful it may be that allocations of valued and contestable matters between them will be equitable and neither would have serious grievances. But being equal, either may misjudge and think a marginal advantage can be obtained with only a little effort. Thus, too, if the parties are equal they may deter each other so that coercion is not exercised but in order to maintain the equality they may engage in a power race which evokes fear and hostility in each until coercion is used preemptively by one side.

When so many contradictory but plausible implications of power differences can be suggested, it cannot be used alone to explain the emergence and expression of social conflicts. Obviously power relations are of central importance in struggles; the consequences of differing degrees of power inequality, however, depend upon many other circumstances. Extended discussion must await later chapters.

CHARACTERISTICS OF THE ADVERSARIES

In considering the dimensions of conflicts we have been concerned particularly with relations between the disputing parties. Since social conflict is a kind of relationship this attention is appropriate. However, conflicts also differ in their emergence and course depending upon the nature of the antagonists and the issues in contention. The issues in contention will be discussed in the next chapter. Here we will consider the characteristics of the conflicting units.

Most typologies of conflicts are made in terms of the units involved. Analysis is often limited to disputes within or between particular units: communities, classes, races, religions, nations, factories, or universities. At the end of this book we will examine the special qualities of conflicts in particular settings: organizations, societies, and the world. To do so consistently with the orientation of this book, we will look for general dimensions of those settings relevant to conflicts. At this point we are considering the parties to the dispute. Here, too, we will consider the characteristics of adversaries in terms of dimensions particularly relevant to social conflicts rather than in everyday terms. This makes it possible to study social conflicts in general and to specify the conditions which relevantly affect the course of a struggle.

Boundary Clarity. The boundaries of each conflict party may be more or less visible. They may be recognized by varying proportions of all the members of the social system containing the antagonists. Boundaries may be more or less permeable to the movement of persons between the parties and open to interaction and communication between people on both sides. Furthermore, the boundary between the parties may involve more or less of the lives of the members of each party; that is, it may vary in comprehensiveness. Each of these variations may be briefly illustrated. In a collective bargaining dispute between labor and management, the membership in each party is relatively visible and clear, not readily permeable, and not very comprehensive.

The units to an underlying conflict must be considered in terms of their potential emergence as adversaries. The boundaries between social categories which are potential conflict units also vary in the previously mentioned ways. Thus, the difference between males and females is visible and generally recognized; it is not permeable in the sense that persons change membership from one category to another (although it is permeable in the sense that there is considerable interaction across the boundary) and is comprehensive in the sense that many aspects of persons' lives are affected by their belonging in one category rather than another. In terms of self-conscious conflict groups the boundaries are not as high. Thus, within the women's liberation movement there are a variety of organizations. Females and males vary considerably in their involvement in one or another organization, in the women's movement generally, or as antagonists to the movement.

It is important to keep in mind that boundedness is a matter of degree. In the political world today, nation-states are particularly highly bounded. There is general agreement that everyone belongs to one or another nation-state and there are formal procedures for determining membership. Furthermore, interaction is channeled by such membership and many aspects of a person's life are determined by membership in a nation-state. Even in this case the boundaries are not impermeable and total. Not all transnational interactions are controlled and directed by the national governments. Ideas, goods, and people cross political borders; people feel some commonalities with persons of similar ages, occupations, religions, and ideologies in other political jurisdictions. On the other hand, in local community conflicts the contending groups are relatively unbounded. It is even difficult to distinguish the social categories which serve as the recruiting ground for active participants in opposing groups. People shift back and forth, tend to interact with each, and have many relations with each other disregarding what an observer might determine to be the boundaries between adversary groups. Again, even in such local cases there is some boundedness. Members of a community have some shared understandings about what kinds of people are likely to be on different sides of particular issues.

Disputes between parties with varying degrees of boundedness tend to be studied differently. In the case of relatively unbounded conflict units, as in community struggles, we usually give special attention to how potential participants in conflict groups become aware of their grievances, what the underlying grievances may be, and how people are mobilized and organized to engage in conflicting behavior. In the case of fights between relatively bounded units, as in international or industrial conflicts, the mobilization of members is taken as less problematic and the emphasis tends to be upon the means used in pursuit of conflicting goals. One value of studying many kinds of social conflicts and developing a paradigm for a whole range of conflict is that it should make us more ready to consider problematic what might otherwise be neglected. It is worthwhile to consider how governments actually mobilize and maintain constituent support for conflicts with other governments. The Vietnam war has certainly helped remind us of the pertinence of this matter. Comparably, it is worthwhile to consider how conflicting behavior can be, and is, pursued in cases with less clearly bounded parties such as in women's liberation or black liberation movements.

Degree of Organization. Related to the boundedness of the parties to a conflict is their degree of organization. At one extreme are two social categories which an observer regards as the recruiting ground for two conflict groups. The members of those categories may have no sense of common identity and little or no organization. At the other extreme are highly bounded groups with members of each group conscious of their adherence. In the more organized groups there tends to be considerable differentiation among the members as they play different roles in the maintenance of the organization. What concerns us here is the degree of differentiation for external affairs. In every social group there is likely to be some differentiation such that particular roles are more implicated in relations with nonmembers. For some groups this differentiation also takes the form of some degree of specialization in conflicting relations with external groups and with particular kinds of external groups.

The nation-state again can serve as a prototypal illustration. There is considerable differentiation within the society and special agencies dealing with "foreign affairs." Those agents are further specialized so that they deal with cooperative and exchange as well as conflict relations. They tend to be specialized to deal with comparable counterparts. Thus, governments deal with governments and armies with armies; in a conflict between a nation-state and an international religious or ideological movement, or between an army and a guerilla force, there are peculiar difficulties.

Trade unions, too, have developed specialized agencies for dealing with their regular adversaries. Some conflict groups are much less organized. Thus, university students protesting some aspect of their lives in the university are usually not highly organized.

One of the important implications of the degree of organization and differentiation is the variation in the position of leaders. In more organized and differentiated conflict groups the leaders tend to claim, and tend to have acknowledged, the authority and legitimacy to represent the entire group. They are likely to be so recognized by the other side and their role as spokesmen is accepted by the adversary. They are also more likely to be able to effectively commit the group as a whole and control and direct their conflicting behavior.

The degree of organization of conflict groups is affected by a number of factors. As the illustrations might suggest, larger and more autonomous groups tend to be more organized. Furthermore, the longer a conflict relationship persists, the more organized the parties become. The degree of organization of each conflict group affects the degree of organization of its adversary. Union-management relations illustrate this development. The point is also illustrated by the efforts of university administrators during a student strike to find leaders who represent the students and therefore with whom they can negotiate. The students themselves, however, may resist any formalization in which some of them are spokesmen and leaders. If the struggle persists in an active form and with conflicting behavior, such differentiation and organization cannot be completely resisted.

This discussion of organization should raise a general question which may have been evoked by the previous discussion of boundedness. Who are the parties to a conflict? Are they the large categories of potential partisans or the self-conscious groups purporting to represent that larger category? Are they those groups who consciously try to coerce each other and regard each other as adversaries or are they the opposing leaders or the entire groups? For example, consider only one side in the current American conflict about equality between whites and blacks. This side might be all American blacks, those whites and blacks favoring greater equality, the National Association of Colored People, the Southern Christian Leadership Conference, the Black Panthers, CORE, some combination of the organizations, or the leaders of some of them.

If analysis is to be cumulative and effective, it is necessary to be explicit about the units which are involved in the disputes being studied. The answer to the question, then, depends upon the issue in contention and the time period used to delimit the conflict. For example, are we considering a conflict about full racial equality in America or about discrimination by a local bus company? Are we considering a three-day confrontation or a decade of struggle? There is no correct or wrong answer to these kinds of questions; they should suggest some of the factors that affect the determination of what groups are in contention.

System Contexts. Another major variation in the types of units which may be in conflict is their systemic relations to each other (Angell, 1965). The conflict units may be independent of each other and of any unit superordinate to them; or both units may be within a larger entity; or one unit may be *part* of the other unit which claims jurisdiction over it. For example, nation-states are relatively autonomous and unsubordinated, unions and management are under some governmental control, and a black caucus may be a faction in a trade union.

Although as an observer one may decide what the systematic relationship is between the conflicting units, the participants themselves may not concur. Indeed, they are likely to contend with each other about the nature of their place in the system. A government claiming jurisdiction over some segment of the society is often attacked by the segment as being the agent of an opposing segment and not representative of the total society. For example, the government may be viewed as the instrument of large business corporations, of whites, of the rich, or of the elderly. The government may contend it is for all the people, business management may assert it is above the conflict between workers, supervisors, and other segments within the company, and university administrators may argue that they represent and mediate all the interests of the university community and do not themselves constitute a separate interest.

These contentions are important aspects of social conflict; in part they are efforts to persuade the adversary and potential allies about the nature of the struggle and they are partly efforts to mobilize support and gain allies to coerce the adversary. As the illustrations mentioned suggest, the superordinates in any system are more likely to claim to represent all parties than are the subordinates. Sometimes the subordinates, being relatively numerous, may claim to be the total system and their adversary an exploitive, unnecessary appendage.

The possible contentious quality of any characterization of the system context of adversary units should be kept in mind by us as students of social conflicts. We must be thoughtful in making assertions about the system relations between units. Keeping in mind the discrepant views of the conflicting units should help prevent us from making an implicitly partisan assumption.

In the light of these considerations, it seems advisable to consider potential and actual conflict units as autonomous, but with varying degrees and kinds of integration between them and within social contexts in which other units have varying degrees of involvement. That is, the conflict units may have complementary and cooperative relations as well as conflicting ones. These complementary and cooperative relations may be institutionalized in the form of shared organizational structures or they may simply be expressed in the transactions between members of the two units, as individuals or as collectivities. For example, consider a university. A variety of units can be discerned by an analyst of social conflict; for the present, consider only students and administrators. The members of these two units have a variety of relations which make them interdependent and in conflict. The administrators in some ways can and do act in the name of the collectivity of the university, including the students. The same is true of the students. The extent to which each does this depends upon understandings between them and the expectations and prescriptions of many other people: state legislators, alumni, taxpayers, and other intersecting sets of people. In short, for any units in conflict, the actual systemic relations are matters of degree. We have suggested three major dimensions of possible systemic relations: (1) the degree of subordination to third parties, (2) the degree of integration or autonomy from each other, and (3) the degree to which one unit claims and the other acknowledges an authority relationship based upon representing an entity broader than (but including) the other unit.

DEFINITION AND STAGES OF CONFLICT

Having discussed many dimensions of social conflict and some of the characteristics of units which may be in contention, it is possible to state more meaningfully how the term social conflict will be used here. *Social conflict is a relationship between two or more parties who (or whose spokesmen) believe they have incompatible goals.* The phenomena included and excluded by this definition should be noted.

This definition does not say anything about the means used in trying to attain the goals. This may seem odd. If parties have incompatible aims, each can induce the other side to yield only by coercion. It would seem appropriate to include as one of the defining characteristics of a conflict relationship that one or both parties threaten or attempt to exercise coercion. If there were pure conflict, the restriction of the term to include attempts or threats to use coercion would be appropriate. But we have seen that in actuality, social relationships are never purely zero sum. Therefore, we must consider noncoercive means to reach incompatible goals in our analysis of social conflict.

In this book we will consider two major ways of pursuing conflicting aims in addition to coercion. One way is persuasion; that is, one or both parties try to convince the other side that it should accede to the goals it desires not out of fear or in return for some reward, but because of its own interests and values. The other way is by contingent rewards; that is, one side (or both) offers the other a positively desired inducement in exchange for a concession toward its goal. Although social conflicts do not necessarily involve coercion and violence, we will be particularly interested in their use. Insofar as a relationship is conflicting, coercion is potential and often actual.

Conflict is related to competition; but the two are not identical. Competition may or may not involve awareness; conflict does. In the case of competition, parties are seeking the same ends whereas conflicting parties may or may not be in agreement about the desirability of particular goals. In addition, competing units generally seek that which is not already part of or dominated by the competitor. They seek it from third parties rather than directly from each other.

Situations which an observer assesses to be conflicting but which are not so assessed by partisans do not constitute social conflicts. We refer to such situations as objective, potential, or latent conflicts. If the parties come to *believe* that they have incompatible goals, a social conflict has emerged. The objective conflict situation underlies a dispute and persists regardless of the partisans' awareness of it. Once the parties believe they have incompatible goals each or both may try to attain them. In seeking to reach their goals, coercive and noncoercive means may be tried. There will follow some termination of the attempted means and a recognizable outcome. Such terminations and outcomes may be more or less permanent and accepted by the participants. A general ongoing conflict relationship can continue while several disputes are terminated and begun in a neverending, overlapping series. Often it is the observer who decides for purposes of his own analysis when a specific conflict is terminated.

The term social conflict, as used here, refers to a situation in which parties believe that they have incompatible goals. The term also refers to the interactional sequence or process in which the parties contend with each other. A comprehensive analysis of social conflicts should include the objective conditions underlying a conflict situation and the processes which lead to the emergence of a partisan awareness. A comprehensive analysis would also encompass the pursuit of conflicting goals, the termination and outcomes of social conflicts, and the consequences of those outcomes.

These distinctions suggest a series of possible stages in the course of struggles, as diagrammed in Figure 1.4. All conflicts do not go through every step. Of all the relations between parties some are objectively conflicting. *Some* of those underlying conflicts become manifest. And only in some of *those* conflicts do the parties actively pursue their conflicting goals. Even then coercion is not always used.

It will prove helpful to consider social conflicts in a series of stages

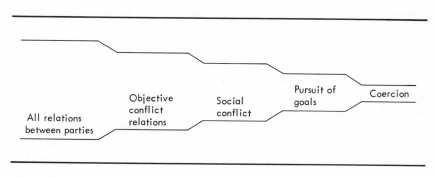

FIGURE 1.4

and with stages which precede and follow the conflict itself. A simplified diagram of this entire range is shown in Figure 1.5. With this range in mind we can study the factors which affect the movement from one stage to the next and the alternatives within each stage. It is also important to recognize that the stages are not independent of each other. One or another alternative followed in one stage affects the alternative

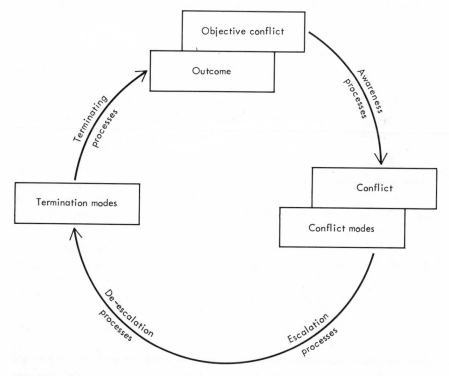

FIGURE 1.5

followed in the next. Moreover, anticipation of alternatives in later stages sometimes affects the choices made in earlier stages.

The book is organized to follow the flow of stages before, during, and after specific conflicts. In chapter 2 we examine objective conflict situations and the bases of social conflicts. In chapter 3 we consider how conflicts emerge, focusing upon the conditions and processes leading to awareness. In chapter 4 we analyze the various means of pursuing conflicting goals and what affects the means used. In chapter 5 we examine the changes in the means used as the parties each seek to gain their ends, attending to escalation and deescalation of the struggle. In chapter 6 we discuss the termination and possible outcomes of social conflicts and what affects the outcomes. In chapter 7 some of the consequences of different outcomes and modes used are examined; special attention is given to the consequences for other conflicts. In chapter 8 we consider the peculiarities of social conflicts in different settings: organizations, whole societies, and the world of nation-states; the chapter also provides a review and synthesis of the major themes of the book and discusses the policy implications of the approach taken here.

As we go along we shall use several current social conflicts as cases to which we can apply, and by which we can illustrate, the ideas presented. We will consider two conflicts within organizational settings: labor–management strife and university student–administrator disputes. We will consider two society-wide conflicts: black-white and male-female struggles. At the world level we will examine the Arab–Israel and the U.S.–U.S.S.R. hostilities.

By juxtaposing conflicts as diverse as women's liberation, American trade unions, the Cold War, and black liberation we shall see how useful an examination of social conflicts in general actually is. Perhaps at the present stage of knowledge or because of the nature of the phenomena it is not illuminating to examine the processes and conditions of social conflicts in general. Obviously in writing a book about social conflicts, I believe that there are enough commonalities in all struggles that it will advance our understanding of each to have an approach that is applicable to all.

Thus far we have argued that social conflicts are social relationships. This means that at every stage of conflict the parties socially interact; each party affects the way the other acts, not only as each responds to the other but as each side may *anticipate* the responses of the other. Even the ends each party seeks are constructed in interaction with adversaries. Furthermore, we have argued that conflicting relations are mixed together with exchange and cooperative relations in concrete cases of inter-unit relations. We have suggested several other characteristics of conflicts and about the stages from which they emerge, through which they move, and the stages that follow. These arguments, assertions, and suggestions will be developed as the analysis proceeds.

BIBLIOGRAPHY

ANGELL, ROBERT C., "The Sociology of Human Conflict," in E. McNeil (ed.), *The Nature of Human Conflict* (Englewood Cliffs, N.J.: Prentice-Hall, Inc., 1965) pp. 91–115.

ARON, RAYMOND, *Peace and War* (Garden City: Doubleday & Company, Inc., 1966).

BERNARD, JESSIE, "Parties and Issues in Conflict," *Conflict Resolution,* 1 (June 1957), 111–21.

BIERSTEDT, ROBERT, "An Analysis of Social Power," *American Sociological Review,* 15 (1950), 6, 730–38.

BLAU, PETER M., *Exchange and Power in Social Life* (New York: John Wiley & Sons, Inc., 1964).

BOULDING, KENNETH E., *Conflict and Defense* (New York: Harper & Row, Publishers, 1962).

COLEMAN, JAMES, *Community Conflict* (New York: The Free Press, 1957).

COSER, LEWIS A., *The Functions of Social Conflict* (New York: The Free Press, 1956).

DAHRENDORF, RALF, *Class and Class Conflict in Industrial Society* (Stanford: Stanford University Press, 1959).

FINK, CLINTON F., "Some Conceptual Difficulties in the Theory of Social Conflict," *The Journal of Conflict Resolution,* 12 (December 1968), 412–60.

FISHER, ROGER, "Fractionating Conflict," in R. Fisher (ed.), *International Conflict and Behavioral Science* (New York: Basic Books, Inc., 1964).

GAMSON, WILLIAM A., *Power and Discontent* (Homewood, Illinois: The Dorsey Press, 1968).

GOLDHAMMER, HERBERT AND EDWARD A. SHILS, "Types of Power and Status," *The American Journal of Sociology,* 45 (September 1939), 171–82.

HAGGSTROM, WARREN C., "The Power of the Poor," in F. Riessman, J. Cohen, and A. Pearl (eds.), *Mental Health of the Poor* (New York: The Free Press, 1964), pp. 205–23.

KRIESBERG, LOUIS, "Internal Differentiation and the Establishment of Organizations," in H. S. Becker, et al., (eds.), *Institutions and the Person* (Chicago: Aldine-Atherton, Inc., 1968), pp. 141–64.

LENIN, V. I., *Left-Wing Communism, an Infantile Disorder* (New York: International Publishers, 1940). Originally published in 1920.

MADISON, JAMES, "The Federalist No. 10 (1787)" in A. Hamilton, J. Jay, and J. Madison, *The Federalist* (Washington, D.C.: Home Library Foundation, 1937), pp. 53–62. Originally published in 1787.

PARK, ROBERT E. AND ERNEST W. BURGESS, *Introduction to the Science of Sociology* (Chicago: University of Chicago Press, 1924).

RAPOPORT, ANATOL, *Fights, Games, and Debates* (Ann Arbor: University of Michigan Press, 1960).

SIMMEL, GEORGE, *Conflict and the Web of Intergroup Affiliations* (New York: The Free Press, 1955). Originally published in 1908 and 1922.

STOUFFER, SAMUEL A. et al., *The American Soldier: Combat and Its Aftermath*, Vol. 2 (Princeton, N.J.: Princeton University Press, 1949).

SUMNER, WILLIAM GRAHAM, *What Social Classes Owe Each Other* (Caldwell, Idaho: Caxton Printers, 1952). Originally published in 1883.

TITTLE, CHARLES R., "Crime Rates and Legal Sanctions," *Social Problems*, 16 (Spring 1969), 409–23.

VON NEUMANN, J. AND O. MORGENSTERN, *Theory of Games and Economic Behavior* (Princeton, N.J.: Princeton University Press, 1944).

WEBER, MAX, *The Theory of Social and Economic Organization*, translated by A. M. Henderson and Talcott Parsons (New York: Oxford University Press, 1947). Originally published in 1921.

chapter two

The Bases
of Social Conflicts

The task of this chapter is to assess the underlying conditions of social conflicts, those conditions which constitute a potential dispute. In order to do this we must recognize and overcome some difficult conceptual and substantive problems. In the preceding chapter we defined social conflict as a relationship in which parties (or their spokesmen) believe they have incompatible goals. We might then argue that the bases of social conflicts are the parties' beliefs that their goals are incompatible. Such truths-by-definition are not very illuminating. Potential conflict must refer to conditions which underlie and which result in beliefs regarding incompatible aims.

Here is the problem. How does one know what those conditions are before they produce the anticipated consequences? One can know them only in the sense that they are theoretical constructs. Empirical indicators must be indirect and depend upon a chain of theoretical links. It is necessary to be clear about this before we proceed. Informally and commonly, we see some conflict behavior, presume a conflict relationship, and then conjecture that there probably is and was an underlying conflict situation. But not all conflicts are expressed in conflict behavior; the antagonistic parties may be aware of their opposition but neither side attempts to coerce the other in order to reach the incompatible goals. Furthermore, of the innumerable potential conflict situations few become manifest. We must also take into account the possibility of "unrealistic" conflict. That is, it might be argued that some coercion is unrelated to a conflict relationship; it is simply expressive or accidental. It might be argued that some struggles are based upon misunderstandings about the incompatibility of the participants' goals. If such "unrealistic" struggles can exist, discerning what is a potential or underlying conflict situation is even more difficult.

Ultimately, it comes down to this. As analysts, we must attempt to construct a reasonable and consistent explanatory scheme for what we are trying to understand and then see how useful it actually is. This requires making assumptions about phenomena and processes which cannot be directly tested. We can test an interrelated set of ideas if they are ordered so that they lead to a particular observable result. In discussing the underlying bases of social conflicts we will be considering theoretical constructs. The bases lie in the mind of the student of social conflict, not necessarily in the mind or heart of the persons observed. This assumption is then tested by seeing whether or not a struggle emerges under conditions specified in the theory.

We begin with the idea that an objective conflict is a situation in which two parties are likely to come to believe that they have conflicting goals. The term "likely" needs elaboration. One might say that any social situation has the potentiality of conflict under some conceivable circumstances. The emphasis upon likely indicates the advisability of giving special attention to those conditions which according to the theory are most frequently going to be recognized as conflicting by participants in the social situation. Given our concerns in the study of social conflict, we are particularly interested in those potential disputes which, when they are actualized, are likely to involve coercion. The assumption of the existence of an objective conflict is still confirmed if either of the following two outcomes occurs: (1) the participants come to believe that they are in conflict, or (2) they do not, but for reasons specified in the theory. In either case the evidence is consistent with the assumption and in that sense supports it.

In order to argue that certain situations are likely to have particular consequences some assumptions about human nature and universal social processes are necessary. Again, how good those assumptions are can be assessed only by examining their implications. I shall not try to enumerate all the assumptions. From time to time, when it is particularly important, I will be explicit about them. At this time a few comments are in order as they relate to the issues already raised concerning unrealistic conflict.

Since social conflicts are ubiquitous it might seem reasonable to seek for the underlying bases of conflicts in an inherent characteristic of the human species. Indeed there is a recurring interest in explanations of social conflicts in terms of biological instincts. A recent formulation of this idea has been made by Ardrey about what he calls the "territorial imperative":

> We act as we do for reasons of our evolutionary past, not our cultural present, and our behavior is as much a mark of our species as is the shape of a human thigh bone.... If we defend the title to our land or the sovereignty of our country, we do it for reasons no different, no less innate, no less ineradicable, than do lower animals (Ardrey, 1966, p. 5).

Even in these formulations room is left for learning what our country is and how it is to be defended. The more open the formulation, to take into account the actual variations in human conduct, the less distinct and meaningful is the idea of instinct.

Take the idea of an aggressive instinct. Presumably that idea is even more open. Now we are discussing only a drive. For observers stressing such instinctual drives, aggression is the source of social conflicts. But such writers also recognize other human needs and drives and obviously they do not say that all persons are constantly and only seeking to harm or kill each other (Freud, 1939; Lorenz, 1963; Tinbergen, 1968). The human species would hardly have survived in that case. The assertion, then, is that aggression is innately gratifying but does not require constant satisfaction and can be expressed in a variety of ways. Accepting such an instinct, one then needs to study what conditions affect its expression in various ways. Some of the ways may be quite ritualistic and not in any way endanger the physical security of any of the partisans.

Nevertheless, in this work we do not assume that aggression is innate. To do so would be to draw our attention to the inner drives of the struggling partisans; channeling and transforming their drives would be the focus of concern. But conflicts are about something; parties are contending about matters of importance to them. Conflict management involves development of ways of handling these contentious issues, not simply ritualizing the expression of aggressive instincts. Essentially, conflicts are part of social relations; they depend upon the relationship between people not upon drives or instincts within a person without reference to others. This is increasingly being recognized by contemporary psychoanalysts.

There is another implication to an emphasis upon human aggression. It follows from the idea that aggression may be free floating or displaced from one target to another. This can be discussed best in considering the frustration-aggression relationship (Dollard, Doob, Miller, Mowrer and Sears, 1939). It might appear to be obvious that if persons are frustrated they will become aggressive, seeking to inflict harm upon somebody or something. If frustration always resulted in aggression and aggression were always caused by frustration, we would have a fundamental premise upon which to base a theory of conflict. It turns out not to be so simple.

Research on frustration and aggression makes it clear that what is frustrating depends upon the goals and intentions of the persons supposedly being frustrated. Those goals may not be evident to the observer. Studies also indicates that aggression depends upon the availability of a target which seems appropriate. The target is attacked partly because of its stimulus quality and not only because of some need of the attacker to express his frustration (Berkowitz, 1969). In other words, frustration and aggression really involve a social relationship; frustration and aggression involve social interaction.

All this still does not deny that a person or a group of persons, feeling frustrated, may attack another group that is a safe and exciting target but is unrelated to the frustration. Taking out their anger on an "innocent" third party certainly would seem to be a case of unrealistic conflict. That may make it seem impossible to ever develop a theory of social conflict utilizing the concept of underlying or objective conflict situations. Several observations need to be made about this matter.

First, if any group should act to injure another, the injured party is likely to respond as if it were being attacked—since it is. The first group may then find that a realistic conflict has begun. For some purposes of analysis the source of attack may not be important. For any general theory about social conflicts, however, it does matter. The means chosen to pursue goals and the possible outcomes are all affected by the underlying basis for the conflict. As Coser (1956) has argued, in unrealistic conflicts injuring another party is an end in itself. In realistic conflict, conflict behavior is a means and alternative means may be tried; additionally, a readjustment in the relationship may terminate the particular conflict.

The theoretical implications of the possibility that hostility is displaced and unrealistic conflict occurs must be faced more directly. We should acknowledge one fundamental difficulty. Suppose a group attacks another and gives a reason, upon what basis do we call it displacement and unrealistic? We do so only because we have a theory about what *really* are the determinants of their distress and the irrelevance of their targets to those determinants. Thus, if a group attacks Jews as exploiters undermining Western Civilization, how do we know that it is not a valid explanation of the ills of the world? We think we know better. But take the case of the populists after the American Civil War. If farmers blamed Eastern business interests for their economic difficulties, was this a matter of displacement and unrealistic conflict or an expression of the underlying conflict situation and a realistic conflict?

We cannot call something an unrealistic conflict without having some idea about what a realistic conflict is. Furthermore, we can assume that everyone has some free-floating hostility and that it can be directed at a large number of targets. What is interesting for us is the channeling of deprivation into particular social conflicts. For such developments, social processes at the group level will be more important than the human capacity to displace feelings or make erroneous diagnoses of their situation.

The point can be made in another way. Displacement may be a common process among humans and still not help very much to explain intergroup conflicts. For collective action, some shared experience and therefore common situation is necessary. In other words, some characteristics of the situation in which a category of people live must underlie the emergence of its members' consciousness of a grievance. Thus a worker's family distress may be displaced and his anger at his wife may be directed at his foreman. But that is not the basis on which a group of factory workers organize a trade union.

With these observations in mind, we can begin to analyze the bases of conflicts. We shall consider the conditions underlying possible social conflicts from the perspective of outside observers. But the validation of the analysis must be found in the thoughts and actions of the people in those conditions. It is they who do or do not create a social conflict from the underlying conditions.

In discussing the bases of conflicts we will be considering large categories of persons and not conflict groups. We are interested in quasi groups or categories which are the recruiting ground for organizations. How persons in quasi groups are mobilized will be analysed in the next chapter.

The boundaries between relevant social categories are not inherent in the categories. The divisions which are particularly important depend in part upon the social definitions of the partisans. In assessing potential conflicts, however, we as observers must gauge what those social definitions will be, how successfully they will be propagated, and under what circumstances given forms of conflict behavior will arise. For example, if we are considering struggles between blacks and whites, should we consider the categories to be all blacks and all whites in the U. S. as two categories? Should we compare poor blacks and rich whites, blacks and whites in professional occupations, blacks and whites in different metropolitan areas, or blacks and whites in different regions? Even in international conflicts, the parties are not fixed. For example, in the Arab-Israeli conflict the parties varied with different time periods. In 1947–48, was one of the parties to the conflict composed of all Jews, Jews in Palestine, Jews in refugee camps in Germany, all persons living in Palestine, Jews in Yemen and North Africa, or some combination of these? Is the other side currently all the countries bordering Israel, all Arab countries, all Muslim countries, all anti-Zionists, or Arab Palestinians in Israel or wherever they or their children may be? These possibilities could be extended. It is the task of this book to at least systematize these possibilities for all kinds of conflicts.

Two kinds of circumstances underlie social conflicts. One is consensus and the other dissensus (Aubert, 1963). In the case of consensus the parties agree about what they want but in situations such that if one side obtains more of what it wants, the other receives less. Dissensual conflicts exist when the parties want different things but the requirements of coordination make those differences incompatible or one side wants the other to accept the values, beliefs, or way of life it professes and thus makes unacceptable claims upon the other.

In this chapter, we will examine the kinds of issues involved in both types of social conflict. We will consider each type separately for analytic purposes, although particular struggles are based upon both consensus and dissensus. For example, students and administrators in universities value power in determining the actions of the university as a whole and in regard to each of them. This is the basis for a consensual conflict. The students and administrators may also disagree about how each should live, what they should strive for, or what they should learn. Such differences could be the basis for a dissensual conflict. Although these two bases of conflicts are mixed together, it is useful to consider them separately for their origins and consequences are not the same. Furthermore, one or the other basis is dominant in certain disputes.

DISSENSUS

People differ about a wide range of values and beliefs. Such differences are the bases for dissensual conflicts only if certain other beliefs are also held. Thus, members of two units may adhere to different religions. If each unit is indifferent to the other's religious convictions, thinks them quaint, or even thinks that it is useful that the other side has them, then no potential conflict exists. Suppose, however, that one or both units feel that the other's religious convictions are morally outrageous. Then an underlying conflict exists. The outraged persons presumably want those who hold such improper views to alter them or stop exhibiting them. Or suppose that one unit is so convinced of the virtue and importance of its views that it wishes the members of the other unit to agree. In other words, the truth of its views are to be accepted by the others for their own good or for their salvation. In such circumstances a potential conflict also exists. Or suppose one group feels the members of another are contemptible because of the values they hold. The basis for a conflict would still exist because those scorned would want that view of themselves altered so long as they had something to do with the other group. We need to consider both what people differ about and the sources of such differences.

Issues in Contention. People differ about what is worth striving for and how to get what they want. Disagreements about what is desirable are particularly relevant to conflicts which are expressed in violence and we will consider these disagreements first. We will then consider disagreements about beliefs.

One fundamental value issue concerns the bases of evaluations. People may differ about the criteria or standards by which they judge or evaluate each other. Should we judge each other by our actions or by our intentions? Should we judge each other by our beauty, intelligence, moral character, generosity, power, wealth, or by the degree of consideration we show towards others? Even if we agree upon a criterion, how are we to agree on an appropriate measure of that criterion? Is black more beautiful, just as beautiful, or less beautiful than white? Claims, counterclaims, and the rejection of other people's claims about these values indicate that the actual conflicts are about many things. We will persevere in looking at value differences which in themselves are potentially conflicting.

We can consider any of the above differences and note that those who rank high according to one standard are likely to urge its importance and thus the bases for a dissensual conflict would exist for every imaginable criterion. That hardly helps our comprehension of the bases of social conflicts. What helps us decide which criteria are more or less relevant is an understanding about which ones will emerge into awareness and which are likely to be pursued coercively. That is discussed in many parts of this book. For the present we will simply point to value differences from among the cases used illustratively in this book.

Some people may believe it is good to be aggressive, dominating, unexpressive of emotions, risk-taking, and physically tough and they label such characteristics masculine. Then, with a few elliptical steps in reasoning, they argue that feminine means the opposite of masculine, as characterized previously. If males must be "masculine" and females "feminine," then values are likely to be imposed upon people. Some persons in the Women's Liberation movement, partly on the basis of such imposed value differences, contend that males as well as females are constrained and are denied much of themselves as they are forced and force themselves to be only part human, only part of what they might otherwise be. In that case, the liberation of women from the restricted roles they learn and must play would also mean the liberation of men. Other people may insist that indeed there are value differences between men and women, but differ in the evaluations of those values. In a male-dominated society masculine ways of living would be highly valued; if females disagreed and thought expressiveness and consideration of others were to be highly valued, then the value differences would be part of an objective dissensual conflict.

In addition to values involving criteria of evaluation, some values pertain to ways of life or goals which are intrinsically meaningful and valuable. They are ultimate ends. Differences in such values often imply an objective conflict because their believers are likely to make universal claims. They seek to convert the nonbeliever. Such conflicts may be seen in international and national ideological struggles. Believers in political democracy, free elections, a multiparty system, nongovernmental means of expression, and limits on governmental power may come to regard such arrangements as intrinsically valuable, desirable for themselves and for all other people. It is then the obligation of the believers to provide tutelage to others so that they can attain the state in which these arrangements are also theirs. Others may believe that a political party which possesses the truth should not be handicapped in realizing that truth by those with erroneous views. They may also believe in the desirability of people working together, submerging egocentric personal wishes for collective purposes; equality and solidarity may be prized as ends in themselves.

Thus far we have discussed dissensual conflicts in terms of the values of the potential partisans. Dissensus may also be about beliefs concerning how to reach agreed upon goals. In a sense, every struggle might be defined as one in which contending parties simply disagree on how to reach an agreed upon goal: salvation, the good life, or security. But there are such profound disagreements about the meaning of salvation, the good life, and security that to argue that all struggles are over means obscures important differences. It is possible, however, that persons share a goal and disagree about how to attain it. The disagreement is a potential conflict if collective action affecting all the parties is needed to pursue the specific goal. Such potential conflicts are not usually given much attention in the study of social conflict because coercion and violence are not as frequently used as in dissensual value conflicts. This is true because the cooperative aspects of the relationship are more prominent in cases of dissensus over means than in dissensus over ends. Disagreements about means, however, are of special interest in the study of the course of conflict development. The dynamics of conflict escalation and deescalation are affected by disagreements within each party about the best way to attain their goal.

Sources of Issues. People develop values and beliefs from their experiences. Insofar as persons in every social category live in a particular environment, they develop a unique set of values and beliefs. This may be true for members of one society compared to another and for members of an age, sex, ethnic, class, or other social category within a society. Thus, the opportunities and constraints of men, of students, of workers, of blacks, of Israelis, of Americans, or any other entity differ from those not in the same category. Many factors affect the uniqueness of the experiences of the members of a social category and its elaboration into a potential conflict. We are most interested in what is especially pertinent: those factors associated with the relations between the categories which may come into conflict.

One factor is the degree of isolation of the members of one category from the members of another. Insofar as the members of a given category have much to do with others in the same category, to the relative exclusion of others, the elaboration of unique values and beliefs will be facilitated and hastened. The isolation of persons in a category increases the likelihood that peculiar world views will emerge and even a set of beliefs and values so distinctive and interrelated as to constitute a culture.

Such isolation may occur naturally as when physical barriers reduce communication and interaction—as occurs between societies. Even within a given society, different circumstances produce different experiences and, insofar as these experiences are not communicated and shared, further differentiation develops. For example, frequently the difference between rural and urban life provides a basis for dissensus. The traditional and virtuous life of the village is contrasted with the libertine and worldly cosmopolitan life of the large urban centers by leaders of conservative or reactionary movements. Such dissensus played a role in the Nazi movement in Germany. The rural-urban difference in some societies is augmented by ethnic differences associated with area of residence. For example, the prohibition struggle in the United States was in part a struggle between rural Protestants and urban Catholics (Siegfried, 1927, pp. 70–90).

Isolation between members of social categories does not only depend on nonsocial barriers. Isolation may be self-imposed as by religious sects seeking to avoid contamination from a surrounding evil. Isolation may also be imposed by nonmembers of a social category. Significantly, social isolation may even exist when there is social interaction. The interaction may be so stylized and coerced that little beyond the role relations are expressed or communicated. For example, blacks and whites in the American South have had considerable interaction but with limited understanding of the others' feelings and ideas because racial etiquette has been extreme (Dollard, 1937; Johnson, 1943). Behind the masks distinctive world views could mature. Moreover, the dominant group has created conditions which required accommodation by members of the subordinate group. That accomodation often took forms which were ridiculed by the dominant group while becoming part of the rationale for continued subordination. The ways of accommodation involve manipulation rather than confrontation—evasiveness, and the appearance of witlessness; these ways are not uncommon among other subordinate groups and the guile of women may be viewed in this way (Myrdal, 1944, appendix 5, pp. 1073-78; Bird and Briller, 1968, pp. 110-25).

Distinctive values or beliefs are a necessary condition for a conflict of dissensus but they are not sufficient. In addition the differences must be such that the values or beliefs are incompatible. Incompatibility has two basic sources. One is that the persons with the different views are in a social relationship which places the views in opposition. The other source is that persons with at least one set of views assert objectionable claims upon persons not sharing the views. These two sources need elaboration and illustration.

Although isolation provides the opportunity for different views to develop, it also precludes opposition. There can be no conflict between groups who have nothing to do with each other. When groups of people enter into a social relationship which requires joint action or actions which affect both groups, and they hold different views, pertinent to that relationship, the basis for a dissensual conflict exists. Such social relationships may come about through a variety of means. People with a distinctive set of views may move into a governmental jurisdiction previously dominated by persons with another set of views. This is the basis of many community conflicts (Coleman, 1957). For example, waves of immigrants to New England villages in the nineteenth century and migrants from the cities to suburban villages during the 1950s provided the basis for community controversies over taxes, churches, and school appropriations. Universities, previously dominated by persons from one social background, may become the setting for an objective dissensual conflict when significant numbers of persons enter them with different views resulting from differences in class or ethnic backgrounds. This can take many forms. For example, consider a university drawing students from the local community and training them for businesses in the community. A new administration may try to change the orientation of the university to the demands of the national market; the selection of students and the competition among them may then be increased despite the objections of the local students and their families. Or consider the changes which a religiously based university undergoes as it becomes secular, or the changes introduced when an elite college broadens its social base. Remember, most potential dissensual conflicts do not become actualized with the parties using coercion.

The development of social relations which require joint action also occurs in the course of the life cycle. Thus, young persons have distinctive experiences as children at home. Some of them may be reared to have values which they then find are inconsistent with adult values when they enter universities or the labor market. This disjunction between the values learned in the family and those of the work-a-day world varies in magnitude in different societies and periods. In economically developing societies the disjunction between traditional family values and the demands of the new society place a strain upon persons seeking to find a place in the new society (Flacks, 1970; Eisenstadt, 1956; Parsons, 1962). This may be a source of student movements in opposition to their governments. As we shall see, there are alternative or supplementary explanations as well (Westby and Braungart, 1966).

In addition to people coming together so that they must coordinate their activities, the circumstances affecting potential conflict groups may alter and affect them unequally so that differences in views become incompatible. People may be accommodated to their value and belief differences or mutual dependence until conditions require more intense coordination; then the value or belief differences are revealed as incompatible. For example, the military elites in each society develop special views as a result of their training and experience. A foreign military threat or defeat or a period of economic dislocation may make their differences in orientation and ways of thinking result in incompatible goals. Consequently, those differences may even be expressed in a military coup.

Another kind of external change which reveals dissensus and makes it become an objective conflict is the appeal by contending parties for support and assistance. Thus, any disagreement between adversaries can evoke wider dissension among others who differ in relevant ways. For example, students in a university may make certain demands of administrators and the differences among the faculty become a potential dissensual conflict insofar as it is expected that the faculty will participate or consciously avoid participating in making a decision about the demands. Or a civil war in Africa may aggravate the ideological dissensus between the U.S. and the U.S.S.R.

The other major source of incompatibility in values or beliefs is the claim by the adherents of one set of views that nonadherents are subject to the same views. One form that this takes is the claim that others should share the views held by the adherents of a particular religious or political ideology. Convinced of the moral or spiritual supremacy of their views, the denial or nonacceptance of their views is repugnant and the true faith must be brought to the nonbeliever. As the language suggests this kind of claim is most clearly made in reference to religious views. Political ideologies, however, may also assume a similar universal and insistent quality.

Some views, on the other hand, cannot be shared. They are part of a culture or identity which is ascribed and not achieved. This produces incompatible values when one party claims superiority for its identity and insists that others acknowledge the claim. The issues can be illustrated by considering the claims of nationalities and ethnic groups. Between national societies with relatively autonomous governments, each may be somewhat relativistic; that is, none insists that it is superior and that its superiority be acknowledged by all other peoples. Yet, such insistence has been made. The Nazi ideology proclaimed the racial superiority of Germans over Slavs, Jews, and others. Within each society, racism or sexism may make claims which are not acknowledged by those who are placed in an inferior status. Even religious differences may take on this character. Thus, Protestants and Catholics may regard their religious views as superior and yet not seek or expect conversion by the others. Religious adherence is taken as an ascribed status which cannot be altered.

CONSENSUS

In consensually based conflicts the adversary parties agree about what they want. Consensus, however, can be the basis for cooperation as well as conflict. When two parties want the same thing and each can attain it only or insofar as the other does, the basis for a cooperative relationship exists. This may exist because of a sense of identity between the two parties. It may also exist because the attainment of the goal for each depends upon the other's attainment as well. For example, the control of a communicable disease may require its control and elimination in adjoining territorial jurisdictions. Or the effective use of a river for power and irrigation may require the cooperation of parties sharing the river as a border. Parties within a business corporation or a society also have a basis for a cooperative relationship since increasing the total wealth of the organization or society depends upon each party getting more wealth.

Consensus, then, underlies social conflict only in conjunction with certain other conditions. In addition, there must be a basis for at least one party to experience or view the distribution of the consensually desired values as unsatisfactory. Furthermore, the basis must exist for one or both parties to believe that the unwanted distribution is attributable to an adversary or at least cannot be altered without a loss to the other side.

In other words, there must be a basis for viewing the distribution and alterations of it as a zero-sum situation. In this chapter we will consider the kinds of issues which often are involved in consensual conflicts. We shall also consider the circumstances in which consensually shared values underlie social conflicts.

Issues in Contention.   Any value which two parties agree about can be a basis for social conflict between them. We need to consider the circumstances and beliefs which must accompany consensus in order for it to constitute an objective social conflict. Our attention will be focused upon those values which most frequently provide the basis for consensual conflicts. We will begin by analyzing one such value to serve as a proto-type of other possible ones.

Consider wealth. Obviously, consensus about the desirability of wealth is widespread among many sets of adversaries. What circumstances or beliefs make such consensus the basis for a struggle? One possibility, as we have already noted, is that each party wants more wealth and each can obtain it only at the expense of the other. The extent to which such a condition actually exists, however, is itself subject to dispute among partisans. Consider a factory with several departments and several levels of hierarchy within each department. If each department is allocated a fixed amount of money by the central management, then the persons in each hierarchical level would seem to be in a position where the gains of one level must balance the loss of another. The levels are in conflicting relationship. But this reasoning makes certain assumptions which may or may not be valid. It assumes allocations will be made by levels, that there can be no alteration of the total amount available, and that funds from external sources are not differentially available to various levels. It also assumes that everyone is thinking in terms of the same period, presumably the budgetary year. Under other assumptions, the relationship need not be a conflicting one.

Some values might seem to be inherently conflicting if both parties have the same one. Imagine that each party wants to have more wealth than the other has. Now what they want is relative to the adversary and by definition both cannot attain their goal simultaneously. However, even in this case the conflict need not be pure and zero-sum. For the conflict to be pure and zero-sum, all the wealth must be possessed by the two parties and additional wealth can come only from the other party. In actuality, wealth is likely to be obtainable from third parties and it can be increased by the internal actions of the party itself. The more autonomous the party, the more likely any increases of wealth will depend on internal developments rather than be at the expense of an adversary.

Some values, however, are necessarily assessed relatively and assume a closed system. Consider, for example, wanting prestige or deference. How much a given unit has can only be measured relative to the amount which others have in the same system. Remember, we are discussing values about which the members of the units are in agreement—they agree about the desirability of attaining the same resource and are assessing it the same way.

Desiring power is another such value. As discussed in chapter 1, social power is relative. The amount of force one party has at its disposal does not determine its power—that depends upon how much it has *compared* to its adversary. This gives a struggle over power its essentially zero-sum quality. It is true that power over subordinates makes it possible for superiors to utilize collective resources more effectively for the welfare of the entire collectivity (Parsons, 1951). The increased gain for the collectivity is relative to some other collective and it may mean more goods or other gains can be divided within the collectivity. But all this does not alter the zero-sum character of the power relations *within* the collectivity. This characteristic is one of the reasons why so many social conflicts arise from and about power differences and also why such disputes are so often handled coercively. The inherent nature of power differences within any hierarchical organization or social system is the basis for asserting that conflicts are inevitable. Dahrendorf (1959) defines classes in terms of possession of authority and hence differences in authority underlie class conflicts. Presumably, people with less power are relatively disadvantaged and, under appropriate conditions, recognize that.

There is another major reason why consensus about the value of power so often underlies social conflicts and ones in which coercion is often used; power is a means to attain many other resources. Power sought as a means can readily become an end in itself. If conflict were defined as necessarily involving the use of coercion, then a power struggle would be part of every conflict (Weber, 1947, p. 132). Given our definition of social conflict, power struggles do not underlie *every* social conflict. Contentions about power become more common and significant when the conflict becomes manifest and as coercion is used.

In addition to valuing power, prestige, and comparative wealth there may be consensus about resources which are not assessed relatively. These are usually quite specific, such as Israeli and Jordanian contentions over Jerusalem or Soviet and American disagreements about Berlin. Even contentions about these places, insofar as they are consensual conflicts, have large amounts of power and prestige components in them. In the discussion of objective consensual conflicts we will concentrate on the abstract and generally conflict-pertinent dimensions of power, prestige, and wealth.

For conflicts based upon consensus to exist, people must want the same thing. They may want it as individuals or as members of a collective, as a people, a race, or a social class. Our first question, then, is how does the consensus necessary for conflict come about? One way is that people in a society are socialized as to what is desirable. As sharers of the same culture they want the same things. Thus, in American society workers and managers in a factory want money and the things money can buy. Success has many conventional meanings and we are brought up in each society to know what they are and what is worth striving for (Kriesberg, 1953). The very consensus essential for social life, then, is also the basis for conflicts.

In each society people are also socialized to "know their place," to *be* different and *want* different things. It will prove helpful to assume that despite such variations, there are some universal human experiences and hence universal sentiments. One which is of particular pertinence for the study of social conflicts is the preference for self-regulation or autonomy (Arendt, 1965, pp. 259–78). We shall assume that despite socialization into subordination, even by ascription, people prefer autonomy to subordination. This is true for individuals and for collectivities with which persons identify. That is, it is assumed not only for persons regardless of age, sex, ethnicity, or rank in a hierarchy, but also to *groups* of persons who think of themselves as having a collective entity and seek some control over their own group, as a group, whether this be by age, sex, ethnicity, or class.

Some of the issues underlying these assertions can be illustrated by considering very young children. They are perhaps the last category of persons which others still regard as being incapable of having much control over their own lives. Despite adult claims, however, children do not abandon all claims to control their own activities. We need not decide whether children or their adult masters have better judgment about the way children should behave. Clearly, there is no inherent nor fully successful inculcation of children's acceptance of adult control. It may be won by coercion or be exchanged for affection and material rewards.

Consensus, then, may be based upon the shared culture of a particular social system. The social system may be a society with extended means of socialization. It may be an organization, such as a factory or university, with much more limited opportunities for socialization into a common culture and with only a rudimentary common culture to share in any case. Consensus may also be the result of universal human experiences (Shibutani, 1961, pp. 393–401; Cooley, 1922). These result from being raised by other humans, usually in a family setting. They also result from the similarity of experiences as persons in a variety of social relations. This is the case for experience within a hierarchical order. Some of these may not be universal, but they can transcend the limits of a given social system. An example of this might be the experience of impersonal interaction as occurs in urban settings or in highly formalized bureaucracies.

Sources of Issues. We need to consider the circumstances which, in conjunction with consensus, constitute objective consensual conflicts. As social observers, we must be able to discern a distribution of some consensually desired resources which will be unsatisfactory to one or another potential partisan *and* which is likely to be viewed as a zero-sum relationship between the potential partisans. In this chapter our task is to outline what affects those circumstances. In the next chapter we will consider how the partisans become aware of these circumstances and come to believe that they are in conflict.

Whatever the distribution of what is valued, it can conceivably be part of a consensual social conflict. Although people in one category may have more than people in another, they may believe that they should have *even more*. Conversely, members of a category with less than another may feel that the inequality is satisfactory, legitimate, or essentially fair in terms of their moral criteria. We must consider what affects each group's satisfaction with the allocation between them.

Satisfaction depends upon the criteria used in evaluating a position and an assessment of how well the standards are being met. For example, members of a category may believe that they should have at least enough money for an adequate living given their training and efforts in their task. What is enough depends partly upon a comparison with others with similar preparation and efforts.

A variety of criteria may be used to evaluate the allocation of consensually desired resources. The criteria may be in terms of rewards for efforts or for outputs, in terms of intensions or of consequences, or they may be in terms of being or of doing. They may have built-in comparisons such as equality—whether of opportunity or of attainment or of advancement over the past.

For people to assess how well their standards are met, they must have some basis of measurement and a point of reference. Other persons often are the basis for determining how well the criteria have been met. The point of reference also may be the group's own past; how close they are to meeting their aspirations depends upon how far they were from reaching these standards in the past.

The first step is to consider the differences between parties in what they have or what they agree is desirable. We must reflect, if only briefly, upon possible degrees and kinds of differences. Suppose we consider two categories of people; we can compare them in two basic ways: as collectivities or as aggregates of individuals. The members of one category can be compared to another as part of a group that has more or less wealth than another group. On the other hand, the members of each group can be compared in terms of the characteristics of their individual members. For example, the People's Republic of China may have a large gross national income, but the per capita income may be much less than in countries with a collectively small income.

The relative position of two categories, even as aggregates, can be compared in several ways, for example, by comparing averages or distributions. A sampling of some distributions is shown in Figure 2.1. You may consider A and B to be different ethnic groups within a society or organization. When we compare the distribution of income, we might find that all members of the category have less than every member of the other category. This is depicted in part 1 of Figure 2.1. Or, as shown in part 5 of Figure 2.1, the members of one category may have almost the same distribution of the desired positions as do the members of the other category. The average income of A and B is much different in part 5 than in part 1. But the average is more alike in parts 2, 3, and 4, although the distributions are different.

The criteria people use are partly a matter of what they learn are appropriate. There is often considerable consensus about the criteria for the *allocation* of what is desired as well as about *what* is desirable. But consensus about the criteria of allocation is less likely to be high than is consensus about what is desirable. People with different experiences develop their own criteria and apply them. When people in different categories do not agree upon the criteria or upon the basis for evaluating their fulfillment, the members of at least one category will feel dissatisfied.

For example, whites in the United States may view the discrepancies in income between blacks and whites and argue that their criterion of equality is being met. They might argue that there is equality of opportunity and the differences in income are simply a consequence of differences in ability and motivation for which they share no collective re-

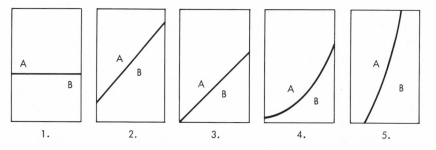

FIGURE 2.1 Patterns of Distribution.

sponsibility. The blacks, however, might hold that the society should so operate that the distribution of income does not differ between blacks and whites. Viewing the same differences between blacks and whites, they would feel that their criterion of equality was not being met and feel dissatisfied.

In addition to feeling dissatisfied, for a social conflict to occur some other set of people must be held responsible. A natural disaster can cause a great deal of dissatisfaction and not a social conflict. The selection or creation of a target is a major topic of concern in the next chapter. Our concern here is with the conditions which tend to make a group of persons believe that they have a zero-sum relationship with another group. This leaves aside the questions about displacement of feelings of anger arising from dissatisfaction. In analyzing the bases for social conflicts we are especially interested in the conditions which underlie two groups actually being in a zero-sum situation.

Three interrelated conditions affect the extent to which groups are in a zero-sum relationship. First, people may believe that what is consensually valued is more or less scarce (Stanley, 1968). Such beliefs depend upon the nature of what is valued and the sources for its creation. Insofar as what is valued is less than the desired amount and is not increasing, groups are more likely to believe that the increase in one party's share necessarily diminishes the other side's attainment of what is valued. As we noted in discussing power and prestige, their scarcity seemed inherent. Now we emphasize that the scarcity of any resource also depends upon the boundedness of the social system. This is the second condition which markedly affects the extent to which the parties are in a zero-sum relationship. Insofar as the parties constitute a closed system and insofar as they are mutually dependent, a change in one group's possession of what is consensually valued will affect the other side. If, in addition the resource is scarce and changes in its magnitude are confined to the social system which the parties constitute, they are in a zero-sum relationship. For example, labor and management may be in a zero-sum relationship within the confines of a given set of markets, but they might, under other market conditions, each increase or both jointly increase what they want at the expense of third parties.

Finally, insofar as one party has taken by coercion, manipulation, or in some other nonlegitimate fashion—its share from the other side, the other side will have experienced a zero-sum relationship. Conceivably, the allocation of values between the two parties might be dictated by impersonal natural forces or processes. Third parties and external nonsocial factors might seem to have determined the allocation. Of course, whether the allocation is determined by nature (e.g. the "natural" differences between the races or sexes) or by exploitation is a matter of contention among the parties in conflict.

Karl Marx's ideas about class conflict can be illustrative of the formal analysis presented here (Marx, 1964). He argued that technological developments resulted in the emergence of large-scale capital investments. Under capitalism, the ownership of that capital by a few resulted in the relative disadvantage of the workers, those who did not own the means of production. The workers had less of the resources they and the capitalist owners all wanted. His analysis pointed out the conditions which would make the workers realize that they were exploited; that they should feel dissatisfied and that the capitalists and their ownership of the means of production was the source of their deprivation.

In summary, we are arguing that there are conditions which underlie consensual conflicts and the observer selects the aspects most pertinent to social conflicts. Within the context that the analyst chooses he or she can discern agreement about the desirability of a particular resource. He or she conceives of possible contending parties and notes the allocation of the desired resources between the two parties and then considers how likely one or both parties are to be dissatisfied with that allocation. Finally, the analyst must assess the likelihood that one party will regard another as the cause of the dissatisfaction and the possessor of resources which, if given up, would reduce its own dissatisfaction.

THE MIXED NATURE OF ACTUAL CONFLICTS:
SOME CASES

In any specific dispute the contending parties have both consensual and dissensual bases for conflict. The relative importance of each varies in different conflicts; it also varies among different segments of each party and probably changes in the course of a struggle. Thus, a religious difference between two groups may be a part of an objective dissensual conflict. In addition, however, the leaders of each religious group may agree about the value of certain resources and for them a large component of the conflict is consensual.

We will discuss some of the dissensual and consensual aspects of objective conflicts in university and industrial organizations, in the American society, and in the current international system. These cases will be used illustratively in this book.

Labor-management.   Let us begin with industrial organizations. What is the objective conflict between quasi groups? A host of problems is immediately apparent. Between what strata should we draw any lines? Should we compare persons working in a single factory, a corporation, an industry, or in major occupational strata across a single city or society? All these are important questions and they are not independent of each other. Thus, the general position of members of the working class affects the way workers tend to think of themselves and act together within any particular factory (Riddell, 1968). For example, factory workers who do not conform to collegual norms tend to have less typically working-class backgrounds than other workers (Dalton, 1948). Working-class self-consciousness affects the development of unions in a particular occupation and the growth of trade union participation affects class consciousness.

The underlying basis for society-wide class conflicts, for conflicts of one particular occupational group against its employers and for conflicts of the manual employees of a particular company against its management all exist. Which become manifest, how they are expressed once the conflicts are manifest, and how they are related to each other all depend upon numerous particular conditions. In this chapter we will provide only a few illustrations of objective conflicts between workers and managers.

First, consider the prestige of different occupations. We can safely assume that people in every society value prestige. This does not mean that some people would not rather have security, safety, or high income to compensate for low prestige, but prestige is valued. Furthermore, there is considerable evidence that at least within the United States there is high agreement about how occupations are ranked in prestige (Kriesberg, 1962; Hodge, Siegel, and Rossi, 1966; Reiss, 1961). The occupations within any given company have society-wide prestige value. The variations in ranking of general occupational titles which may be found in companies are presented in Table 2.1. The scores are taken from a national U.S. survey conducted in 1963; the respondents were asked to rate 90 occupations. Scores were compiled for each occupation and ranged from 94 for a Supreme Court Justice to 34 for a shoe shiner.

Similarly, within each company and across the society as a whole,

TABLE 2.1 Prestige Scores of Selected Occupations

Occupation	*Score*
Member of a board of directors of a large corporation	87
Accountant for a large business	81
Owner of a factory that employs about 100 people	80
Trained machinist	74
Machine operator in a factory	63
Night Watchman	50

Source: Data from Hodge, Siegel, and Rossi, 1966.

TABLE 2.2   Annual Earnings of Males in Selected Occupations and Offices

A. *Occupations*	*Median Earnings in Dollars, 1969*
Salaried managers, officials	11,284
Foreman	9,522
Operatives and kindred workers	6,248
Laborers, except farm and mine	2,483

B. *Offices**	*Annual Salaries, about 1971*
Chairman, General Electric	252,250
Chairman and president, International Telephone and Telegraph (ITT)	382,494
Chairman, General Telephone and Electronics	100,000
President, Xerox Corporation	325,063
Cable and pipe repairman, New York Telephone Company	5,460

*Does not include expense allowances, stock options, or bonuses. In 1971 the chairman and president of ITT received a bonus of $430,000.

Sources: *A*: U.S. Bureau of the Census, 1971, p. 229; *B*: Tetlow, 1972.

material benefits are not equally distributed among different occupational strata. There are many ways of comparing even income among different occupations: weekly, monthly, yearly, or life-time earnings or income before or after taxes. Let us consider the most frequently used measure: annual gross earnings. Part A of Table 2.2 shows variations only between large heterogenous occupational categories. Within a large corporation, the variation is greater, as indicated in part B of Table 2.2.

Another way of looking at the earnings of different occupational strata emphasizes the relative nature of earnings and the collective character of occupational groups. We could examine the proportion of the national income which various groups receive compared to their proportion in the population. We could also look at the percentage distribution of a company's earnings.

Power differences among occupations are even more difficult to quantify, but they exist in many different ways. First, there is the degree to which members of different occupational groups can control their own work activities. In some occupations neither the mode of work nor its pace are under the workers' control—as for example, in assembly line work (Blauner, 1964). The workers can have varying amounts of control over their own activities depending on the technology of the occupation and the amount and kind of supervision to which they are subject. Control over one's own work is closely related to power relations with others in relevant occupations. Thus, within a factory or corporation, there may be clear lines of authority associated with different occupational roles; roles at each rank being superior to some and subordinate to others.

The control may not only refer to the work activities themselves but to claims about the incumbency of the occupational role. In some occupations the members largely determine entrance (this is particularly true of professions). Once entered the rights to the position may depend upon customers, colleagues, or superiors. In industrial employment, in the past, superiors in authority have determined entrance and duration of employment; the major constraints upon the arbitrariness of such decisions were the nature of the competitive market for each occupation and the customary standards of appropriate notice. With the development of trade unions, unionized workers have gained some collective control over the terms of employment (Foote, 1953; Hildenbrand, 1953).

Power among occupational strata also differs in the determination of policy for the larger units of which they are a part. Thus, we can consider the relative power workers and managers have in determining the policies of the factory or corporation in which they work. Even with unionization, workers as a group have relatively little power in decisions about matters such as investments, mergers, marketing choices, or new product developments. We can also ask about their relative power in formulating policy in the community and society in which they live. In these spheres we are usually considering broad occupational strata. On the whole, wage earners are practically unrepresented in the U.S. Congress and hardly represented in state legislatures (Mathews, 1954, table 7). Even considering the occupational origins of political elites, we find that few are children of wage earners (Keller, 1963, p. 312).

Differences in power are likely to be the bases of conflicts insofar as the parties with different amounts of power disagree about the decisions to be made. That is, when dissensus about collective values is added to consensus about the desirability of having power we have the basis for conflict. Thus, if workers and managers agreed about what the factories, companies, and society should do, then the differences in allocation of power would not be fraught with serious implications for them. In the case of factories or companies, we do not know a great deal about how different the goals of workers and managers actually are for the whole enterprise. There are certainly some differences. Managers, given their identification with the firm and their specific roles within it, are likely to consider the size, rate of growth, or percentage of the market held by the firm to be more important concerns than would the workers. But, there is probably considerable consensus, within this society, about the basic aims of the firm.

The dissensual conflicts between workers and managers are generally based upon incompatibility arising from their social relationship which requires coordination. They are much less likely to arise from claims about values or life styles made upon each other. The disdain of workers and managers about each other's way of life is not so strongly held that it would generally lead to efforts to impose their own views.

University Students-Administrators. People are college and university students on a transitory basis, unlike persons in ethnic, sexual, national, or even occupational categories. Related to this is the fact that most students are of similar ages. Administrators (and faculty) are more like persons in any occupational category within an organization.

Given the nature of students and administrators within colleges and universities, differences in prestige and money are generally not significant conditions underlying conflict. Their relative prestige and money is in great measure derived from their social and economic positions outside of colleges and universities. In societies where attendance at institutions of higher learning is severely restricted to children of the highest socioeconomic stratum, the prestige of the students is high and they may be able to maintain a high standard of living as well. In these cases their prestige and income is not based on their position as students. In countries such as the United States, where attendance is widespread and the students are not drawn from a homogeneously high stratum, the prestige of students has some independent value. Although the prestige of students and administrators has not been assessed in any systematic way, it is probably safe to infer from our own experience that students have much lower prestige within the university organizational structure. Given the view of students as uneducated recipients of knowledge and skills from the faculty, the low prestige of students relative to faculty and administration is integral to the setting in which they operate.

Power differences between students and administrators are clearly an integral characteristic of colleges and universities as organizations. Students have relatively little individual or collective power. The general difficulties in the assessment of power are compounded because power relations are always in flux and they vary widely among organizations and in different spheres of organizational life. In curricular activity such as course selection, course conduct, and grades, the students have little direct power. They can and do affect such matters by essentially aggregate market conduct: the choice of college and the choice of courses and programs of study. There is also some control by group definitions of what is appropriate and necessary work, but this is done within very powerful constraints essentially constructed by the faculty and administration (Becker, Geer, and Hughes, 1968). Currently there is increasing formal student participation in curriculum decisions (Freidson, 1955; McGrath, 1970). There has been very little individual or collective control over many spheres of extracurricular activities such as housing and drinking. This too is changing, largely in the direction of increased student autonomy. Finally, there is the matter of relative power in determining the general policy of the university or college. The issues here relate to the organization's investments, expansion into surrounding neighborhoods, and kinds of research constraints imposed or not imposed. Students generally have had little influence in making such decisions.

Dissensus in values between administrators and students is typically present in universities. For one thing there is a generational difference in experience and interest. Furthermore their respective positions within the university structure result in different perspectives. Finally, differences in social, economic, and ethnic backgrounds accentuate the existing dissensus.

As we noted earlier, dissensus constitutes objective conflict when differences in values and beliefs are incompatible. Incompatibility may arise from the need to act in coordination or from the claims which one group makes upon the other regarding their differences. Both kinds of incompatibility exist in universities. Joint coordination is required as the various groups within universities must work together. Actually, much of the work of various categories within a university can and must be done relatively autonomously; close coordination is unnecessary or impossible. This reduces the objective dissensual conflicts. Nevertheless, there is increasing questioning of the role of universities as collectivities which affect the neighborhoods in which they are located and the policies of governmental units, and even how they invest their endowment. Dissensus about major societal issues, then, has implications for university decisions.

The kind of relationship in colleges and universities, the age differences, and the societal context all make it likely that dissensus in values will be incompatible because people make unacceptable claims on each other. Within a college where administrators feel they are responsible for the lives of their students they will make judgements about their moral conduct and try to channel it in accord with their own values. Arrangements about aspects of living such as those pertaining to sexual relations, drinking, and ways of dressing all can become issues of contention. As we shall see, one outcome of conflicts about such issues is an alteration in the moral claims people make on each other. To some extent there may now be a decrease in dissensus, but this may simply be the result of more tolerance for differences.

Females-Males. Although the physiological differences between males and females are usually unambiguous, the social differences between men and women are not. For some purposes it may be appropriate to consider the lines of cleavage for potential conflict to be those of males and females. But the social meaning of male and female is diverse and for purposes of studying social conflict we have to recognize that a woman's position is dependent not only on her sex, but on the social role of women. That social role is partly defined in relation to male roles. Therefore, in noting possible lines of cleavage by sex, it may be appropriate to consider categories based on age, marital status, and employment in conjunction with sex.

One assumption should be made explicit. We assume that there are no innate differences between men and women about what they would consider to be desirable. Males and females are presumed to be equally capable of valuing power, prestige, and material goods. Aside from differences directly and necessarily involved in human reproduction—conception and pregnancy—we can assume that whatever the differences, they are a matter of degree. Even if there were innate differences on the *average* between males and females in some human capacity, the overlap in that capacity between men and women is so great that the differences could be socially ignored. The differences which we observe between men and women in values and conduct is largely a product of the social structure which they have created and in which they live (Weisstein, 1968). As in all asssumptions, the test of this assumption must be in its usefulness for understanding the variations in the genesis and development of conflicts.

As for other quasi groups, we will consider differential allocations of prestige, power, and economic resources. Measures of the relative prestige of men and women, aside from associated characteristics, is not obtainable. Under current conditions there is evidence that men and women agree that men have higher status. One kind of evidence is the degree to which women talk much less than men when in groups of men and women (Strodtbeck, James, and Hawkins, 1957). Furthermore, girls, asked if they wished they could have been boys, are ten times as likely as boys to say they wished they were of the other sex (Watson, cited in Millett, 1970, p. 57). Even among adults, women are more likely than men to admit to having wished that they belonged to the opposite sex, 16 percent compared to 4 percent (Erskine, 1971, p. 290).

The basic peculiarity of men and women as conflict groups is that they live more intimately with each other than among themselves. It is within the family as well as in their relations in the larger society that the objective conflict must be considered. First of all, legal subordination of wives to husbands exists even in the United States. In some states a wife does not have any legal claims upon her husband's earnings or property while they are married aside from the right to be supported (Mead and Kaplan, 1965, p. 153). In other states a wife has an interest in the property which is commonly owned but exclusive authority to manage and control that property generally belongs to the husband. In some states she is not an independent legal agent in a variety of ways (Schulder, 1970).

Outside the home women are not equal beneficiaries of the various distribution and ranking systems in the society. In the past women were excluded from higher education. Even now, there is a remarkable attrition as the levels of education progress. Thus, in 1965 women constituted 50.6 percent of the high school graduates, 40.7 percent of the B.A. (or first professional degree recipients), 32.1 percent of the M.A. recipients, and they received only 10.8 percent of the doctor's degrees awarded (Epstein, 1970, pp. 57–58). The attrition within one field may be illustrative. Thus in sociology, women make up:

43 per cent	of the college seniors planning graduate work in sociology;
37 per cent	of the master's candidates in graduate school;
30 per cent	of the Ph.D. candidates in graduate school;
31 per cent	of the graduates who are teaching undergraduates;
27 per cent	of the full-time lecturers and instructors;
14 per cent	of the full-time assistant professors;
9 per cent	of the full-time associate professors;
4 per cent	of the full-time full professors;
1 per cent	of the chairmen of graduate sociology departments;
0 per cent	of the 44 full professors in the five elite departments (Rossi, 1970, p. 11).

When employed, despite some legislation requiring equal pay, women still earn less money than men for the same jobs (Mead and Kaplan 1965, p. 57). Within every occupational stratum women earn less than men on the average. Finally, in terms of political power it should be recalled that in the United States it was not until 1920 that women obtained the right to vote. Even now, women are very markedly underrepresented at all levels in holding public office. In the actual operations of the legal system, women tend to be treated as less valuable as well as protectively (Nagel and Weitzman, 1972).

Dissensus between men and women in values and beliefs is popularly judged to be highly compatible. Men are more oriented toward, and committed to, concerns about physical courage and aggressiveness, to instrumental efforts and rationality while women are directed toward nurturance, expressiveness, intuition, and emotion. As long as each thinks that what the other wants is good for those others and useful for oneself, the dissensus can be complementary and the basis for exchange. Persons in each category may tend to associate with others in their own group, enjoying and developing their own special qualities. Within contemporary American society there is considerable variation in values and beliefs among men and among women and great overlap between them. Nevertheless, given the differences in socialization and the different social experiences of each, some dissensus is widespread.

For dissensus to be part of the basis of a social conflict, the members of the different categories must think that the differences between them are incompatible. One source of incompatibility arises from the need for coordination. Despite considerable segregation between the sexes, coordination is necessary in many spheres. Most obviously, within each family unit coordination between men and women is needed. The difficulties in achieving a satisfactory level of coordination does not concern us in this book except insofar as these are seen as part of societally shared difficulties between major social categories requiring social changes and not simply the need for improved interpersonal relations and more love between husband and wife.

Within other institutional spheres, such as the economy or politics, the dissensus generally seems irrelevant to the needs for coordination. It is possible that insofar as there are differences, for example, in aggressiveness, then men and women might find it difficult to agree in choosing among policies which differ in possible violence. Thus it might be that support for goals which might entail violence will be a source of contention between men and women. Later in the book we will have reason and opportunity to consider this possibility further.

The other source of possible incompatibility is that men and women make claims upon the other which are mutually objectionable. Sometimes this takes the form of arguing that the others should hold values and beliefs like their own. Witness the anguished cry from *My Fair Lady*: "Why can't a woman be more like a man?" Thus, too, some feminists argue that men also need liberation—to be freed of the role pressures that they be assertive, domineering and unemotional (Roszak, 1969). As liberated persons they could be more expressive, more openly loving of their children, and generally freer to develop a wider range of tastes and abilities than presently. Sometimes this incompatibility arises from the asserted superiority of one's own group's values, beliefs, and patterns of conduct. Again, this might be clearer if we point to an example from the Women's Liberation movement. Some of them argue that the non-hierarchical, equalitarian solidarity of sisterhood is superior to the more typically hierarchical rankings insisted upon by men.

Dissensual and consensual conflicts can, and often do, exacerbate each other. Sometimes, however, aspects of each can mitigate the other's effects. If men and women agree that power is good and if women demand that men have less power over them, it follows that if women's demands are met, men must lose something which is desirable. But, if one values autonomy and freedom, women might argue that if men could stop trying to have so much power over women, they themselves would also be freer. Such inconsistencies do not invalidate each claim. Rather, different people at different times, and to different audiences, may stress one or the other value. The elaboration and specification of the many claims into an integrated program is what leaders of organizations do in formulating the ideology for a particular conflict group. In considering objective conflicts, we need simply discern the *possible* relations between consensual and dissensual conflicts.

Blacks-Whites. To illustrate differences among ethnic groups as a possible basis for social conflicts, we will consider blacks and whites in America, especially in the 1960s. First, we should note that the differences between blacks and whites is social, not biological. Who is white and who is black is a matter of self and other definitions. We will use the popular and conventional definitions because they have social meaning. Given the nature of certain kinds of data, we will sometimes use information about whites compared to nonwhites; most nonwhites in the United States are blacks.

We will discuss objective consensual conflict before considering dissensual conflict. We assume that there are no genetic differences among the many socially defined "races" relevant to their valuing power, prestige, or material well-being. Persons, regardless of "race," are equally capable of desiring such resources.

In regard to prestige or social status blacks are accorded less than are whites. The assertion that black is beautiful is part of an effort to reduce that status difference, at least in the eyes of the blacks. In the past, blacks have acknowledged the status hierarchy which placed them below whites. Efforts to lighten skin color and straighten hair were indications of this. It is in this connection that denial of access to public facilities, segregation of public facilities, and unequal provision of public services is particularly oppressive.

The availability of public services and of the goods and services which can be bought on the private market is, of course, intrinsically important. That is, differences in the ability to eat well, have adequate shelter and clothing, and enjoy what people in a given society think appropriate have inherent value to members of a society. The differences between whites and nonwhites in these regards have been, and are, great. Thus, in 1969, 9.5 percent of all white persons were living in poverty compared to 31.1 percent of nonwhite persons. In part this reflects differences in employment rates, family structure, kinds of jobs held, and wages paid for similar employment. To illustrate: in 1969, 3.1 percent

TABLE 2.3 Occupation and Median Earnings of Males 25 to 64 Years Old in the Experienced Civilian Labor Force with Earnings in 1959, by Education and Color.

Occupation and Education	Median earnings in dollars	
	White	Nonwhite
Accountants and auditors (all)	6,834	5,771
with 4 yrs. or more of college	7,311	6,115
Civil engineers (all)	7,952	6,800
with 4 yrs. or more of college	8,691	7,817
Elementary school teachers (all)	5,471	4,476
with 4 yrs. or more of college	5,601	4,565
Laborers (except farm and mine)	3,871	2,666
Elementary: 0 to 7 yrs.	3,229	2,379
8 years only	3,932	3,044

Source: U.S. Census, 1963.

of the white civilian labor force was unemployed compared to 6.4 percent of the nonwhites (U.S. Bureau of the Census, 1971, pp. 210, 322).

These problems are reflected not only in poverty rates. Even in the same occupations whites generally earn more money than nonwhites. See Table 2.3. Related to such income differences are inequalities in the distribution of food, housing, health care, and education, and mortality rates.

Finally, we must consider the distribution of power between blacks and whites. Two aspects of power relations are pertinent here—for collectivities and for aggregates of individuals. In both regards, blacks have less power than whites. Individually, for example, blacks have had fewer civil rights than whites: thus, they have tended to receive more severe punishments for similar convictions and until recently had been largely disenfranchised in some sections of the country. Collectively, there has been a disproportionately low representation of blacks in various levels of government. After the 1970 congressional elections blacks had the highest representation since Reconstruction yet they constituted three percent of the House of Representatives and one percent of the Senate.

The extent to which there are potential dissensual conflicts between whites and blacks is more difficult to assess. A way of life different from their own is attributed to blacks by many whites; they allege widespread differences in family life, child rearing, patterns of consumption, and personal moral qualities. Many blacks also see themselves as an ethnic group with its own distinctive way of life, but they see different distinctive characteristics than do many whites. The experiences of oppression

are not purely ennobling; if they were, we might all wish to be oppressed. Nevertheless, many blacks perceive an admirable and distinctive
style which has developed from the peculiar experiences of blacks in
America. This distinctive way of life is shown in warmth, spontaneity,
solidarity, courage, and "soul" (Rainwater, 1970).

In actuality, American blacks and whites generally share fundamental
values and beliefs. Differences between them in the distribution of certain values and beliefs are in large part attributable to differences in
economic class and social status. Still, there are enough differences and
beliefs in the differences for objective dissensual conflicts to exist.

Dissensual conflicts depend on the incompatibility of differences in
values and beliefs. Such incompatibility arises from the necessity of
coordinating programs in education, welfare, and even foreign policy; it
arises from the need to coordinate activity in specific organizations such
as factories, schools, and political agencies.

Incompatibility also arises from claims whites and blacks may make on
each other in regard to their distinctive values and beliefs. Thus, whites
and blacks might feel that the way of life they perceive the others have
is morally outrageous. This might be expressed in avoidance, but it may
also be expressed in desires to bring the others to the correct and morally
proper way of life. The differences in values and beliefs and the simple
sense of collective ethnic identity give added purpose to desires for more
power for ethnic collectivities. The power desired may be for control
over the other group or it may be for greater autonomy to assure the
opportunity to maintain and pursue the distinctive styles of one's
own ethnic group.

Again, we can see that in specific conflicts as between blacks and
whites, consensual and dissensual components are mixed. The emphasis,
however can and does vary over time and among different segments of
each category.

International. In considering objective international conflicts we will
focus our attention on the relations between the U.S. and the U.S.S.R.
and between Israel and the neighboring Arab countries. But, given the
interrelations of all nations and the vast amount of relevant information,
I will only outline the bases of conflict among these particular sets
of countries.

Hopefully the value of considering a wide range of units in understanding social conflicts will be more apparent as we study international
conflicts, sensitized by the consideration of objective conflicts among
very different kinds of units. In discussing the previous categories of
people who were in potential conflict, we observed that we had to consider collective power, status, and wealth, as well as the distribution of
such resources among individuals in each category. When we think about

international conflict, we should think about the availability of such resources for the individuals of each society as well as the amounts available to each society as a collectivity.

Let us begin by considering objective consensual conflicts. The first question we must ask is whether or not there is enough consensus among the nation-states of the world about values concerning power, status, and material well being for a conflict about them to exist. There is probably a very high degree of consensus among government leaders and the populace of societies throughout the world about the value of material wealth and about how it is measured. It is also, undoubtedly, of great importance in the value hierarchy of the peoples of the world (Gellner, 1964; Shimbori et al., 1963). There probably is considerable consensus about the desirability of status, prestige, or national honor, but less agreement about its assessment than in the case of material wealth or power. Power is undoubtedly an important value about which there is a high level of consensus. Agreement is even high about its assessment, total military expenditures being a very good indicator of popular perceptions of power (Alcock and Newcombe, 1970).

Now we must consider the possible conditions for one or more countries in our sets of adversaries to be dissatisfied with the allocation of these values *and* believe that improving the allocation must be at the expense of the other side.

We begin by considering material or economic values and their distribution between Israel and the neighboring Arab countries. As can be seen in table 2.4, the per capita wealth of Israel is much greater than the per capita wealth of, for example, Egypt. This in itself, however, does not constitute an objective conflict. Probably the peoples and governments of each country are dissatisfied with the per capita wealth, but not because they use each other as reference groups; the United States, other countries of more similar character, and their own past are more significant points of reference. Even more fundamentally, they do not consider that per capita wealth will be increased at the expense of the other side. Within the nation-state framework, there is not much that one country can coerce or take from the other to improve its per capita standard of living. Increased trade or decreased military expenditures would generally benefit both sides. Relative total wealth (gross national product) is easier to consider as a constituent of potential struggles. Its relative size is important because it is so closely related to power. Furthermore, it is possible to alter the relative amounts of GNP two neighboring countries have by taking some land and its resources from one country and adding them to the other. This is a basis for consensual conflict between Israel and its neighbors (Khouri, 1968).

In the case of the U.S. and the U.S.S.R., the governments and peoples may be more conscious of each other as standards of comparisons for per capita wealth, but the nonzero-sum quality of the each one's per capita wealth is as true as in the case of Israel and its neighbors. Gross national product differences are less clearly alterable at the expense of the other side than is the case for Israel and the surrounding Arab countries. Conceivably, control over other countries may affect trade and investment opportunities. Insofar as each major power is economically exploitative of territories it dominates, then the denial of such territories to the other side increases its total GNP at the expense of the other side. Any assessment of wealth is complicated by the ambiguity about the composition of the adversaries. Is the Soviet Union pitted against the U.S. or are the North Atlantic countries pitted against the Warsaw bloc countries? The relative wealth of two sides in a potential conflict obviously varies with the composition of the two sides.

Status differences are another possible source of potential consensual conflicts between Israel and neighboring Arab countries. Thus, some Egyptians, especially those most directly involved in military relations with Israel may feel a loss of status and need to regain honor which can be obtained only at the expense of Israel—by militarily defeating her. Even control over religiously significant places, for example in Jerusalem, may have status considerations. Objective consensual conflicts regarding status are less present in the relationship between the U.S. and the Soviet Union.

The final basis of consensual conflicts to be considered here pertains to power. Without question, given the nature of the units involved and the nation-state system of which they are parts, the relative power between the various sets of adversaries constitute objective conflicts. Neither Israel nor the surrounding countries have enough power relative to the other to feel secure, given the magnitude of the issues in contention between them. Each side's relative power can be increased only at the expense of the other within the context of a simple dyadic system. The same is the case for the U.S. and U.S.S.R. if they are considered superpowers in a world system (Kissinger, 1960).

Objective dissensual conflict is present between at least some segments of the Soviet and American societies. Not only do they have differing views associated with Marxism-Leninism and communism or Americanism and capitalism, but those views have universal claims (Kennan, 1961). Even here, however, there are important similarities among some elites in both countries (Angell et al., 1964). The Israeli-Arab differences in religious, social, and political views are great, but they do not entail universal claims on each other. Consequently there are no significant objective dissensual conflicts between Israel and the surrounding states.

It is gross and brutal to the truth to attempt to describe the bases

TABLE 2.4   The Arab-Israel Zone: Economic, Social, and Military Indicators

	Population (millions)		Literacy		Students Enrolled in Technical Schools (per 10,000 population)		Electric Energy Production (per capita kwh)	
	1955	1965	1948[a]	Early 60s	1959	1964	1955	1965[a]
Egypt	22.9	29.6	20	27	39	47	60	180
Iraq	6.0	7.4	10	18	11	10	95	170[e]
Jordan	1.4	2.0	5	33	8	13	n.a.	80
Lebanon	1.4	2.4	70	n.a.	4[c]	5	160	380
Syria	3.9	5.6	20	36	1[d]	14	40	100
Israel	1.8	2.6	94[b]	87[b]	75	135	740	1600

	Force Levels (thousands)		Force Levels (per 1,000 population)		Defense Expenditures[g] (in millions of $ U.S.)		Per Capita GNP (in millions of $ U.S.)	
	1955	1965	1955	1965	1955	1965	1955	1965
Egypt	80	180	4	6	286.91	461.84	134	171
Iraq	40	82	7	11	56.00	243.60	160	259
Jordan	23	45	6	23	29.40	58.80	91	252
Lebanon	6.2	13	4	5	12.19	29.35	530	370
Syria	25	60	6	11	29.47	95.50	145	194
Israel[f]	250	3375	134	144	45.46	315.93	659	1308

[a]Estimates.
[b]Jewish community only.
[c]1961.
[d]Provisional.
[e]1964.
[f]Including citizen reserves; the regular services consisted of about 75,000 in 1965.
[g]Including international security and justice.
Source: J. C. Horewitz, *Middle East Politics: The Military Dimension.* Copyright © 1964 by the Council on Foreign Affairs Relations, Inc. New York: Frederick A. Praeger, Inc., Table 18. Reproduced, with adaptations, · by permission of the publisher and author.

underlying conflicts between all these countries in a few paragraphs. But I am counting upon the reader to add the information needed to elaborate and qualify what I have sketched out. In the course of the book more elements of circumstances among these countries will be discussed. But this will be done to illustrate and examine the ideas being presented, not to provide comprehensive case studies.

SUMMARY AND CONCLUSIONS

Objective conflicts may be consensual or dissensual or have varying proportions of both components. Neither consensus nor dissensus can underlie social conflicts, however, unless a set of related conditions are also present. Consensus underlies social conflict when there are bases for one or both sides to view the distribution of what is desired as unsatisfactory and to believe that they can reach a more satisfactory position at the expense of the other side. Dissensus underlies social conflicts when it is the source of incompatibility. This may arise from the requirements of social coordination or when the differences in values and beliefs are accompanied by other views which would lead one or both sides to make unacceptable claims upon the other.

In specific conflicts consensual and dissensual components are combined in varying proportions. Consensual elements may be more important to some segments of each party to a potential struggle than for others, as in the case of leaders compared to the rank and filers. The proportions are also likely to vary as a fight runs its course.

As students of social conflicts we should be sensitive to the objective conflicts which underlie manifest conflicts and the variety of objective conflicts which may be part of what appears to be a single fight. This sensitivity should help us understand the likely course and outcome of specific conflicts. It should help us discern important differences within what might appear to be a single struggle.

This may mean that the "same" people engaging in conflict behavior may or may not be expressing the "same" underlying issue. Thus, students demonstrating at a college may be doing so for a variety of underlying reasons. For some students in relations with some administrators the issue is essentially consensual—a struggle over power and autonomy; for other contending parties, the dissensus about life styles is more central. Furthermore, there is the possibility that one side in the struggle misunderstands the goals that the other is pursuing.

Even when partisans are struggling for the same goals, the underlying conflicts may be different for the segments constituting each side. This is particularly apparent when we consider groups who are allied together during a specific conflict. For example, in the civil rights struggle for equal material well-being and power between blacks and whites in America, the underlying conflict may be quite different as viewed by the various groups struggling for that end. Consider even the variety of underlying bases for whites to be allied with blacks. For some there may be dissensual bases for the conflict with other whites: the commitment to values about equality are compelling. They feel that their own moral character is corrupted by being part of a system in which they are oppressing other humans, in which they can feel superior for no reason except belonging to a large social category by accident of birth. Other whites may agree that material well-being is a primary value but believe that their own material interests would best be served by adding the possible contribution blacks could make to the collective output. Finally, other whites may feel in ultimate agreement with whites and blacks about the value of power but believe that their political party or faction would have more power with the support of blacks as allies than they would by turning aside such support.

We have suggested a wide range of possible bases for social conflicts. This should sensitize us to the complexities of any particular struggle. The clinical diagnosis of a specific fight requires much detailed information but that information must be combined with an understanding of the processes and conditions common to all kinds of social conflicts.

Thus far, we have considered objective conflicts and the conditions which constitute them. Clearly, the conditions are manifold and many different ones may be combined to underlie social conflicts. Not all potential conflicts are actualized. How objective conflicts become manifest is the topic of concern in the next chapter. As we proceed we shall see the implications of different kinds of objective conflicts for the way social conflicts emerge, how incompatible goals are pursued, and what the outcomes are.

BIBLIOGRAPHY

ALCOCK, NORMAN Z. AND ALAN C. NEWCOMBE, "The Perception of National Power," *Journal of Conflict Resolution*, 14 (September 1970), 335–43.

ANGELL, ROBERT C. et al., "Social Values and Foreign Policy of Soviet and American Elites," *Journal of Conflict Resolution*, 8 (December 1964), 329–85.

ARDREY, ROBERT, *The Territorial Imperative* (New York: Dell Publishing Company, 1966).

ARENDT, HANNAH, *On Revolution* (New York: Viking Compass Edition, 1965).

AUBERT, VIHELM, "Competition and Dissensus: Two Types of Conflict and Conflict Resolution," *Journal of Conflict Resolution*, 7 (March 1963) 26–42.

BECKER, HOWARD S., BLANCHE GEER, AND EVERETT C. HUGHES, *Making the Grade: The Academic Side of College Life* (New York: John Wiley & Sons, Inc., 1968).

BERKOWITZ, LEONARD, "The Frustration-Aggression Hypothesis Revisited," in Leonard Berkowitz (ed.), *Roots of Aggression* (New York: Atherton Press, 1969), pp. 1–28.

BIRD, CAROLINE WITH SARA WELLES BRILLER, *Born Female: The High Cost of Keeping Women Down* (New York: David McKay Co., Inc., 1968).

BLAUNER, ROBERT, *Alienation and Freedom: The Factory Worker and His Industry* (Chicago: The University of Chicago Press, 1964).

COLEMAN, JAMES, *Community Conflict* (New York: The Free Press, 1957).

COOLEY, CHARLES H., *Human Nature and the Social Order* (New York: Charles Scribner's Sons, 1922).

COSER, LEWIS A., *The Functions of Social Conflict* (New York: The Free Press, 1956).

DAHRENDORF, RALF, *Class and Class Conflict in Industrial Society* (Stanford, Calif.: Stanford University Press, 1959).

DALTON, MELVILLE, "The Industrial 'Rate-Buster': A Characterization," *Applied Anthropology*, 7 (Winter 1948), 5–18.

DOLLARD, JOHN, *Caste and Class in A Southern Town* (New Haven: Yale University Press, 1937).

DOLLARD, J., L. DOOB, N. MILLER, O. MOWRER, AND R. SEARS, *Frustration and Aggression* (New Haven: Yale University Press, 1939).

EISENSTADT, SAMUEL N., *From Generation to Generation* (New York: The Free Press, 1956).

EPSTEIN, CYNTHIA FUCHS, *Woman's Place: Options and Limits in Professional Careers* (Berkeley: University of California Press, 1970).

ERSKINE, HAZEL, "The Polls: Women's Role," *The Public Opinion Quarterly*, 35 (Summer 1971), 275–90.

FLACKS, RICHARD, "Social and Cultural Meanings of Student Revolt: Some Informal Comparative Observations," *Social Problems*, 17 (Winter 1970), 340–57.

FOOTE, NELSON N., "The Professionalization of Labor in Detroit," *The American Journal of Sociology*, 58 (January 1953), 371–80.

FREIDSON, ELIOT (ed.), *Student Government, Student Leaders, and the American College* (Philadelphia: United States National Student Association, 1955).

FREUD, SIGMUND, "Why War," in John Rickman (ed.), *Civilization: War and Death* (London: Hogarth Press, 1939) pp. 13–30. Originally written in 1932.

GELLNER, ERNEST, *Thought and Change* (Chicago: University of Chicago Press, 1964).

HILDENBRAND, GEORGE H., "American Unionism, Social Stratification and Power," *The American Journal of Sociology*, 58 (January 1953), 381–90.

HODGE, ROBERT W., PAUL M. SIEGEL, AND PETER H. ROSSI, "Occupational Prestige in the United States: 1925–1963" in R. Bendix and S. M. Lipset (eds.), *Class, Status, and Power* (New York: The Free Press, 1966).

HUREWITZ, J. C., *Middle East Politics: The Military Dimension* (New York: Frederick A. Praeger Inc., 1969).

JOHNSON, CHARLES S., *Patterns of Negro Segregation* (New York: Harper and Brothers, 1943).

KELLER, SUZANNE, *Beyond the Ruling Class* (New York: Random House, Inc., 1963).

KENNAN, GEORGE F., *Russia and the West Under Lenin and Stalin* (Boston: Little, Brown & Company, 1961).

KHOURI, FRED J., *The Arab-Israeli Dilemma* (Syracuse: Syracuse University Press, 1968).

KISSINGER, HENRY A., *The Necessity for Choice: Prospects of American Foreign Policy*. New York: Harper and Brothers, 1960).

KRIESBERG, LOUIS, "The Retail Furrier: Concepts of Security and Success," *The American Journal of Sociology*, 37 (March 1953), 478–85.

———, "The Bases of Occupational Prestige," *American Sociological Review*, 27 (April 1962), 238–44.

LORENZ, KONRAD, *On Aggression*, translated by Marjorie Kerr Wilson (New York: Bantam Books Inc., 1967). Originally published 1963.

MCGRATH, EARL J., *Should Students Share the Power?* (Philadelphia: Temple University Press, 1970).

MARX, KARL, *Selected Writings in Sociology and Social History*, translated by T. B. Bottomore, T. B. Bottomore and M. Rubel (eds.) (New York: McGraw-Hill Book Company, 1964). Originally published 1844–1873.

MATTHEWS, DONALD R., *The Social Background of Political Decision-Makers* (Garden City, N.Y.: Doubleday & Company, Inc., 1954).

MEAD, MARGARET AND FRANCES BAGLEY KAPLAN, *American Women, The Report of the President's Commission on the Status of Women and other Publications of the Commission* (New York: Charles Scribner's Sons, 1965).

MILLETT, KATE, *Sexual Politics* (Garden City, N.Y.: Doubleday & Company, 1970).

MYRDAL, GUNNAR, "A Parallel to the Negro Problem," in *An American Dilemma* (New York: Harper and Brothers, 1944), Appendix 5, pp. 1073–78.

NAGEL, STUART AND LENORE J. WEITZMAN, "Double Standard of Justice," *Society,* 9 (March 1972), 62–63.

PARSONS, TALCOTT, *The Social System* (New York: The Free Press, 1951).

————, "Youth in the Context of American Society," *Dædalus*, 91 (Winter 1962), 97–123.

RAINWATER, LEE (ed.), *Soul* (Chicago: Aldine Publishing Company, 1970).

REISS, ALBERT J., JR., *Occupations and Social Status* (New York: The Free Press, 1961).

RIDDELL, DAVID S. "Social Self-Government: The Background of Theory and Practice in Yugoslav Socialism," *British Journal of Sociology*, 19 (March 1968), 47–75.

ROSSI, ALICE S., "Status of Women in Graduate Departments of Sociology," *The American Sociologist*, 5 (February 1970), 1–12.

ROSZAK, BETTY, "The Human Continuum" in B. Roszak and T. Roszak (eds.), *Masculine/Feminine* (New York: Harper & Row, Publishers, Inc., 1969), pp. 297–306.

SCHULDER, DIANE B., "Does the Law Oppress Women?" in Robin Morgan (ed.), *Sisterhood is Powerful* (New York: Vintage Books, 1970), pp. 139–57.

SHIBUTANI, TAMOTSU, *Society and Personality* (Englewood Cliffs, N.J.: Prentice-Hall, Inc., 1961).

SHIMBORI, MICHIYA, et al., "Measuring a Nation's Prestige," *The American Journal of Sociology*, 69 (July 1963), 63–68.

SIEGRIED, ANDRE, *America Comes of Age* (New York: Harcourt, Brace, and Company, 1927).

STANELY, MANFRED, "Nature, Culture and Scarcity: Foreword to a Theoretical Synthesis," *American Sociological Review*, 33 (December 1968), 855–70.

STRODTBECK, FRED, RITA M. JAMES, AND CHARLES HAWKINS, "Social Status in Jury Deliberations," *American Sociological Review*, 22 (December 1957), 713–19.

TETLOW, KARIN, "How Much Can a Person Make for a Job Like That?" *New York*, 5 (May 1972), 28–35.

Tinbergen, N., "On War and Peace in Animals and Man," *Science*, 160 (June 28, 1968), 1411–18.

U.S. Bureau of the Census, *U.S. Census of Population: 1960 Subject Reports. Occupation by Earnings and Education.* Final Report PC (2)–7B (Washington, D.C.: U.S. Government Printing Office, 1963).

———, *Statistical Abstract of the United States: 1971*, 92nd edition (Washington, D.C.: U.S. Government Printing Office, 1971).

Weber, Max, *The Theory of Social and Economic Organization*, translated by A. M. Henderson and T. Parsons (New York: Oxford University Press, 1947).

Weisstein, Naomi, " 'Kinder, Kuche, Kirche' as Scientific Law: Psychology Constructs the Female," in Robin Morgan (ed.), *Sisterhood is Powerful* (New York: Vintage Books, 1970), pp. 205–20.

Westby, David L. and Richard G. Braungart, "Class and Politics in the Family Backgrounds of Student Political Activists," *American Sociological Review*, 31 (October 1966), 690–92.

chapter three

The Emergence
of Social Conflicts

For social conflicts to exist groups of people must believe that they have incompatible goals. Our concern in this chapter is to analyze what makes people have such beliefs. In the last chapter, as observers, we discerned circumstances which could and probably would lead to social conflicts. But not all potential conflicts emerge into awareness. In this chapter we shall examine what determines that emergence. Despite all the reasons for social conflict, why do some, but not others, emerge?

For social conflicts to emerge three major aspects of awareness are needed. First, the groups or parties to the conflict must be conscious of themselves as collective entities, separate from each other. Second, one or more groups must be dissatisfied with their position relative to another group. Finally, they must think that they can reduce their dissatisfaction by the *other* group acting or being different; that is, they must have aims which involve the other group yielding what it would not otherwise yield. Before trying to explain how these subjective states emerge we should analyse them in more detail.

A group's self-awareness as a collective entity in opposition to another group is formed and transformed in the course of a conflict. Nevertheless, some awareness is necessary at the struggle's outset. Awareness may be expressed in social movements or in organizations within a social movement. We should keep the problematic character of conflict groups in mind. As noted in the first chapter, parties to a conflict may be more or less clearly bounded. The members of a group themselves determine that they are an entity with boundaries and therefore exclude some kinds of people as well as include others. Even in the case of nation-states, the parties should not be taken for granted. In a dispute between the U.S. and the U.S.S.R., are the contending parties the two govern-ments, the people supporting each government's goals, all the citizens of the two nation-states, or all the supporters of each side's general ideology? The mobilization of people into self-conscious groups which are in op-position to another group is a primary aspect of any social conflict. Without self-conscious groups, discontented persons may express their dissatisfaction individually but not engage in a social conflict. Workers in a factory may be discontented and therefore frequently absent, or leave after a short time on the job; such a factory would have a high absentee or turnover rate, but not necessarily a high degree of social conflict.

The second part of the subjective conditions which must exist for a social conflict to arise is for members of one or more groups to have a grievance. This entails having less than what is wanted. That requires a standard by which they can judge what is appropriate and desirable for them to have. In addition, a grievance requires that people think that it is possible to have more. This conceptualization should make it clear that people may have less than they would like but not feel that they have a grievance. They think the discrepancy exists because that is the way the world is, it is God's will, or because of the limits of tech-nology and of humans. This conceptualization should also make it clear how objective conflict relationships may not necessarily be experienced subjectively.

The third aspect of a manifest conflict is that at least one party be-lieves some redress of its grievances and some lessening of its dissatisfac-tion depends on another group. That is, a dissatisfied group thinks that *if* its claim on another group is met, it will be less dissatisfied. In addition, for a manifest conflict to exist that claim must be unacceptable, objec-tionable, or undesired by the other group. In other words, the parties must have incompatible goals. We will discuss the formulation, trans-formation, and implications of different conflicting aims in other chap-ters of the book. At this time we need only outline the major kinds of aims.

Basically, we can distinguish two types of conflicting goals—to term-inate the relationship between the groups *or* to alter it. The aim of terminating a relationship may involve either withdrawal or the ob-literation of the other unit. Thus, in the case of consensual conflicts a group may seek to flee from the claims made by the other side or it may hope to destroy or exterminate the other party as an adversary (this may mean the destruction of it as an organized group or killing all its members or its leading segments). In the case of dissensual conflicts the relationship may be terminated by secession or by converting the other party so that it no longer exists as a dissensual conflict group.

More commonly the goal of a conflict group is to alter the relationship with its adversary. The alteration may involve changing who occupies certain positions in the relationship or it may mean changing the structure of the relationship. In consensual conflicts a group might wish to become the occupants of the dominant positions and displace the current holders of the position, as in a palace revolution. There is no counterpart for this in dissensual conflicts. There are a variety of goals involving changing the structure of the relationship in consensual conflicts. Many of them involve redistributing the values which all parties agree are desirable. The poor may want more money or the rich may want even more. In the case of dissensual conflicts an aim which involves changing the relationship may be to seek autonomy or tolerance for its own way of life.

In this chapter we are primarily concerned with understanding how conflict groups become conscious of themselves as groups, come to perceive that they have grievances, and formulate goals which would lessen their dissatisfaction, at the apparent expense of another party. Actually, these three aspects of a manifest conflict are highly interdependent. Who we are, what we have to complain about, and who is to blame for it are all related and help determine each other. For example, if we are women and subjugated, it must be men doing it. If capitalists are in charge and we are underpaid, we are proletarians.

In studying these aspects of manifest conflict we are interested in accounting for basic variations in these subjective states. We want to account for the intensity and extensiveness of conflicts. Thus we can study variations in the proportion in a given category who are organized into conflict groups and the proportion who are mobilized as supporters of the goals of the organizations. We can study variations in how strongly the members of a category feel dissatisfied; i.e., how intense is the feeling of grievance among the members of the movement or organizations in conflict. Finally, we can consider variations in the radicalism of the aims pursued. That is, are the goals considered relatively minor modifications of the current relationship or a fundamental restructuring? The measure of this is likely to be the way in which the other side regards the goals.

The bases for consensual and dissensual conflicts should help account for the extent and intensity of manifest conflicts. But they cannot provide a complete explanation. Additional factors must be introduced. Three sets of factors will be considered: (1) the characteristics of the units, (2) the whole set of relations between the units, and (3) the units' environment or context. As we discuss each set of factors we will try to see how they relate to the conditions underlying conflict to produce or not produce manifest conflicts.

To support the contention that a particular condition makes conflict more or less likely or more or less intense and radical we will point to empirical evidence. The evidence, however, is more available about the conflict *behavior* of units than their subjective states. Yet the state of mind which defines the existence of a social conflict may not be expressed in conflict behavior. As we shall see in the next chapter, still other factors must be taken into account to explain whether or not parties in conflict use coercion and violence. We should be careful, therefore, when we test the ideas with reference to coercive *conduct* and conflict *behavior,* rather than more direct measures of what people are thinking and feeling.

ADVERSARY CHARACTERISTICS

We begin by considering how characteristics of a unit affect its entering into a conflict relationship with another unit. It might be argued that whether or not a group enters into conflict with another depends entirely on the relationship between them. Alternatively, it might be contended that some units, or their members, are basically aggressive or hostile and such characteristics account for social conflicts. On the whole, in this analysis, we emphasize the relationship between parties as the explanation for their disputes. But we also need to examine the role of internal or domestic factors which affect the emergence of conflict groups. Even in this discussion, however, many characteristics of a unit cannot be assessed independently of an opponent.

Collective Identity. We begin considering internal factors by examining how characteristics of the people in a given social category affect the likelihood that they (or some of them) come to view themselves as having a collective identity. We ask what about them makes them think that they share a common fate, that they have more in common with each other than they have with members of other social categories?

A prerequisite for a sense of common identity is communication among the members of the category. Insofar as communication among members is hindered or handicapped relative to nonmembers, so is the likelihood that a sense of commonness and collective identity will develop. Many factors affect the ease of communication. The proximity and density of the members of a category, their absolute number, the social and nonsocial barriers between them, and the social and technical skills the members possess all affect the rate of communication.

Thus, factors which bring persons of a social category into large concentrations facilitates their communication with each other and the development of common perspectives. For example, industrial employment in large factories provides such opportunities; similarly the concentration of ethnic groups in particular regions or parts of a city provides this opportunity. Less physically concentrated people are handicapped in developing collective self-awareness. For example, women in this society are not concentrated in any particular locations.

Communication, of course, does not depend entirely on physical distance. Access to the technology of communication and the possession of the social skills for communication are more critical. Social categories which have members with such resources more readily develop collective self-consciousness and express this in some organizational form. One of the factors which accounts for the order in which trade unions have been established is the ability of the workers to communicate and organize; printers, shoemakers, and other skilled craftsmen were the first to form trade unions.

Significantly, when we consider consensual conflicts it is those who have more status, power, or material wealth who are also most likely to have more of the requisite skills and resources for communication (Parkin, 1971). Furthermore, those with more power, if they have enough, may use their power to limit the possession and development of the skills needed for communication among the groups with less power. For example, education has been forbidden or limited for slaves, and even since slavery, American blacks have not had equal access to education. Women, too, have not had equal educational opportunities (Flexner, 1959, pp. 23–40).

The availability of the means of extensive communication also favors the dominant groups. Thus, the mass media generally convey the perspectives of whites, of males, and of upper-white collar occupations (e.g., Johnson, Sears, and McConahay, 1971). Similarly, within organizations, newspapers are often controlled by the dominant groups in the organization (witness the traditional pattern of control even over student-run college publications). Members of sub-dominant categories, then, have less opportunity to develop a collective identity. In the case of dissensual conflicts, however, the restrictions of media often help the growth of ingroup solidarity. This may be reenforced by language differences as between societies or between ethnic groups within a society.

Communication is also affected by the size of the units under consideration—but in contradictory ways. The larger the unit, the greater is the communication problem to reach common understandings and a sense of common interest. But in larger units the chances are greater that interaction will be contained within the unit rather than with outside persons. This is illustrated by the finding that the ratio of intra-society transactions to intersociety transactions increases with the population size of societies (Sawyer, 1967).

Homogeneity of the members in a social category tends to facilitate communication and the growth of a sense of solidarity and common fate. For example, Landecker (1963) found that class consciousness was more frequent among persons with high status crystallization than among those with low status crystallization. One of the frequently observed difficulties in the formation of worker solidarity in the form of trade union membership or of class consciousness in America has been the extensive immigration and ethnic heterogeneity of the American workers (Perlman, 1928, pp. 162–69; Bok and Dunlop, 1970, p. 30). This may also be seen in variations among different occupational groups or within organizations. For example, in a study of teachers and administrators in 28 high schools, it was found that incidents of disputes among teachers was correlated with heterogeneity of the faculty (Corwin, 1969).

Solidarity among women as a conflict group is handicapped by their heterogeneity. Not only do they have the diversity of men in terms of ethnicity, region, and occupation, but their marital status and the status of their husbands have great salience for them. In dissensual conflicts some homogeneity in values must exist within each of the conflict groups, but it may be relatively trivial compared to the differences within and the similarities across group lines. Groups in dissensual conflict often seek to create a homogeneity based upon past experience. Thus, national and ethnic groups emphasize a common historical origin or basic experience that distinguishes them from nonmembers.

Finally, the boundedness and degree of organization of the category affect the growth of group solidarity. The more clear and unchanging are the boundaries of a social category, the more likely are the members of the category to develop a sense of common fate. Members of a caste are more likely (everything else being equal) to think of themselves as a collective group with a common interest than are members of a social class. Social categories based upon ascribed and unchanging status, such as race or sex, are conducive to solidarity. However, we have already noted and will note additional factors associated with those of lower rank which operate in a contrary direction. National societies are highly bounded and internally organized. This helps explain why their members have a relatively high sense of common interest and solidarity with their compatriots.

The more highly interdependent and integrated are the members of a category, the more likely they are to see themselves as a collectivity with common interests. This can be seen in variations among members of different occupations (e.g., L. Kriesberg, 1953; Seidman, London, Karsh, and Tagliacozzo, 1958). Miners, for example, are vitally interdependent in their work activities and historically have had a high sense of solidarity compared to other occupational groups (Gouldner, 1954). Of course, the solidarity of the miners is reenforced by many factors, such as isolation and concentration.

Finally, we must observe that the more highly organized the group is and the more it precedes and transcends a particular conflict, the less problematic is the issue of mobilization of support for any particular conflict. In many ways, self-consciousness of the group is less important; it can be taken for granted. Thus, in conflicts between established conflict groups (e.g., governments or trade unions), acquiescence or support of a constituency can generally be assumed.

Sense of Grievance. The aspect of social conflict which has received the most attention among students of conflict is the degree of discontent or dissatisfaction among the members of a partisan group. This is understandable. Seeing a group pursue an aim which is incompatible with another group's desired position, it seems natural to ask what is making the group do that and look for the answer in the bases of dissatisfaction of that group. Even if that cannot provide a comprehensive explanation for the emergence of social conflicts, it is an essential component.

The sense of grievance must reside among the members of one, or both, adversary groups, but the sources of the sense of grievance may reside in the relations between the parties in contention, in their environment, or in the characteristics of the members themselves. We will consider the third source first. Dissatisfaction, discontent, or a sense of grievance analytically entails people having less than they think they *should* have and conceivably could have. Stated this generally, the formulation is appropriate for dissensual conflicts as well as consensual ones. But, in discussing and illustrating the sources for the discrepancies, we will concentrate our attention upon consensual conflicts.

Our concern is with a sense of grievance or discontent, and it might seem reasonable that such feelings are at the opposite end of a continuum from happiness or a sense of well-being. Research has revealed the inaccuracy of this idea (Bradburn and Caplovitz, 1965; Bradburn, 1969). The research indicates that self-assessed happiness or well-being is based upon the balance of positive and negative feelings. Furthermore, positive and negative feelings are not correlated with each other; that is, a person may have a lot of both, a lot of one and little of the other, or little of either. In addition some factors make for satisfying or positive feelings while others make for negative or dissatisfying ones.

These findings suggest that we should not interpret indicators of satisfaction or dissatisfaction alone as the measure of a general sense of grievance or level of discontent. For a particular social conflict, however, specific dissatisfactions probably have special pertinence. Unfortunately, there is little research or even speculation about the components and structure of feelings of discontent as an aspect of social conflict. The complexities are mentioned here because they can help to reconcile what otherwise would be inconsistent findings.

There are several formulations of the bases of a sense of inequity (Goodman and Friedman, 1971; Homans, 1961). We will organize the discussion in terms of three approaches to the sources of discontent. These approaches might be viewed as competing or supplementary. The first approach we will consider emphasizes the absolute magnitude of the deprivation the members of a group endure and the number of spheres in which the people are deprived (Dahrendorf, 1959). The second approach to be considered emphasizes the inconsistent levels which people have in different status dimensions (Lenski, 1954; Goffman, 1957). The third approach emphasizes the changes over time in what people have or what they think they should have (Gurr, 1970; Davies, 1962).

DEPRIVATION.   The general idea is that there is enough agreement in consensual struggles that the more deprived people are, the worse they feel. They do not need any particular insight to know that they are deprived. In any case, other groups of people are readily available for comparison; reference groups can always be found. The important corollary of the idea is that people who are low ranking in several dimensions are more deprived, and feel that they are, than are persons who are high in some ways even if they are low in others.

There are additional reasons why we might expect that insofar as groups are deprived, and uniformly so, they will be dissatisfied. First, the homogeneity of the members of the group facilitates their interaction and the likelihood that they view themselves as a collective entity.

In addition, if members of a given category do not share some other positions with persons in adversary groups, conflict lines will be superimposed. Instead of being bound together by crosscutting ties they will find each conflict issue reenforces the other. Feelings of dissatisfaction will not be muted. Suppose all poor people lived in one region of the country, were of the same low status ethnicity, and had little political power. Then, in the event that a conflict along income lines arises, all the other bases of cleavage would be drawn into the struggle. If these various categories were not superimposed, then people of low income might be of a different ethnic, regional, or political position and have ties of friendship or calculative interest which see them as allies at another time, on another issue.

Furthermore, we might expect that persons who are deprived in one sphere, without satisfactory redress, will generalize their dissatisfaction from one area of discontent to another. They have fewer compensating satisfactions. In short, the more deprived people are, the more likely are they to have general feelings of frustration.

On the bases of these arguments we would expect that lower ranking persons will be more likely to be dissatisfied and to feel it more intensely, compared to higher ranking persons. There is evidence consistent with these expectations. Inkeles (1960) reviewed data from many societies and found that persons of lower occupational or economic levels tend to be generally dissatisfied as indicated by responses to several different kinds of questions. Similarly, occupational studies generally find that the lower the prestige, income, or work autonomy of an occupation, the more likely are its incumbents to be dissatisfied with it and wish to leave it (e.g., Friedmann and Havighurst, 1954; Blauner, 1964).

We would also expect that the more spheres in which people are ranked low, the more likely are they to feel dissatisfied. Thus, in studies of happiness the findings generally indicate that education and income each are directly related to being happy and to having a higher ratio of positive to negative feeling (Bradburn and Caplovitz, 1965, pp. 10–11; Bradburn, 1969, p. 95). Furthermore, these two variables generally have cumulative effects.

There are other reasons, however, to expect that greater deprivation is not directly related to greater sense of grievance and dissatisfaction. First, people who rank low on a consensually valued dimension tend to think poorly of themselves and wish to avoid identifying themselves in terms of that dimension. This means they would avoid interacting with others similarly placed or at least avoid making any collective identification. The absence of solidarity then interferes with collectively recognized and experienced dissatisfaction.

If deprivation is severe, persons will be preoccupied with the day-to-day private efforts at coping rather than develop collectively shared discontent. Even moderate deprivation can be mentally restricting. Buchanan and Cantril (1953, pp. 20–22) in a public opinion study in nine countries found that workers were *less* likely to identify with persons of their nation not of their own class *and* less likely to identify with persons of their own class in other countries, compared to middle class respondents. Related to this, is the fact that if deprivation is severe the deprived tend to accommodate to the deprivation. This may take the form of suppression and denial of hostile feelings and of placating and ingratiating behavior (Karon, 1958; Parker and Kleiner, 1970). These reactions do not aid in the development of a collective sense of grievance. Another, related point deserves mentioning. Severe deprivation may make people despair of changing the conditions. As an accommodation to such despair, even the self-recognition of collective discontent may not occur.

All these arguments indicate that the issues in contention, the stage in the course of a struggle, and other aspects of social conflict must be taken into account to assess the impact of deprivation.

Another difficulty with the degree of deprivation as an explanation of discontent must be considered. In many struggles the party which seems to initiate pursuit of contentious goals is the relatively advantaged party. It is the stronger, the richer, or the higher status group which seeks an increasingly unequal distribution of what is consensually valued. It may be that these groups are not so much more discontented than the others, but they are more able to pursue their desires. We need to consider other possible sources of discontent and their consequences before making a judgment on this matter.

RANK DISEQUILIBRIUM.   Another major theme in contemporary discussions of sources of discontent is rank disequilibrium, status inconsistency, or rank incongruence. The idea is that persons who are high in some rank dimensions and low in others will be particularly dissatisfied. There are several alleged reasons for this. First, it is argued that there is a tendency within social systems for people to have approximately equivalent ranks in different ranking systems; therefore, a person who is high on some ranks and low on others is odd, is treated as odd, and feels so himself. Social interaction is uncomfortable and this discomfort is communicated to the persons with inconsistent ranks (Lenski, 1954; Hughes, 1944). Consequently, rank disequilibrium is experienced as a source of strain.

This strain is compounded by the tendency of others to try to relate to people in disequilibrium in terms of their low ranks and the persons in disequilibrium themselves trying to relate to others in terms of their high ranks (Galtung, 1964). This might be seen in a male worker "putting down" a woman supervisor as just a woman and the supervisor treating the worker as just that. Relations among workers in restaurants abound in such problems (Whyte, 1948).

The third major reason that status inconsistency is a source of grievance is that it makes people feel that their low rank is particularly objectionable. This is partly because people treat them in terms of it when that is not the major way they see themselves. It is also the case because if they use the high ranks as a reference or comparison level, the low rank is more objectionable than if they used a lower rank as the reference level. The low rank is particularly grievous, in addition, because the high rank provides a claim for an equal level on the other ranks. Moreover, the high rank makes it credible that the same level be attained on other ranking dimensions. As we have noted earlier, just having less than you would like is not enough to make a grievance; people must also think that it is *possible* for them to have what they think they should have.

A final consideration deserves noting. If people have high ranks along some dimensions, they are likely to have resources and skills which give them reason to think that they might alter their circumstances, at least compared to those who are uniformly deprived. The sense of competence or possible efficacy would make it easier for persons to admit, recognize, and collectively acknowledge their dissatisfaction.

Many writers argue that not all patterns of rank incongruencies have the same consequences. Thus, persons ranked high on ascribed dimensions (e.g., ethnicity) or dimensions which are considered investments (e.g., education), but low on achieved or reward dimensions (e.g., occupation or income) may be called underrewarded. They will experience failure and disappointment (Jackson, 1962; Geschwender, 1967). They are likely to feel anger. On the other hand, persons ranked low on ascribed or investment dimensions and high on achieved or reward dimensions should feel a sense of success and not be discontented. They may feel guilt.

There is some evidence consistent with these arguments. Geschwender (1968) for example, studied unrest among male manual workers; unrest was indicated by questions about job satisfaction, neighborhood satisfaction, participation in voluntary associations and several other activities. He found that underrewarded inconsistents did tend to exhibit symptoms of individual unrest. Similarly, there is some indication from the happiness studies that older persons with high education but low income are less likely to be happy than one would expect from a simple additive model (Bradburn and Caplovitz, 1965, pp. 10–11; Bradburn, 1969, p. 96). Presumably among young persons the possibility of raising their income to the appropriate level for their education is viewed as still available.

There is another kind of specification of rank disequilibrium which should be introduced. This is related to the idea of relative deprivation and reference groups (Hyman, 1942; Merton and Kitt, 1950; Runciman, 1966). The idea is that people judge how well they are doing by reference to some groups to which they may or may not belong. This is applicable to any explanation of a sense of grievance since that depends upon a discrepancy between what people think they *should* have and what they *do* have.

The idea's particular relevance for rank disequilibrium can be briefly noted. Each status to which people belong can serve as a reference group. The basic difficulty with reference group theory is that it does not tell us which of the many possible groups will be selected as the reference group. Thus, among status inconsistents, people could choose a high status as their reference and feel deprived. But it is also possible for them to choose a low rank and, using that as a standard, feel relatively well off.

As we have noted, some students of status inconsistency presume people will generally choose their high ranks as standards; that is why inconsistents would generally be more dissatisfied than consistents. Other students of the matter argue that statuses which entail investments will serve as the standard. Another line of reasoning stresses that certain statuses have particular importance in each society or group; it is the "master" status (Hughes, 1944). Thus, in American society occupation is salient. Socially, we use it to locate each other. Consequently, we might expect that a person would use his occupation as the standard of reference. Thus, the manual nonmanual occupational distinction is a fundamental one in this society; the distinction is a kind of boundary behind which each group conducts the important social relations. Assessments of income or of work role are made relative to oneself and one's friends as manual workers. Therefore, high income manual workers might be expected to think they are not doing so badly compared to others who are socially relevant to him and hence be satisfied. There is some evidence which lends credence to this reasoning (Runciman, 1966, pp. 188–208; Bradburn, 1969, p. 196). It might be expected, by the same reasoning, that low income white-collar workers would be especially dissatisfied. The same studies do not indicate any such affect. Apparently these conditions are relevant to satisfactions but not (at least in the same manner) to dissatisfactions.

Although the reasoning by which status inconsistency is a source of discontent and therefore a basis for the emergence of social conflict seems plausible and evidence can be cited in support of it, there are methodological and substantive considerations which limit its utility as an explanation for the emergence of social conflict. First, consider an important methodological issue, called the identification problem by Blalock (1967*a* and 1967*b*). The difficulty arises from trying to distinguish an interaction affect from an additive effect of two or more variables. In an additive model each variable affects the dependent variable independently of the other; hence one can simply add together their effects. In an interaction model the effects of each variable depends on the other. The difficulty may be more easily understood by discussing some illustrative (and hypothetical) data.

Suppose we were interested in the effects of earnings and job autonomy on work satisfaction. We might expect that high job autonomy and high earnings would each make for work satisfaction, regardless of the other. In that case, we would expect results such as those presented in Table 3.1. The sums of the consistent and inconsistent cells each add to 100; they are equal and this indicates no interaction effects. Suppose, however, that

TABLE 3.1 Percent Feeling Dissatisfied

	Earnings	
Power of Autonomy	*High*	*Low*
High	20	50
Low	50	80

TABLE 3.2 Percent Feeling Dissatisfied

	Earnings	
Power of Autonomy	*High*	*Low*
High	20	60
Low	70	80

the results are as shown in Table 3.2. Now the sum of the inconsistent cells (60 + 70) is greater than the sum of the consistent cells (20 + 80). This indicates that an interaction effect does exist. We might interpret Table 3.2 to mean that being high on either earnings or autonomy and being low on the other dimension is about as dissatisfying as being low on both because the discrepancy between being high in one way and low in another is very distressing.

The identification problem arises because other possible combinations of additive and interaction effects could produce the table. Thus, in Table 3.3, we can see a variety of possible interaction effects. The significance and meaning of the main effects of the independent variables also vary depending on the presumed contribution made by the interaction of the two variables. Thus in the case of combination C, it appears

TABLE 3.3 Results and Possible Components

					Possible Components				
Results					*Additive*			*Interaction*	
	H	L							
H	20	60	=		20	50	+	0	10	A
L	70	80			50	80		20	0	
			=		20	40	+	0	20	B
					60	80		10	0	
			=		20	30	+	0	30	C
					70	80		0	0	

that earnings do not markedly affect satisfaction and that persons with high power and low earnings are particularly outraged—presumably feeling that they are particularly underpaid given their power.

Clearly, an infinite number of possible combinations of additive and interaction components can be constructed to yield the results shown. Several implications follow from this identification problem. First, it demonstrates that contentions between deprivation and status inconsistency should not be thought of as mutually exclusive. Empirical findings can be consistent with both ideas at the same time. Second, the identification problem cannot be solved by any methodological device (Hornung, 1972). It is necessary to develop precise theoretical statements about the impact of each variable. That is, in order to argue that there is an interaction effect one should be very clear about the expected main effects of the independent variables under specific conditions and at particular magnitudes. Thirdly, since there is considerable ambiguity about interpreting any single set of empirical findings, one might be well advised to choose the simpler explanation as long as it is plausible; this is the additive model (Blalock, 1967b). Another alternative is to develop a comprehensive set of specific interpretations and consider a wide variety of empirical findings to assess the usefulness of the set of interpretations. It is this latter course which we will be trying to chart.

Thus far, in discussing the limits to the applicability of status inconsistency as an explanation for the emergence of social conflict, we have only considered the ambiguity of interpreting empirical findings. There are substantive reasons for expecting that rank disequilibrium does not help account for the emergence of conflict or more specifically a sense of grievance. Some of the reasons are the very ones we offered to account for the effects of simple deprivation as a basis for discontent. First, being high in some hierarchies could serve as a compensation for being low in others. Second, belonging to incongruent statuses subjects people to inconsistent claims and directives. A general reaction to such cross-pressures is to reduce attention and withdraw interest from the issues in contention among the status groups (Lazarsfeld, Berelson, and Gaudet, 1944; M. Kriesberg, 1949). This may have more relevance for modes chosen to express grievance or in the formulation of conflicting objectives, but lack of certainty in these areas might also tend to dampen self-acknowledgement of discontent. Finally, experiencing rank disequilibrium could result in feelings of self-inadequacy or failure rather than a grievance directed at some other group. Thus, Jackson (1962) found that "persons whose inconsistency is due to high racial-ethnic status and low occupational or educational status tend to respond to their stress" with high levels of psychophysiological symptoms. These inconsistents are "underrewarded" and would be expected to be dissatisfied. Worrying and having symptoms of anxiety are related to dissatisfaction but as such do not seem to be a direct stimulus for collectively defined grievances.

In considering deprivation and rank disequilibrium we presented evidence that each is the basis for the feelings of discontent which are components of a conflict situation. But we also saw that these factors have contradictory implications. Before proceeding further it is advisable to try to integrate the two sets of ideas. The integration is tentative but it may serve as a basis for elaboration or reconstruction.

On the whole, within a common culture we expect that persons will feel dissatisfied in relation to the number of areas in which they are deprived or have low ranks. The additive model is assumed to be fundamental for the overall sense of grievance. Empirical comparisons of additive and interaction models have usually been consistent with the additive model; it seems to explain more of the variance in the dependent variable than the interaction model (Treiman, 1966; Lauman and Segal, 1971; Laslett, 1971; Goffman, 1957; Hornung, 1972). Certain kinds of inconsistencies, under specific conditions, have interaction effects upon particular aspects of the sense of grievance. The belief in the ability to improve one's condition, for example, is supported by being high in some regards or at least not being generally very low.

Landecker (1970) has suggested that rank disequilibrium will be a source of disturbance in the small group where it affects face-to-face interaction but in a larger social system, such as the society at large, the resulting crosscutting ties would be integrative. It is true that the presumption of strain resulting from status inconsistencies is dependent upon certain kinds of social interaction. The gross measures of status inconsistency at a societal level include many people who normally do not experience strain as a result of "status inconsistency." Status categories are necessarily very broad at the societal level. A wide range exists within each status category and many persons therefore do not experience status inconsistency. Within organizations, status categories are narrower; measurement of inconsistency should be closer to incumbents' experiences. Status inconsistency effects, then, should be greater within organizations than within entire societies.

Related to the size of the unit being studied is the nature of the boundaries among the status categories within the unit. For example, the distinction between manual and nonmanual workers is still socially significant in Great Britain and this affects the patterns of social interaction and the bases of reference (Parkin, 1971). There observations are pertinent to the findings that higher paid manual workers are somewhat more satisfied with their income than one would expect on a purely additive model (Runciman, 1966). We should also expect that higher income American blacks would tend to be more satisfied with their income than equally well off whites or poorer blacks. But it is not so. At every income level, nonwhites (almost entirely Negroes) are more dissatisfied than whites (see Table 3.4). Perhaps the nonwhites are using the whites as a comparison group and given their education, occupation, and other social characteristics evaluate their income as inequitable (see Table 2.3). They do not seem to evaluate themselves only within the black community and say in effect, "I'm doing fine for a black." It is also possible that the results are at least partly due to blacks having less income than whites within each broad income stratum.

TABLE 3.4 Percent Dissatisfied with Family Income, by Race and Income, November 1966

Annual Family Income	Race	
	White	Nonwhite
$ 4,999 or less	37.5 (360)	52.0 (50)
5,000 to $6,999	41.1 (243)	50.0 (16)
7,000 to $9,999	27.0 (407)	59.0 (22)
10,000 or more	18.6 (476)	31.2 (16)

Question: "On the whole, would you say you are satisfied or dissatisfied with your family income?"
Source: National U.S. sample survey, conducted by American Institute of Public Opinion (Gallup); cross-tabulation was provided by The Roper Public Opinion Research Center.

CHANGES IN ATTAINMENTS AND EXPECTATIONS. The third major source of grievance arises from a decline in what people have or an increase in what they expect. Stated more generally, dissatisfaction rises as people have a decreasing proportion of what they feel they should and could have. This gap or discrepancy is argued to be the fundamental basis for revolts and other kinds of turmoil and violence (e.g., Gurr, 1970; Feierabend, Feierabend, and Nesvold, 1969; Davies, 1962; Tanter and Midlarsky, 1967). We need to elaborate this deceptively simple idea in more detail.

A variety of changes in either expectations or attainments can increase an unwanted discrepancy between them. Figure 3.1 presents the basic types. Type A is the most obvious; the members of a society, organization, or segment of a society have decreasing amounts of what they previously possessed. This might be due to a bad growing season and a poor harvest or it might be due to another group reducing the autonomy, income, or honor of these people. The expectations are presumed to persist, at least for a while. That is, having attained a certain level, that level is felt to be appropriate, desirable, and certainly attainable. A fall from that level in actual attainments, then, would produce dissatisfaction and a sense of grievance.

Type B is stressed in many studies of revolutions (e.g., Davies, 1962;

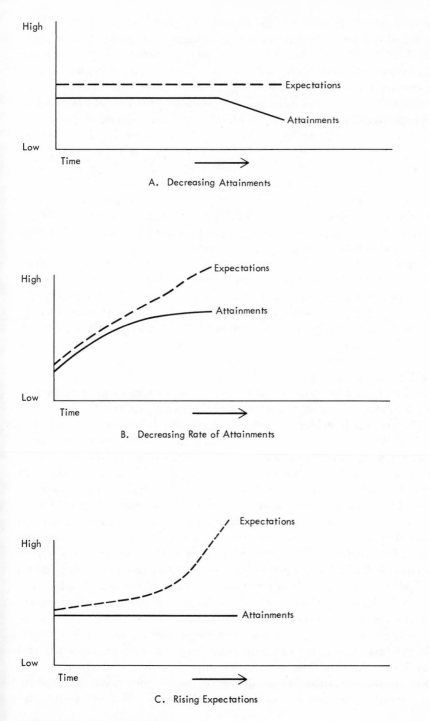

A. Decreasing Attainments

B. Decreasing Rate of Attainments

C. Rising Expectations

FIGURE 3.1 Types of Changes.

Brinton, 1955). It accounts for revolutions occurring not after a long period of constantly bad times, but as conditions improve. It is improving conditions which then deteriorate that particularly creates a sense of grievance. Expectations continue to advance at the rate which past experience dictates. Even a leveling off of progress and certainly a fall in attainments is experienced as a deprivation. This line of reasoning is appropriate to precipitants of conflict as well as to general discontent underlying a social conflict. Thus, the precipitating incident for the student protest at the Berkeley California campus in 1964 was the university administration decision to forbid the continued use of an area then being used for political activities (Lipset and Wolin, 1965).

The third major type of discrepancy arising from changes in expectations and attainments is type C, that of rising expectations. For a variety of reasons, people may raise their expectations about what they could and should have and hence discover that what they have is intolerably inadequate. The phrase "revolution of rising expectations" refers to this idea particularly in regard to the economically underdeveloped countries. The peoples in these societies are increasingly dissatisfied with their conditions as they become familiar with what there is to have and what people in economically advanced societies already have. Within every society leaders may promise gains and even begin programs which raise expectations that then are unmet. For example, in the United States, the expectations of the blacks and of the poor were raised in regard to racial equality and to the ending of poverty by federal governmental actions and words in the early 1960s.

The systematic evidence for these arguments is indirect. That is, the studies have related revolutionary efforts, violence, or domestic turmoil to changes in previous conditions. The feelings of dissatisfaction and of grievance are inferred. But we have already seen that dissatisfaction can arise from other sources than that of changes in attainments or expectations. On the other hand, dissatisfaction may not always be expressed in conflict behavior or in coercion. Even if groups are pursuing conflicting goals they may seek to pursue them by noncoercive means or through nonviolent coercion. The emergence of a conflict relationship and a group's choice of how to pursue its aims depends on many other factors in addition to feeling dissatisfied and having a grievance. Finally, conflict behavior may be undertaken, not because dissatisfaction has grown, but because redress now seems feasible.

Later in the book, as we discuss the use of coercive and violent means, we will examine again the data regarding changing expectations and conditions. At this time we restrict our discussion to feelings of discontent and grievance. We need research which uses many series of indicators of social and economic conditions for conflict units. We also should have more direct measures of grievances and discontent. Public opinion surveys provide such data as do content analyses of speeches, sermons, and newspapers. To test the relationships posited, we need data for at least three time periods: before, during, and after a major change.

We should also consider the limitation of changes in expectations and conditions as an explanation of discontent which leads to conflict behavior. First, poor conditions may be made more endurable by the promise of better things to come in the future. The raised expectations of a glorious future often have made people willing to endure current sacrifices. It is also conceivable that if conditions have been improving people are more able to absorb a setback with less bitterness than they would a more consistently deprivational condition. Under still other circumstances, a new deprivation may be experienced as a failure which induces guilt or self-hate such that an outwardly directed greivance does not even emerge. Or, the deprivation may lessen positive feelings and yet not increase negative ones (Bradburn, 1969). This, in balance, would make people feel less happy, but not appreciably raise the level of conflict-relevant discontent. Finally, the improvement of conditions may be of sufficient magnitude to satisfy rather than intensify appetites. For example, European immigrants found American industrial employment sufficiently better than their previous conditions to be much less dissatisfied than American-born workers (Ellsworth, 1952).

These possibilities indicate that the level of deprivation *and* the degree of equilibration among different ranks affect how changes in attainments and expectations are related to conflict-relevant grievances. For example, a fall in economic well-being from an already low level may impose such severe burdens that expectations quickly fall also. However, if high levels in other rank systems were sustained, the reaction might still be strong.

This discussion of sources of discontent suggests that we could find reasons for any group anywhere to be dissatisfied. And as a matter of fact everybody can report grievances. No one and no group can be without *any*. In order for grievances to be pertinent to the emergence of social conflicts the discontent must be intense, shared by a significant number of persons, and channeled into the pursuit of an end which is opposed by some other social group. The conditions we have discussed as sources of discontent also affect the formulation of goals and the mode of their pursuit; we will consider them again in those contexts.

We can further integrate the sources of discontent as explanations for disputes by specifying the effects in terms of unit characteristics and the nature of the discontent. Thus, discontent can vary in intensity. It may be useful to assume that simple deprivation is the best predictor of the intensity of the feeling of dissatisfaction. But expression of such dissatisfaction depends on the belief that some alteration is possible. It is in *this* regard that status inconsistency, relative deprivation, and changes in expectations and actual conditions have particular pertinence.

For example, consider the findings about the level of satisfaction in different societies as related to socio-economic conditions in those societies (Cantril, 1965; Stone, 1970). A cross section of persons in fourteen countries were interviewed using a self-anchoring–ladder rating technique. In this technique each respondent is asked to imagine his future in the best possible light and then in the worst possible light, he then describes each. Taking these two points as extremes on a ten-step ladder, the respondent is asked to rate where he stands now, where he was five years ago, and where he expects to be five years hence.

Cantril found that the rank correlation between the socio-economic level in the countries and the average *present* rating of the people in the countries is $+.67$ ($+.52$ Pearson product moment correlation). In other words, the general level of deprivation in the society is strongly related to the level of satisfaction. Stone then examined the relationship of these data to the degree of inequality in the societies based on the distribution of agricultural land. Inequality is not highly related to present self-ratings. Inequality, however, is significantly related to ratings of the *future*; the correlation is $+.53$ and the correlation between the inequality and the degree of shift between the present to the future is $+.59$. In other words, in societies with much inequality people tend to expect greater improvements in their lives than in countries with more equality. Nevertheless, even in this study the current socio-economic level in the society was just as strongly related to expectations of improvement: the poorer the country the greater was the expectation of change.

The different explanations also have varying pertinence for different segments of a conflict party. Thus, as we noted earlier, there is evidence that in status systems with clearly marked boundaries, those toward the top of a low ranking stratum tend to be relatively satisfied. We noted this for higher income manual workers (Runciman, 1966). Yet, it is usually from these levels that the leaders of mass organizations of the entire stratum emerge (e.g., Lipset, 1950, pp. 179–98). This is partly a matter of the higher ranking persons within each stratum having the social status and skills which make them more likely to be leaders for their stratum. It may also be that they are particularly responsive to changes in expectations and conditions. Furthermore, such persons are in some ways marginal; they do not fit clearly in the low ranking nor high ranking strata. Marginality can be a source of insight and facilitate a questioning posture, useful for a leader (Shibutani and Kwan, 1965, pp. 351–61).

Of course the leaders or would-be leaders play a critical role in arousing discontent and making people aware of their grievances. Some issues are more dependent than others on the interpretation of leaders or a vanguard. For example, Rossi and Berk (1970) found in their study of black neighborhoods that popular discontent with the police could be accounted for without recourse to the role of black community leaders, but feelings of economic exploitation by local businessmen were more dependent upon the role of an elite.

The selection of the particular grievance whose redress is sought may be influenced by the leaders. Therefore, the leaders' own special circumstances may affect the basis of discontent which becomes paramount. We assume that the leader can increase sensitivity to grievances but not, at least in the first instance, create the grievance. The leaders may help increase awareness or raise the consciousness of the members of a social category, and in doing so may emphasize deprivation, or the discrepancies in the status that the people themselves hold, or they emphasize the people's deprivation compared to others or their own past. The leaders play a special role in the analysis of what is wrong and what is to be done.

In every social conflict some persons who "belong" to one side of the conflict ally themselves with the adversary group. Explanations for such "class traitors" may well be different than for most members of the adversary group. Thus, status inconsistencies and changes in expectations or conditions may be particularly important explanations for the whites who join with blacks in the struggle for racial equality, for nonmanual workers who ally themselves with manual workers, or for faculty who are sympathetic to student protests. For example, Donald (1956) found that the white abolitionists of the 1830s were from old and prominent Northeastern families who were being displaced in leadership by urban manufacturers.

The three approaches to grievances arising from internal characteristics of the conflict unit pertain to consensual conflicts. They may contribute to dissensual conflicts as additional issues in contention or by the displacement of feelings. The sources of grievances in dissensual conflicts are best considered later when we examine grievances as they arise from the relationship between conflict groups.

The different explanations for conflict-relevant discontent also pertain to the formulation of goals. The present discussion of this final aspect of a manifest conflict relationship is still focused upon the characteristics of the unit. The formulation of incompatible aims clearly depends in large part upon the interaction between the parties to a conflict; we will consider that later in the chapter.

Goals. For a social conflict to emerge, groups must believe that they hold incompatible goals. Not all aims sought to redress grievances are oppositional and incompatible with those of a potential adversary. A working-class goal of other-worldly salvation, for example, may be compatible with managerial goals, although an observer might regard the two groups as being in a potential conflict relationship. In this section we will examine group characteristics which affect the formulation of incompatible aims. Before doing so, we should note a few dimensions of goals particularly relevant to social conflicts.

First, a necessary component of any goal is the *belief* that it is attainable or at least that the present unhappy conditions can be altered in the direction of the desired future position. In other words, for any group to become aware of a grievance and pursue an aim to rectify the grievance against the wishes of an adversary, the group must have some expectation that its efforts will reduce the grievance. Without any such hope or belief, rectification of grievances will rarely be attempted and the grievance itself may not be admitted into awareness. The belief may vary from complete confidence to desperate hope.

Second, collective or group goals are of special importance. That is, we are interested in aims which pertain to an entity and not only to its constituent members. For example, workers, students, women, or the United States seeking power or status *as a group* relative to another group have collective aims; seeking opportunities to allow members to leave the group is not a collective goal.

The third dimension and the one whose variation is particularly relevant to later stages in the course of a social conflict is the nature and radicalism of the goals. As outlined earlier, an aim may be to terminate or to alter the relationship. Termination may be attained by withdrawal, as in secession, or by obliteration of the adversary. The relationship may be altered by exchanging occupants of certain positions in the relationship or restructuring the relationship. Restructuring is often along the dimension of more or less equality—the most pertinent meaning to "left" and "right" (Lipset, 1960). Terminations or alterations may be more or less radical depending on what the parties previously believed was appropriate and how opposed the other group is to the goal. In this sense there can be radical "right" and radical "left" goals.

All goals are ideas about what might be; they are mental constructs of a future condition which is desired. As such they are embedded in a set of ideas about the present plight and what can be done about it. These ideas may be more or less well articulated. When they are explicit and elaborated we refer to them as an ideology. They may also be so unformulated that they are implicit and must be inferred from indirect verbal expressions and actions. Thus, Hobsbawm (1959, pp. 108–16) observed that although the classical city mobs were a prepolitical phenomenon, some ideas were manifested in their actions. For example, participants in mobs expected to achieve something, assumed that the authorities would be sensitive to their actions, and directed their activities selectively against the rich and powerful.

Many unit characteristics are intimately involved in shaping purposes: the degree of differentiation in the group, the qualities of the leaders and their followers, and the size and nature of the unit's boundaries. Our attention will be focused on explicit goals, but implicit ones can be similarly analyzed.

LEADERS. Any discussion of goals and ideology must include some reference to leadership. The spokesmen of a conflict group play a primary role in the formulation of aims. Discontent may be dormant and fester; unhappiness may appear to be a necessary part of the human condition. Often, it is. But leaders can also point to possible changes and future conditions in which the grievances lessen or disappear.

Goals differ in the anticipated time and effort for their realization and the certainty of their attainment. Thus a group may hope in some future generation to achieve a grand purpose, but meanwhile seek only a limited goal for next year. In order to reach that great end it is trying to attain a prerequisite now. In other words, there are strategic and tactical goals.

For a conflict organization to mobilize support and sustain itself, let alone expand, the succession of goals must be closely related to the group's capacities. An appropriate balance must exist between the aims to be attained and the effort needed to attain them.

Particularly for newly emerging conflict organizations, the choice of immediate goals is important in building support for the organization (Haggstrom, 1968). The organization, as part of a larger social category and social movement, must choose goals whose support will increase group awareness and sense of grievance if it is to grow. To say that the sense of grievance must be increased for the movement to succeed sounds strange. There is a paradox here. In one sense the organization must succeed in meeting the demands of the supporters but success obviates the basis for support of the organization. Leaders, the opposition, and fortuitous circumstances may or may not conjoin to yield a combination of distant goals and immediate achievements which sustain the emerging conflict organization. Some cases will help illustrate how the paradox actually works.

In organizing the poor in community action programs during the 1960s organization building was more successful if demands were met with initial resistance and later yielding by the opposition. Resistance is important because it seems to confirm the validity of the analysis which claims that a conflict organization is necessary. Yet failure to attain any benefits would also reveal the invalidity of the diagnosis of the problem or the way of solving it.

Leaders also play an important role in the articulation and integration of diverse interests. For example, George Wallace, like Barry Goldwater, in 1964, may have appealed to white fears about racial integration and "crime in the streets." But Wallace combined this with expressions of concern about the welfare of the working man and of the little people. Wallace received a larger measure of support from workers and trade union members than Goldwater (Lipset and Raab, 1970, pp. 362–67).

The dynamics of events in the social movement stage may make it difficult for the leadership to establish itself or develop goals which meet the paradoxical requirements. Let us briefly consider the May 1970 university student strikes following the U.S. invasion of Cambodia and the killing of students at Kent State and Jackson State. The wave of protests had many purposes reflecting a variety of student interests. One immediate aim came to be "no business as usual." Many students could be mobilized for that goal, but for different reasons. For some it was the beginning of a national strike in which *all* business would be stopped, the war ended, and a radical social transformation of the society brought about. For others it was an opportunity to educate fellow students and the community about the war and other social issues. For still others it was a way to bring pressure upon the Federal government to end the war. For some it was pressuring the local university administrators to shift the relative power of segments of the university. For some others it was a way to end the semester early without final examinations and with no academic penalty. This mixture of interests and goals made it sometimes seem that all students were trying to make a revolution and still get good grades.

Some universities did shut down and this meant that dormitories and university facilities were closed; students had no base to work from and left the campus. In other universities, after a few days of interruption in normal procedures, business as usual returned. At still other universities a compromise was reached: classes were to continue as usual for students who wanted to attend and for those who wanted to engage in special activities, workshops and community action could be conducted and grades would be given by arrangement with the instructor, usually on the basis of work already done. After a few days of activity, students began to drift away once arrangements for grades had been made and as the momentum of a massive social action disappeared.

In the case of the labor movement one can trace a variety of formulas that leaders constructed to build a viable conflict organization. During the nineteenth century in the United States, many national trade unions began but did not survive: the Knights of Labor, the National Labor Union, and the Industrial Workers of the World (Perlman, 1928). The "pure and simple trade unionism" of the American Federation of Labor provided a set of immediate and long-term goals which were always partially attainable. Thus, when the founder-leader, Samuel Gompers, was asked what the workers wanted, he answered, "More, more, more, and more."

In elaborating goals, beliefs about the past as well as the present and the future are promulgated. Certain beliefs about the past can make ends seem more legitimate and attainable. Leaders can argue that the desired future position is attainable because such a position once existed; for example, land and other property were once communally owned; in early human history women were socially superior to men and were worshipped by them (Steinem, 1971); or our ethnic group once had an autonomous and high culture compared to the barbarians of the time.

Beliefs about the contemporary events are relevant when they indicate the possibility of attaining the sought-for ends. Thus, leaders often seek to convince the supporters that the adversary is weak or weakening while the supporters are strong and getting stronger. For example, Palestinian Arab leaders claimed many victorious guerrilla attacks after the Six-Day War of June 1967 in order to promote the growth of the Arab Palestinian movements (Peretz, 1970).

Leaders agitate, then, not only by trying to increase the sense of grievance or discontent, but also by holding out a better and attainable future. There is another paradox here. To depict how exploited and victimized people are seems to contradict the possibility of such a weak group bettering itself against the desires of the group doing the victimizing. One way out of the paradox is to use the power of weakness. People who really have nothing are invulnerable from threats and coercion. Having nothing, they can lose nothing. As the Communist Manifesto exhorted the workers to unite in struggle, "you have nothing to lose but your chains" (see Blau, 1964, pp. 230–31).

BASES OF GRIEVANCE.   The nature and direction of the goal is strongly shaped by the grievance underlying it. Considering how the previously discussed sources of discontent affect aims will help to integrate the apparent contradictions in the ideas about the sources.

People who are deprived or whose conditions have deteriorated are more likely to support radical goals and large changes in their relationship to the presumed adversary than people with status inconsistency or improved conditions. For example, during periods of severe economic depression in the United States relatively radical aims have been voiced by some, albeit small, groups within the labor movement; but during the economic upswing after the depression trade union organizations, with much more reformist goals, expanded (Dunlop, 1951). Or, we might consider blacks in the United States during the 1960s. Blacks with higher education and income tended to be conventional militants while those who were more uniformly worse-off tended to be disproportionately in support of black separatist objectives (Marx, 1969, esp., pp. 57, 117).

The direction of goals, whether to the left or right, toward increasing or decreasing inequalities, also depends on the nature of the discontent. Deteriorating conditions for the formerly high ranking persons, even if the deterioration is only relative to those lower than themselves, makes them favor aims which restore previous inequalities. It is from such groups that reactionary political movements have drawn disproportional support. We also expect status inconsistents with ascribed or investment statuses lower than achieved or reward statuses to support goals which would be conservative or reactionary compared to persons with over-rewarded kinds of inconsistencies, who would support more liberal or equalitarian aims (Schmitt, 1965; Broom and Jones, 1970).

The pattern of status inconsistency also affects the content of the goal. People will try to raise themselves along the dimensions in which they have relatively low status. Hence they will be challenging those who are above them on *that* dimension. This helps determine the goal and the adversary. Thus, persons with low ethnic status and high occupational and income levels might try to raise the status of their ethnic category and challenge those who presume to have higher ethnic status or individuals may try to "pass" and deny their ethnicity.

Fundamentally, the content of the grievance determines the goal. If economic deprivation is experienced, then efforts usually will be directed at improving those conditions. But how that is to be done and who is the opponent to those efforts depends in part on the leaders' ideas as well as the prevailing ideas among the members of the category. This requires bringing the relations between the conflicting parties and their environment into the analysis. This will be treated later in this chapter.

SIZE, CULTURE, AND OTHER GROUP CHARACTERISTICS.   Many attributes of the social category or conflict group affect the formulation of purposes. Many of these attributes have significance relative to the adversary and will be considered in that context. For example, the size of a group is meaningful in large part only in relationship to the size of its adversary. But in another sense, the size of a social category in itself has consequences for the formation of explicit goals. Thus, making aims clear and elaborated is facilitated by the interaction among a number of persons; a critical mass of similarly thinking persons must be present. The concentration of a large number of possible supporters gives a sense of power (even if inaccurate when compared to the adversary) that strengthens the belief that a grievance can be redressed and therefore one can dare to formulate a goal of a better future. These are part of the reason why the size of the student body is the best predictor of student protest demonstrations in universities (Scott and El-Assal, 1969). Similarly, a comprehensive study of racial disturbances in the U.S. in the 1960s found that the number of blacks in a city was most highly related to disorders (the correlation was .59) (Spilerman, 1970; Spilerman, 1971).

Certainly the experience that the members of a group have had with previous efforts at redressing grievances affects the formulation of new aims. A history of failure may inhibit formulating any goals of a better future; but if one is made, it is likely to be more radical than for groups with a history of past success.

Within any social category there is considerable variation, at the personality level, in the ability to imagine radical transformations, to desire collective solidarity, or to hold other values and beliefs which are relevant to the nature and direction of aims. That is, a small percentage within every large social category might support radical goals but widespread support requires the convergence of many appropriate conditions. Therefore, organizations may be able to find a small number of members to support extreme goals but as members join, the aims are likely to become less extreme; moderate goals may even be formulated in order to attract popular support. Units may also differ in the proportion of persons with given personality traits. For example, people differ in the degree to which they are intrapunitive or extrapunitive. That is, some people tend to blame themselves while some people tend to blame other persons when things go wrong. Groups with many extrapunitive members would tend to believe that their dissatisfactions are attributable to an adversary and therefore they would formulate goals which are incompatible with the other group's aims (Gurr, 1970, pp. 164–68).

Many unit characteristics, then, interact to affect the ends to be pursued. Goals however, are not merely the expression of the inner desires of the members of a social category or a group. Rather, we must take into account the relations between the unit and its adversaries and the context with which the parties interact.

RELATIONS BETWEEN THE ADVERSARIES

As in analyzing the unit characteristics and the emergence of social conflicts, we want to consider how relations between adversaries affect collective identity, the sense of grievance, and the formulation of goals.

Collective Identity. Groups wittingly and unwittingly define each other as well as themselves. Qualities become salient in relationship to other persons. Within the United States, being an American is not a salient identification; it is when an American is in another country. Identity is partly established in contrast to others (Voegelin, 1940; Shibutani and Kwan, 1965, pp. 383–91.) Thus there is some evidence that persons living in ethnically heterogeneous neighborhoods take their ethnicity more seriously than do those in ethnically homogeneous neighborhoods (Borhek, 1970; also see Barth, 1969).

Not only the awareness, but also the content of collective identity is established in interaction. Each self-conscious collectivity defines nonmembers. If a group is relatively powerful it will try to impose its definitions upon other groups. Where whites are dominant they seek to define who is nonwhite. The criteria and variety of nonmembers may be more or less clearly delimited and imposed. The Nazis' attempt to define Jews and other groups stands as one of the most gross efforts of this kind. The definitions may entail trying to assert how the other group acts and thinks as well as who is and who is not a member. Thus, men say what women are like; university officials define what students are; and whites say how blacks behave.

In cases with salient power inequalities the subordinate group will try to reject the definitions imposed by superordinates. What ensues is a struggle over who has a right to define membership and the qualities of each group. But, interestingly, if there has been long experience of mutual involvement, even when the subordinate group rejects the definition of the superordinate, it may accept the terms of evaluation. This is the self-hatred syndrome in which members seek to deny that they are different in the ways the dominants assert. Under circumstances of more autonomy, the subordinated group may actually reject the criteria of evaluation and assert the superiority of its own way as compared to that of the superordinants. Even then, however, its own way may be defined in opposition to the way of the dominants.

To illustrate: students, blacks, and women have sometimes tried to refute allegations that they were less responsible, hard working, or committed than administrators, whites, or men. At other stages of collective identity, some segments of the group may argue that they really have the characteristics attributed to them, but that these are good—being black then entails being expressive and warm in human relations. The matter gets even more complicated when one group tries to define the other as a way of arguing to itself about what it should be. For example, in the Women's Liberation movement, some persons feel that the masculine way of life is so wrong that efforts should be made to avoid taking over its qualities. This is the case with presumed male concern about hierarchy and domination. As some feminists put it:

> In order to assert our principles and prevent their co-optation
> by the male power structure, we must, within the movement,
> fight the development of a class system based on skills which
> are not available to everyone. We must fight the ascendancy

of leaders in order to encourage the development of leadership skills in all women. We fear that the artificial creation of
leaders, as has always been the case in male-dominated societies, will inevitably suppress the initiative of the majority
(The Feminists of New York City, 1970).

From this interplay of assertion, repudiation, acknowledgement, and reinterpretation of one's own group as viewed by others and of others from
the perspective of one's own group, identities with new content emerge.

Sense of Grievance. In considering how relations between adversaries
make a potential conflict become manifest, one fundamental and obvious way should be acknowledged first. That is, the coercive pursuit of a
conflicting goal by one side will make both sides aware that they have
incompatible aims. But the mode of pursuing goals needs separate
analysis and that will be done in the next chapter. Here we wish to
examine what qualities of the relationship between adversaries affect
either side feeling dissatisfied and aggrieved.

INTEGRATION. The entire gamut of relations between members of
two social categories affects the salience and even awareness of each particular relationship within the gamut. Relations between members of
groups may vary widely in scope and quality. They may have much or
little to do with each other and they may have a small or large proportion
of conflicting relations relative to cooperative ones. We will use the term
integration to refer to both components combined, although the two are
not always associated with each other. In analyzing the effects of integration upon conflicts emerging we will sometimes discuss the components separately.

On the whole, we expect that with larger proportions of nonconflicting
relations, any particular objective conflict is less likely to become manifest. Presumably the cooperative relations compensate for the conflicting
ones; therefore an issue in contention is not felt to be as grievous as it
would be if unmitigated by common and complementary relations
(Morris and Jeffries, 1968).

As diagrammed in part A of Figure 3.2, this reasoning yields a linear
inverse association between the likelihood of recognizing a conflict and
the proportion of nonconflicting relations between adversaries.

Integration also involves the extent of the relationship—the number
of ways in which people interact and relate to each other. Everything
else being equal, the more groups have to do with each other, the more
they have to quarrel about. If they have nothing to do with each other,
they have no basis for a social conflict. We are also presuming, however,
that the proportion of nonconflicting relations increases as the extent of
interaction increases. Consequently we would expect a curvilinear association between the likelihood of becoming aware of a conflict and

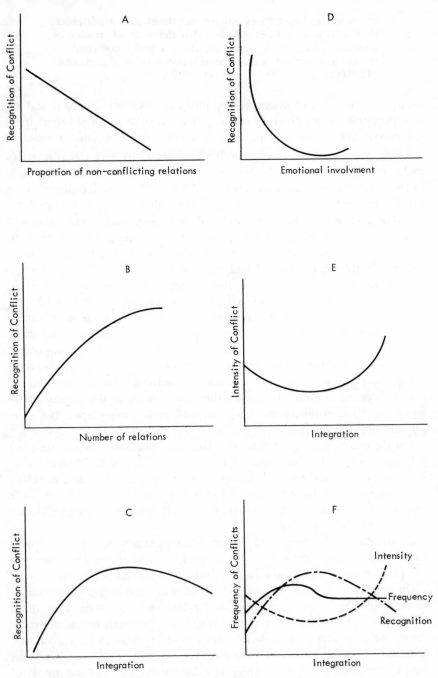

FIGURE 3.2 Integration and Manifest Conflict.

the number of relations between the parties. This is illustrated in part B of Figure 3.2.

On the whole, integration beyond a low level would be expected to inhibit recognition of conflicts. See part C of Figure 3.2. The idea is that with increasing integration, crosscutting ties of conflict as well as cooperation bind people together and tend to inhibit open acknowledgement of each particular conflict (Coser, 1956). At a more interpersonal level, people with social relations across conflict-group boundaries are less likely to perceive issues as contentious. For example, in one community allegations about Jews were raised in a local election. Jews with cross ties with Gentiles tended not to respond with ethnocentrism, especially if they spoke about the issue with Gentiles (Weinberg and Williams, 1969).

There is even an additional possible inhibiting mechanism. The more emotionally involved people become with each other, the more reluctant they are to admit that they have issues of contention between them. Coser (1956, p. 62) writes, "The closer the relationship, the greater the affective investment, the greater also the tendency to suppress rather than express hostile feelings." In less interpersonal, psychological terms, the tendency to suppress hostile feelings and the awareness of conflict may be due to shared identification. That is, insofar as groups feel that they are part of the same larger entity, they tend to deny the issues that divide them. However, at very high levels of involvement there may be higher demands made of each other for responsiveness which are likely to be unmet and hence provoke disappointment. The result is a somewhat curvilinear relationship between involvement and conflict recognition, as shown in part D of Figure 3.2.

Herein arises another paradox. If hostility is suppressed and if divisive issues are unrecognized, the intensity of the hostility and the gravity of the issue grow. The grievance then can burst forth in greater magnitude than if the issues had been recognized earlier. As illustrated in part E of Figure 3.2, we posit that at low levels of integration, intense hostility and a sense of grievance can be acknowledged, unchecked by other considerations and at high degrees of integration; *once a conflict becomes manifest* it will also be of great intensity. There is another mechanism which helps account for this. It is particularly relevant in dissensual conflicts. This is the additional outrage people feel about disagreements with others who are supposed to be close. This is one of the reasons for the intensity of feeling often noted in conflicts regarding what seem like small doctrinal differences when factions break away from larger political or religious groups. This potentially intense sense of grievance adds to the chances that a struggle will emerge.

All of these factors affect the frequency of disputes. Since they do not have the *same* effect upon the frequency of conflicts, however, there is not a linear association, nor even a simple curvilinear one, as may be seen in part F of Figure 3.2. The resultant line may also help make it clear why social conflicts do not disappear with integration.

POWER INEQUALITY. If one group has much more power than another, the more powerful may suppress the weaker to such an extent that the weaker may not acknowledge its dissatisfactions and formulate any goal which challenges the stronger. Repression and intimidation may make any such formulation seem futile and self-defeating. Of course the intimidation and repression in themselves are sources of discontent among those experiencing it and additional repression may be needed to suppress that discontent. Herein lies one check upon continued aggrandizement by the superordinate.

Superior power, particularly in large and total social systems like a society, can also be used to try to convince the weaker that they are not deprived and have no grounds for grievance. Formal and informal means of education or indoctrination may be employed to convince the weaker that allocation of whatever is consensually valued conforms with standards of equity and legitimacy (Mann, 1970). Interestingly, arguments in terms of such standards also become restraints upon the superordinates. Suppose it is argued that the subordinates owe obedience because of the benefits being given them by the superordinates or, in other words, a fair exchange exists. In that case, the superordinates are constrained to honor the terms of the exchange in order to maintain their claims against the subordinates.

The degree of power inequality also affects the likelihood of a grievance becoming manifest because it is related to the magnitude of the grievance. The weaker one side is, the more reason its members have to complain. For example, Schuman and Gruenberg (1970) found that the smaller the proportion of blacks in a city the more likely are blacks to feel dissatisfied; presumably where blacks are a smaller proportion of the city population, there is less political responsiveness to them.

This implies that a deprived group will use whatever power it has to press its demands and it needs power to do so. On the whole, then, we must conclude that great power inequalities increase dissatisfaction at the individual level but for this to be collectively recognized, some power and some expectation of improvement by one's own efforts in opposition to an adversary is necessary. Thus, trade union organizations were first developed among the most strategically located workers in each industry: locomotive engineers in the railroad industry, loom fixers in textiles, molders in casting, and cutters in the garment industry (Dunlop, 1951, pp. 49–50).

Goals.   Each side helps shape the other side's purposes. One way this happens is a conflict party responds to the way it is being defined and what is being sought from it. The other way is that a conflict party shapes its goals in terms of the anticipated responses of the other side.

REACTIONS. A collectivity shapes its goals in response to an adversary by imitation or by contrast. In consensual conflicts the members of a collectivity deny the differences attributed to them and their aim is to attain the conditions which make that denial valid. In dissensual conflicts, the members of a collectivity may exaggerate the differences along the very lines stressed by the adversary. Some illustrations should make these possibilities clearer.

The intensified persecution of Jews in Russia toward the end of the nineteenth century spurred and helped shape the Zionist aim. A national home and a normal social and economic life, an emphasis upon productive work and especially labor on the land was one kind of response to the anti-Semitic allegations and persecutions. Zionism was based partly on the argument that the Jews should be like other peoples; if they could not be accepted as Russians or as Germans because they were Jews, then they were indeed Jews who also had a national identity and needed a national homeland. In a sense, too, college students who argue against the *in loco parentis* doctrine contend that they are responsible and can control themselves just as well as adults or others living away from a college.

The response can also be one of contradiction. If the other side alleges immorality, looseness, lack of discipline, and hedonism, then the response is the glorification of spontaneity, warmth in human relations, soul, and a counterculture. Sometimes people emphasize a presumed goal of the other side pertaining to themselves as a way of directing their own collectivity. Thus, some people stress the antireligious elements in Soviet ideology as a way of arguing that America has religious and specifically Christian goals.

ANTICIPATIONS. The other side can affect its adversary's aims a great deal by making clear what it will, and will not, allow its adversary. This is particularly the case when other side is relatively strong. In some cases, what is allowed are opportunities for individuals "letting off steam," "griping," "bitching," or ridiculing what they do not like (Coser, 1956, p. 41). This may reduce some pressure and make the adversary seem more human. It may even provide a way of communicating challenges and desires for change which would not otherwise be communicated. Such vents may even be institutionalized as in the office party when people can get drunk and tell the boss off or in student skits when they lampoon the faculty. But this may dissipate rather than generate collective goals.

In order to understand how anticipated reactions affect the development of conflicting purposes we need to recall one of the fundamental components of an emerging social conflict: it must seem possible to improve one's lot, to get closer to what is desired, at the expense of some other party. There are several ways in which the other party gives credence to such beliefs. If the other side seems weak and incompetent it not only may be giving evidence that indeed it is responsible for the unsatisfactory conditions, but also that it is subject to pressure and to change. Students of revolutions generally agree that one of the immediate causes of revolts against the authorities is the appearance of hesitancy, uncertainty, and self-doubt among the authorities. This may be signaled by verbal signs of panic and by defections. Such signs invite more radical formulations of goals—fundamental restructuring of authority relations rather than reforms seems possible and necessary.

Aside from such signs of collapse by the adversary, a group or its leaders may try to formulate its goals for maximum impact upon the other side. An ideology is not only directed at the constituency to make them believe that an aim is desirable and attainable, it is also directed toward the adversary. If the adversary can be convinced of, or at least question, the morality and justice of its position, then chances of inducing defections, uncertainty, and guilt in the adversary increases. That in turn would yield further evidence to the members of the group that they can get what they want from the adversary. Consequently, aims are often formulated in terms of shared values: of freedom, justice, and equality. For example, leaders of national independence movements lay claim to the rights of a people to rule themselves.

This also means that immediate goals may be chosen from among the array of possible goals partly in terms of which one is most likely to be yielded by the adversary. Thus, consider white opposition to the different possible integration aims of blacks in the 1960s. According to a 1963 national survey, about 80 percent of the whites conceded that Negroes ought to have as good a chance as white people to get any kind of job; about three-fourths favored equal access to public facilities; about 60 percent thought white and Negro students should go to the same schools; but less than half disagreed with the statement that white people had a right to keep Negroes out of their neighborhoods if they wanted to (Sheatsley, 1966, p. 224). On that basis, striving for equal jobs might seem to be a most promising goal for blacks. Support for legal and political equality probably would be even more generally found (Williams and Weinir, 1967). But the vulnerability of those who control these different spheres of life to the kinds of tactics available to the blacks also dictates the choice of goal, as well as considerations of the major dissatisfactions and organizational needs of blacks and their leaders.

Finally, we should note that the utility of pursuing a particular goal is affected by how the group feels about the other side and its reaction to yielding a particular goal. This has been called "vicarious utility" (Valavanis, 1958). For example, if one group has strong animosity toward another, it will derive extra pleasure from pursuing an aim which humiliates its adversary. Vengeance can be sweet. Without such feelings a less extreme end might be chosen. On the other hand, if there is a high mixture of positive feelings or common interests, a goal may be chosen which will minimize the harm to the other side, even if it fails to maximize the group's own values independently of considering the vicarious value of the other side's satisfaction.

The gratifications of getting retribution and humiliating the other side may sometimes lead a group to pursue aims which would otherwise seem to be self-defeating or which inflict self-losses not commensurate with what might be won.

ENVIRONMENT OF ADVERSARIES

In addition to the characteristics of each unit and the relations between them, the social context within which the conflict parties exist helps shape their identities, grievances, and goals.

Collective Identity. The prevailing ways of thinking at any given time profoundly affect the categories by which people think of themselves. Identifications in terms of religious beliefs, material well being, political relations, ethnicity, or ways of life may be more or less salient in different times and places.

Such prevailing ways of thought have significance beyond the way parties think of themselves. They define each other in terms of prevailing categories. Moreover, people who are not immediate actors in the conflict recognize and support actors in terms of the shared understandings of which categories are important. Thus there is often popular support to claims for separatism and national autonomy by ethnic groups. Yet governments are reluctant to support such movements because they or other friendly governments are vulnerable to secessionist movements. Nevertheless, appeals for support in terms of ethnicity, nationality, or in terms of political oppression have some built-in audience. This may be seen in the support which Jews received in recognition of a claim for a homeland and more recently that Palestinian Arabs received in *their* claims (Avineri, 1970).

Sense of Grievance. The social context in which the parties to a conflict exist is not the source of their sense of grievance, but it helps provide the criteria for evaluating conditions and possible changes. The available alternatives and their relative salience helps explain why some conditions become manifest grievances at certain times and not others.

As previously discussed, for a social conflict to emerge from an objective conflict relationship, at least one side must feel that the condition is not satisfactory according to its standards. Its standards of equity, however, are drawn from the prevailing tone, from the *Zeitgeist*. Presently we seem to be experiencing a worldwide increase in the value of equality (Beteille, 1969). Leaving aside the sources of this rising standard, its rise makes less tolerable inequities based upon age, race, nation-state, or sex.

Related to this general increase is the example that each group provides every other group of what is acceptable. Deprivations accepted as legitimate are questioned if others question what *they* had accepted as proper. Thus, the increase in standards of equity by blacks, by the poor, by women, by the youth, each reverberate upon each other and confirm to each that they have a right to be dissatisfied.

Finally, standards may be directly raised by actions and words of others who are not immediate partisans to a conflict. For example, many observers have remarked that the 1954 U.S. Supreme Court decision declaring segregated schools unconstitutional raised the hopes of blacks in the U.S. (e.g., Bell, 1968, p. 6, and The National Advisory Commission on Civil Disorders, 1968, p. 226). Second-class citizenship was not good enough.

In addition to raising standards of what should be, a sense of grievance can become manifest when objectionable conditions become unnecessary. That is, people may come to believe that it is possible for improvements to be made. Here, too, the gains others are making elsewhere raises expectations. The mass media certainly help to quickly spread the word about what is possible. But clearly there are many self-insulating factors which inhibit people from simply feeling aggrieved because they do not individually or collectively have what some others have. We have already reviewed variations in many such factors.

A basic component for a conflict-relevant sense of grievance is that a collectivity can improve its position at the expense of another collectivity. Viewing the relationship as one which has a zero-sum payoff is crucial for the emergence of a social conflict. Such views are dependent upon the actual parameters of the system within which the parties are operating and the parties' perceptions of the parameters. For example, Gurr (1970, pp. 125–26) reports several studies indicating that believing parameters are fixed, that what one group gets another must lose, is particularly widespread in Latin America. That expanding parameters reduce the belief that contending parties are in a zero-sum relationship is also indicated by the finding that European states had fewer wars with each other when colonial empires were expanding than during other historical periods (Rosecrance, 1963). The expanding U.S. economy and the open frontier, even if exaggerated in its effects, probably has mitigated the sense of grievance.

One other contextual condition significantly affects the emergence of manifest social conflicts. This is the degree to which conflict regulation is institutionalized. If there are generally supported and well-understood procedures for handling disputes, matters of possible contention are more likely to be viewed as competitive and not conflicting or as part of larger exchange relationship and not simply as a zero-sum relationship.

Goals. The formulation of goals is channeled by the contexts within which the contending parties exist. First, the terms in which aims are formulated depends upon the contemporary way of thinking. They depend upon the analysis of problems and the solutions which are available. Thus, in much of the world today, issues are politicized (Gurr, 1970, p. 179). Grievances are often diagnosed as pertaining to power and authority. For example, one of the influential books in the Women's Liberation movement is titled *Sexual Politics* and indeed the theme is that women are oppressed in a power relationship (Millett, 1970, pp. 125–27). Even within the politicized realm, societies may differ in styles of analysis and hence solutions. In the U.S. extremist and populist thought is sufficiently widespread that this can effect the formulation of goals for a variety of grievances. Analyses of the McCarthyism of the 1950s in the U.S. testify to this (Shils, 1956, pp. 98–185).

The formulation of goals is dependent upon the current way of thinking; but what is current changes. There may even be intellectual fashions in what is the appropriate kind of solution to grievances. Insofar as this is the case, leaders of conflict groups or those with more access to the surrounding social world will tend to keep up with these changes more than the rank-and-file constituency. This can be a source of discrepancy in goals within a conflict unit. It is also a reason why leaders can sometimes appear to be even more radical than their rank-and-file constituency.

Which goals are chosen depends upon possible adversaries who are believed able to redress grievances. The social environment, in this sense, provides targets for displaced dissatisfactions. In general, the environment helps each conflict group determine who the adversary can and ought to be. We observed above that currently issues are often viewed as involving power and authority relations and requiring political solutions. This is also true in the sense that the government itself tends to be viewed as the place to find redress for grievances. Thus, in societies where the government is the major employer of university graduates, dissatisfactions of underemployed intellectuals or of university students are directed at the government.

The visibility and salience of different groups in a society make them more or less likely adversaries. Some, like governments make themselves available as targets by presuming to be responsible for a wide range of social, economic, as well as political conditions. But societies vary in the ethnic groups, the kinds of economic institutions, family structures, and so on, in ways which make different groups more or less likely as adversaries. For example, in a study of revolutions in Latin America, Midlarsky and Tanter (1967) report evidence indicating that hostility toward the U.S. increased with higher levels of U.S. aid and investment. This seemed to be true, however, only in countries with nondemocratic governments; presumably in these countries, the U.S. could be readily viewed as co-opting the local government.

Third parties and their likely evaluations also affect the way in which conflict groups formulate their goals. Taking into account how others feel may not be readily compatible with the group's own requirements and hopes. For example, the Arab Palestinian organizations have disagreed about their aims. Recognizing that asserting their goal to be "throwing the Jews into the sea" has done "grave damage" to the Arab position, debate has focused upon the goal of creating a "democratic Palestinian state" in which Arabs and Jews will live in Peace (Circular of the Popular Democratic Front for the Liberation of Palestine, 1969). But opposition to that aim by some Arab factions "was based on the claim that the slogan contradicts the Arab character of Palestine and the principle of self-determination which was established in the National Covenant of the [Palestine] Liberation Organization, and that it also advocates a peaceful settlement with the Jews of Palestine."

Finally, the degree and form of the institutionalization of conflict regulation affects the formulation of goals, particularly their radicalism. Units which are part of a larger system with institutionalized means of reaching collective decisions tend to formulate reformist goals.

SUMMARY AND CONCLUSIONS

Significantly, as we have moved in this chapter from underlying to manifest conflict, we have given increased attention to leaders and to the aware segments of the social categories in contention. Not all members of a conflict unit exhibit complete or even appreciable awareness of the social conflict. Most university students are not generally in a manifest conflict relationship with administrators. Most women are not aware of being part of an objective collective conflict relationship with men. Most Americans may be basically indifferent to the pursuit of most foreign policy aims of the United States government. The extent and degree of mobilization varies by time and issue. The modes used in pursuing goals may be violent and may produce a variety of consequences even if only a small segment of a social unit is in manifest social conflict. But these are matters for succeeding chapters.

In this chapter we have analyzed three major elements of every social conflict: collective identity, sense of grievance, and incompatible goals. We have tried to understand what conditions and processes lead a category of people to think of themselves as a collectivity with a common identity and what factors affect the content of that collective identity. We have examined what makes people think they do not have what is appropriate for them and what is possible for them to have; that is, how people come to feel dissatisfied in not attaining what they think they should and could have. Finally, we studied what determines the formulation of goals which would be objectionable to another collectivity. We wanted to see what conditions and processes made one group believe that its grievances could be reduced by another group yielding something or altering its conduct.

In examining the determinants of collective identity, sense of grievance, and incompatible goals, we considered three sets of factors: unit characteristics, relations between the units, and the social environment of the units. The various determinants are complexly related to each other and to the various components of a social conflict. But what is most important to recognize here is that each factor does not have the same kind of effect upon every aspect of a struggle. The forces do not all operate in the same direction.

Any given change in conditions may have contradictory effects upon the probability of a dispute emerging from an objective conflict situation. For example, consider a social category whose power is deteriorating relative to another social category which has been, and still is, superior. As the magnitude of the deterioration increases, we would expect the sense of grievance and the degree of dissatisfaction to do so also. The belief that something can be done about it, that it is possible to improve one's position may also rise as conditions deteriorate but only up to a point, then further deterioration may weaken such beliefs. Thus studies of unemployed workers reveal that many become apathetic (Sheppard, Ferman, and Faber, 1960; Lazarsfeld-Jahoda and Zeisel, 1933; Kornhauser, 1959, pp. 163–67). These studies also indicate that with deteriorating conditions workers are increasingly isolated from each other, avoid social contacts and generally exhibit less solidarity. Finally, as conditions deteriorate the nature of the goals change: they are likely to be more radical. These various consequences are diagramed in Figure 3.3.

What this means is that the actual behavioral outcome of a deteriorating condition will depend on the responses of the other side and the

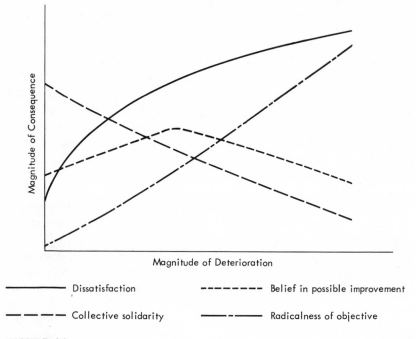

—————— Dissatisfaction	– – – – – – – Belief in possible improvement
— — — — Collective solidarity	——-——- Radicalness of objective

FIGURE 3.3

social context within which both sides are operating. It is also likely that a variety of conflict organizations, following different modes of action, will coexist. One of them may become more dominant than the others depending on the appropriateness of the strategy it follows given the constituency, the opponents, and the developing circumstances. This serves as a transition to the next chapter. The level of satisfaction or dissatisfaction is not simply and directly translated into one or another mode of conflict behavior. Other factors must be taken into account in order to understand the recourse to coercion and to violence. That is the task of the next chapter.

BIBLIOGRAPHY

AVINERI, SHLOMO, "Israel and the New Left," *Transaction*, 7 (July/August 1970), 79–84.

BARTH, FREDERIK (ed.), *Ethnic Groups and Boundaries* (Boston: Little, Brown and Company, 1969).

BELL, INGE POWELL, *CORE and the Strategy of Non-Violence* (New York: Random House, Inc., 1968).

BETEILLE, ANDRE, "The Decline of Social Inequality?" in Andre Beteille (ed.), *Social Inequality* (Baltimore: Penguin Books, Inc., 1969), pp. 362–80.

BLALOCK, H. M., JR., "Status Inconsistency, Social Mobility, Status Integration and Structural Effects," *American Sociological Review*, 32 (October 1967a), 790–801.

————, "Status Inconsistency and Interaction: Some Alternative Models," *American Journal of Sociology*, 73 (November 1967b), 305–15.

BLAU, PETER M., *Exchange and Power in Social Life* (New York: John Wiley & Sons, Inc., 1964).

BLAUNER, ROBERT, *Alienation and Freedom: The Factory Worker and His Industry* (Chicago: The University of Chicago Press, 1964).

BOK, DEREK C. AND JOHN T. DUNLOP, *Labor and the American Community* (New York: Simon and Schuster, Inc., 1970).

BORHEK, J. T., "Ethnic-Group Cohesion," *American Journal of Sociology*, 76 (July 1970), 33–46.

BRADBURN, NORMAN M., *The Structure of Psychological Well-Being* (Chicago: Aldine Publishing Co., 1969).

————, AND DAVID CAPLOVITZ, *Reports on Happiness* (Chicago: Aldine Publishing Co., 1965).

BRINTON, CRANE, *The Anatomy of Revolution* (New York: Vintage Books, 1955). Originally published in 1938.

BROOM, LEONARD AND F. LANCASTER JONES, "Status Consistency and Political Preference: The Australian Case," *American Sociological Review*, 35 (December 1970), 989–1001.

BUCHANAN, WILLIAM AND HADLEY CANTRIL, *How Nations See Each Other* (Urbana: University of Illinois Press, 1953).

CANTRIL, HADLEY, *The Pattern of Human Concerns* (New Brunswick, N.J.: Rutgers University Press, 1965).

Circular of the Popular Democratic Front for the Liberation of Palestine, 1969. Cited in Yehoshafat Harkabi, "Liberation or Genocide?" *Transaction*, 7 (July/August 1970), 63.

CORWIN, RONALD G., "Patterns of Organizational Conflict," *Administrative Science Quarterly*, 14 (December 1969), 507–20.

COSER, LEWIS A., *The Functions of Social Conflict* (New York: The Free Press, 1956).

DAHRENDORF, RALF, *Class and Class Conflict in Industrial Society* (Stanford: Stanford University Press, 1959).

DAVIES, JAMES C., "Toward a Theory of Revolution," *American Sociological Review*, 27 (February 1962), 5–19.

DONALD, DAVID, "Toward a Reconsideration of Abolitionists," in David Donald, *Lincoln Reconsidered, Essays on the Civil War Era* (New York: Alfred A. Knopf, Inc., 1956), pp. 19–36.

DUNLOP, JOHN T., "The Development of Labor Organization," in Joseph Shister (ed.), *Labor Economics and Industrial Relations* (Chicago: J. B. Lippincott Co., 1951), pp. 48–56.

ELLSWORTH, J. S., JR., *Factory Folkways* (New Haven: Yale University Press, 1952).

FEIERABEND, IVO K., ROSALIND L. FEIERABEND, AND BETTY A. NESVOLD, "Social Change and Political Violence: Cross-National Patterns," in Hugh Davis

Graham and Ted Robert Gurr (eds.), *Violence in America* (New York: Bantam Books, 1969), pp. 632–87.

THE FEMINISTS FROM NEW YORK CITY, "Kate Millet Please Understand," reprinted in *It Ain't Me Babe* (October 8, 1970).

FLEXNER, ELEANOR, *Century of Struggle* (Cambridge, Mass.: Harvard University Press, 1959).

FRIEDMANN, EUGENE A. AND ROBERT J. HAVIGHURST, *The Meaning of Work and Retirement* (Chicago: University of Chicago Press, 1954).

GALTUNG, JOHAN, "A Structural Theory of Aggression," *Journal of Peace Research*, 2 (1964), 95–119.

GESCHWENDER, JAMES A., "Continuities in Theories of Status Consistency and Cognitive Dissonance," *Social Forces*, 46 (December 1967), 160–71.

———, "Status Inconsistency, Social Isolation, and Individual Unrest," *Social Forces*, 46 (June 1968), 477–83.

GOFFMAN, IRWIN W., "Status Consistency and Preference for Change in Power Distribution," *American Sociological Review*, 22 (June 1957), 275–81.

GOODMAN, PAUL S. AND ABRAHAM FRIEDMAN, "An Examination of Adams' Theory of Inequity," *Administrative Science Quarterly*, 16 (September 1971), 271–88.

GOULDNER, ALVIN W., *Patterns of Industrial Bureaucracy* (New York: The Free Press, 1954).

GURR, TED ROBERT, *Why Men Rebel* (Princeton, N.J.: Princeton University Press, 1970).

HAGGSTROM, WARREN C., "Can the Poor Transform the World?" in Irwin Deutscher and Elizabeth J. Thompson (eds.), *Among the People* (New York: Basic Books, Inc., 1968), pp. 67–110.

HOBSBAWM, E. J., *Primitive Rebels* (New York: W. W. Norton & Company, Inc., 1965). Originally published in 1959.

HOMANS, GEORGE CASPAR, *Social Behavior: Its Elementary Forms* (New York: Harcourt, Brace & World, Inc., 1961).

HORNUNG, CARLTON ALBERT, "Status Consistency: A Method of Measurement and Empirical Examination," unpublished Ph.D. dissertation, Department of Sociology, Syracuse University, 1972.

HUGHES, EVERETT C., "Dilemmas and Contradictions of Status," *American Journal of Sociology*, 50 (March 1944), 353–59.

HYMAN, HERBERT H., "The Psychology of Status," *Archives of Psychology*, No. 269 (1942).

INKELES, ALEX, "Industrial Man: The Relation of Status to Experience, Perception, and Value," *The American Journal of Sociology*, 66 (July 1960), 1–31.

JACKSON, ELTON F., "Status Consistency and Symptoms of Stress," *American Sociological Review*, 27 (August 1962), 469–80.

JOHNSON, PAULA B., DAVID O. SEARS, AND JOHN B. MCCONAHAY, "Black Invisibility, the Press, and the Los Angeles Riot," *The American Journal of Sociology*, 76 (January 1971), 698–721.

KARON, BERTRAM P., *The Negro Personality* (New York: Springer Publishing Co., 1958).

KORNHAUSER, WILLIAM, *The Politics of Mass Society* (New York: The Free Press, 1959).

KRIESBERG, LOUIS, "Customer versus Colleague Ties among Retail Furriers," *Journal of Retailing*, 29 (Winter 1953–54), 173–76.

KRIESBERG, MARTIN, "Cross-Pressures and Attitudes," *The Public Opinion Quarterly*, 13 (Spring 1949), 5–16.

LANDECKER, WERNER S., "Class Crystallization and Class Consciousness," *American Sociological Review*, 28 (April 1963), 219–29.

———, "Status Congruence, Class Crystallization, and Social Cleavage," *Sociology and Social Research*, 54 (April 1970), 343–55.

LASLETT, BARBARA, "Mobility and Work Satisfaction: A Discussion of the Use and Interpretation of Mobility Models," *American Journal of Sociology*, 77 (July 1971), 19–35.

LAUMAN, EDWARD O. AND DAVID R. SEGAL, "Status Inconsistency and Ethno-religious Group Membership as Determinants of Social Participation and Political Attitudes," *American Journal of Sociology*, 77 (July 1971), 36–61.

LAZARSFELD-JAHODA, MARIE AND HANS ZEISEL, *Die Arbeitlosen von Marienthal* (Leipzig: Verlag von S. Hirzel, 1933).

LAZARSFELD, PAUL F., BERNARD BERELSON, AND HAZEL GAUDET, *The People's Choice* (New York: Columbia University Press, 1944).

LENSKI, GERHARD E., "Status Crystallization: A Non-Vertical Dimension of Social Status," *American Sociological Review*, 19 (August 1954), 405–13.

LIPSET, SEYMOUR MARTIN, *Agrarian Socialism* (Berkeley and Los Angeles: University of California Press, 1950).

———, " 'Fascism'—Left, Right, and Center," in S. M. Lipset, *Political Man* (New York: Doubleday & Co., 1960), pp. 131–76.

——— and Sheldon S. Wolin (eds.), *The Berkeley Student Revolt* (New York: Anchor Books, 1965).

LIPSET, SEYMOUR MARTIN AND EARL RAAB, *The Politics of Unreason: Right Wing Extremism in America, 1790–1970* (New York: Harper & Row, Publishers, Inc., 1970).

MANN, MICHAEL, "The Social Cohesion of Liberal Democracy," *American Sociological Review*, 35 (June 1970), 423–39.

MARX, GARY T., *Protest and Prejudice* (New York: Harper & Row, Publishers, Inc., 1969).

MERTON, ROBERT K. AND ALICE S. KITT, "Contributions to the Theory of Reference Group Behavior," in R. K. Merton and P. F. Lazarsfeld (eds.), *Studies in the Scope and Method of "The American Soldier,"* (New York: The Free Press, 1950), pp. 70–105.

MIDLARSKY, MANUS AND RAYMOND TANTER, "Toward a Theory of Political Instability in Latin America," *Journal of Peace Research* 3 (1967), 209–26.

MILLETT, KATE, *Sexual Politics* (Garden City, N.Y.: Doubleday & Company, Inc., 1970).

MORRIS, RICHARD T. AND VINCENT JEFFRIES, "Violence Next Door," *Social Forces*, 46 (March 1968), pp. 352–58.

National Advisory Commission on Civil Disorders (Kerner Commission), *Report of the National Commission on Civil Disorders* (New York: Bantam Books, 1968).

PARKER, SEYMOUR AND ROBERT J. KLEINER, "The Culture of Poverty," *American Anthropologist*, 72 (June 1970), 516–27.

PARKIN, FRANK, *Class Inequality and Political Order* (New York: Frederick A. Praeger, Inc., 1971).

PERETZ, DON, "Palestine's Arabs," *Transaction* 7 (August 1970), 43–49.

PERLMAN, SELIG, *A Theory of the Labor Movement* (New York: Augustus M. Kelley, 1928).

ROSECRANCE, RICHARD N., *Action and Reaction in World Politics*, (Boston: Little, Brown & Company, 1963).

ROSSI, PETER H. AND RICHARD A. BERK, "Local Political Leadership and Popular Discontent," *The Annals* (September 1970), 111–27.

RUNCIMAN, W. G., *Relative Deprivation and Social Justice* (Berkeley and Los Angeles: University of California Press, 1966).

SAWYER, JACK, "Dimensions of Nations: Size, Wealth, and Politics," *The American Journal of Sociology*, 73 (September 1967), 145–72.

SCHMITT, DAVID R., "An Attitudinal Correlate of the Status Congruency of Married Women," *Social Forces*, 44 (December 1965), 190–95.

SCHUMAN, HOWARD AND BARRY GRUENBERG, "The Impact of City on Racial Attitudes, *American Journal of Sociology*, 76 (September 1970), 213–61.

SCOTT, JOSEPH W. AND MOHAMMED EL-ASSAL, "Multiversity, University Size, University Quality and Student Protest: An Empirical Study," *American Sociological Review*, 34 (October 1969), 702–9.

SEIDMAN, JOEL, AND JACK LONDON, BERNARD KARSH, AND DAISY L. TAGLIACOZZO, *The Worker Views His Union* (Chicago: The University of Chicago Press, 1958).

SHEATSLEY, PAUL B., "White Attitudes Toward the Negro," *Daedalus*, 95 (Winter 1966), 217–38.

SHEPPARD, HAROLD L., LOUIS A. FERMAN, AND SEYMOUR FABER, *Too Old to Work—Too Young to Retire: A Case Study of a Permanent Plant Shutdown* (Washington, D.C.: U.S. Government Printing Office. U.S. Senate Special Committee on Unemployment Problems, 1960).

SHIBUTANI, TAMOTSU AND KIAN M. KWAN, *Ethnic Stratification* (New York: The Macmillan Company, 1965).

SHILS, EDWARD A., *The Torment of Secrecy* (New York: The Free Press, 1956).

SPILERMAN, SEYMOUR, "The Causes of Racial Disturbances: A Comparison of Alternative Explanations," *American Sociological Review*, 35 (August 1970), 627–49.

———, "The Causes of Racial Disturbances: Tests of an Explanation," *American Sociological Review*, 36 (June 1971), 427–42.

STEINEM, GLORIA, "A New Egalitarian Life Style," *The New York Times* (August 26, 1971), p. 37.

STONE, PHILIP J., "Expectations of a Better Personal Future," *Public Opinion Quarterly*, 34 (Fall 1970), 346–59.

TANTER, RAYMOND AND MANUS MIDLARSKY, "A Theory of Revolution," *The Journal of Conflict Resolution*, 11 (September 1967), 264–80.

TREIMAN, DONALD J., "Status Discrepancy and Prejudice," *The American Journal of Sociology*, 71 (May 1966), 651–64.

VALAVANIS, STEFAN, "The Resolution of Conflict when Utilities Interact," *The Journal of Conflict Resolution*, 2 (June 1958), 156–69.

VOEGELIN, ERIC, "The Growth of the Race Idea," *Review of Politics*, 2 (1940), 283–317.

WEINBERG, MARTIN S. AND COLIN J. WILLIAMS, "Disruption, Social Location and Interpretive Practices: The Case of Wayne, New Jersey," *American Sociological Review*, 34 (April 1969), 170–82.

WHYTE, WILLIAM F., *Human Relations in Industry* (New York: McGraw-Hill Book Company, 1948).

WILLIAMS, J. ALLEN JR. AND PAUL L. WIENIR, "A Reexamination of Myrdal's Rank Order of Discrimination," *Social Problems*, 14 (Spring 1967), 443–54.

chapter four

Pursuing
Conflicting Goals

If two parties are in a conflict relationship it might seem that either side, in pursuit of its goals, would have to use coercion. How else could one side induce the other to yield what it does not wish to? In simple zero-sum relationships that may be the case. But, as we noted in chapter 1, by extending the time range, widening the number of issues in contention, or fractionating the single conflict issue, the zero-sum payoff is transformed into a variable-sum payoff. As we shall see in more detail in this chapter, even in a conflict relationship there are alternatives to coercion as well as varieties of coercion.

We shall discuss the alternative ways in which conflicting parties may pursue their aims and what affects the choice of alternative. The use of the word choice should not be interpreted to mean that all alternatives are consciously weighed by each party and, after due calculation, a course of action selected. Rather, we will be concerned with the factors which influence and constrain the course followed. As observers we may consider alternatives, even if those were not thought of or were quickly rejected by the participants. It may be that the constraints are generally so great that little thought is given to the selection. The conflicting parties may appear to be only doing the obvious and taking unreflective action.

The point is that conflict behavior is a means to move toward some desired goal. We are not interested in simply expressive action, even violence. Again, this is not to deny that some modes have expressive elements; people do use coercion because it feels good to express hostility or to hurt someone else. We must consider such actions and their determinants but they are not conflict behavior. For the coercive action to be conflict behavior there must be some intention to induce the other side to yield some of what the coercer wishes to obtain. The choice of alternative may seem counterproductive to an observer or the intention may not be recognized by the opponent, to whom it appears irrational and simply expressive. But it may not appear that way to the actors. For example, the blacks have generally seen the recent riots in the ghettos as protest actions which would affect white policies (Brink and Harris, 1969, p. 264; Feagin and Sheatsley, 1968; Erskine, 1968, p. 524; Sears and Tomlinson, 1968).

ALTERNATIVE MODES

The modes used in conducting a conflict will be analyzed in terms of the types of inducements applied and the degree to which the application of the inducements is regulated. We will first discuss the inducements.

Types of Inducements. A party in conflict with another has three basic ways to induce the other side to move toward the position it desires. It may try to persuade, coerce, or reward the other side to do so. Each of these ways, and their varieties, will be discussed separately. In actual conduct, as we shall see, the ways are combined in varying proportions.

PERSUASION. We should not confuse persuasion in the analytic sense with the persuasion attributed to guns in Western movies. Persuasion as it is used here means to convince the adversary that it really is not in conflict about the goal being pursued. The conflict party argues, in effect, that the adversary should comply because what is sought is consistent with his own longer term or more general interests and values. The idea is to appeal to more abstract principles, shared identifications, or previously neglected values and considerations.

These various appeals can be advanced in a variety of forms and arenas. The persuasive efforts may be more or less explicit. They may be done mutually in varying degrees; that is, one side may make such efforts with or without the acceptance of the other side. If done against the wishes of the spokesmen for one side, they call such efforts subversive. In that case the appeals may be hidden or conducted with subterfuge. The persuasion may also vary greatly in the degree to which it utilizes symbolic means of communication or tries to convince the other side by deeds and demonstrations. Thus, efforts by missionaries, or less obviously by members of each group in dissensual conflict, may be to convince the other side of the rightness of their own views by what must be recognized as exemplary conduct and rich reward.

COERCION. Coercion involves trying to make the other side yield from feared or actual injury. In attempting to coerce the other side the coercer is trying to change the reality in which the other side exists so that it believes that the pains of not complying will be greater than those of complying. Coercion is punishing. It also is conditional; that is, it depends upon the conduct of the other side. Compliance obviates the need to coerce.

Coercion, too, has many forms and arenas. One significant distinction is whether it is threatened or implemented. Given its conditional character, it generally is threatened before being applied in the hope that the threat will suffice. This also means that the threat must be convertible to action. The threat may be implicit in the relationship and hardly evoked to induce compliance. In that case, however, we are back at the objective conflict stage.

Coercion also varies in the content of the negative sanctions which may be applied. Sanctions could include interpersonal efforts at shame and ridicule. In this study, however, we are especially concerned with sanctions which involve physical harm to adversaries, which entail economic sanctions in the form of withdrawal of goods or services, and which physically prevent or impede the opponent from doing what it wishes. We shall use the term violence to refer to actual efforts at coercion which involve the immediate and direct physical damage to people or their possessions. This is a conventional meaning of the word violence and more appropriate for the theoretical position taken in this work. I wish to point out, however, that some recent writers would broaden the term violence to include any actions or inactions by people which prevent others from living a complete life (Galtung, 1969). In this sense the deaths from malnutrition due to inequitable distribution of the resources of a society is violence. Although this extension of the term violence is inapplicable to the theoretical stance of this work, the definition used here would include actions not always popularly covered by the term violence (Blumenthal, Kahn, Andrews, and Head, 1972, pp. 71–95). Thus, when a state's military forces fires upon a group challenging the state's authority, that is violence as defined here. The role of government as a partisan to conflict and as an arbitrator of it, however, is not a simple matter and will need a closer examination later in this chapter.

REWARD. The idea of reward as inducement is an obvious one, but may seem strange at first in relationship to social conflicts. The idea is that one side offers the other a reward for compliance rather than a punishment for not complying. There is an extensive literature about the differences between punishment and rewarding as inducements to learning and to socialization in general (e.g., Hilgard and Bower, 1966; Becker, 1964). The implications for using rewards rather than punishments in handling conflicts, however, has not been systematically considered and the research on the topic is tangential.

Rewards, like punishments, must be conditional upon the action of the other side if they are to serve as inducements. It must cost something to a party to offer rewards or they might be given even if the other side did not comply. Given freely, as in love and identification, the rewards are not an inducement to follow a particular course of action that is objectionable.

Rewards or positive sanctions can take a variety of forms. Commodity exchanges are the clearest example. In these cases, one group will offer money, land, or payments of another kind in exchange for obtaining what it seeks. The positive sanction may also involve nontangible positive sanctions such as approbation or deference.

Actual Inducements. In any concrete case, these major types of inducements are generally combined. Inducements may be explicitly combined, for example, when one government promises benefits *and* threatens punishment to get compliance. The combination is also often implicit. Thus threats to an adversary are usually cloaked in justifications and those might have a persuasive effect.

In Figure 4.1, the three dimensions of inducements are diagrammed and we can imagine the variety of actual means taken as different points within that field. One such set of points will be discussed here because they are often neglected in general analyses of social conflict. That is, the variety of nonviolent means of pursuing objectives.

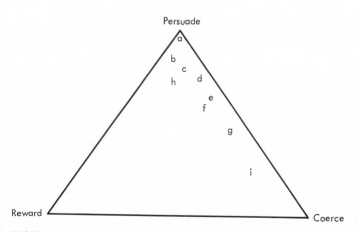

FIGURE 4.1 Means of Inducement.

Sharp (1959) has outlined nine different types of nonviolence. These range from nonresistant (in which people withdraw into their own purity) to nonviolent revolution (a and i, respectively, in figure 4.1). Between these are active reconciliation, (c) such as engaged in by Quakers, passive resistance or noncooperation (e), nonviolent direct action in which people intervene to disrupt unacceptable procedures (g), and satyagraha as formulated by Gandhi (h). These types vary in the degree of coercion. They all involve some persuasive element, but again, in varying degrees. Some even include rewards in the sense that there is promised a better life, a more ethical life, a closer approach to God by compliance. Some are buttressed by elaborate reasoning and some are almost spontaneous impulsive acts of people in response to conditions which they will not accept. Satyagraha or "Truth-force" as developed by Gandhi is one of the most influential applications and theoretical analyses of nonviolence as a way of bringing about a desired change against the opposition of others (Gandhi, 1940; Bondurant, 1965).

Three concepts are fundamental in satyagraha: truth, nonviolence, and self-suffering. For Gandhi, truth is God; it is an end which we seek, but since we cannot know absolute truth its pursuit excludes the use of violence. Nonviolence does not imply the negative action of not harming, but positive love, of doing good to the evil-doer, but it does not mean acquiescence to the wrong, it means resisting the wrong-doer, even if that injures him. Self-suffering means inviting suffering upon oneself but not out of weakness; it requires courage and refraining from violence when it is possible to use violence. It is directed at moral persuasion; it is a means.

Expediential and coercive arguments are associated with other forms of nonviolence. Coercion is a fundamental aspect of many kinds of nonviolent actions. Passive resistance and noncooperation raise the costs to the other side of pursuing its goals. The costs are those of diverting resources to overcome the resisters and of bearing the moral burden of repression.

Institutionalization of Conflict Regulation.   Another dimension of the means used to pursue conflicting goals cuts across the three kinds of inducements already discussed. This is the degree to which the regulation of conflict behavior is institutionalized. Conflict behavior is often conducted within a set of norms or rules. The norms prescribe what inducements are legitimate for what purposes. Thus, there are even rules of war. The norms may even state which kinds of inducements are appropriate for different conflicting parties. Thus a government is allowed to use violence in circumstances which are not allowed to nongovernmental actors. Rules vary in scope and specificity among different arenas of conflict.

These rules may be more or less institutionalized. Institutionalization is great insofar as the rules seem to have an external existence, independent of the actors, insofar as they are internalized within the actors, and insofar as they are supported by sanctions (Blau, 1964, pp. 273–77). Each aspect of institutionalization requires a little elaboration.

Rules which are embodied in written form or orally transmitted beyond one generation take on an independent quality which helps maintain the rules and constrains adherence to them. Codification by precedent or by law makes the rules less vulnerable to each conflict unit's partisan interpretations.

Such externality is not at all incompatible with the internalization of the rules through socialization. People learn rules and if they accept them as legitimate they may become so internalized that violation would be shunned in order to avoid the feelings of guilt or shame which would follow violation.

Sanctions to punish violations of the rules are crucial for their maintenance. Such sanctions vary in magnitude and in the certainty that they will be imposed. The likelihood that they will be imposed depends greatly upon it being in somebody's interest that they be imposed. Since the content of the rules generally are in accord with the interests of the dominants in a relationship they are the ones who are most interested in maintaining them and have the resources to do so. In other words, rules which favor the dominants will be maintained by the dominants and these are the generally extant rules.

To illustrate: American trade unions were considered illegal conspiracies until the middle of the nineteenth century; at the turn of the century a standard procedure was the labor injunction by which workers intending to strike were issued a restraining order forbidding it; and when the Sherman Antitrust Act was enacted in 1890 it was implemented against the trade unions (Leek, 1952; Taft, 1964). Thus, the employers enlisted the power of the state in maintaining rules for perpetuating the existing pattern of labor-management conflict.

VARIATIONS IN CONFLICT REGULATION. Each means of inducement previously considered can be more or less regulated and institutionalized. Let us first consider regulation of persuasive inducements. In relations between parties with great power differences, the regulations are likely to facilitate ways in which the dominants can take persuasive actions against the subdominants and protect the dominants from persuasive incursions from the other side. Between relatively equal parties, the rules generally permit mutual persuasive efforts. This may take the form of mutual agreement not to interfere with each other, as when governments agree to limit the access of the people of each country to the persuasive efforts of the other. Where there is also a relatively high integration and many shared understandings, the rules may proscribe too high levels of subterfuge.

The regulation of coercion, too, can vary in degree and content. Even in wars, coercion may be very limited and reduced to a ritual. European societies, themselves, have engaged in warfare under more restrictions about the use of violence than has recently been the practice. Thus, in the wars of the seventeenth and eighteenth centuries, fighting was halted to gather harvests, fighting did not involve the populace at large, and there were restraints upon exploitation of technological innovations (Nef, 1950). Even in contemporary wars, certain restraints can be found. For example, bacteriological weapons have not been employed. Chemical warfare has been restricted to chemicals used against plants and to ones which are used for domestic riot control purposes. The scope of operations has been limited; in the Korean war the U.S. did not bomb extensively north of the Yalu River. Of course, in such cases it is difficult to argue that these restraints were due to adherence to rules. Rather, they could spring from calculations of self-interest. The limited character of wars may depend upon mutual deterence. Bombing China north of the Yalu was eschewed and the Chinese did not interfere with the movement of supplies between Japan and Korea. The assessment of whether or not rules are adhered to because of acceptance of their legitimacy or because of self-interested calculations is certainly very difficult in any single case. In the long run, theoretically and empirically, the two conditions are highly related.

Rewards, too, may be more or less regulated. Rules tend to be about what is a fair exchange and what the terms of the exchange should be. The economic market place is controlled by a complex set of rules, adhered to from common understandings, self-interest, and high levels of institutionalization. On the whole, there is relatively little regulation about rewards in conflict relations. The exchange seems to be worked out in a bargaining situation with persuasive and coercive inducements also used. There may be extensive regulations, however, about the procedures to be followed in the negotiations through which the bargain is made.

BASES OF REGULATION AND INSTITUTIONALIZATION. Perhaps the most fundamental factor underlying the content of the rules governing conflict behavior and the institutionalization of the rules are the recurrent practices preceding explicit rules. Repeated practices come to be expected and after a while deviations become not only violations of expectations but illegitimate (Sumner, 1906, pp. 2 30). The way things are done is the way they should be done because that is the way they have been done. There is a kind of social logic to that statement since rules grow from expectations.

Anticipated continuing relations also promotes the regulation of conflict behavior. If the parties expect that they will be in contention over and over again, they develop understandings about how they should each pursue their objectives (Sayles and Strauss, 1953). Certain kinds of inducements may come to be regarded as out of bounds. It also follows, all things being equal, that patterns which are stable and are anticipated to remain stable are more likely to become institutionalized than are those patterns which are rapidly changing.

Other aspects of the relationship between the parties greatly affect the development of rules regarding conflict behavior. In general, insofar as the parties are integrated and have shared understandings, conflict behavior will be regulated. The way in which the relative power of the contending parties affects the regulation and institutionalization of conflict behavior is more difficult to assess. Presumably if the parties are relatively equal, rules about conflict behavior will be more equitable and adherence to them will be more acceptable to all parties. Thus it is only with the increased power of the trade unions that collective bargaining becomes highly regulated and institutionalized. On the other hand, if power inequalities are great it may be possible for the dominant to impose rules about conflict behavior.

Characteristics of the parties to a conflict and their general context also greatly affects the degree of institutionalization and regulation. Thus, insofar as the conflicting parties each are clearly bounded and autonomous, institutionalization of conflict behavior will be impeded. Nation-states provide a clear example of this. On the other hand, if the parties are within a larger social system, which has the ability to impose sanctions and guide conduct, then the conflict behavior between the contending parties will be regulated.

Finally, the kind of issues in contention affects the degree to which conflict behavior will be regulated. The elaboration and institutionalization of ways of handling conflict are more likely in cases where the contending parties are dealing with issues which they think require speedy and definite resolution. That is, some issues can be left to simmer, others come to a boil quickly. For example, Wright (1957) studied the kinds of markets which did and did not have commercial arbitration. That is, he analyzed those commodity exchanges, such as fabric makers selling to clothing manufacturers, to see in which ones the buyer and seller made agreements that any disputes would be handled by arbitration rather than through the usual legal procedures of suing through the courts. He found that one factor was very highly related to the use of commercial arbitration: the perishability of the commodity. Presumably, for goods which quickly lose their value, such as fish or vegetables, it is important to reach a speedy decision about a dispute. Almost any decision is better than no decision. In addition, issues which are viewed as crucial to the actors are less likely to be regulated than are issues which are not so viewed.

A variety of factors, then, affect the content and degree of regulation of conflict behavior and the extent to which the regulations are institutionalized. In this work, however, we will usually take the level of regulation and institutionalization as given. The parties in any particular conflict do not modify them greatly. Only toward the end of the book, in the chapters discussing the outcomes of conflicts and their consequences will we consider the levels of regulation and institutionalization as something to be explained rather than as part of an explanation.

Adjudication. Thus far, in discussing the ways in which parties pursue their conflicting goals, we have not considered how third parties may arbitrate or otherwise adjudicate the conflict and make an award to one side or the other. Many conflicts are settled under the supervision or through the actions of a social unit which encompasses the contending parties. Thus, there may be arbitration of labor-management conflicts by the government; student and administrator conflicts may be appealed to, and settled by, the university board of trustees; and contending organizations of blacks and whites may petition congress for legislation to advance their respective aims. Obviously, the partisans to such conflicts do not always accept the neutrality of the third party in making such adjudications.

From the perspective taken in this book, the adjudication of social conflicts is one of the ways in which third parties participate in conflicts. That is, the would-be adjudicator will be considered a potential or real ally of one of the contending parties. Within that framework, each conflict group will try to persuade, reward, or even coerce the third party to support it in the pursuit of its goals. This is part of the subject of the chapter on terminations and outcomes.

This perspective does not rule out the possibility of the third party playing an impartial role in conflict management and settlement. Usually, in such cases, the conflict behavior is highly regulated and institutionalized. The contending parties are likely to emphasize persuasive inducements as they contend they are correct in terms of some generally shared principles.

The point is, however, that the neutrality of the third party is not to be taken for granted or to be regarded as absolute. It is more likely to result from a power equilibrium than anything else. The extent to which it exists also depends on the nature of the issue in contention, the character of the units in conflict, and most importantly, the general context within which the parties exist.

One final observation must be made. Sometimes one of the parties to a conflict claims to be above the conflict and this claim is not recognized by the other side. The other side argues that the claimant is an adversary. In the perspective used in this book, we will have to regard both contentions as persuasive efforts.

SELECTING THE MODE

As soon as a conflict unit begins to move toward its goal, some way of inducing the other side to yield has been chosen. The choice may not have been a matter of much reflection by anyone or it may have been the result of long and extensive deliberation. We will examine four sets of factors which, in either case, jointly determine how a goal is pursued. They are: the issue in contention, the characteristics of the conflict unit, the whole set of relations between the conflicting units, and the environment or context of the units.

The mode chosen in pursuing an aim is a blend of all the inducements with varying degrees of regulation and institutionalization. But the choice is made and remade as long as the conflict is manifest. The parties shift the modes of pursuing their goals as they change, as the other side responds, and as the entire environment alters, partly as a response to their previous choices. We cannot possibly discuss this complex, ever shifting interplay altogether and all at once. We are limited to analyzing the basic components.

The Issue. The basic factor which affects how a conflict party pursues its goal is the goal itself. How people try to get what they want depends upon what they want. Or that is what they wish were so. Actually there is often much dissension within a conflict unit about the appropriateness of a given means for the end sought. Some means, if utilized, may be counterproductive, indeed may deny the attainment of what is desired. As Kennan (1961, pp. 390–91) writes regarding international conflicts, "Outright war is itself too unambivalent, too undiscriminating a device to be an appropriate means for effecting a mere change of regime in another country. You cannot logically inflict on another people the horrors of nuclear destruction in the name of what you believe to be its salvation, and expect it to share your enthusiasm for the exercise." He even goes on to say:

> ... modern warfare in the grand manner, pursued by all available means and aimed at the total destruction of the enemy's capacity to resist, is, unless it proceeds very rapidly and successfully, of such general destructiveness that it ceases to be useful as an instrument for the achievement of any coherent political purpose. Such warfare ... involves evils which far

outweigh any ... purpose at all ... short of sheer self-preserva-
tion, and perhaps not even short of that (p. 391).

Yet wars continue to be waged as if for some political goal. This is most
likely, for limited wars for limited aims (Blechman, 1966).

Nevertheless, in general one can discern some relationships between
the goals in contention and the ways in which they are pursued. First,
efforts at persuasion are more frequently and extensively exercised in
dissensual than in consensual conflicts. After all, what is often sought
in dissensual conflicts is an alteration in the values or beliefs of the
other side. In that case, some degree of conversion of the other side is
needed. Furthermore, there is a psycho-logic which compels a party to
emphasize either persuasion or coercion, depending on its analysis of the
conflict. For example, consider the alternative approaches that black
liberationists or women's liberationists might take. If the consensual
nature of the conflict is stressed, then it is argued that both sides want
the same thing and the other side is getting more of it at the expense
of the exploited, deprived side. If that is the case, the other side would
not be induced to make concessions and reduce the exploitation without
some coercion. But if the dissensual nature of the conflict is stressed, then
it must be argued that the other side is not gaining by the deprived
position of women or blacks. The analysis and the argument must then
argue that both sides are suffering and that they have some common
interests. The possibility of mobilizing one's own side in terms of its
exploitation is weakened.

Second, the magnitude of the incompatibility of the goals undoubtedly
affects the mode chosen. If what is being sought is a fundamental change,
then rewards and bargaining are not likely to seem adequate and in this
society, at least, neither is persuasion. Bell (1968, p. 59) in her study of
CORE observed that the choice of nonviolence was based on the liberals'
belief that discrimination rested on isolated attitudes that were not very
deeply rooted.

Even the degree and nature of coercive violence varies with the ends
pursued. Thus, in an analysis of civil strife in over a hundred nations
in the early 1960s, Gurr (1969, Table 17.7) found that turmoil (strikes,
riots, demonstrations) was disproportionally associated with promoting
or opposing a specific governmental policy; but conspiracy was disproportionally associated with the seizure of political power; and internal
war was especially likely when there were several, or diffuse, political
aims.

Lammers (1969) in his study of strikes and mutinies found that two
main goals could be distinguished: (1) promotion of interests, or (2) secession or seizure of power. In the former case the main weapon is a work

stoppage and in the latter case it is violence: imprisonment or killing of superiors.

Thirdly, aims tend to be collective or aggregative; that is, the benefits may be sought for the group as an entity or for the constituent members. Persuasion and conversion or reward and exchange are possible and likely to be tried for the latter aims. But for collective goals, coercion is more likely because collective goals require more open acknowledgement from the adversary and once a struggle has begun, coercion is likely to seem necessary.

Finally, the very content of the goal may seem to dictate the means used. To some extent a party may try to attain its aim by demonstrating their movement toward the goal. For example, if the end is equality and respect from the other side, one might seek that by presuming it already exists. Or, for example, if a group seeks a way of life in which people act spontaneously—if they seek to overthrow what they regard as rigid social conventions—then acting freely themselves might seem a way of bringing that change about. Even the provocation of using obscenities seems appropriate. Indeed the use of obscenity as a way of pursuing a conflicting goal is a kind of social invention. It both coerces the other side and serves as a way of demonstrating what is being sought; it may even be persuasive by demonstrating how much one can get away with. By being so outrageous it casts doubts upon many conventions, even upon the legitimacy of authority. Or so it might seem to those using this technique.

Similarly, people who want to attain self-respect and lose fear may think that one way of doing so is to act tough and intimidate the op- position. Thus, Fanon (1966) has argued that exercising violence against oppressors gives people a new sense of power and self-respect. If the aim becomes simply to remake oneself, then there is no longer social conflict. The other side is treated as an object upon which one acts in order to change oneself. In social conflicts this is never the only quality of the mode used.

The Adversaries. Popularly, the way in which an adversary pursues its goals is attributed to the character of that party. It *is* a determinant, but not the sole one. The nature of the adversary limits the range of modes it uses and affects the chances that each will be used under spe- cified conditions. We now turn to consider how this may be so.

PREDISPOSITIONS. The group's cultural traditions or historical pre- cedents suggest what alternatives exist and which are relatively acceptable for certain issues. Governments make wars. Other units do not generally have that as a readily available alternative; they must escalate up to the point at which large-scale, organized violence is employed by specially trained agents in the exercise of violence. Within any society, previous usage of a particular mode of pursuing conflicting goals often increases the likelihood of its usage again. Thus, in a study of civil disorder in 114 nations during the 1960s, the magnitude of current civil strife was correlated (.29) with historical levels of such strife, within each nation (Gurr, 1969, Table 17.12). We shall consider such matters in more detail in chapter 7 when we analyze the consequences of social conflicts.

Various categories of people may be predisposed to favor some modes rather than others. A 1969 national survey of American men found that more highly educated men were less likely to favor violence either for social control *or* for social change than were men with fewer years of schooling (Blumenthal, Kahn, Andrews, and Head, 1972). It has been suggested that middle class distaste for violence helps account for the use of nonviolence by CORE when there was a high proportion of middle-class persons participating in CORE activities. (Bell, 1968, p. 80). Presumably the involvement of lower-class blacks in organizations striving for the betterment of the conditions of blacks makes the use of coercion and of violence more likely. There is some evidence that persons of lower education, income, or occupational status are more willing than others to resort to violence in pursuit of their ends (McCord, Howard, Friedberg, and Harwood, 1969, p. 95). A national survey of Negroes conducted in 1963 reveals the same difference; but when the questions were repeated in 1966, there was no longer any difference outside the South by strata: the higher-income blacks were just as likely (21 percent) as low-income blacks to say that Negroes will have to use violence to win their rights (Brink and Harris, 1969, p. 260). In the 1966 survey, the respondents were asked for the first time whether they would join in something like riots. If anything, low income blacks outside of the South were more likely to say they would *not* than were middle and upper-income respondents.

Such changes over time help to explain the differences by socioeconomic strata in the propensity to use violence. Even if a difference is found, at a given time for a given sample, the meaning is not self-evident (Kriesberg, 1970, pp. 5–24). If low-status persons are more ready to use coercion and violence, it may be that they are pursuing goals which seem amenable to attainment by no other means; they may have fewer resources needed for other modes; coercion and violence may have some inherent gratifications or be gratifying because they provide an outlet for more generalized and displaced frustrations; or it may be that persons of different social strata are socialized in ways which make some modes seem proper and others improper. The meaning of the relationship between socioeconomic rank and readiness to use coercion and violence in the pursuit of collective ends is not at all clear. Detailed analyses of attitudes and conduct about a wide variety of goals and in different historical periods are needed to make any interpretation with confidence. It should also be noted that the relationship is only a moderate one.

Similar differences exist between men and women. Men generally are more likely to favor and to use coercion and violence in the pursuit of conflicting goals than are women. Some of the ambiguities in interpreting the meaning of this difference are like those outlined for the differences by socioeconomic rank. The immense cultural component in sexual roles, however, would argue for a difference in socialization and cultural expectations in explaining the differences between men and women in this regard. Generally, in this and many other societies, masculinity includes being physically tough in the sense of being able to take and give bodily pain. The cult of masculinity or of *machismo* emphasizes physical bravery, inducing and accepting challenges to fight, and risking bodily injury. There is also some evidence that an emphasis upon this kind of masculinity is disproportionally found in the lower socioeconomic strata (McKinley, 1964) and also varies by society.

One way of testing some of these ideas is to look at preferences of different strata and sexes regarding pursuing the same goals. A problem here, of course, is that every goal has different import to people of different strata and sexes. To reduce this problem we can look at views within one society about a conflict with another country. According to the cultural interpretations suggested above, we would expect men and lower socioeconomic persons to tend to favor more aggressive pursuit of foreign policy aims *and* the difference between men and women should be greater among the lower than the higher socioeconomic strata.

Israelis, in 1962, were asked, "To what extent would you prefer a policy of 'agression' (toughness) on the part of the Israeli Government toward the Arab States?" Men did tend to favor a more aggressive or activist policy. Moreover, the less educated, the poorer, those with lower status occupations, and those of lower ethnic status did tend to favor a more aggressive policy. The difference between the men and women was greatest in the skilled worker stratum and among persons with less than a secondary education. The pattern was particularly clear and supportive of a cultural explanation in the case of ethnic differences. In Israel, the national backgrounds of the Jews are ranked, with the European Jews having higher status than the Oriental Jews. In Table 4.1 we see that the differences by sex are particularly great in the lower status and more traditional ethnic groups.

In the U.S. in 1964, support for a stronger stand in Vietnam, even if it meant invading North Vietnam, was also more likely among men than among women and the differences between them were greater in the lower socioeconomic strata. For example, see Table 4.2. But, unlike Israel, support for a stronger war stand was expressed more frequently

TABLE 4.1　Percent of Israelis Who "Very Much" Prefer a Policy of "Aggression" (Toughness) toward the Arab States, by Sex and Ethnicity, 1962

Country of Father's Birth	Sex		Difference
	Male	Female	
Russia, Poland, Rumania, Galicia	15.5	10.7	4.8
U.S., Germany, Great Britain, etc.	9.5	10.0	−0.5
Palestine	24.0	16.3	7.7
Bulgaria, Greece, Yugoslavia, etc.	26.8	20.9	5.9
Egypt, Syria, Lebanon, Yemen, etc.	40.1	26.8	13.3
Morocco, Algeria, Tunisia, Libya	35.7	25.8	9.9

Source: Secondary analysis of 1962 national survey, probability sample of 1170 cases and an additional sample of 300 kibbutz members. In this analysis, the kibbutz members are included with appropriate weighting. The study was conducted by the Israel Institute of Applied Social Research as part of comparative studies under the direction of Hadley Cantril (1965). The data were made available by The Roper Public Opinion Research Center.

the more income, the higher the occupational status, and the more years of formal education respondents had (Hamilton, 1968).

Even if there is a tendency for males and lower socioeconomic strata to favor more coercive conflict modes, clearly, these are not powerful determining factors. In the U.S. in 1964, the higher socioeconomic strata tended to support a stronger stand because they tend to be more attentive to and supportive of official leadership (Rosi, 1965; Gamson and Modigliani, 1966). Taking stronger action seemed to be closer to governmental policy than the other alternatives in the question and the Republican opposition was in favor of taking stronger action. The sex differences can also be reversed on issues of greater significance to women than men; or the differences may disappear within particular groups at particular times. For example, consider blacks in the U.S. In a 1964 national survey men appeared to be more militant than women (Marx, 1969, p. 53–54), and in 1966 in Houston, men were less likely than women to say that violence was never justified; but in 1967 in Watts, informal interviews did not reveal any differences between men and women (McCord, Howard, Friedberg, and Harwood, 1969, pp. 74, 91–93). In the 1967 Milwaukee riot, women were less often arrested for rioting, but among the arrestees and among an inner city sample, they were equally likely to admit to having participated (Flaming, 1971). In certain revolutionary situations women may be in the forefront of violent action, as during the French Revolution in the march on Versailles of October, 1790 and in later food riots (Coser, 1967, p. 68).

In summary, there is some evidence that groups differ in their predisposition to use coercion and violence. This indicates a variation in cultures, for example in ideas regarding masculinity. The evidence also

TABLE 4.2 Percent of Americans Who Support "Taking a Stronger Stand" in Vietnam, by Sex and Education, 1964

Education	Sex		Difference
	Male	Female	
Less than 8 yrs.	44.4	8.3	36.1
	(45)	(24)	
8 yrs.	46.2	21.7	24.5
	(39)	(46)	
9–11 yrs.	55.0	31.6	23.4
	(80)	(95)	
12 yrs.	62.8	43.9	18.9
	(86)	(123)	
12 yrs. and some	62.6	50.4	12.2
college	(131)	(123)	
College completed	60.8	50.0	10.8
or More	(74)	(56)	

The question was: "Which of the following do you think we should do now in Vietnam?" 1. Pull out of Vietnam entirely, 2. Keep our soldiers in Vietnam but try to end the fighting, 3. Take a stronger stand even if it means invading North Vietnam. The question was asked of those interested enough to have opinion; those uninterested in the issue are not included in this table.
Source: Secondary analysis of Survey Research Center, 1964 election survey. National, cross-section sample of voting age citizens, 1,571 interviews were completed. The data were kindly made available for analysis by the Survey Research Center.

indicates that such variations may be relatively unimportant in accounting for positions about and uses of violence in social conflicts. The goals being sought, the nature of the adversary, and the availability of alternative conflict modes all affect the preference and the choices. These other factors can overwhelm the cultural determinants. Culture often seems to be an important determinant because it is consistent with and supported by many other relevant factors.

IDEOLOGY. More specifically than the culture or historical precedents, the group's ideology may embody prescriptions and proscriptions about how to pursue its goals. In general, the elaboration of an ideology tends to objectify the struggle and the adversary. This makes the conflict seem more impersonal and therefore greater militancy and more severe sanctions can be imposed upon the adversary (Coser, 1956, pp. 115–16). But, if we think of ideology as merely the explicit and elaborated ideas about what is wrong, what would be a solution, and how one can attain the desired goal, then the content of the ideology is more important than its mere existence.

Thus, the nonviolent ideology of the civil rights movement in the United States during the 1950s and early 1960s helped divert efforts toward integration, equality, and freedom away from violence. The availability of the ideology of nonviolence, as interpreted and applied by Martin Luther King, Jr., undoubtedly affected the choice of method to pursue conflicting aims. King's leadership was important in this regard, but it should be recognized that CORE was using nonviolent direct action for many years prior to the Montgomery, Alabama bus boycott. Yet, the prior existence of the ideas and tactics of nonviolent direct action by and for blacks in America did not produce nor sustain widespread action using such means. Many other conditions had to be present for the wider participation in the civil rights movement of the early 1960s.

There have been, and are, defenders and even praisers of violence. They seem to revel in the heroics and solidarity of those who would indulge in it; they see it as an expression of profound ideas and emotions and as the way to bring about apocalyptic transformations. As Sorel (1950, p. 302) wrote:

> The conception of the general strike, engendered by the practice of violent strikes, admits the conception of an irrevocable overthrow. There is something terrifying in this which will appear more and more terrifying as violence takes a greater place in the mind of the proletariat. But, in undertaking a serious, formidable, and sublime work, Socialists raise themselves above our frivolous society and make themselves worthy of pointing out new roads to the world.

Sorel, although intellectually influential, was not a leader of any social conflict groups. Adolf Hitler was. He wrote in *Mein Kampf* (1941, p. 784):

> The lack of a great, new, creative idea means at all times a limitation of the fighting power. The conviction of the justification of using even the most brutal weapons is always dependent on the presence of a fanatical belief in the necessity of the victory of a revolutionary new order on this globe. A movement which does not fight for such highest aims and ideals will therefore never take the ultimate weapon.

Nazism, according to Hitler, was such an idea; therefore terror and violence, domestically and internationally, was possible, justified, proper, and even a kind of evidence for the idea (Arendt, 1951, pp. 334–428).

LEADERSHIP. The development of an ideology embracing violence or nonviolence, or any other means, requires the presence of ideological leaders or ideologists close to the leaders. This is one basis for leadership variation in preference for coercive ways of pursuing collective goals. Certainly, there are times when leaders seem to be cautioning and constraining their followers not to employ violence or, at any rate, only a moderate amount. But at other times leaders seem to be urging reluctant followers to forego persuasive efforts or bargaining and to strike violently. No simple and constant difference between leaders and followers in these regards exists. But some conditional regularities may be suggested.

Generally, in conflicts which are highly regulated and institutionalized, leaders are more likely to support the rules than are their constituencies. This means that the *followers*, or a faction of them, are more often in favor of extreme modes of pursuing their ends than are the leaders. On the other hand, when the conflicts are not so regulated and institutionalized, particularly if the conflict parties are just getting mobilized, the leaders will tend to support more coercive means compared to the rank and file. Actually this is still too crudely stated. There is more differentiation than simply between leaders and followers. At least one should distinguish between active leaders of different levels, active rank and file members, nominal members, the constituency or possibly active rank and file, and the potential leadership. With these additional specifications, we can suggest further regularities in the relationship between kind of participation in the conflict group and selection of ways of pursuing goals.

In highly regulated and institutionalized conflict relationships, such as collective bargaining in the contemporary U.S., the highest trade union leaders are likely to be less militant than lower ranking union officials. There is some evidence that lower ranking officials are more suspicious of management intentions (Mills, 1948, p. 141). Presumably the national leaders are more deeply involved in negotiations and other interactions with management and therefore develop mutual dependence and understanding. Rank and file members probably are less militant than the local leaders except at the outset of direct coercive action. On the other hand, union members are undoubtedly more supportive of militant action than nonmembers even of similar economic status. For example, union members are much more likely to support the idea of sympathy strikes than are nonmembers, even if they are poor or have low education (Cantril and Strunk, 1951, p. 828).

DIVERSITY.   The diversity or heterogeneity of the conflict group can, in itself, affect the mode selected for the pursuit of goals. A mode must be found which is acceptable to the diverse members. If the group is long established and has a consensus about what are the appropriate means, then the diversity may not be an important inhibitor, just as it does not inhibit national governments in their pursuit of foreign goals. But in less clearly bounded and newly emerging organizations, diversity usually results in less coercive means. For example, in the civil rights movement during the late 1950s and early 1960s, blacks and whites of different social strata and of different regions were working together. It is true that there was considerable selectivity within each group. Still, the diversity made attractive the emphasis upon nonviolence within CORE, SNCC, and SCLC and the emphasis on traditional procedures—such as persuasive attempts in direct conversations with leaders and adversary proceedings within established legal rules. As we shall discuss when we consider escalation, the movement to greater coercion and to new modes is often associated with changes in the composition of the membership of conflict groups.

PARTICULAR RESOURCES. People's preferences for one mode rather than another also are affected by the costs they have to bear to use one rather than another mode. Every mode involves peculiar risks and expenditures. In general, violence is risky because there is often a good likelihood that violence will be reciprocated. Particularly in challenging superior power, there is the risk of having to absorb heavy sanctions. It is partly for such reasons that youth are so often found to be involved in violent disruptions (Coser, 1967, pp. 65–71; National Advisory Commission on Civil Disorders, 1968, p. 172; Sears and McConahay, 1969). Young people not only tend to feel invulnerable because of their youth, but they actually have fewer assets which are hostage to those with superior power. They are less likely to have children and spouses to whom they would feel an obligation "to be careful." Their careers do not yet seem so fragile. Even as students they are generally less vulnerable to sanctions wielded by authorities than are employed persons. It is partly for these reasons that students are so generally reported to be involved in civil turmoil (Gurr, 1969, Table 17.5) and why they are so disproportionally represented in organizations like CORE (Bell, pp. 76–79). Young people are usually less dissatisfied with their own condition than are older persons because they still anticipate improvements. This hope and the freedom to take risks can mean greater participation in conflict behavior despite dissatisfaction being less widespread among them.

Being free of encumbering commitments facilitates people's participation in conflict behavior, apart from, or as well as, being a motivating source. Thus the socially isolated and those lacking family and friendship ties may be particularly likely to support extremist objectives (Ringer and Sills, 1952–1953), belong to conflict organizations with more provocative tactics, and themselves be particularly likely to engage in conduct which risks heavy sanctions against them. For example, during the 1967 Detroit riot, neighborhoods in which residents had little social interaction with each other had more severe rioting than other neighborhoods in the riot area (Wanderer, 1969).

Finally, adversary characteristics affect the selection of the ways to pursue conflicting goals. Each mode has special requirements and some kinds of people have the appropriate resources to utilize those ways and others do not. First let us consider the implications of the simple numerical size of the conflict group.

Conspiracies or terrorism can be carried out by relatively few people. Indeed, for conspiracies to succeed, the number of persons cannot be large. But in order to wage internal warfare, large social strata must become engaged (Gurr, 1969, Table 17.5). Similarly, nonviolent direct action, to be effective, requires a large number of participants. Even aside from effectiveness, a goodly number is needed for mutual support and protection. Rioting, too, requires a large number of participants. This gives each person a sense of security and support. Thus, Spilerman (1970) studied racial disorders in the United States between 1961 and 1968 and found that the absolute number of nonwhites in a city was by far the single most important factor in accounting for disorders. Community variables were not markedly related to the disorders. Presumably, the grievances of blacks are sufficiently diffuse in the society and rioting a widely enough accepted form of expression, that the more blacks there are available, the more incidents which might trigger a riot will occur and the more people there are who are available for rioting. Riots, depending in part on milling and contagion, require congeries of people. Streets filled with people who are young enough to take a little risk can begin engaging in activity which draws in other participants. Thus, what is crucial is the number of persons *appropriate* for a given mode. There may be many elderly persons in a society, but old age inhibits engaging in a variety of coercive actions. Despite the grievances which the elderly may feel, their tactics in pursuit of their goals are generally moderate. When they are concentrated in particular areas so that they constitute a significant proportion of the electorate, they may exercise *political* influence.

It should also be observed that the number of appropriate people may not be sufficient to determine the use of a given mode. How acceptable that mode is to the possible utilizers is also important. Spilerman (1970) studied racial disorders which occurred when they were a prevailing pattern. When riots are not as widespread, *and when the rioters are usually white*, then the absolute number of blacks is not likely to explain the incidence nor the severity of racial riots. This is the finding of studies of riots from 1913 to 1963 (Lieberson and Silverman, 1965).

In general, the particular resources available to a group channels the mode selected for its pursuit of its goals. Groups with resources which can be traded with an adversary can try that method. Groups skilled in manipulating symbols are likely to try persuasion. The degree and form of organization similarly helps determine which form of coercion will be attempted. Social categories without well developed organizations are likely to resort to or utilize riots, uprisings, and other somewhat spontaneous outpourings of pressure and grievance. Deprived and with few resources to use in nonviolent means, with little left as hostage to attacks by the adversary, and with few alternative courses, persons who are finally moved to protest are likely to do so violently.

The many studies of the participants in the American ghetto riots of the 1960s provide pertinent information. Involvement in collective behavior depends partly on being on the scene and becoming caught up in events, but there is some self-selection in who actively participates, particularly in large-scale rioting which persists for more than several hours. On the whole, comparisons of either arrestees or self-admitted participants in riots with a sample of persons in the same residential areas reveal considerable similarity in socioeconomic characteristics such as education, income, and occupation; but there are some differences even in these regards. Thus, black rioters tend to have experienced more unemployment, have lower occupational status, and have lower education (if age is controlled) than nonrioters (Geschwender and Singer, 1970; National Advisory Commission on Civil Disorders, 1968, pp. 173–77; Flaming, 1971).

A further specification of the reasons for differential participation in riots can be found by bringing together three disparate reports. First, the Los Angeles County Probation Department reported that only 27 percent of the juveniles arrested during the Watts riot came from intact homes (*New York Times,* November 24, 1965, p. 22). Second, between 1960 and 1965 the real income of female-headed black families declined as did that of blacks who lived in the ghettos of Cleveland and Los Angeles; but at the same time real income of male-headed black families and those living elsewhere increased (Williams, 1970). The poor blacks suffered an actual fall in real income and the gap between them and better-off blacks increased. Finally, as Caplan and Paige (1968, p. 20) note on the basis of survey responses, "Rioters are particularly sensitive to where they stand in relation to other Negroes, not to whites."

In summary, the nature and magnitude of the grievance does not in itself determine the mode of pursuing goals. Violence is not simply an expression of grievance. As we noted previously, deprivation in many ways inhibits awareness of grievance and open pursuit of desired goals. The deprived have limited resources for making demands and seeking them, whether coercively or not. Some data from a study by Gurr of civil strife throughout the world in the early 1960s is revealing in this regard (Gurr, 1969, Table 17.11). Among nations with low levels of economic development there was little or no correlation between short-term or long-term deprivation and either turmoil or conspiracy. Among societies which have high or medium levels of development there are moderate correlations between each kind of deprivation and each kind of civil strife. Presumably a minimal level of resources are needed to react to deprivation with coercive efforts. Furthermore, the correlations, if anything, are higher for short-term rather than for long-term deprivation. Presumably long term deprivation, although more cause for grievance, weakens the possibilities for protest.

The Relations Between the Adversaries. The degree and kind of integration between the contenders, the feelings people in the conflicting groups have toward each other, and their relative power, all affect the mode selected by conflict groups in pursuit of their aims. Let us consider the degree of integration first.

INTEGRATION. As used in the preceding chapter, integration refers to the degree of interaction between the members of different groups and to the extent to which they have common and complementary relations relative to conflicting ones. The latter itself has many possible bases. One which is of special pertinence here is that of crosscutting ties, whether these be of crosscutting conflicts or of positive bonds. In social systems with many lines of cleavage which are not superimposed, groups who are adversaries along one conflict line may be allies or have constituents who are allies on another issue (Dahrendorf, 1959; Berelson, Lazarsfeld, and McPhee, 1954, pp. 305–23).

In the preceding chapter we discussed some of the ways in which crosscutting ties affect the likelihood of conflicts becoming manifest and the form of their manifestation. The extent to which persons in conflict groups share some common and complementary interests also has important consequences for the mode chosen. On the whole, the greater the overlap of statuses between groups, the less likely is either party to utilize coercion against the other, and if it does, the coercion is more likely to be nonviolent. For example, compare societies with patrilocal and matrilocal residence patterns (LeVine, 1965). If the people do not marry within their own village and follow the patrilocal residence pattern, the bride would come to her husband's village to live. The husband and all his brothers would remain in the same village. If they follow matrilocal residence, the groom would go to his wife's village. The wife and her sisters remain in the same village with husbands from several villages. Consequently, if there is an intervillage conflict, under the matrilocal system the men in each village would be faced with the possibility of fighting their brothers in the other village. But under the patrilocal system, they would be allied with all their brothers (it is their in-laws who might be in the other village). In conjunction with other factors, matrilocal societies tend to have a sense of solidarity and lack of intervillage warfare while patrilocal societies are plagued by more dissension, fights, and feuds (Murdock, 1949, pp. 204–6).

This idea of crosscutting ties is broader than, but includes, the concept of status inconsistency. Now we are considering nonranked as well as ranked statuses. As discussed in the preceding chapter, status inconsistency might be expected to be a source of intensified grievance and hence of more coercive and violent modes of seeking redress. On the whole, however, we are arguing that crosscutting ties, even when associated with, or arising from, status inconsistency, serve to inhibit violence and may even provide the basis for noncoercive pursuit of goals (Ross, 1920, p. 164ff; Coser, 1956, p. 72ff; Galtung, 1966b, pp. 121–61).

Illustrative evidence can be seen in studies of industrial conflict. Let us consider strikes as more coercive than collective bargaining conducted without recourse to strikes. Kerr and Siegel (1954) studied the rate of strikes in different industries in eleven industrial countries. They found that certain industries generally had much higher rates of strikes than did others. For example, the propensity to strike was generally high in mining and the maritime and longshore industries; medium-high in lumber and textiles; medium in the chemical, construction, and printing industries medium-low in clothing and services; and low in railroad, agriculture and trade.

Kerr and Siegel considered a variety of possible explanations for the interindustry differences in the propensity to strike. They concluded that one important determinant was the location of the worker in society. Workers who form "isolated masses" are particularly prone to strike. For example, miners, sailors, and longshoremen tend to have separate communities, have their own codes, and have few neutrals to mediate the conflicts. The workers are relatively homogeneous in work roles and mobility out of the occupation is difficult.

Another kind of evidence to test these ideas can be found in studies of community conflicts. A systematic study of 18 New England communities revealed that low interaction between opponents was related to rancorous conflicts (Gamson, 1966). The flouridation of water and two other issues were studied in each community. The use of illegitimate tactics, as volunteered by informants, identifies rancorous conflicts. Acquaintanceship between opponents was substantially lower in rancorous than in conventional communities. Furthermore, communities in which there was high crosscutting on the issues were more likely to have conventional conflicts than communities with high cleavage. Crosscutting ties were measured by the degree to which people of the same background shared the same position on the issues. Background was measured in terms of length of residence, nationality background, education, and religion.

In international relations, too, the nature and degree of interaction between adversary countries affects the mode chosen to pursue conflicting goals. For example, since the Korean war, the American and North Korean governments have had few relations and the peoples of each country do not engage in exchange transactions of any sigificant nature. When the North Koreans seized the U.S.S. Pueblo, in 1968, the U.S. Government did not have an array of sanctions which could be used to cajole, exchange, or force the return of the vessel and its crew. The option of a large-scale military venture to force their return seemed out of proportion and might punish the adversary and yet fail to safely retrieve the ship and crew. There even was speculation about seizing a North Korean vessel so that the U.S. government would have something to exchange for the release of the U.S.S. Pueblo. Interaction, then provides the basis for applying negative sanctions short of violence, by disrupting the interaction, just as well as providing reasons for not pursuing an issue coercively in order to prevent further disruption of the relationship.

There is an interesting set of data about the level and nature of integration between societies and the occurrence of war between them. Naroll (1969) studied states and their rivals, selecting 20 pairs from 25 B.C. to 1776. He found that general cultural exchanges were negatively related to war frequency ($-.40$); he did not find, however, that mere trade was related to war frequency.

Deutsch, et al. (1957) studied the emergence of "security communities" —groups of people within a territory with a sense of community and with institutions and practices which assure, for a "long" time, that social problems will be resolved without recourse to large-scale physical force. Examples of such security communities include "amalgamated" cases such as the United States since 1877, England-Scotland since 1707, Italy since 1859 and Switzerland since 1848 and "pluralistic" cases such as Norway-Sweden since 1907, United States-Canada since the 1870s, and England-Scotland between the late 1560s and 1707. Their analysis and findings are too complex to be summarized here, but the major findings which pertain to our concerns can be cited. A few conditions seemed essential for the success of both amalgamated and pluralistic security communities. The first was the compatibility of major values relative to political decision making; the second was the capacity of the participating units to respond to each other, and third was mutual predictability of behavior. What is of special interest here is that the mobility of persons, at least among the politically relevant strata, was also found in successful cases. Furthermore, in amalgamated security communities they also found that there were unbroken links of social communication both geographically between territories and socially between different strata and there was a wide range of communication and transaction between the peoples.

Integration has consequences for other aspects of the relationship between parties and these consequences in turn affect the mode selected for handling conflicts. Thus, high levels of integration tend to increase the levels of mutual trust, understanding, and legitimacy. Such feelings and beliefs tend to reduce the intensity of any given conflict as well as make the pursuit of goals by means of persuasion or of exchange seem more likely to be successful and intrinsically attractive.

Blumenthal, Kahn, Andrews and Head (1972, pp. 135–78) studied opinions about violence and identifications with white student demonstrators, black protesters, and police. They found that identification with a group is positively associated with justifying its use of violence and identification with the opponents or victims was negatively associated with justifying violence used *against* it. Furthermore, their analysis suggests that identification with the victims of violent action is more important than identification with its performer in accounting for justifications of violence.

There is a variety of experimental and field evidence that belief in the legitimacy of leaders or their directives inhibits aggression and violence directed against them (Gurr, 1970, pp. 189–91; Rothaus and Worchel, 1960; Tanter and Midlarsky, 1967). For example, Bwy (1968) found that in Latin American countries legitimacy was negatively correlated $(-.71)$ with organized violence (but insignificantly, $-.14$, with turmoil). Gurr (1969) found that measures of legitimacy correlated $-.58$ with civil strife in Latin American countries with a *caudillo* type of government and $-.45$ in pluralist, democratic countries. But in elitist and authoritarian countries, the correlations are much weaker, $-.26$ and $-.08$ respectively. Presumably, coercion by the government can suppress civil strife.

Although integration generally reduces the likelihood that violence will be employed in the handling of any given social conflict, this should not be interpreted to mean that integration is a safeguard against all violence nor even that the intensity of violence will be minimized within the social system. Issues in contention may come to be so formulated that among the alternatives available to the parties concerned, violence may be attempted by one or the other party even with relatively high levels of integration. Indeed, once a conflict becomes manifest and coercion is attempted, the violence may be particularly intense because of the added resentments, sense of betrayal, and pains suffered in the course of the conflict emergence. In a sense, integration means mutual dependence and vulnerability. The extensive brutalities of civil wars testify to these dangers.

RELATIVE POWER.   Undoubtedly, the difference in power between adversaries affects the means of conflict each uses. But if the effects are measured by the use of coercion, then the magnitude of the power differences cannot have uni-directional consequences. If large power differences deter the weaker from using coercion against the stronger, then they invite the stronger to use coercion for further aggrandizement against the weaker. We need to consider each set of possibilities before trying to reconcile them.

On the whole, it should be clear that with the vast preponderance of power which a government has over any segment of the population under its administrative authority, even extreme deprivations will be endured with only occasional outbursts of violent protest. Thus, soldiers, seamen, and prisoners mutiny or riot relatively infrequently, if one considers only the poor conditions which they generally have endured (Lammers, 1969).

On the whole, it is when the weaker party believes it is gaining power relative to the stronger adversary that it will venture the use of coercion. This can be illustrated in several contexts. Coercion is used calculatively insofar as it is institutionalized; if that is the case, we would expect strikes to be employed by trade unions when their chance of success is greatest. Strikes should be chosen and employed, then, during upturns in the economy and therefore when labor is in shorter supply. This seems to be the case (Knowles, 1954; Rees, 1954). Note, that in such cases, it is not increased grievances which explain the pursuit of conflicting goals, but the *opportunity* to improve one's conditions. It is true that business upturns may also be accompanied by price increases and a fall or slowing down of real income. But the relative power interpretation seems particularly compelling in that strikes to organize the unorganized show the same pattern as do strikes to secure wage increases and other benefits.

These considerations throw additional light upon the findings that revolutions and uprisings often occur when previously improving conditions show a downturn (Feierabend, Feierabend, and Nesvold, 1969; Davies, 1962; Gurr, 1970). This is usually interpreted as an expression of increased dissatisfaction resulting from an increased gap between attainments and expectations. In the preceding chapter, we discussed how a decrease in the rate of improvement could be the basis for increased dissatisfaction. But dissatisfaction is not directly and uniformly expressed in the coercive pursuit of a redress of grievances. It can be accepted as an unfortunate but natural calamity. It is when some other group, like the ruling government, is held responsible that coercive action or violence in the form of revolutionary uprisings may occur. In that case, the downturn is attributable to the incompetence of the leaders. Such incompetence not only weakens their legitimacy but makes them weak and vulnerable. Assuming that there are always grounds for dissatisfaction, the weakness of the formerly stronger party invites rebellion. The deteriorated conditions and lack of authority also mean that the super-ordinates have fewer resources available to be traded off for continued obedience.

Even a government which brings about an improvement in the sense that it reduces its repression of its own citizens may invite rebellion. The loosening of restrictions may facilitate communication among and mobilization of the previously oppressed groups; in this way the emergence of awareness of the many remaining grievances would be facilitated. But the government may also appear weak in allowing these things; it seems an admission of error and thus gives new credence and validity to the arguments of the dissidents. Sometimes concessions may be made as if to forestall violence and thus seem to admit that its utilization would be successful.

The anti-Communist uprisings and rebellions since the death of Stalin and the moderating of totalitarian controls in the Soviet Union and in East Germany, Poland, and Hungary testify to the risks to leaders of totalitarian regimes of a little liberty (Kecskemeti, 1961; Gurr, 1970; pp. 118–19; Crozier, 1960). In many times and places evidence of an "inadequate police and military control apparatus" is followed by periods of hostile outbursts (Smelser, 1963, p. 233).

Even within an authoritarian organization, when superiors appear weak and frightened of coercion from subordinates, the chances that subordinates will attempt to use force increases. Thus dissension among superordinates may appear and actually be an indication of the inability to act cohesively (as well as effectively) in using established ways of handling conflicts. If the subordinates believe that they will not suffer severe negative sanctions, they will be more likely to risk collective protest and coercion outside of established channels. Lammers (1969) in his study of mutinies and strikes, found:

> In several of the mutinies in the sample, ... the mutineers knew that more or less successful promotion of interests' movements had taken place recently on other ships of war. The factors here may not only be doubt that authorities would apply coercive sanctions but also awareness that authorities could neither quickly nor easily crush the uprising by force. This may be the reason why army units are so underrepresented in the sample and why air force units are completely absent. A ship, particularly a ship at sea, is not easily boarded or taken if its crew offers resistance, and the arrival of opposing ships may take days or weeks. In the case of army or air force units, military police or loyal troops can usually be rushed to the spot at short notice (p. 565).

The argument is not that substantive concessions invite violence but that responsiveness to that mode or its threatened use makes that mode more attractive. Of course the same would be true of any other mode.

On the other hand, refusing to make substantive responses to non-coercive or nonviolent modes and trying to insist upon maintaining current power differences can provoke more coercive actions by the subordinates. Thus, prison riots are generally preceded by attempts of prison authorities to tighten security (Ohlin, 1956, pp. 24–25) The way in which a flaccid, permissive reaction by the supposed stronger party or the harsh imposition of severe sanctions by the stronger party each may escalate the use of coercion and violence will be discussed in the next chapter.

The analysis thus far may seem to indicate that the greater the power differences and the greater the certainty that the stronger party will use its coercive force, the less likely is there to be violence. That is not the whole truth. The weaker side may often be intimidated, deterred, and its use of violence suppressed. But that does not mean that the stronger will not be tempted to use its superior force for further aggrandizement. Consequently, coercion and violence may be frequently employed because the weaker does not deter the stronger.

Evidence for this possibility is readily available. When the Negroes in the U.S. were even weaker compared to the whites than is the case today, they were subject to a variety of violent and terroristic acts by the dominant whites. Race riots meant whites rioting and attacking blacks; the police often did little or nothing to suppress the violence (Lee and Humphrey, 1943; Meier and Rudwick, 1969). Group violence against individual blacks occurred as in lynchings and was not subjected to governmental intervention. The very law and its enforcement could be implemented in a repressive manner.

Not only is the stronger party freer to indulge in coercion and violence than the weaker in seeking its aims, but it may formulate goals which result in the exchange of violent acts even if that was unintended. The powerful unit may act more imperiously and impetuously, more boldly and more aggressively; the consequence is violence. The evidence in support of these arguments can be found particularly in studies pertaining to international wars.

One kind of evidence may be seen in the results of a series of "inter-nation simulations" (Raser and Crow, 1968). In "inter-nation simulations" persons assume particular roles in a nation's government, each nation may have two or three roles, and there are several nations in the system. The actions of the persons in the simulation are unstructured but they are given information about the other nations and their own population's response to their decisions in accord with processes which are programmed and carried out on a computer. In this particular study there were two blocs, the leader of each had nuclear weapons. One of these powers, for some of the games in the series, had the capacity to delay its nuclear response. That is, its nuclear weapons system was secure from enemy attack and could survive any attack. According to many students of such matters, such a capacity would obviate preemptive strikes and reduce the chances for a nuclear exchange. In the simulations there was confirmation of some of the reasonings about deterrence. But the capacity to delay response actually increased the chance of war. What was not foreseen was the tendency for the nation with the capacity to delay response to be seen and to act more powerfully; its consequent aggressive posture precipitated nuclear war.

There are a few studies using historical and cross-sectional data which examine the relationship between deterrence or power and the incidence of war. Naroll (1969) studied 20 periods selected from 2,000 years of history in which one state, while in a defensive stance, was militarily stronger than its conspicuous rival. He then compared the same pair of states for periods when the same state was not militarily stronger than its conspicuous rival. Four different ways of assessing military strength were used. He found wars were not "less frequent during the periods when the conspicuous state, while in a defensive stance, enjoyed the specified military advantages than during other periods. . . . If anything, armament tends to make war more likely" (p. 152). In a study of primitive societies, Naroll (1966) also found no support to the deterrence idea; rather, military orientation was positively correlated with war frequency. Weede (1970) studied 59 nations from 1955 to 1960 and found that militarization was correlated with violent foreign conflict. He also found that total national power was somewhat related to violent conflict behavior. But holding *verbal* foreign conflict constant, the powerful states were less likely to engage in violent foreign conflict.

Russett (1963) analyzed 17 instances between 1935 and 1962 in which a potential attacker threatened a smaller country that was, to some degree, under the protection of another state. He found that military superiority by the defender was not a sufficient condition to deter attack. If the protector was highly integrated with the pawn then successful deterance did occur. Such integration presumably increased the probability, in the mind of the potential attacker, that the protector would indeed use force against the other state if it attacked the pawn country.

The analyses of arms races and the way in which one side's military preparations are matched by the other in escalating movement toward war will be examined in the next chapter. It is sufficient here to note that evidence of arms races ending in war is evidence against the idea of deterrence.

The evidence we have reviewed about power differences and the utilization of coercion in the pursuit of goals does not seem consistent. We argued that in many spheres the rising strength of a previously subordinate group would tend to be associated with the use of coercion, but very great differences in power tended to be accompanied by the use of coercion by the stronger party; yet, we then saw that superior power did not generally deter attack—rather preparing for war was associated with waging war. Clearly, power differences per se do not determine the use of coercion; we must consider other factors simultaneously.

One of the crucial additional considerations is the issue at stake. Deterrence is likely to be successful, not only if the threatened force is powerful and certain, but what is being demanded is not too severe a deprivation. For example, during the six-day war of June, 1967, while Israel was engaged in military actions against Egypt, Jordan and Syria, the Premier of Lebanon, Rashid Karami, ordered the army to attack Israel. But the commanding general, Emile Bustani, refused, reportedly saying, "When you wear this uniform you can condemn the army to destruction. But while I wear it, you cannot" (*New York Times*, June 21, 1967). Lebanon did not attack; it was deterred and suffered no losses. Compare this with explaining why Japan was *not* deterred by the military might of the U.S. and launched its attack on Pearl Harbor in 1941. Russett (1967) has concluded that at the time Japan was deeply involved in a war with China; it was faced with a severe shortage of war materials, particularly after the U.S. stopped shipping oil and scrap iron to Japan. The needed resources were available in the British and Dutch Pacific colonies. Believing the U.S. would defend those colonies against attack and convinced that the U.S. would not retract its demands for the Japanese withdrawal from China and Indochina, the Japanese leaders perceived only unsatisfactory alternatives. The status quo was not long endurable; withdrawing from China would be a defeat, attacking the colonies without attacking the U.S. would make it subject to powerful American military intervention, and attacking the U.S. in addition to the colonies was a dangerous escalation, particularly if the U.S. waged a prolonged war. They chose the risky alternative at least partly because the alternatives, given the system within which they were operating, domestic and international, were at least as bad.

The Soviet-American Cold War can also be considered in this context. Did the U.S. deter the Soviet Union from aggression? Or has the Soviet Union deterred the U.S.? Or has each deterred the other? Perhaps the threat of a nuclear holocaust has frozen both sides in terror. The avoidance of full-scale war between the U.S. and the U.S.S.R. may well owe something to this terror. But it also owes something to the limited claims each side made upon the other. Neither side sought to destroy the other side's government. If each side were basically defensive and sought only to consolidate its gains, then deterrence of expansionism could be easily attained (Gamson and Modigliani, 1971).

In general, *the effectiveness of deterrence depends upon the goals sought as well as the differences in power.* The more that the stronger power demands of the weaker, the less deterred is the weaker. An oppressed and exploited group, feeling that there is some increase in its relative power may well risk strong negative sanctions by using coercion to redress long standing grievances.

In addition, other aspects of the relationship between the conflicting parties and the general context of the parties, affect the meaning and significance of the power difference. Thus relative power equality between parties within a larger integrated and highly organized social system tends to produce more equitable procedures for handling conflicts, and mutual tolerance between the parties. Under those conditions noncoercive and nonviolent means are likely to be used. In the international system, with its relative absence of institutionalized conflict regulation, power is less likely to be a safeguard against other's coercion and violence (Singer and Wallace, 1970).

RESPONSIVENESS OF THE ADVERSARY.   In addition to the level of integration and the degree of power differences, conflict parties have particular relations with each other that affect the way each pursues its goal vis a vis the other. The basic matter here is the alternative conflict modes that are available to each party. What is available depends on the other side. If both parties agree about the procedures, conflicting goals may be pursued with little violence or even with little coercion. What is crucial is the extent to which the other side is responsive to the demands made through the channels and in accord with understandings (Smelser, 1963, pp. 236–41).

The content of the understandings and the joint expectations, then, affect which mode each side will attempt to use. For example, American employer hostility to trade unions helps account for the violent and often bloody history of trade union organization in the U.S. (Taft and Ross, 1969). It also helps account for the relatively high proportion of nonorganized workers in the U.S. (Bok and Dunlop, 1970, p. 50). Compared to other industrial and democratic societies, collective bargaining is less well established in the U.S. American union members are more likely to be involved in strikes and for longer periods than in other pluralistic industrial societies (Ross and Irwin, 1951). Another indication of the importance of institutionalization of the relationship is the finding that over the decades, the average length of strikes has been reduced.

There are, finally, idiosyncratic qualities to the relationship between two parties which affect the choice of mode. How each party defines the other affects the way each responds to the other and limits the ways each can pursue its goals. For example, Nazi ideology held that the Slavs were inferior to the Germans. Even when anti-Soviet Russians wished to aid the German invaders in World War II, they received little encouragement from the Nazis (Fischer, 1952). The Nazis were hardly in a position to persuade Russians of the desirability of the ends they sought. Their extraordinary violence against the Russian people was a basis for Russian support of the Soviet government.

The Environment. In addition to the issue, the nature of the units in the conflict, and the character of the relationship between the conflicting parties, the context in which the units exist affects the way in which the parties pursue their aims. Any two parties in a social conflict are within a larger social system. That system includes other groups, encompassing understandings and patterns of interaction, and alternative means by which parties can pursue their objectives.

OTHER PARTIES.   The conflict units do not stand alone. There are possible allies, expanded constituencies and more encompassing organizations and groups. In the preceding chapter we discussed how the very aims of a conflict group are shaped in part by third parties as well as adversaries and internal factors. Similarly, the choice of the way to pursue conflicting goals is affected by third parties.

First, let us consider how the pursuit of a conflict group's goals is affected by third parties when they are possible allies of the conflict groups. Each conflict group tends to shape its pursuit of goals in persuasive as well as coercive terms because there is an audience and potential allies. For example, in the civil rights movement of the 1950s and early 1960s nonviolent direct action and large demonstrations appeared to be appropriate means because carrying them out was educational and persuasive to large sections of the population and to governmental leaders who on the whole were not hostile to the demands for equality and integration in the South. Police attempts at repression in Birmingham and elsewhere vividly revealed the prevailing oppression. This brought support for the Negroes' demands and aided in the passage of civil rights legislation by the U.S. Congress. The effects of demonstrations upon others throughout the nation was not forgotten in planning, conducting, and interpreting nonviolent direct action (King, 1963).

We should also seek to explain why the segregationists of the South did not choose means of pursuit which would not bring allies to the blacks. As Kenneth Clark observed,

> ... it would probably be all too easy to abort and to make impotent the whole King-SCLC approach, if white society could control the flagrant idiocy of some of its own leaders, suppress the more vulgar, atavistic tyrants like Sheriff Jim Clark, and create instead a quiet, if not genteel, intransigence.... When

> love meets either indifference or passive refusal to change, it
> does not seem to have the power to mobilize the reactions of
> potential allies (1966, pp. 256–57).

Indeed, in cities where such quiet intransigence was followed, the program was less successful. It may be that Sheriff Jim Clark of Selma and Commissioner of Public Safety Eugene "Bull" Conner of Birmingham were particularly and personally prone to use extreme violence against demonstrators. But the explanation must go deeper: they were public officials and part of another conflict group. Perhaps these groups did not understand the role and likely response of third parties in their own city, state, and nation. They were also committed, in part by past success, to the use of intimidation; it was consistent with their view of blacks. And fundamentally, the issue was not negotiable for them. They understood that what the blacks were ultimately asking for meant the ending of a kind of tyranny; that could not be compromised. Violent coercion was an appropriate means for the maintenance of their position.

Third parties affect the choice of means to pursue conflicting ends in another, quite different, way. The modes used by one comparable party can serve as a model to others; there can be what is almost a fashion in the techniques used to advance a party's cause. Demonstrations, strikes, riots, even revolutions seem to spread as if by contagion. For example, Skolnick (1969) writes:

> Despite the differences among student movements in developed
> and underdeveloped countries, however, it is clear that a
> process of mutual influence is at work among them. For ex-
> ample, the white student movement in America received in-
> spiration in its early stages from dramatic student uprisings
> in Japan, Turkey, and South Korea. More recently, American
> activists have been influenced by street tactics learned from
> Japanese students and by ideological expressions emanating
> from France and West Germany. The French students were
> certainly inspired by the West Germans, and the Italians by
> the French (p. 86).

The Kerner Commission also argued that geographic contagion was observable in the riots of 1967, particularly for the disorders centering around Newark and Detroit (National Advisory Commission on Civil Disorders, 1968, p. 114).

Groups also follow historical precedents. The experience and techniques women used in the Abolitionist movement were applied in the beginning of the women's movement (Flexner, 1959, p. 41). The techniques of the woman's suffrage movement provided examples to Gandhi and were taken back from there by the civil rights movement in the U.S. (Millett, 1970, p. 82).

Because like-appearing events appear closely related in time and space does not in itself demonstrate a causal connection. Demonstrations, revolutions, riots, or other ways of pursuing conflicting goals may be employed in one place for the same reasons they were employed elsewhere; that is, there is convergence of means. This point is made by Knowles (1954, p. 223) in regard to trade union strikes. The theoretical and empirical links from one place to another must be demonstrated to argue that groups follow models of other's conduct in pursuit of their goals. There are several ways in which the use of a particular technique in a conflict relationship can induce imitation or adaptation of the technique by others. Its success will tend to make it attractive; if a group sees that others have attained at least something of what they wanted it is likely to use the same tactic. Even the demonstration that people could have dared to try a certain act, like a revolution, makes it conceivable as an alternative to other groups. Sometimes, the tactic appears to be a social invention, a way to do something that had not been utilized before and which seems appropriate to others; for example, sit-ins.

SOCIAL PATTERNS AND UNDERSTANDINGS. The general system of which the adversaries are parts also affects the selection of conflict modes. Included here are the general understandings shared by all or many units in the social system about what means are appropriate for what purposes by which kinds of actors. Also included here are the social structural patterns which characterize the system and how collective decisions are reached by its members. Illustrative evidence about how these aspects of the social system affect the way groups pursue their goals will be briefly reviewed.

The opponents as well as the other units, may share cultural traditions or general understandings; for example, about the propriety of using violence of different kinds and the justifications for it (Smelser, 1963, pp. 79–130). Governments at the national level are generally considered, by other governments, to have the prerogative of using force. This means that war is generally considered a legitimate means of pursuing foreign policy. Even within the territory under a government's jurisdiction, its use of violence to put down rebellion is not a matter which other governments feel they have an obligation to limit. On the whole, nonintervention in the internal affairs of other states is the principle which governments assert. Intervention, then, is based more upon expedient calculations of which side is likely to win and which side's victory is desired than upon the enforcement of shared norms. Nevertheless, intervention in internal wars is more common than not (Kende, 1971, Table 7).

The course of action pursued by a conflict group depends on the range of alternatives available for the issue at stake. Those alternatives depend on the whole set of interrelated structures within the social system. For example, consider the variety of settings within which trade union–management relations may operate. The trade unions may be more or less closely tied to political parties, in a two-party, multi-party, or one-party political system. There may be one or more trade unions representing workers within an enterprise. Management may be more or less closely tied to political parties and more or less autonomous of government. The ways in which workers seek redress of their grievances depends on the way such variable conditions are combined. Efforts at reform or restructuring of labor-management relations could be channeled through political action and legislation, through lobbying within governmental agencies, or by strike action.

Similarly, the ways in which universities are related to other institutions in a society affect, for example, the means which students use to pursue their goals (Weinberg and Walker, 1969). Societies differ in the extent to which the government controls university finances and structure and societies vary in the extent to which political parties sponsor student groups and recruit students into political careers. In the United States, government control is relatively weak and there is relatively little political party recruitment through university groups. Consequently there is local political activity, as in student governments. But, relatively isolated from the main political system in the society, students may resort to non-institutionalized channels when they do become involved in society-wide issues. Where there is strong government control and low political recruitment, for example, as in France, powerful unions of students are more likely.

One of the fundamental aspects of the social patterns which affect the mode used in conflicts is the degree to which the system as a whole has crosscutting ties, a sense of common identity, and institutionalized means of collective decision making. We have discussed, for example, crosscutting ties previously, but from the perspective of a conflict unit or from the perspective of the relations between units in conflict. Now we are considering the import of crosscutting ties at the social system level as a factor affecting the mode of pursuing conflicting goals.

Conflict parties also share adherence in larger entities and such adherence might be expected to shape the means of struggle. This can occur through many processes. If the shared membership is with a legitimate and strong superordinate, the conflict modes are likely to be regulated and institutionalized. The parties to a conflict will tend to follow the procedures for conflict resolution. This may include legal and political procedures in which persuasive means would be important; persuasion would be directed at the superiors in terms of the values and standards they maintain. Within stable societies or organizations, these procedures may operate so readily that little coercion and no violence occurs. Such highly institutionalized means of conflict might not even be regarded as conflict behavior by the partisans and are not of central importance here. If one of the conflict parties claims to be the superordinate and all encompassing entity and this is not recognized by the other party, the institutionalized and regulated means of conflict resolution will be followed under duress or the conflict will be pursued outside the established procedures. This kind of issue arises, for example, when management claims to speak for the whole enterprise and the workers believe they have interests which are in opposition to the management.

Shared membership also is a forum in which integrative transactions can transpire. Participating in common enterprises may be the basis for common interests and the development of shared understandings, perspectives, and values (Alger, 1963). Shared memberships may also provide the basis for crosscutting bonds. All this should make persuasion and bargaining more possible, more likely to be successful, and therefore more likely to be utilized. Coercion will be mitigated.

Even aside from shared memberships, the general level of integration in the social system in which the conflict parties are contending may constrain the conflict parties. The more integrated the entire social system is, the more implicated are third parties in the conflict between any two; and yet not being as involved in the issue in contention, the third parties would tend to limit the disruptiveness and coercion of the means used by the parties in conflict.

There is little systematic evidence testing these ideas. Plausible as they may seem, the evidence is not unequivocal. We will consider evidence from the study of international relations. Smoker (1967) studied the relationship between arms races and international integration. International integration was measured by the growth in the number of international nongovernmental organizations (INGO's). Three arms races were studied: the one preceding and terminating in World War I, the one preceding and terminating in World War II, and the one between the U.S. and the U.S.S.R. after World War II. Smoker argues that the level of integration before the two world wars was not sufficient to prevent the arms race from escalating to the point at which war broke out: the growth of INGO's stopped and fell back as the arms race grew in intensity. The same pattern existed before World War II. But after World War II, there was a very large increase in the rate of establishment of INGO's and the level of integration apparently was sufficiently high to absorb and halt the arms race which did fall off after 1951–1952.

Singer and Wallace (1970) used a different approach to the same issue and reached different conclusions. They related international governmental organizations (IGO's) with wars between 1816 and 1964. They correlated the number and the growth of IGO's in each five-year period during those years with the onset of war, number of battle dead, and number of months of war in the next five-year period. They found no relationship between the two and conclude that "war is basically inherent in the continued coexistence of the nation-state and the international system as we know it" (p. 545). In other words, the level of integration and the strengths of international organizations cannot overcome the forces which bring nation states into conflicts which are pursued by means of organized violence.

The findings of Smoker and of Singer and Wallace might not be inconsistent. The measures of each study are necessarily gross; more importantly they cover different periods. Smoker is arguing that the post World War II increase in NGO's indicates a significantly greater level of integration than the past which constrains current war-making. But that should hold for conflicts among all countries and not just between the U.S. and U.S.S.R. Yet, the number of wars has been large and, if anything, increasing since 1945 (Kende, 1971). Furthermore, Holsti (1966) examined the ways in which major conflicts were handled in two time periods: 1919–1939 and 1945–1965. He found that in 31 percent of the 38 conflicts during the earlier period, settlements by international organizations were attempted, compared to 41 percent of the 39 conflicts in the later period. But they were no more likely to be successful in the second period than the first. Furthermore, military force was employed in 71 percent of the conflicts during the first period and was hardly less frequent in the second period when 64 percent involved the employment of military force.

On the whole, then, it appears that it is not a change in the international system which accounts for any halt or slowing down of the arms race between the U.S. and the U.S.S.R. It may have contributed some, however, to the other factors, for example, the mutual fear engendered by the weapons and the arms race (Smoker, 1966). Other factors may include the technological developments in weapons systems and economies in cost of weapons production. More importantly, there may be increasing routinization of crises (Galtung, 1966a), lessening cohesion of their respective alliances, and the growth of third forces. Fundamentally, there may be increasing belief in the essentially limited and defensive nature of each other's aims.

The international system, made up of nation-states with claims of sovereignty and with control over the means of mass destruction has such low levels of overall integration that the variations in system integration have only a small effect upon the overall probability of armed conflict. The integration between *pairs* of adversary nations has more pertinence for the modes of settling conflicts between them. There is some evidence, however, that system characteristics in terms of the entire set of power relations, alliances, and resulting crosscutting ties and cross-pressures has some effect upon the incidence and severity of war. Thus, when countries are generally not committed to alliances, all countries are subject to pressure from more countries and war was not found to be as likely as when countries were tied into nonoverlapping alliances (Zinnes, 1967). Haas (1968) focusing on patterns of relative power, studied 21 international subsystems and compared unipolar, bipolar, and multipolar systems. He found that systems with one dominant power were most pacific. International systems with several major powers have shorter wars, but more of them, than do systems with only two major powers.

Evidence from community studies are also pertinent to the issues raised here. There is some evidence that in cities with more direct representation of the citizens in the government, where presumably there are more channels for expressing grievances, riots by blacks and by whites are somewhat less likely (Lieberson and Silverman, 1965). At the societal level there is also evidence that the general level of civil strife is related to the nature of the overall political structure, although we should keep in mind that nearly all such strife has a political purpose and hence is directed at the government (Gurr, 1969). Four major types of political systems are distinguished: *polyarchic*—nations with Western democratic political structures; *centrist*—authoritarian regimes (includes communist); *elitist*—small, modernizing elites, predominantly African; and *personalist* —characterized by unstable personal leadership, predominantly Latin American. The total magnitude of strife is lowest in the polyarchic system, particularly strife in the form of conspiracies and internal wars; centrist systems also tend to have low magnitudes of strife, partly because of higher coercion. Elitist systems have high magnitudes of strife, particularly in the form of internal wars; and personalist systems have particularly high levels of strife in the form of turmoil (strikes, demonstrations, and riots). The strength of institutions is also negatively related to civil strife. The strength of institutions was measured by "the proportion of gross national product utilized by the central government; the number and stability of political parties; and the relative size of trade unions" (p. 614). So measured, the strength of institutions is positively related to civil strife in personalist systems, apparently in such systems trade union activity and some political parties are strongly opposed to the government and its policies; in the other systems strength of institutions is inversely related to civil strife.

We must conclude that the level of integration of the system, its degree of shared understandings, and the extent to which there are strong encompassing organizations do not have simple, direct, and unilinear effects upon the conflict modes used. Even if we consider only the variations in the use of violence, the absolute level and nature of the integration, the content of the understandings, and the character of the encompassing organizations have their own significance.

TECHNOLOGY AND ECOLOGY. We have been discussing the essentially social aspects of the system within which conflicting parties contend. There are also nonsocial aspects of the environment. Actually, the distinction is a matter of degree. Thus, physical distances between units have significance only as they are mediated through the technology of the time. Who is next to whom, depends partly on the means of communication available to the people involved.

In any case, what one party can do to another, by way of persuasion, coercion, or reward, depends partly on the technology available. In general, countries have fought wars by marching armies against each other. In historical perspective, then, we would expect that countries would tend to fight with their neighbors. The more neighbors to fight with, the more frequent the wars. This is indeed what Richardson (1960, p. 176) found in his study of wars between 1820 and 1945. The number of borders was one of the few characteristics he found to be correlated with the incidence of war. Using the same data, Wesley (1962) calculated the geographical opportunity for warfare by combining the length of the frontier and the number of people along the frontier and found that that matched the number of battle deaths. Weede (1970) studied international conflicts from 1955 to 1960 and found that contiguity was moderately correlated with foreign conflict.

Queen Victoria provides a different kind of evidence. Offended at the behavior of the Bolivian government, she ordered a naval blockade of the country. She was told that the country was landlocked and therefore could not be blockaded. (Instead she resorted to having the offending country taken off English maps.)

We should keep in mind, however, that countries which are close together probably also have more objective and manifest conflicts simply because they have more to do with each other. We should really examine the proportion of social conflicts which result in war and the proportion which are handled in other ways. It may be that the *proportion* does not vary with propinquity. It is also possible, particularly in the past, that wars could be waged against nonneighbors only with great difficulty, but other conflict means are not so geographically constrained.

The geographic distribution and concentration of people of different social categories within a nation or a city also affects how its members can pursue their goals at a given technological level. This is pertinent for the organization and tactics of industrial workers and of managers, of blacks and whites, of students, faculty and administrators, and of women and of men.

One final aspect of the system within which the contending parties exist must be considered. The entire system may be changing in a way which channels the modes of struggling between conflicting groups. For example, if a group of nations, like those of Europe, can expand overseas by building empires, they might not find war among themselves to be as useful a way of pursuing their aims against each other. Each would seek to advance its interests vis a vis the other by actions directed at third parties outside the system. Indeed, during this period of expanding empires, wars were less frequent in Europe (Rosecrance, 1963).

The possibility of an expanding pie so that each group could have more and more is an alluring prospect for finding noncoercive modes of conflict or for using regulated or nonviolent coercion. This might be a factor in labor-management relations in an expanding economy or an imperialist one, or in an expanding industry or company. At the same time such expansion raises expectations and often increases the power of the relatively weaker party. Consequently there may be more demands being made and therefore more conflict behavior, some of which will be coercive. Thus, there may be an absolute increase in the number of cases in which intense coercion is used, but it may still be a smaller proportion of the cases of manifest conflicts.

We should not be mechanical in interpreting data about the incidence of any particular mode of conflict handling. Increases in the incidence of nonlegitimate coercion or of violence can indicate that more is being demanded than heretofore. It may be the dominants as well as the subdominants who are making these new demands. In any case, a higher incidence of violence need not mean that a larger proportion of conflicts are being pursued in more extreme fashion. More issues or more profound ones may be being raised, that's all.

SUMMARY AND CONCLUSION

Four sets of factors affect the mode chosen in pursuit of a goal: the issue, the characteristics of the conflict party, the relationship between the contending parties, and the environment of the parties in contention. It is important to keep in mind that these factors are interrelated, in the sense that they affect each other. Moreover, they all jointly affect the mode. Certain modes are especially attractive to particular kinds of people; some, all would agree, are especially appropriate to a particular end and with a given adversary.

Sometimes one or another factor is predominantly determining of the mode. For example, the relationship between opponents may be such, in terms of integration, power, and responsiveness, that certain modes are precluded and only a few options are really viable. Or, the characteristics of a unit are so overwhelming that certain modes are adhered to regardless of other considerations. If this were completely the case, we would consider the mode chosen as expressive rather than instrumental.

Not only are these different factors interrelated and jointly determining of the mode; the mode itself affects the unit, the relations between the adversaries, and the goal itself. This is part of the subject of chapter 7, on the consequences of social conflicts. What is of singular importance at this point is that means and ends affect each other. If people choose a way of pursuing their goal because it seems appropriate for what they are trying to get, then, if they are using a particular mode, it must signify that there is an end which justifies the means.

There is a very important implication of these arguments. If one kind of factor affects the selection of a mode and the mode affects the other factors, every conflict unit can affect what its adversary seeks and how the adversary goes about getting it.

Gregg, (1966, pp. 30–35) describes the success of the Norwegian sports strike against the Nazis during the German occupation of Norway. The ability of a people to wage a nonviolent resistance effort even against the Nazis is clearly an impressive achievement. But note how the many factors we have considered in this chapter intertwine to explain the phenomena. The Nazi occupation did not offer many alternative modes of expressing grievances about the Nazi occupation. The power difference, measured in military strength, was very great. Open warfare against the Nazis had been defeated. By not participating in Nazi organized sports events, masses of people could indicate their refusal to cooperate with the Nazi occupation. This kind of noncooperation is a relatively weak means, but it was one of the few available, given the adversary. The issue was also one which could take on high significance to those conducting it and not become so significant to the opponents. For the Norwegians this expressed their opposition to the Nazis. The aim was to demonstrate defiance to the Nazis and support to the other forms of resistance. It was a difficult tactic for the Nazis to overcome and as they tried and failed, the significance of the defiance, even in this area, took on greater importance to the Norwegians. Undoubtedly massive sabotage of more directly relevant military efforts would have been responded to differently by the Nazis and would have recruited a more select group of Norwegians.

In ths chapter we have generally considered a means of pursuing a conflicting goal as a single choice. Actually, of course, it is constantly being made. As the means change in sequence we think of the social conflict as escalating or de-escalating. That is the subject of the next chapter.

BIBLIOGRAPHY

ALGER, CHADWICK F., "United Nations Participation as a Learning Experience," *Public Opinion Quarterly*, 27 (Fall 1963), 411–26.

ARENDT, HANNAH, *The Origins of Totalitarianism* (New York: Harcourt, Brace & Company, 1951).

BECKER, W. C., "Consequences of Different Kinds of Parental Discipline," pp. 169–208 in M. L. Hoffman and L. W. Hoffman (eds.), *Review of Child Development Research*, vol. 1 (New York: Russell Sage Foundation, 1964).

BELL, INGE POWELL, *CORE and the Strategy of Non-Violence* (New York: Random House, Inc., 1968).

BERELSON, BERNARD R., PAUL F. LAZARSFELD, AND WILLIAM N. McPHEE, *Voting* (Chicago: University of Chicago Press, 1954).

BLAU, PETER M., *Exchange and Power in Social Life* (New York: John Wiley & Sons, Inc., 1964).

BLECHMAN, BARRY M., "The Quantitative Evaluation of Foreign Policy Alternatives: Sinai, 1956," *Journal of Conflict Resolution*, 10 (March 1966), 408–26.

BLUMENTHAL, MONICA D., ROBERT L. KAHN, FRANK M. ANDREWS, AND KENDRA B. HEAD, *Justifying Violence* (Ann Arbor: University of Michigan Press, 1972).

BOK, DEREK C. AND JOHN T. DUNLOP, *Labor and the American Community* (New York: Simon and Schuster, Inc., 1970).

BONDURANT, JOAN V., *Conquest of Violence: The Gandhian Philosophy of Conflict*, rev. ed. (Berkeley and Los Angeles: University of California Press, 1965).

BRINK, WILLIAM AND LOUIS HARRIS, *Black and White* (New York: Simon and Schuster, Inc., 1969).

BWY, DOUGLAS P., "Political Instability in Latin America: The Cross-Cultural Test of a Causal Model," *Latin American Research Review*, 3 (Spring 1968), 17–66.

CANTRIL, HADLEY, *The Pattern of Human Concerns*, (New Brunswick, N.J.: Rutgers University Press, 1965).

————, AND MILDRED STRUNK, *Public Opinion: 1935–1946* (Princeton, N.J.: Princeton University Press, 1951).

CAPLAN, NATHAN S. AND JEFFERY M. PAIGE, "A Study of Ghetto Rioters," *Scientific American*, 219 (August 1968), 15–21.

CLARK, KENNETH B., "The Civil Rights Movement: Momentum and Organization," *Daedalus*, 95 (Winter 1966), 239–67.

COSER, LEWIS A., *The Functions of Social Conflict* (New York: The Free Press, 1956).

————, *Continuities in the Study of Social Conflict* (New York: The Free Press, 1967).

CROZIER, BRIAN, *The Rebels: A Study of Post-War Insurrections* (London: Chatto & Windus Ltd., 1960).

DAHRENDORF, RALF, *Class and Class Conflict in Industrial Society* (Stanford, Calif.: Stanford University Press, 1959).

DAVIES, JAMES C., "Toward a Theory of Revolution," *American Sociological Review*, 27 (February 1962), 5–19.

DEUTSCH, KARL W. et al., *Political Community and the North Atlantic Area* (Princeton, N.J.: Princeton University Press, 1957).

ERSKINE, HAZEL, "The Polls: Speed of Racial Integration," *Public Opinion Quarterly*, 32 (Fall 1968), 513–24.

FANON, FRANTZ, *The Wretched of the Earth* (New York: Grove Press, Inc., 1966).

FEAGIN, JOE R. AND PAUL B. SHEATSLEY, "Ghetto Resident Appraisals of a Riot," *The Public Opinion Quarterly*, 32 (Fall 1968), 352–62.

FEIERABEND, IVO K. AND ROSALIND L. FEIERABEND AND BETTY A. NESVOLD, "Social Change and Political Violence: Cross-National Patterns," pp. 632–87 in Hugh Davis Graham and Ted Robert Gurr (eds.), *Violence in America* (New York: Bantam Books, 1969).

FISCHER, GEORGE, *Soviet Opposition to Stalin: A Case Study in World War II* (Cambridge, Mass.: Harvard University Press, 1952).

FLAMING, KARL H., *The 1967 Milwaukee Riot: An Historical and Comparative Analysis*, unpublished Ph.D. dissertation, Department of Sociology, Syracuse University, 1971.

FLEXNER, ELEANOR, *Century of Struggle* (Cambridge, Mass.: Harvard University Press, 1959).

GALTUNG, JOHAN, "East-West Interaction Patterns," *Journal of Peace Research*, no. 2 (1966), pp. 146–76.

———, "International Relations and International Conflicts: A Sociological Approach," pp. 121–61 in *International Sociological Association. Transactions of the Sixth World Congress of Sociology* (1966b).

———, "Violence, Peace, and Peace Research," *Journal of Peace Research*, no. 3 (1969), pp. 167–91.

GAMSON, WILLIAM A., "Rancorous Conflict in Community Politics," *The American Sociological Review*, 31 (February 1966), 71–81.

——— AND ANDRE MODIGLIANI, "Knowledge and Foreign Policy Opinions: Some Models for Consideration," *Public Opinion Quarterly*, 30 (Summer 1966), 187–99.

———, *Untangling the Cold War* (Boston: Little, Brown and Company, 1971).

GANDHI, MOHANDAS KARAMCHAND, *An Autobiography or The Story of My Experiments with Truth*, translated by Mahadev Desai, 2nd ed. (Ahmedabad: Nevajivan, 1940).

GESCHWENDER, JAMES A. AND BENJAMIN D. SINGER, "Deprivation and the Detroit Riot," *Social Problems*, 17 (Spring 1970), 457–63.

GREGG, RICHARD B., *The Power of Nonviolence* (New York: Schocken Books, 1966).

GURR, TED ROBERT, "A Comparative Study of Civil Strife," in Hugh Davis Graham and Ted Robert Gurr (eds.), *Violence in America: Historical and Comparative Perspectives* (New York: Bantam Books, 1969), pp. 572–632.

————, *Why Men Rebel* (Princeton, New Jersey: Princeton University Press, 1970).

HAAS, MICHAEL, "International Subsystems: Stability and Polarity," paper presented at the American Political Science Association Meeting, September 1968.

HAMILTON, RICHARD F., "A Research Note on the Mass Support for 'Tough' Military Initiatives," *American Sociological Review*, 33 (June 1968), 439–45.

HILGARD, E. R. AND G. H. BOWER, *Theories of Learning*, 3rd ed. (New York: Appleton-Century-Crofts, 1966).

HITLER, ADOLF, *Mein Kampf* (New York: Reynal and Hitchcock, 1941). Originally published in 1925.

HOLSTI, K. J., "Resolving International Conflicts: A Taxonomy of Behavior and Some Figures," *Journal of Conflict Resolution*, 10 (September 1966), 272–96.

KECSKEMETI, PAUL, *The Unexpected Revolution: Social Forces in the Hungarian Uprising* (Stanford, Calif.: Stanford University Press, 1961).

KENDE, ISTVAN, "Twenty-Five Years of Local Wars," *Journal of Peace Research,* 1 (1971), 5–22.

KENNAN, GEORGE F., *Russia and the West Under Lenin and Stalin* (Boston: Little, Brown and Company, 1961).

KERR, CLARK AND ABRAHAM SIEGEL, "The Interindustry Propensity to Strike— An International Comparison," in A. Kornhauser, R. Dubin, and A. M. Ross (eds.), *Industrial Conflict* (New York: McGraw-Hill Book Company, 1954), pp. 189–212.

KING, MARTIN LUTHER JR., *Why We Can't Wait* (New York: Harper & Row, Publishers, Inc., 1963).

KNOWLES, K. G. J. C., " 'Strike-Proneness' and Its Determinants," *The American Journal of Sociology*, 60 (November 1954), 213–29.

KRIESBERG, LOUIS, *Mothers in Poverty* (Chicago: Aldine Publishing Company, 1970).

LAMMERS, CORNELIS J., "Strikes and Mutinies: A Comparative Study of Organizational Conflicts Between Rulers and Ruled," *Administrative Science Quarterly*, 14 (December 1969), 558–72.

LEE, ALFRED MCCLUNG AND NORMAN D. HUMPHREY, *Race Riot: Detroit, 1943* (New York: Dryden Press, 1943).

LEEK, JOHN H., *Government and Labor in the United States* (New York: Rinehart & Company, 1952).

LEVINE, ROBERT A., "Socialization, Social Structure, and Intersocietal Images," in Herbert C. Kelman (ed.), *International Behavior* (New York: Holt, Rinehart & Winston, Inc., 1965), pp. 45–69.

LIEBERSON, STANLEY AND ARNOLD R. SILVERMAN, "The Precipitants and Underlying Conditions of Race Riots," *American Sociological Review*, 30 (December 1965), 887–89.

MARX, GARY T., *Protest and Prejudice* (New York: Harper & Row, Publishers, Inc., 1969).

MCCORD, W., J. HOWARD, B. FRIEDBERG, AND E. HARWOOD, *Life Styles in the Black Ghetto* (New York: W. W. Norton & Company, Inc., 1969).

McKINLEY, DONALD GILBERT, *Social Class and Family Life* (New York: The Free Press, 1964).

MEIER, AUGUST AND ELLIOTT RUDWICK, "Black Violence in the 20th Century: A Study in Rhetoric and Retaliation," in H. D. Graham and T. R. Gurr (eds.), *Violence in America* (New York: Bantam Books, 1969), pp. 399–412.

MILLETT, KATE, *Sexual Politics* (Garden City, N.Y.: Doubleday & Company, Inc., 1970).

MILLS, C. WRIGHT, *The New Men of Power* (New York: Harcourt, Brace & Company, 1948).

MORRIS, CHANDLER (ed.), *Modernization by Design* (Ithaca, N.Y.: Cornell University Press, 1969).

MURDOCK, GEORGE PETER, *Social Structure* (New York: The Macmillan Company, 1949).

NAROLL, RAOUL, "Does Military Deterrence Deter?" *Transaction*, 3 (January/February 1966), 14–20.

———, "Deterrence in History," in Dean G. Pruitt and Richard C. Snyder (eds.), *Theory and Research on the Causes of War* (Englewood Cliffs, N.J.: Prentice-Hall, Inc., 1969), pp. 150–64.

National Advisory Commission on Civil Disorders (Kerner Commission), *Report of the National Commission on Civil Disorders* (New York: Bantam Books, 1968).

NEF, JOHN V., *War and Human Progress* (Cambridge, Mass.: Harvard University Press, 1950).

OHLIN, LLOYD E., *Sociology and the Field of Corrections* (New York: Russell Sage Foundation, 1956).

RASER, JOHN R. AND WAYMAN J. CROW, "A Simulation Study of Deterrence Theories," in L. Kriesberg (ed.), *Social Processes in International Relations* (New York: John Wiley & Sons, Inc., 1968), pp. 372–89.

REES, ALBERT, "Industrial Conflict and Business Fluctuations," in A. Kornhauser, R. Dubin, and A. M. Ross (eds.), *Industrial Conflict* (New York: McGraw-Hill Book Company, 1954), pp. 213–20.

RICHARDSON, LEWIS F., *Statistics of Deadly Quarrels* (Pittsburgh: The Boxwood Press, 1960).

RINGER, BENJAMIN B. AND DAVID L. SILLS, "Political Extremists in Iran," *Public Opinion Quarterly*, 16 (Winter 1952–1953), 689–701.

ROSECRANCE, RICHARD N., *Action and Reaction in World Politics* (Boston: Little, Brown and Company, 1963)

ROSI, EUGENE J., "Mass and Attentive Opinion on Nuclear Weapons Tests and Fallout, 1954–1963," *Public Opinion Quarterly*, 29 (Summer 1965), 280–97.

ROSS, ARTHUR M. AND DONALD IRWIN, "Strike Experience in Five Countries, 1927–1947: An Interpretation," *Industrial and Labor Relations Review*, 4 (April 1951), 323–42.

ROSS, EDWARD A., *The Principles of Sociology* (New York: The Century Company, 1920).

ROTHAUS, PAUL AND PHILIP WORCHEL, "The Inhibition of Aggression under Non-Arbitrary Frustration," *Journal of Personality*, 28 (March 1960) 108–17.

Russett, Bruce M., "The Calculus of Deterrence," *Journal of Conflict Resolution*, 7 (June 1963) 97–109.

Sayles, Leonard R. and George Strauss, *The Local Union: Its Place in the Industrial Plant* (New York: Harper & Brothers, 1953).

Sears, David O. and T. M. Tomlinson, "Riot Ideology in Los Angeles: A Study in Negro Attitudes," *Social Science Quarterly*, 49 (December 1968), 485–503.

Sears, David O. and John B. McConahay, "Participation in the Los Angeles Riot," *Social Problems*, 17 (Summer 1969), 2–20.

Sharp, Gene "The Meanings of Non-Violence: A Typology," *The Journal of Conflict Resolution*, 3 (March 1959), 41–66.

Singer, J. David and Michael Wallace, "Intergovernmental Organization and the Preservation of Peace, 1816–1964: Some Bivariate Relationships," *International Organization*, 24 (Summer 1970), 520–47.

Skolnick, Jerome H., *The Politics of Protest* (New York: Simon and Schuster, Inc., 1969).

Smelser, Neil J., *Theory of Collective Behavior* (New York: The Free Press, 1963).

Smoker, Paul, "Fear in the Arms Race: A Mathematical Study," *Journal of Peace Research*, 1 (1966), 55–64.

———, "Nation State Escalation and International Integration," *Journal of Peace Research*, 1 (1967), 60–74.

Sorel, Georges, *Reflections on Violence*, translated by T. E. Hulme and J. Roth (New York: The Free Press, 1950). Originally published 1906–1919.

Spilerman, Seymour, "The Causes of Racial Disturbances: A Comparison of Alternative Explanations," *American Sociological Review*, 35 (August 1970), 627–49.

Sumner, William Graham, *Folkways* (Boston: Ginn and Company, 1906).

Taft, Philip, *Organized Labor in American History* (New York: Harper & Row, Publishers, Inc., 1964).

——— and Philip Ross, "American Labor Violence: Its Causes, Character, and Outcome," in Hugh Davis Graham and Ted Robert Gurr (eds.), *Violence in America* (New York: Bantam Books, 1969), pp. 281–395.

Tanter, Raymond and Manus Midlarsky, "A Theory of Revolution," *The Journal of Conflict Resolution*, 11 (September 1967), 264–80.

Wanderer, Jules J., "An Index of Riot Severity and Some Correlates," *American Journal of Sociology*, 74 (March 1969), 500–505.

Weede, Erich, "Conflict Behavior of Nation-States," *Journal of Peace Research*, 3 (1970), 229–35.

Weinberg, Ian and Kenneth N. Walker, "Student Politics and Political Systems: Toward a Typology," *American Journal of Sociology*, 75 (July 1969), 77–96.

Wesley, James Paul, "Frequency of Wars and Geographical Opportunity," *Journal of Conflict Resolution*, 6 (December 1962), 387–89.

Williams, Walter, "Cleveland's Crisis Ghetto," in Peter H. Rossi (ed.), *Ghetto Revolts* (Chicago: Aldine Publishing Company, 1970), pp. 13–29. Originally published in 1967.

WRIGHT, CHRISTOPHER, "The Self-Government of Commercial Communities," A Report for the Arbitration Project, University of Chicago Law School, 1957.

ZINNES, DINA A., "An Analytical Study of the Balance of Power Theories," *Journal of Peace Research*, 3 (1967), 270–88.

chapter five

Escalation
and De-Escalation

Any high level of conflict behavior will have been preceded by conflict behavior of a lesser magnitude. Not that all conflict behavior inevitably escalates. Struggles terminate and ways of conducting them may de-escalate or remain frozen. But a good predictor of high levels of coercion and violence is conflict behavior of a lesser magnitude earlier. Thus, Tanter (1966) studied various kinds of conflict in 1955–1957 and related them to other conflicts in 1958–1960 in 83 countries. He found that anti-government demonstrations, guerrilla warfare, and revolutions in 1955–1957 had a multiple correlation of .60 with revolutions in 1958–1960. Similarly, expulsion of foreign diplomats, severance of diplomatic relations, and the number killed in foreign conflicts in 1955–1957 had a multiple correlation of .66 with war in 1958–1960.

In this chapter we seek to understand how conflict behavior waxes and wanes. We will examine the several processes which make for conflict escalation and those which make for de-escalation. Then we will examine the conditions that determine which processes are operative and to what extent. What we have discussed in the previous chapter regarding the selection of conflict modes should be helpful in our present quest. We can now examine the conditions and processes during a struggle which alter the issue, the conflict parties, the relationship between them, and their social environment in ways which lead to the selection of modes that constitute escalation or de-escalation.

First, we must be more precise about the meaning of escalation and de-escalation. Escalation means movement toward greater magnitudes of conflict behavior; de-escalation means movement toward lesser magnitudes. Several dimensions of magnitudes must be distinguished. The conflicting parties' feelings toward each other is one dimension. We might consider that conflict behavior is of a higher magnitude if it is accompanied by greater feelings of animosity, hostility, or hatred toward an adversary. But feelings do not always match behavior. It will be best to restrict the magnitudes of conflict behavior to overt conduct; feelings may be helpful in explaining changes in conduct.

Two dimensions of conflict behavior can be usefully distinguished—how conflicting goals are pursued and the scope or extent to which there is participation in the conflict behavior. In the first dimension, insofar as the parties increase coercion rather than persuasion or rewards, the magnitude of conflict behavior has risen. Similarly, insofar as violence is used rather than other forms of coercion, the magnitude of conflict behavior is greater. In the case of persuasion or rewards it is not possible to calibrate increases in the magnitude of a conflict. The amount of resources devoted to each way is one indicator, but the quality of the appeals in persuasion or the significance of the resources offered for exchange, are also relevant.

In addition to changes in conflicting modes the scope of the conflict behavior may increase. This may involve more widespread participation by the members of each contending social category. It may also involve an increase in the number of conflicting relations between adversary parties. Finally, the scope of a conflict may increase in the sense that other parties become involved as partisans in the fight.

These several ways in which conflict behavior may vary in magnitude are not necessarily related to each other. Thus, participation in conflict behavior may become more restricted within a social category as its reliance upon violence becomes greater. Therefore, references to escalation or de-escalation should specify the sense in which it is used. In this work, our concern is largely with changes in the mode of pursuing conflicting goals, especially the use of coercion and particularly violence. When other meanings of escalation or de-escalation are discussed they will be explicitly stated.

We can argue that escalation occurs as people in a struggle believe that the gains if they triumph and the losses if they are defeated are greater than the costs of raising the magnitude of their own conflict behavior and absorbing the increased burdens which the other side places upon them. This should not be seen as a simple calculation which each side regularly and carefully undertakes. But it may prove helpful to keep such a formula in mind as we consider what makes people willing to expend more resources to put pressure on an adversary and what makes them able to absorb more pressure from their adversary. We will also be asking what increases the hopes and expectations of victory and the fears and expectations of defeat in the course of a social conflict. Such changes underlie the movement toward escalation or de-escalation.

PROCESSES OF ESCALATION

Changes Within a Conflict Unit. Once a struggle has begun, each party to the conflict tends to undergo changes which make for escalation. We will discuss the social-psychological and the organizational changes which have this effect.

SOCIAL-PSYCHOLOGICAL MECHANISMS. In many ways, once conflict behavior has started, mechanisms are triggered which tend to increase the magnitude of conflict behavior. Having expressed hostility and coercive action against another party, the alleged reason for it assumes importance commensurate with the action taken. The cause is endowed with additional significance and there is increased commitment to it. In addition, as the other side reciprocates with coercion, the threats and injuries suffered also induce feelings of loyalty and commitment to the cause pursued (Lewin, 1948, p. 199; Deutsch and Kraus, 1960). Increased commitment to the goals pursued justifies increased effort toward their attainment and the willingness to absorb, without yielding, the coercive efforts of adversaries; hence these mechanisms are sources of escalation. Finally, engagement in conflict behavior is often accompanied by a sense of crisis. There is a feeling of anxiety and of limited time in which to act. Under such circumstances, fewer alternative courses of action are considered than in periods which are not viewed as a time of crisis (Hermann, 1969; Holsti, 1971) Constricted in the range of alternatives considered, each side tends to persist in the course of action already undertaken.

ORGANIZATIONAL DEVELOPMENTS. Engaging in conflict behavior in itself tends to alter the group in ways which promote persistence and even escalation of the behavior. These alterations involve changes in the leadership and their relations with their constituencies, changes in the partisan supporters as they are mobilized, changes in the ideology about the struggle, and changes in the organizational goals. Each of these changes warrants separate discussion.

Leaders are particularly prominent in organizational relations with nonmembers. An entire organization can act as a single entity in relation to another organization only through representatives or spokesmen. Collectivities with any organization at all have differentiation which includes roles for dealing with the social environment. Such differentiation is a basis for escalation.

First, there is a tendency for leaders to be particularly committed to goals and the means used to attain them, once they have made the goals and means visible to their constituency. In effect, they have made a public assertion that in their judgment the purpose and the ways used to serve that purpose are sound and beneficial. Consequently, once a course of action is entered there is a tendency to persist upon the same course. If coercion is begun, persistence in it, without success, leads to escalation. These tendencies exist in any public acts of leaders but they are exaggerated in coercive external relations. "Mistakes" in foreign policy are rarely admitted. There are several reasons for this. Acts against an adversary will be condemned and opposed by the adversary; to reverse the course of action seems to be catering to the enemy. Furthermore, in taking actions against an adversary, the leaders have acted as representatives of the entire collectivity and this tends to bind the internal constituency. Mistakes are also denied in external relations because it is easier to do so than in regard to internal issues. Since a course of action is directed against another party, the effects of that policy are more difficult for its partisans to assess than when the course of action is domestically oriented. The leaders can argue that the adversary is beginning to yield or has changed in ways which require even more of the same pressure.

This discussion presumes that the leaders are conscious of the possibility of being replaced by another group of leaders. Competition and rivalry with alternative leaders can be a factor making for escalation. For example, McWorter and Crain (1967) studied civil rights leaders in 15 American cities in 1964–1965. On the basis of interviews with civil rights leaders and others in each city, they assessed the extent of organized and individual competition for civil rights leadership in each city. Organized competition refers to competiton between groups or organizations committed more or less permanently to different programs or ideological stances. Individual competition refers to the competition among individuals for leadership in such a way that the leaders are not permanently committed to one side. They found that militancy, as measured by responses to four agree-disagree questions, was least among leaders in cities with minimal competition and higher in cities with either individual or group competition. Demonstrations were also more frequent where there was competition; but they were short-lived; organized competition weakened the ability to sustain the demonstrations.

The threat of being outflanked by more militant rivals for leadership puts pressure on the leaders of both sides to escalate the means of struggle. Leaders may also face the threat of being outflanked by rivals who argue for moderation, admission of defeat, or less intensive efforts in pursuit of the goal. Competition is likely to promote escalation under several circumstances. Notably, if the conflict is emerging, then the leaders of the challenging party are likely to have a constituency which would support more intense action to get quicker results. Another circumstance in which competition may promote escalation is when the conflict relationship between adversary parties has become institution-alized. Even if only informal, the understandings, mutual respect, and interdependence which leaders of parties in recurrent conflicts develop makes them vulnerable to more radical rivals. Thus the constituency may be suspicious of its representatives who regularly traffic with the enemy and may even become suspicious that the leaders are being co-opted by the opposition, are getting "soft," or are "selling out." Under such circumstances the threatening rivals are likely to be those who argue for more forceful means and competition is likely to result in escalation of conflict behavior once a struggle has begun. Competition also tends to be escalatory when the conflict party is homogeneous and is treated as a unified antagonist by the adversary.

Another process explains why competition for leadership is a source of conflict escalation. Specialists in the use of coercion come to the fore. In international relations, the military assume predominance once armed forces are engaged (Ikle, 1971). Even in less organized conflict parties, as a conflict moves toward more coercive action, additional persons are likely to become actively involved in the struggle. These new partisans are a source of competitors for leadership and may try to assume leader-ship positions. They are less likely to have had nonconflicting relations with the adversary and they are less likely to have some stake in the status quo. For example, in community conflicts the new leaders who tend to take over the dispute are rarely former community leaders, do not have the constraints of maintaining a previous community position, and are not subject to the cross-pressures felt by members of community organizations (Coleman, 1957, p. 12).

The McWorter and Crain (1967) study should remind us, however, that even if competition is an inducement for more intense and coercive conflict behavior, it may be sufficiently divisive that the ability to con-duct sustained forceful action is reduced. This seems to be the case, at least in part, among the various Arab states and organizations in their conflict with Israel.

Under some circumstances, competition may be the source of pressures for de-escalating a conflict. This is most likely to be the case in later stages of a struggle, in particularly heterogeneous conflict units, with an adversary who is divisively conciliatory, and in conflict relationships which are regulated but not institutionalized to the point of rigidity.

Changes in the rank and file also may induce escalation. As the con-frontation between adversary groups occurs, the partisans and potential partisans of both sides become more involved in the struggle and more "radicalized." The adversary groups tend to become more committed to the goals pursued and therefore the means used to pursue them can be escalated. This occurs wittingly and unwittingly.

At an early stage of conflict, when awareness is first emerging within a social category, the members begin to share their grievances and, by identification, the sense of deprivation resulting from membership in the social category increases. This may be done by leaders who articulate the deprivations. It may also be done by the members themselves sharing their experiences and mutually interpreting them. For example, in the Women's Liberation movement, an important component is "conscious-ness-raising" groups. In these small groups, women meet to share their experiences as women in the society; what had seemed personal diffi-culties then are recognized as general and societal and therefore requiring societal solutions, not simply personal accommodation.

The membership composition of the partisan groups changes as the conflict proceeds and this can also make for escalation. The development of a struggle may expand participation in the conflict behavior and this expansion brings in not only less moderate potential leaders, but a constituency which is more prone to use intense means. This is true for a number of reasons. First, in the case of oppressed categories, the seg-ments which are most oppressed tend to become involved only when there are visible signs of possible gains. But their sense of grievance, once aroused, is likely to be greater than for persons who had the re-sources to initiate the struggle (Fanon, 1966). The newly aroused are less moderate, not only because their grievances are greater, but also because they are less constrained by understandings with the other side and are less likely to have had experience with finding compromises with organized opponents. For example, a national study of opinions regarding civil liberties for Communists, atheists, and others expressing minority sentiments was conducted during the Joseph McCarthy period in the U. S. (Stouffer, 1955). A cross-section of the population and community leaders was interviewed. On the whole, the community leaders were more tolerant of the rights of nonconformists than was the public at large. A national survey of blacks and of black civil rights leaders con-ducted in 1966 also is illustrative of the same point (Brink and Harris, 1969, appendix D). The leaders, although less satisfied about the pro-gress being made by blacks and more militant about the goals to be pursued, compared to blacks in general, were less likely to say they would engage in violent conduct.

The composition of a group also changes by some people leaving, in-sofar as membership is voluntary. Consequently, if the conflict behavior escalates, the members who are unwilling to engage in more intense conflict behavior withdraw and those who are willing to engage in it become a larger and larger component of the conflict group. Such intensification of the means may be accompanied by a restriction in membership. Broad coalitions dissolve and the scope of the conflict, in the sense of the numbers involved, de-escalates at the same time that the intensity of the coercion increases.

Related to the changes in the leaders and the rank and file, but significant enough to warrant separate discussion, are the changes in the beliefs and expectations of the partisan groups. At the initial stages of a social conflict, each side rallies its forces. Before any test of strength against an adversary, the forces may seem powerful indeed. The conviction in victory may increase at the sight of the massed forces. Within the insularity of the partisan group, reassuring rumors may reinforce the conviction of strength and success in pursuing the course of conduct entered. If, in addition, there is some initial gain, the support for escalation may grow rapidly. This is particularly true for people who are in a state of collective excitement and contagion. Such swellings of feelings may be short-lived but can escalate rapidly as in the form of riots or nonregulated strikes. Thus in the American student strikes of May 1970, almost continuous rallies were maintained at which announcements of "shut downs" at other colleges were proclaimed. The elan and conviction of an ever-grander victory could sustain relatively extreme action, at least for a few days. Some students voiced the expectation that the strike would expand and go beyond the 1968 events in France in which students and workers joined together in a widespread strike.

Once a conflict group has emerged and assumed a differentiated form, the persons committed to the purpose of the organization also become committed to the maintenance of the organization per se. In itself this is not escalatory and indeed, as we shall discuss later, can make for de-escalation. But the maintenance of an organization may require finding continuing activities to sustain participation and involvement in an organization. This is a reason why leaders of an organization must search out new activities; membership may wane and involvement lessen if it is not sustained by activities. If an organization fails in this regard it will wither away or, if part of a larger social movement, lose out in competition to a more active rival organization. In itself, then, concern with maintaining the viability of an organization may help maintain at least a moderate level of conflicting activity.

Changes in Relations Between Adversaries.   Once a conflict emerges, the changes in the relations between the conflicting parties are fundamental for escalation. We shall consider three such changes: the expansion of the issues in contention, the polarization of relations, and third party intervention.

EXPANSION OF THE ISSUES.   Once a struggle has begun about a particular issue in contention, it often brings more general and additional issues into awareness. Often more fundamental disputes are discovered. As Coleman (1957) writes of community conflicts:

> It seems that movement from specific to general issues occurs whenever there are deep cleavages of values or interests in the community which require a spark to set them off—usually a specific incident representing only a small part of the under-lying difference (p. 10).

For example, a community controversy over the kinds of books in the school library is generalized to the whole educational philosophy (Shaplen, 1950).

The deterioration of relations between groups in conflict is self-escalating because as they deteriorate, contentious issues which had previously been ignored or denied are brought out. There is less need to deny them and indeed the overt conflict may seem a good time to "settle accounts" (Ikle, 1971).

Additional issues also arise because as each side pursues its major aim, subgoals or preliminary ones emerge and they soon take on independent importance as issues in contention. In international relations this is clear as when a military base is important not in itself but as a protection of another position. For example, Sharm el Sheik is a matter of contention between Israel and Egypt, not for its intrinsic attractiveness, but because it controls access to the Gulf of Aqabah and hence the port of Eilat. Similar developments occur within societies. Often it is difficult to say which goal is a means to which other goal, all the issues are so inextricably tied together. Thus, blacks in the U.S. may be struggling for integrated housing in order to get integrated schools, strive for income equality in order to increase housing desegregation, and seek integrated schools to get better jobs and more income equality.

In addition, as one side imposes sanctions upon the other, those sanctions become issues. For example, when women were struggling for suffrage in the U.S., they picketed the White House; they were maltreated by the police, many were arrested and when maltreated in prison they went on hunger strikes which resulted in forced feeding (Flexner, 1959, p. 251). As far as the women's movement was concerned, such behavior by the opposition created new issues of contention. Allies were drawn to the women's cause by the repressive police conduct.

Finally, once conflict behavior proceeds to the point that severe coercive threats and actions are employed, there is an interactive dynamic which expands the issues in contention. Threats and coercion reverberate between adversaries. If one side is threatened it tends to respond with hostility and aggression toward the other (Gurr, 1970, p. 35; Berkowitz, 1969, p. 42–46). Then the other side reciprocates and harming the other side becomes an end in itself. Once inflicting harm or indulging in revenge becomes a goal, runaway escalation may ensue.

It is also possible that if the other side responds with a lower magnitude of conflict behavior this results in escalatory behavior. Underreaction may invite expansion of goals. After all, what a conflict party seeks as a goal, what it perceives as an aim, depends at least partly on what it believes it can get. Hence if the other side responds less vigorously and less coercively than anticipated, this may be an indication of weakness and embolden the conflict party to seek more. This then means an expansion of the issues at stake and often a prolongation of the conflict. Whether underresponse leads to escalation or de-escalation depends upon many attributes of the response, as we shall see later in this chapter.

POLARIZATION. As a conflict emerges and develops, the adversaries tend to become increasingly isolated from each other. For example, before war erupts between governments, they tend to withdraw from joint membership in international organizations (Skjelsbaek and Singer, 1971). As conflict parties reduce the number of nonconflicting relations, they are less and less constrained by cross-pressures and crosscutting ties. They are freer to indulge in more intensive coercive means.

Polarization also takes the form of reducing the neutrals and potential mediators. Parties to a conflict generally try to induce others to join them. Insofar as a party feels morally superior and confident that most of the audience are likely to be allies, it will urge everyone to choose sides. As the coal miners in Harlan County, Kentucky, sang in the thirties, "You either are a union man or a thug for J. H. Blair. Which side are you on, man, which side are you on?" Or as Eldridge Cleaver said, "If you're not part of the solution, you are part of the problem." Or, as the German Nazis put it, "If you are not for us, you are against us."

The polarization of relations between antagonists means that there are fewer opportunities to communicate about noncontentious issues and even about issues in contention. In addition, as the magnitude of conflict behavior increases, communication barriers increase in the sense that fear and hostility cause suspicion and hence it is difficult to signal any de-escalation efforts. Tentative efforts to reduce the magnitude of conflict behavior may be viewed as a trap or as weakness and an invitation for applying more pressure. In any case, lack of responsiveness to tentative efforts at decreasing the magnitude of a conflict is likely to be responded to with resentment, increased anger, and taken as an indication that de-escalation is not possible. Whereupon the other side can feel it was correct in rebuffing the gestures which were alleged to be conciliatory.

As coercion increases, the perceptions of the other side and the reality upon which those perceptions are based makes him seem more and more inhuman. In extreme cases, the enemy is degraded and brutalized; he is then held in contempt and regarded as subhuman. The relations between prisoners and guards in concentration camps is an extreme case. But to some extent, the same is true of many conflict relations. What is distressing about such matters is that in these circumstances the pain and suffering of the adversary does not arouse sympathy and compassion. When it does, that is a source for de-escalation. But the point here is that the suffering of adversaries can make them seem despicable. Their pain can be an invitation for further violence. In battle, pleas for pity may make the weaker seem contemptible (Near, 1971).

Similarly, the brutality of the other side makes brutality in return, not only a matter of retribution or vengeance, but perfectly reasonable because the other side is a brute and presumably understands only brutishness. The imagery of nonhuman animals in conflict relations is revealing for it allows treating the enemy in an inhuman fashion; viz., use of words like pigs, dogs, and cattle.

INTERVENTION. The social context of conflicting parties can be the basis of escalation by the involvement of third parties in the struggle. Involvement or intervention could be de-escalatory, as we shall examine later; but it tends to be related to escalation. Thus, Gurr (1970, pp. 270–71) in his study of civil strife in 114 nations, found that external support for dissidents was correlated .37 with the length of the civil strife and .22 with its pervasiveness. Similarly, external support for regimes was correlated .30 with duration and .28 with pervasiveness. External support results in escalation through several mechanisms. External support makes it possible for an adversary with limited resources to persevere and even expand its conflict behavior (Gross, 1966, pp. 162–86). Moreover, if one side is aided by an outside party, its enemy will tend to be aided by a different outsider. Thus, Gurr found that external support for dissidents was very highly correlated with external support for the regime (.83). Finally, the very intervention of third parties as partisans, in itself, means an escalation in the scope of the conflict.

Third parties are drawn into conflicts by a variety of circumstances. As indicated already, if one side is being aided in a conflict by an outside group, adversaries of that outside group would have a reason to assist the other side, following the maxim: my enemy's enemy is my friend. Each side also appeals in terms of values and standards which make claims for others to intervene on its side. More fundamentally, third parties are likely to see some advantage accruing to them by the victory of one side rather than the other and unless constrained by other considerations will try to aid the preferred victor (Eckstein, 1966).

Involvement may also expand because as the partisans pursue their goals, they do so in a way which infringes upon the interests of third parties. If one side, more than the other does this, the offended third party will have increasingly conflicting relations with the more offending side. For example, in World War I, Germany's use of submarines to attack shipping to Great Britain aggravated the emerging conflict with the U.S. Partisans in a struggle may be more or less conscious of the possible effects of their actions upon third parties. Depending upon their expectations of the likely responses of third parties, consideration of those reactions may set limits to escalation. Thus, if third parties hold normative standards about what they regard as intolerable kinds of conflict behavior, the antagonists may limit their own behavior to avoid outraging third parties who might intervene.

PROCESSES OF DE-ESCALATION

Conflict behavior does not increase in magnitude indefinitely. It must de-escalate, stagnate, or stop. In the next chapter we will consider terminations of social conflicts. In this chapter we are interested particularly in escalation of social conflicts, but escalation cannot be understood without understanding *de-escalation*. The processes are the same, but the conditions vary and therefore the direction of change in the magnitude of conflict behavior. Attention by students and observers of conflicts has been directed largely at escalation. It is also important to study the circumstances by which the processes result in de-escalation.

Changes within a Conflict Unit.   As conflict behavior is continued, it triggers mechanisms which can limit its escalation or may produce de-escalation, as well as lead to increases in magnitude.

SOCIAL PSYCHOLOGICAL MECHANISMS.   Earlier, we noted how engagement in conflict behavior may produce a greater commitment to the goals pursued and hence a willingness to persist and even escalate conflict behavior. It should be even more obvious that expending resources in pursuit of a goal becomes increasingly costly as it is maintained without gaining the end sought. The cost for each additional increment of coercive effort may increase at a higher and higher rate as alternative expenditures are foregone. For example, a few hours at the picket lines or at the barricades may be a diversion; days or weeks so engaged threatens other interests.

Increased commitment to an aim resulting from sacrifices trying to attain it makes subjective sense—it is helpful to one's self-esteem to think something is worth the effort as long as the effort is being expended. But it is also soothing to one's self-esteem to decide that something is not desired, when it appears very difficult to attain. This may be called the "sour grapes" mechanism. When the costs for attaining a goal become too great, it may be devalued. When such turning points are reached depends upon a number of other circumstances—which we will be considering in this and the next chapter.

ORGANIZATIONAL DEVELOPMENTS. We noted in the discussion of escalation processes, that competition for leadership may induce increased magnitudes of conflict behavior. Under certain conditions, however, leadership competition hastens de-escalation of conflict behavior. The basic condition is that a segment of a conflict party prefers to reduce the efforts being exercised in pursuit of the conflicting goal; that is, there is a constituency for more moderate action.

A constituency for more moderation is likely to develop after conflict behavior has been pursued at increasing cost without signs of successfully attaining the proclaimed ends. Leaders who can offer a plausible way of attaining the goal by de-escalating the means used would be a source for de-escalation. This increases the risk of not attaining the goal. That is why de-escalation is facilitated by decreasing commitment to the aim being pursued. Even without abandoning the goal downgrading its importance makes more intense coercive action seem inappropriate and wasteful. Potential leaders who can articulate such changes and the new alternatives pose a threat to the established leaders.

Another condition that increases the likelihood of de-escalatory leadership competition is the heterogeneity of the conflict group in regard to the goal. That is, if the segments of a conflict party differ about the goal's importance, potential leaders have the basis for a constituency to support a more moderate means toward the end.

Some ways leaders pursue group aims may promote the very differences which are the basis for de-escalation. Thus, as coercive action is intensified, leaders often increase pressure for greater rank-and-file support of the policies being pursued. Tolerance for dissent declines. Criticism of leaders is made to appear treasonous. Consequently, leaders create more division and dissent than would otherwise be the case. This is done by defining those who disagree as traitors and treating them as such; in that case they will tend to reciprocate and indeed expand their dissent to more general opposition. In times of intense conflict behavior, it may not even be necessary for some segment to express disagreement. They may be viewed as potential or likely dissenters and closely watched, preventively intimidated, or even physically isolated or punished. For example, in the U.S. in World War II, Americans of Japanese descent were removed from their homes and placed in "relocation centers." "Disloyalty" was created (Grodzins, 1956). Would-be loyal followers can be made into traitors and dissension fostered in any conflict group. The creation of such dissent provides the basis for a constituency which would support a more moderate course of action. The rank and file, rather than uniformly becoming mobilized for more intense action, may have segments which become increasingly disenchanted.

Finally, as we noted in the discussion of organizational changes inducing escalation, concern with maintaining the organization is often de-escalating. Once a conflict organization has developed, many persons, especially those in leadership positions, feel a commitment to the survival of the organization. This commitment is in addition to any other purpose which the leaders proclaim for the organization. Concern with survival limits the escalatory tendencies since continued escalation can threaten the continued existence of the organization. Of course, this is true insofar as the adversary is not already seen as threatening the very life of the organization.

Changes in Relations Between Adversaries. Conflict behavior does not only increase polarization between conflict units, expand the issues in contention, and draw in third parties. New ties between adversaries may develop, goals may be devalued, and third parties may act to de-escalate the conflict.

EMERGING TIES. As a social conflict continues, opponents can develop new bonds even while they are struggling against each other. This, of course, is more true for recurring conflicts which have ended with some degree of compromise. As noted in chapter 4, this is one of the bases of institutionalization of conflict regulation. But even in the course of a single, specific conflict, the adversaries may develop mutual respect and understanding. This is especially likely when the conflict behavior being followed is at least somewhat regulated and the issues in contention are not considered vital. Under these circumstances, it is possible for adversaries to respect the skill with which the other side has pursued its goal. Such mutual respect may even develop in international wars. When there is mutual respect, some limits on escalation exist.

Such mutual understanding and respect are particularly likely between those persons on both sides occupying similar statuses, e.g., soldiers, generals, and leaders. Leaders in every conflict situation are in positions which bring them into interaction with their opposing counterparts. The leaders can recognize that they share many problems with the leaders of the other side; they seek to maintain themselves in leadership positions, make some progress toward their proclaimed goals, and not require too much sacrifice of their followers.

Under these circumstances, leaders can reach understandings to de-escalate a fight. Such arrangements usually entail reaching an agreement about the outcome of a conflict as well, e.g., as in the 1962 Kennedy-Khrushchev agreement about the missile bases in Cuba (Holsti, Brody, and North, 1964). But agreements may sometimes be only about the means of pursuing goals. This distinction, in reality, is never absolute. Any agreement about ends must include understandings about means and an agreement about means has at least implications about ends.

Mutual understandings about de-escalating a struggle (without making an agreement about the outcome) may be reached in open negotiations, but they may also be reached surreptitiously. When conflict behavior has reached high levels and a major escalatory change seems about to occur, leaders may covertly seek an understanding to avoid that escalation. Presumably both sides see too great a risk in engaging in the higher level of conflict behavior, but do not want to give any appearance of "backing down" to their own followers.

These points may be illustrated by the events of March, 1963, in Selma, Alabama (Hinckle and Welsh, 1969). The Southern Christian Leadership Conference (SCLC) under Dr. Martin Luther King's leadership, and the Student Nonviolent Coordinating Committee (SNCC) were cooperating in organizing activities in Selma. In conjunction with those efforts they attempted a mass march to Montgomery, Alabama, on Sunday, March 7. They were stopped by the state troopers under Colonel Al Lingo and police under Sheriff Jim Clark. They were beaten and gassed. A second march was planned for Tuesday. Former Florida Governor LeRoy Collins, head of the Federal Community Service and unofficial ambassador of President Johnson, flew in to try to avoid a repetition of Sunday's bloodshed.

> A federal judge had issued a temporary restraining order against the march and Dr. King was in a quandary. His organization prided itself on never violating the law—or a court order; yet, he had pledged to lead this march (King was absent Sunday), and civil rights workers and ministers from all over the South were gathering.... They all wanted to march. Collins offered a typically Johnson compromise; he had conferred with Colonel Lingo and obtained a pledge that the marchers would be unharmed if they turned back a small distance down Highway 80. Lingo had even drawn a rough map, showing where the Union [civil-rights] forces must halt. Collins handed the ... map to King: this way, he said, both sides would save face—and King would have a dramatic moment. King hesitated, then took the map ... The plan worked. The marchers were halted, knelt, said a prayer and turned back. The deal became obvious to SNCC people when Colonel Lingo, in a mild Southern doublecross, pulled his troopers back, leaving the highway to Montgomery open as King rose to lead his followers in retreat to Selma. The move was meant to embarrass King and it did. King's fall from favor was only momentary. The diverse elements ... were united later that week by the death of the Rev. James J. Reeb, a white Uni-

tarian minister from Boston, who died of wounds from a night-time beating at the hands of some Selma white citizens . . . (pp. 108–9).

CONTRACTION OF GOALS.   Each side in a conflict presumably believes that its actions will stop or prevent the escalation of conflict behavior by the other side. For example, the United States' bombing of North Vietnam was intended, according to some American leaders, to impede the movement of soldiers and supplies from North Vietnam to the war in the South. Whatever the intentions of one side may be, the other side may not de-escalate. Indeed, violence and coercion are likely to be reciprocated. For the several reasons already discussed, threats and coercion result in further escalation. Bombing of cities has not led to the intimidation of the people and their withdrawal of support from their own leaders, not in North Vietnam and not in Japan, Germany, or Great Britain during World War II (U.S. Strategic Bombing Survey, 1946–1947; Sheehan, et al., 1971, pp. 307–44).

Coercion by one side *can* lead to de-escalation by the other side in two basic ways. One possibility is that the coercion is sufficient to physically prevent the other side from continuing in *its* conflict behavior. The other side then loses its *capacity* to continue its conflict behavior at the same level and must de-escalate. Thus, a conflict group may be repressed by its much stronger opposition; its leaders may be harrassed and imprisoned. Or the armed forces of one side may so decimate the ranks of the other that it cannot continue to field an effective army. The other possibility is that one side loses its will to persist; it doubts its ability and questions the desirability of continuing its conflict behavior. In actuality, the will to continue conflict behavior is highly related to the capacity to do so. Neither factor alone determines de-escalation. Klingberg (1966) studied war casualties in relationship to the termination of war. He found some evidence that in modern times nations have tended to surrender before suffering population losses of three or four percent; but there is variation: Paraguay may have lost 80 percent of its population in the Lopez War (1865–1870). Surrender is often preceded by unfavorable trends in four indices, when viewed as a whole: casualty percentage ratios between opposing belligerents, army-size ratios, proportion of battle defeats, and intensity of fighting. An abnormal increase in the proportion of soldiers who are taken prisoner or become sick sometimes preceded surrender by several months. These findings indicate some relationship as well as independence of the ability to continue to wage war and the willingness to do so.

However it is brought about, if one side finds that the adversary's coercion has reduced its ability to pursue its goals, it is likely to contract the goals. At least within the limits of a particular conflict, the issues in contention are likely to become more limited. In that sense, de-escalation has happened.

The loss of capacity and will to continue conflict behavior is related to many conditions which will be analyzed in more detail later in this chapter and in the next two chapters. At this point it is necessary only to outline some of the ways in which the interaction between adversaries can affect one side's loss of will and capacity to fight on.

The possibility of one side physically preventing the other side from engaging in conflict behavior depends on the relative resources of both sides (Gurr, 1970, pp. 232–73). In a peculiar but fundamental sense, the opponents help determine the magnitude of each other's resources. That is, one conflict party can define and treat its adversary as a more or less isolated group. The more isolated it is, the more limited are its resources. So each adversary might be expected to try and separate out the "hard core" opposition and attack only it. But, as we discussed in the section on escalation, conflicts tend toward polarization and expansion of the partisans on each side. Now we must add the possibility that either or both sides may consciously try to avoid that expansion in order to keep the adversary isolated and small. This argues for each side being careful to engage in conflict behavior which is not so large in scope as to expand its opposition. A government which tries to put down a small band of dissidents by widespread repression of potential supporters would create more opposition and conflict escalation. More on this later.

We also noted in the discussion of escalation that as a conflict persists, the issue in contention tends to expand and become more general. To de-escalate a conflict, one or both sides may try to "fractionate" the conflict (Fisher, 1964). The general issues in contention may be broken up into more specific ones and dealt with one at a time. One or both sides may come to believe that the expansion of the issues has gone too far and try to concentrate upon a more delimited matter of contention. This is often part of the termination of a conflict as we shall see in the next chapter.

The extent to which a conflict party's actions divides rather than unifies the adversary lessens the adversary's capacity to even sustain the same level of conflict behavior. External pressure can be a source of unity; members of a threatened group may rally together against the enemy. But external pressures can also aggravate internal dissension and large segments of the conflict group may withdraw support from their own leaders. It is easy to point to cases which exemplify each development. Whether external pressure is a unifier or not, obviously depends on many conditions. The matter is important and complex enough that we will discuss it separately in chapter 7. Here we need to point out only that external pressure may be divisive and that depends partly upon the character of the pressures and the context of their application. If a group can engage in conflict behavior which weakens the solidarity of its adversary, then the adversary may de-escalate its conflict behavior.

A conflict group may aggravate the dissension within its adversary in many ways. One way is to be divisively conciliatory. It may phrase or rephrase its demands so that they require sacrifices from some segment of the enemy and not from it as a single unit. Or, the limited nature of the demands may be stressed so that escalation seems increasingly inappropriate. On the other hand, the coercion may be applied divisively. Thus, it may be conducted selectively so that only a segment of the adversary party experiences it. The segment of the conflict group suffering a disproportionate burden of the fight may be especially likely to become disenchanted with the struggle.

INTERVENTION. The social context of a conflict can importantly contribute to its de-escalation. If third parties do not become involved as partisans, this in itself limits the expansion of the conflict. The isolation of the conflict may be agreed upon by the third parties in order to prevent their own involvement. In some cases there are norms about neutrality to support such noninvolvement. This is the case in international relations and the norm against interference in the domestic affairs of other states. Needless to say, the norm is often violated.

Third parties also act as enforcers of possible breeches of understandings about conflict behavior. Violations of norms can bring about the interference of previously uninvolved third parties. The recognition of this possibility serves to limit the tactics used in conflicts and to maintain the boundaries of appropriate action. This is true, for example, in community conflicts (Coleman, 1957, p. 12). Even where all the parties are not members of a relatively integrated social system with relatively institutionalized conflict regulation, third parties sometimes act similarly, as in international relations when a civil war breaks out in one country. In these cases, however, additional considerations affecting interference and noninterference in the internal affairs of other countries are so great that third parties are relatively unimportant in setting limits to the escalation of conflict behavior.

Finally, third parties can act as mediators. Aside from helping to reach a settlement of the issues in contention, mediators may help reach an understanding about the means used in the conflict. Mediation can be particularly helpful when both sides are fearful of further escalation. A mediator can convey the mutual interest in limiting escalation which neither party would be willing to openly and unilaterally communicate to the other. A mediator can also help devise formulas which permit both sides to continue a conflict at a lower level and presumably without changing the relative positions of the two sides. This may occur even in the midst of a rapidly escalating situation. For example, in the 1963 march on Montgomery from Selma, Collins was able to negotiate a compromise between Lingo and King which probably averted widespread violence against the marchers by the state troopers (Hinckle and Welsh, 1969).

CONDITIONS OF ESCALATION AND DE-ESCALATION

We have considered a number of processes which make for escalation and de-escalation of conflict behavior. The same processes are involved in both courses of development. The outcome of the processes, then, depends on a variety of specific conditions. It is to those conditions that we now turn. We will discuss the conflict modes, the characteristics of the adversaries, the responses of the other side, the issues in contention, and the social context.

Consideration of the interaction between conflict parties under varying conditions may be facilitated by using diagramatic formulations as well as verbal ones. Before analyzing the specific conditions affecting escalation and de-escalation, then, we will briefly discuss such formulations. We can best begin with the equations developed by Richardson in regard to arms races (Richardson, 1960; Rapoport, 1957). He reasoned that the amount of arms one side amassed was a function of how much the other side had, modified by the amount of hostility it had toward the other side and the costs of the arms. Therefore an arms race could be described by two simultaneous equations:

$$\frac{dx}{dt} = ky - ax + g$$

and

$$\frac{dy}{dt} = lx - by + h$$

In these equations, defense expenditures of each side, x and y, over time, equal the other side's defense expenditures, minus the cost of the defense effort plus the grievances against the other side.

These equations could fit any process in which a movement by one party changes the field so that the other party moves and thereby alters the situation so that the first party will change its position. This underlies all social interaction and is particularly pertinent to analysis of escalation and de-escalation. Following Boulding (1962), we can present

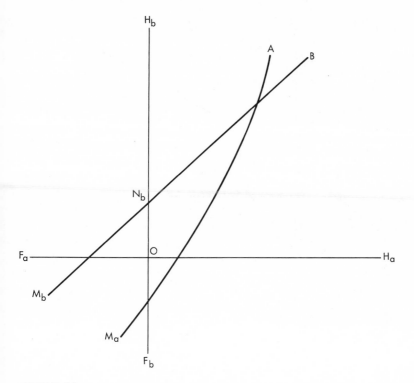

FIGURE 5.1

these equations graphically and examine some properties of such interactive processes. Assume a single dimension of hostility and friendship along which two parties can move toward each other. In Figure 5.1, the origin, marked by an O, is the neutral point for both parties. Any movement upward or to the right is a movement of escalating hostility. Along OH_a, A's hostility to B is measured and B's hostility toward A is measured along OH_b. Similarly, movement downward or leftward is de-escalatory and on the other side of the origin is called friendliness. Now we postulate two curves which show the amount of hostility each side has toward the other at each level of hostility the other side has. Thus, the A curve, $M_a A$, shows how much hostility A has at every level of hostility or friendliness B has. As the curves are drawn, each party has some hostility toward the other initially, that is, even if the other side is neutral. Thus, when B is neutral, A has ON_a hostility. The lines also are drawn with positive slopes or positive reaction coefficients. That is, each party increases its hostility toward the other with more than one unit for each unit the other side increases its hostility. In other words, the higher the reaction coefficient, the touchier is the party.

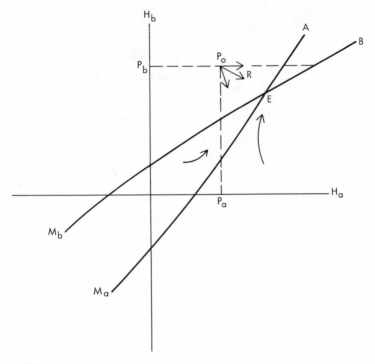

FIGURE 5.2

Figure 5.2 is the same as Figure 5.1, except now we can see the dynamics of the system. The two curves intersect at E. Let us see if that is a stable equilibrium point. Suppose the parties were at point P_o, for A, this is OP_a amount of hostility; for B, it is OP_b hostility. For the amount of hostility A has, B has too much. B would reduce its hostility as indicated by the arrow going down from P_o. A, however, has too little hostility for the amount B has and would increase its hostility, as indicated by the arrow pointing to the right from P_o. The vector for those two directions is the arrow between them, pointing to P_1; this is the direction the two parties would move. Indeed, from each point in the graph, the vector lines would lead to the equilibrium, E, which is thus indicated to be a stable equilibrium point. Given these reaction coefficients, then, the two parties would remain hostile to each other. A more friendly equilibrium would require different reaction coefficients. With still other curves there may be no stable equilibrium; as in a runaway arms race, there may be ever increasing hostility until the limits of the system are reached. Boulding discusses many properties of such graphs and a variety of reaction coefficients, the presentation here should be sufficient to assist us in describing and understanding escalatory and de-escalatory movements.

Mode.   How a conflicting goal is pursued has consequences for future escalation. Having initiated one kind of conflict behavior, the probability of using each other kind is altered. This is true because engaging in any particular conflict behavior affects those conducting it, those against whom it is being directed, and often even third parties. The mode employed has some costs and may have some gratifications to those using it and it imposes burdens upon the adversary. We shall discuss these effects and their implications for conflict escalation and de-escalation. We shall also discuss variations in modes as they have consequences for the conflict party employing the mode for the other side and for third parties.

Although attempting to coerce the other side is costly in many ways, we must also recognize that many persons derive gratification from certain aspects of coercion. Such gratification makes de-escalatory responses to overtures from the other side unlikely. Enjoying engaging in a particular kind of coercive action makes persistence in it relatively independent of the other side's actions.

Gratifications from certain kinds of conflict behavior derive from several sources. One source is the pleasure of solidarity with one's own people. Conflict behavior which brings people together to share some danger in facing an adversary can be exciting and pleasurable. Particularly at an early stage in a confrontation, the massing of persons can create a feeling of brotherhood or sisterhood, of brave comrades standing firm together. At the barricades, in the streets, before storming the enemy's positions, the sense of collective solidarity and even love for those with whom these times are shared arises and is savored. Such feelings not only make for persistence in the behavior because it is pleasurable, but the sense of solidarity also gives a feeling of strength which enables people to continue even when they are suffering setbacks. The sense of solidarity is itself strengthened by seeing how well comrades are behaving. Their sacrifices and strength in the face of the adversary make each person feel proud to be allied with them; their sacrifices make them worth sacrificing for. Some of these points are illustrated by the account of one participant in the civil rights movement. He tells of thousands of students marching to a city jail in support of a group that had been arrested.

> When we had all arrived we started singing "We Shall Overcome" and after we finished there was a peaceful quiet, like I've never heard before in my whole life. We stood there, the police stood there, and the white mob stood there—we all just stood there. And then, in the background, faintly we heard the students in the jail sing to us. We couldn't see them but they chanted, "Oh students don't you mourn." It brought tears to my eyes. . . .

Then the police charged.

> I saw one little girl—weighed about seventy pounds—and the
> policeman gave the command for a dog to leap at her. And
> one of the basketball players—a great big boy—put himself
> in front of her. The dog leaped and came back down with
> his suit and all his clothes torn off and the boy just smiled
> and walked off. I saw beauty that day.

He was blinded temporarily by the tear gas attack.

> When I was able to see again I saw some of the girls getting
> themselves together. Some went back to the campus in an
> ambulance; they had been hit in the legs with nightsticks.
> And all of them—their clothes were torn and they were many
> of them bleeding—they were all standing in line again. In
> that few minutes they had pulled themselves back together
> and they were singing as loud as they could, "I'm gonna sit
> at the welcome table." And the police stood there and didn't
> say a word (Bell, 1968, p. 115).

Another source of gratification which certain kinds of conflict behavior provides is the feeling of being important and being part of
something which is important. Actions which disrupt the routine for
significant proportions of a social system must be important. And it is
gratifying to be doing something important. If it is "important" enough,
"history" is being made and one is part of its creation. This feeling of
excitement and importance can be experienced by persons who are
merely cogs in the great machinery of war or revolution. But the feeling
can animate the leaders too. Even the occupiers of the most powerful
positions in a society feel an extra excitement and pleasure at directing
vast enterprises. They certainly are making history and there is a thrill
in it as indicated in the Hopkins papers about the leaders of the U.S.,
Great Britain, and the Soviet Union during World War II (Sherwood,
1948). People enjoy the excitement of crises and may even help create
them or define some events as a crisis to increase their own importance
and the significance of their coping with it (Argyris, 1967, p. 42).

A third source of gratification which makes for the persistence of some
kinds of conflict behavior is the pleasure people find in "proving themselves." In confrontations with an adversary, courage, stamina, and quick
judgment are all put to the test. Many people enjoy such challenges and
look for them; once found they help sustain people in the conflict behavior. There is the joy of handling heavy and expensive equipment in
international wars, of staying up nights at the barricades, of bravely
enduring pain, of marshalling legions of men, and of conferring long
hours to make grave decisions.

All these feelings of collective solidarity, excitement, making history, and proving one's self cannot be sustained for long and cannot in themselves maintain a group in continuing conflict. Even the extraordinary, if continuously performed, can become routine. But these emotions, aroused by collective action which faces coercion from an adversary, can overcome initial doubts and fears. Once engaged in an exchange of coercive acts, other processes may become operative to sustain the escalation. The feelings also promote escalation at the early stages of conflict behavior since many people may be drawn into the action by the initial excitement. Commitments thus made, have an enduring quality.

Extreme coercive acts, once executed, tend to be justified by their perpetrators. People committing what they regard as great or terrible acts vindicate themselves. For example, if people riot and property is burned and if people are hurt and killed, then a cause worthy of such losses must be found. Sympathizers and participants in a riot are likely to feel even more than before that conditions were very bad to lead to such events.

Riots, however, also have a self-limiting character. Goods and property, once stolen or burned, cannot be taken or destroyed again. Riots can be part of an escalatory development by spreading rapidly to encompass larger and larger segments of the society. Unless the conditions for this extension are present, however, riots may burn themselves out. From the ashes more organized and radicalized groups may emerge to continue the conflict in other ways. How the riots are put down may also increase the sense of grievance and provide the basis for increased levels of conflict behavior at another time.

Modes vary widely in their possible effects upon the other side. The effect depends partly upon the other side's understanding of the meaning of the actions. Modes vary in the clarity of the message. For example, terrorism is particularly unclear. The terroristic acts themselves do not reveal what is being demanded nor of whom it is being demanded. They imply that the other side should "drop dead," go away, or otherwise disappear. That is not a goal which the other side is likely or even able to accede to easily. When the other side is a foreign occupying force, however, there may be more possibility of doing so. Terrorism, because of its accompanying secrecy, is hard to be explained and interpreted by its perpetrators. Faced by unclear but vaguely total demands and no visible adversary with whom discussion is possible, terrorism is likely to provoke strong reactions from the other side. Riots, too, are unclear in meaning. There are no authoritative interpretators. Thus when a national sample of whites was asked in August, 1967, what the two or three main reasons for the ghetto riots were, 45 percent said "outside agitators" (Erskine, 1967–1968, p. 665).

The meaning of acts also depends on the conventions of the other side. In a period of inflation of rhetoric and actions, voices may become shriller and actions more extreme in order to be noticed and to be taken seriously. The other side's conventions also serve as criteria to evaluate the appropriateness of coercive acts. That is, if a party acts in a manner which goes beyond the normative expectations of the other side, the reaction may be one of such outrage that the acts are counterproductive—instead of intimidating, they provoke further escalation. For example, the police "bust" at Columbia University in 1968 served to de-legitimate the university authorities in the eyes of the students and faculty. Actually seeing the police clubbing students and dragging them from the seized buildings was much more likely to make student and faculty regard the police action as brutal than only hearing or reading about it. Thus among those who did not see the police action, 28 percent of the faculty and 41 percent of the students thought the police action was brutal, compared to 66 percent and 74 percent of the faculty and students who did see it (Barton, 1968).

In general, the more severe the action of one side, the more likely is it that escalation occurs. Evidence for this is found in a study of colleges which had their first demonstrations against certain kinds of campus recruitment during October–December, 1967 (Morgan, 1970). The severity of the control measure against civil disobedience was assessed and the frequency of expansion of protest was also assessed. The more severe the control measure, the more likely was it that the protest expanded. For example, in only 2 percent of the cases where there was no confrontation did the protest expand; but in 50 percent of the schools in which police were used, protest expanded, and in 73 percent of the cases where some demonstrators were arrested by the police there was expansion of the protest.

The earlier discussion of the effects upon the perpetrators of conflict behavior suggest that conduct which does not involve such arousal of feelings of solidarity against an adversary permits responsiveness to de-escalatory efforts by the other side. Modes which involve more attention to the ideas and feelings of the other side also makes responsiveness more likely and probably also inhibit rapid escalation. For example, this would be the case insofar as persuasion is used as the way of pursuing conflicting goals.

In general, violence is provocative. It hurts the other side so that the newly created grievance cries for retribution and increased violence may be used to suppress efforts at retribution. Nonviolent acts do not have the same effect. Escalation may occur as more people are drawn in as participants in the nonviolent actions, but increases in the magnitude of coercion are probably less likely than if violence had been used.

Each party to a conflict considers how the other side will be affected by its choice of means and this very anticipation then affects its choice and the likelihood of escalation. Insofar as conflict is regulated and institutionalized, each side can anticipate with relative accuracy the response of the other. Such accuracy lessens the likelihood of rapid escalation. Acts which provoke escalatory behavior from the other side are less likely to be taken mistakenly. This is one reason why stable conditions contribute to the moderation of conflict behavior—accurate expectations can develop.

In two circumstances, however, shared understandings about ways of pursuing conflicting goals may be the basis of escalation. First, one party to a conflict may try to provoke the other side into escalation in order to make the other side behave in a reprehensible manner. Second, boundaries of acceptable conduct are constraining, but once crossed there may be a sense of unlimited license.

Many illustrations of consciously provocative actions can be found, even in cases of governments acting against other governments. For example, in May, 1967, the Egyptian government requested the United Nations Emergency Force (UNEF) to withdraw from Egypt; this meant that Egyptian military forces again controlled Sharm el Sheik and would not permit Israeli vessels to pass through to the Gulf of Aqabah and the port of Eilat in Israel (Nasser, 1970). Hassanain Haykal (1970), the Egyptian spokesman, writing in Al Ahram, interpreted the action thus:

> The closure of the Gulf of Aqabah to Israeli navigation and the ban on the import of strategic goods, even when carried by non-Israeli ships, means first and last that the Arab nation represented by the UAR has succeeded for the first time, vis-á-vis Israel, in changing by force a *fait accompli* imposed on it by force ... Egypt has exercised its power and achieved the objectives of this stage without resorting to arms so far. But Israel has no alternative but to use arms if it wants to exercise power. This means that the logic of the fearful confrontation now taking place between Egypt ... and Israel ... dictates that Egypt ... must wait, even though it has to wait for a blow. This is necessitated also by the sound conduct of the battle, *particularly from the international point of view.* Let Israel begin. Let our second blow be ready. Let it be a knockout (pp. 180, 185; emphasis added.).

Crossing a boundary, however, opens up new vistas of possible means of conflict. Once one side has broken a barrier, it feels relatively unrestrained and so does its adversary. In international conflicts, there may be agreed upon limits, for example, about the use of nuclear, bacteri-

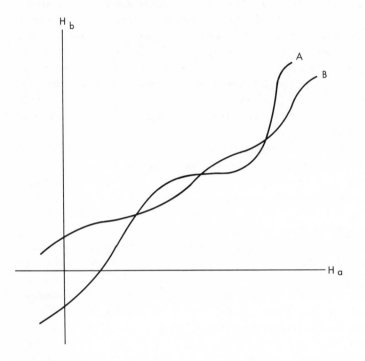

FIGURE 5.3

ological, or chemical weapons. Each side may be careful about using a "little bit" of such weapons because a barrier would be broken. The anticipation of rapid nuclear escalation once tactical nuclear weapons are used inhibits their employment. This was part of the issue in the American utilization of chemical weapons in Vietnam. It was argued that their use in combat, even if only the kinds used in domestic riot control were employed, could easily evolve into the employment of more and more potent gasses. Forces differ in the degree to which clear boundaries may be demarcated; for example, the distinction between some military advisers and special combat units is not as sharp as the introduction of aerial bombing across national borders (Schelling, 1960).

The existence of boundaries in conflict behavior may be shown graphically in irregularities in the curves of the reaction coefficients. That is, there would be step-wise progression in the level of conflict behavior, as shown in Figure 5.3. A number of equilibrium points would be reached and then passed if one or the other side acts in an extreme fashion. A variety of understandings can serve as boundaries in conflict behavior. They may pertain to the weapons used, deception in their use, or their targets. Weapons vary from personal vilification, verbal manipulation, armed violence, to withdrawal of previously provided goods and services.

Finally, one other attribute of conflict modes with implications for escalation and de-escalation should be mentioned. Modes differ in the secrecy with which they are pursued. Typically, secrecy means that the constituency of the conflicting parties' leaders are not allowed to know what the leaders are doing. This is most likely to be the case in an exchange and when a sudden shift is contemplated. Followers are then faced with a *fait accompli*. This subjects them to the claims of collective solidarity and loyalty to the leaders for support. Secrecy may facilitate de-escalation because mobilization and arousal of the rank and file are less likely and then rank-and-file pressure for continued firmness is lessened.

At an early stage of a conflict however, secrecy may permit leaders to act and make commitments which are part of an escalatory movement. Probing an adversary, using subversion, and conducting propaganda may be kept secret from the rank and file, while the adversary experiences their impact and polarization and hostility grows.

Adversary Characteristics. In addition to the conflict mode chosen, several characteristics of the adversaries affect the likelihood of escalation or de-escalation. We will discuss their degree of heterogeneity, the nature of their diversity, and the stability and nature of their organization.

HETEROGENEITY. The diversity of the conflict unit has implications for conflict behavior escalation and de-escalation. Diversity in the unit provides the basis for de-escalation insofar as support for the pursuit of any particular policy will not have the same priority for all segments of the conflict party (Landecker, 1970). In that case, lack of success in the pursuit of the goal will more readily result in devaluing the objective— a "sour grapes" reaction. Those segments which did not give the goal high priority at the outset would then reduce even their moderate support. Diversity also makes it more likely that the conflict unit segments will not suffer costs and burdens of the conflict behavior equitably. Furthermore, the unit is more subject to divisive efforts by the other side.

Finally, diversity facilitates responsiveness to the other side and consideration of more alternatives than would be the case in a more homogeneous unit. We noted in the discussion of escalation processes that as a conflict develops and particularly as coercion is applied, the sense of crisis and feelings of anger and fear restrict the number of alternatives reviewed. People become increasingly rigid in the pursuit of their aims. Plunging forward with more of the same and insensitive to the witting and unwitting signals from the other side, opportunities for de-escalation are missed and the conflict behavior escalates (Quester, 1970). If the adversaries have some components which are not caught up in the same experiences they may be able to consider a number of alternatives and be more responsive to overtures from the other side.

The extent to which this possible consequence of diversity is actualized depends on the organizational form it takes (Wilensky, 1967). Thus, insofar as diverse segments of the unit have their own information gathering, analyzing, and policy development capacities and a way of introducing their ideas into the decision-making processes at the highest level of the unit, then the diversity is likely to be effective and correct in matching the conduct of the other side. Such organizational forms for diverse segments are generally rare. For example, even in large units such as the nation-state, few groups have resources to develop alternative policies to the central government's. The agency which is most likely to have developed a number of detailed contingency plans is the military one. The defense establishment alternatives are then most likely to be drawn upon when changes in courses of action are considered. Plausible as these ideas are, we lack systematic evidence bearing upon them.

NATURE OF DIVERSITY. The critical dimension here is the unit's range of positions regarding possible escalation relative to the unit's operating position. That is, at any given time in a struggle, a group is pursuing its goal with a particular mixture of means; the proportions of persons and their relative influence favoring escalation and de-escalation obviously affects the direction of the unit's movement. This is phrased mechanically. It should be understood in conjunction with the previously discussed processes of escalation and de-escalation. Thus, the consequences of competition for leadership significantly depends upon the relative size of constituencies for escalation and de-escalation. For example, insofar as the bulk of active rank-and-file union members are dissatisfied with recent union gains and ready to exercise more militancy in pursuit of their demands, the union leaders will vigorously seek larger benefits and be willing to use more coercion for a longer time to reach a settlement. Otherwise, the leaders may well find their leadership position challenged by more forceful and demanding competition and find their positions undercut by rank-and-file wildcat strikes.

The relative proportions of each unit favoring different conflict modes also directly affects the means used. Thus, disaffection with the purpose and the means used in its pursuit may result in people withdrawing support. They desert. In Lenin's memorable phrase, they "vote with their feet." This has happened in many wars when even large military units desert to the enemy or simply dissolve (Brooks, 1969; Morison, Merk and Freidel, 1970).

If people favor de-escalation strongly enough, they may actively intervene to bring it about. This can occur even in the midst of violent confrontations, as in a riot. Thus, in the American ghetto riots of the 1960s, some people in the community tried to stop looting and burning. As we would expect from the analysis in the preceding chapter, counter-rioters tend to be better educated and have higher income than the rioters or than the noninvolved (National Advisory Commission on Civil Disorders, 1968, p. 132).

Finally, the diversity which is derived from the coalition character of the conflict party has some peculiar possible consequences. If the coalition has been formed primarily as an alliance against a particular adversary, then pressure from that adversary tends to strengthen the coalition. Thus, Soviet-Chinese political friendship seems to vary directly with hostility toward the U.S. NATO solidarity has also varied directly with presumed threat from the Soviet Union (Holsti, 1969; Hopmann, 1966; Travis, 1970). Coalition solidarity, then, is the basis for more intense and pervasive conflict behavior between adversary coalitions. The strengthening of coalition ties in the face of opposition then becomes the basis of stronger action against the adversary and the reciprocal consequences for the adversary keeps the spiraling escalation going.

The diversity of interests within a coalition can be the basis for escalation inasmuch as the coalition element committed to the highest magnitude of conflict behavior within the coalition may engage in acts which bind other elements in the coalition to the same course. Often it is the smaller or weaker elements in the coalition who do this. They are more vulnerable to attacks from the adversary and therefore they are more likely to have issues of vital importance in contention compared to the stronger elements in the coalition. Moreover, they may believe that a large portion of the burden of pursuing the conflict will be borne by the stronger allies. This may be one of the mechanisms which explain the finding that alliance formation is associated with international wars (Singer and Small, 1968). Illustrative cases abound. The Great Powers honored their alliance commitments and followed Serbia and the Austro-Hungarian Empire into the conflagration which became World War I. But the U.S. and the U.S.S.R., once the Cuban missile crisis emerged, ignored Cuba and its claims (Holsti, Brody, and North, 1964). They reached an accommodation without escalating their conflict behavior to the use of violence. Within societies, too, coalitions which include segments willing to pursue more escalatory actions can commit and bring along the rest of the coalition. For example, relatively small but extreme elements in a coalition may have disproportionate influence toward escalation because the issue in contention is more vital to them and the others in the coalition must be willing to go along with the more radical proposals in order to maintain the coalition.

DIFFERENTIATION AND STABILITY. Units with clearly differentiated leaders who are relatively secure from constituency challenges are freer to escalate *and* to de-escalate than are units with vulnerable and relatively undifferentiated leadership positions. A tradition which supports the leader in pursuing unpopular courses may help the leader persist in actions with the conviction that history will vindicate him. With that assurance he may persevere despite considerable dissension. The American presidency offers some illustrations of this phenomenon, most recently in regard to the Vietnam War. Naroll (1969, p. 158), in his historical survey of wars, found that older rulers, hereditary rulers, and states with greater centralization of political authority, were more likely to be involved in wars than younger rulers, than elective or self-appointed ones, or than states with less centralization. His explanation is that "a ruler who regards his position in the state more possessively is more likely to become involved in war."

The degree to which the conflict party is highly organized and under the control of the highest decision maker also affects the chances of limiting escalation. In many struggles the people in direct confrontation are not under effective control of their presumed superiors. This can readily lead to escalation of conflict behavior. Thus the Chicago police who acted against the demonstrators at the 1968 Democratic Party convention used more violence than was probably intended (Walker, et al., 1968). This in itself was an escalation; in addition, it led to a further polarization between different segments of the society (Robinson, 1970). When the police were called in to remove students from the Columbia University buildings they had occupied, the violence of the police was greater than had been expected by the university administrators (Rader and Anderson, 1969). The shooting of students at Kent State in May, 1970 was an unplanned escalatory act which led to further escalation; it exemplifies the loss of control or lack of control which occurs when violence is threatened (The President's Commission on Campus Unrest, 1970). A final illustration will be cited: General Douglas MacArthur had enough autonomy to act in ways which expanded the war in Korea (Paige, 1968; McCartney, 1954; Friedman, 1969).

Inability to control or coordinate action makes it difficult to de-escalate. If both sides are seeking to reduce the level of conflict behavior without losing relative power, each side wants its messages to the other side to be clear and understood and each must correctly understand the other. The greater the hostility and the higher the level of conflict behavior, the more difficult it is to comprehend the other side's de-escalatory overtures. One source of difficulty is that actions inconsistent with the overtures may occur as subordinates pursue their regular conflict behavior and those actions erupt into major events. For example, in 1960, the heads of government of the U.S., Great Britain, France, and the Soviet Union were to meet in Paris as part of a nascent movement to de-escalate the East-West tension. A high flying U.S. reconnaissance plane, the U2, was shot down over Soviet territory (Wise and Ross, 1962). The resulting tempest prevented the meeting and disrupted the movement.

Finally, the strength and solidarity of each adversary affects the ability to escalate or at least to persist at the same level of conflict behavior. The ability to withstand the pressures which the other side brings to bear depends partly on the partisans' sense of identification with their side in terms of time perspective and the significance of the issue in contention. As we will examine in more detail in chapter 7, if there is considerable dissension within a conflict party, external conflict tends to aggravate the dissension (Coser, 1956, pp. 92–95; Smith, 1970). Such dissension decreases the possibility of pursuing an escalatory policy. They may also encourage the other side, however, to raise its demands and thus reduce the likelihood of a general de-escalation. This brings us to the reciprocal actions of the two sides, the next section of this chapter.

Response of the Other Side.   The basic condition which affects escalation and de-escalation is the way the conflict parties interact. In many current discussions of social conflict, much attention is given to overreaction and underreaction. We have already noted how each can produce either escalation or de-escalation. In short, a very strong reaction can either intimidate the other side and result in conflict de-escalation or it may provoke the other side and cause escalation. On the other hand, a mild reaction can either placate the other side and produce de-escalation or it can invite further escalation by showing weakness. Clearly, we must specify many attributes of responses and conditions of the interaction between opponents if these plausible but contradictory possibilities are to be reconciled. We shall discuss the severity and consistency of the response, the accompanying interpretation, the recipient's expectations, the accompanying actions, and the reciprocity over time.

The first response attribute to be considered is its severity. Increasing severity of response does not produce de-escalation. We saw, for example, in Morgan's (1970) study of colleges, that the more severe the administration response to student demonstration was, the greater was the probability of expansion of the conflict. Part of the explanation is that the response of the other side becomes an issue in itself. If the other side reacts severely, the recipients have a new grievance. An even more severe response is necessary to suppress the reaction to the new grievance. There is a variety of evidence to support this interpretation (Gurr, 1970, pp. 238–51). For example, the very large South Vietnamese army was ineffective in repressing insurgency partly because it was too massive for the task; it acted as an invader in its own country (Thompson, 1966). Yet, at some point, force can and does suppress an adversary. Indeed, quantitative studies indicate a curvilinear relationship between the repressiveness of governments and political violence. For example, Walton (1965) rated 84 nations on the degree of coerciveness or permissiveness of their national political systems and on their degree of political stability in 1955–1961. She found that the most highly coercive countries were either stable or only moderately stable; those with intermediate levels of coercion had a disproportionate number of the most unstable countries; and those which were highly permissive tended to have stable regimes.

This curvilinear relationship may be portrayed in terms of the graphs presented earlier. We may posit two reaction coefficients and initial levels of hostility as presented in Figure 5.4. Note that B (perhaps the burghers) has some initial hostility toward A (perhaps the authorities), but a little friendliness goes a long way; also, it will be quite hostile to A at moderate levels of hostility or coercion by A; but, at higher levels of hostility, it submits and does not exhibit hostility to A. In such a system, there is more than one equilibrium point. One point represents a coercive regime and a coerced populace; the other point represents a responsive regime

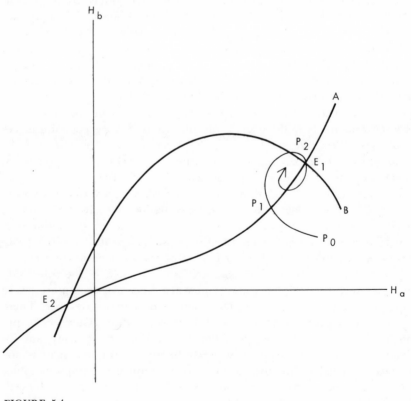

FIGURE 5.4

and a grateful populace. In between is a vast arena for a hostile population and confrontations which might lead to one or the other equilibrium point.

Boulding (1962, p. 32) has noted some peculiar features of an equilibrium point such as E_1. Note that the vector lines circle around it like a spiral. This may be explained as follows: suppose we start at P_0, at that point A is very hostile and B has been cowed into submission, A can afford to be a little more permissive, B becomes less cowed and increases his hostility to P_1. Until P_2 both get more hostile toward each other: A because it fears B's rising hostility and B because A's level is not yet severe enough to suppress it. After P_2, B's hostility begins to decline under pressure.

The *consistency* with which a way of pursuing conflicting goals is exercised helps determine the other side's response. We assumed this in our earlier discussion of a conflict party's ability to coordinate its conflict behavior and hence pursue a convincing de-escalatory effort. A conflict party may include subgroups which make statements or commit acts so inconsistent with the major conflict mode that the adversary does not respond as intended. Persuasive efforts are not convincing if actions are taken at variance with the assertions, for example, of overriding common interests. This is part of the reason, too, why contingency planning for escalation increases the likelihood of escalation—the adversary doubts the commitment to more moderate means.

Consistency is particularly pertinent in the use of coercion by a conflict party claiming jurisdiction over its adversary, for example a government responding to dissension (Gurr, 1970, pp. 250–58). Consistency in this context means that coercion is always applied relative to the violation of some proscriptions. That is, only persons who commit undesired acts suffer negative sanctions and the severity of the sanctions are clearly related to the magnitude of the acts. Governments often do not so respond to dissension. For example, police and military response to riots is typically to seize some participants and bystanders who are close and beat or arrest them, or both. Some are released and the majority, who get away, are ignored. Typically, too, military forces try to control insurgency by shooting a few dissidents and supposed sympathizers. Such actions are often ineffective or counterproductive. Persons who engage in the proscribed activity have not suffered any negative sanctions and others who did no "wrong" have suffered greatly at the hands of the regime.

When massive force is threatened and applied precisely, it has a better chance of limiting escalation. For example, in the 1967 Detroit riot, heavy firing by fearful National Guardsmen was part of an escalatory movement. Army troops with strict orders not to fire unless they could see the specific person at whom they were aiming quickly established order; they then helped residents clean up the streets (National Advisory Commission on Civil Disorders, 1968, pp. 84–108).

Although words may belie actions, the interpretations accompanying actions can affect the other side's reactions. This is most often revealed in assertions regarding limited goals. But interpretations often also accompany a variety of actions which might otherwise be construed as coercive. For example, weapons are alleged to be built and stockpiled only for defensive purposes. Sometimes allies, sympathizers, or subgroups within a conflict organization "explain" the organization's action as being less hostile or coercive than it appears. Thus, it is explained that what seems like a threat is meant only for internal consumption. It need not be taken literally since it is really intended to forestall more severe actions by rival leaders or organizations. Sometimes, leaders themselves may direly threaten an adversary in public and secretly indicate that the threat should not be taken too seriously. Such understandings and comradeship between adversary leaders, of course, make them vulnerable to rank-and-file suspicion and challenge.

In addition to the interpretations made of their own actions, spokesmen for a conflict party try to interpret and define who the adversary is and what *its* characteristics are. Such attempts affect the other side's reaction and the likelihood of escalation and de-escalation. Thus, if the coercion is accompanied by assertions that the adversary is to be *collectively* destroyed or subjugated, that adversary is likely to be solidary and ready to increase the magnitude of coercion in order to maintain its opposition. This is particularly likely when the adversary is defined in terms of an ascribed characteristic such as race or ethnicity. For example, the Nazi definition of the Slavs as lesser beings increased the solidarity of the Russians with the regime and intensified the violence and the extensiveness of the conflict.

One reason that satyagraha or nonviolent direct action (see chapter 4) is likely to inhibit escalation, even when critical and profound issues are in contention, is that it implies and is usually accompanied by assertions that the opponent is recognized as equally human and worthy of consideration. This inhibits the coerciveness of the opponent.

In a sense, interpretations and explanations of one's own action, directed at an adversary, are forms of persuasion. This is even true when a conflict party explains why it is doing what it is doing. For example, Mario Savio, a leader of the Free Speech Movement (FSM) at Berkeley in 1964, said that the movement was directed against bureaucratization of life and against the idea that nothing new can happen and therefore unusual and even extraordinary means are needed to shake people up

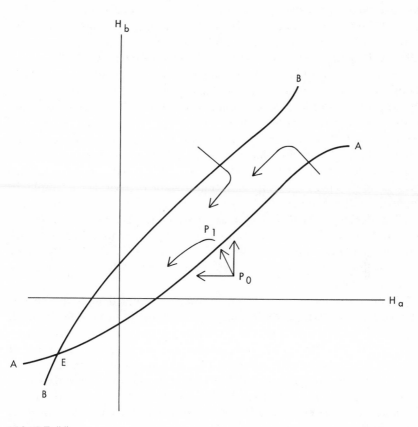

FIGURE 5.5

(Savio, 1965). Such interpretations convey ideas and feelings which constitute appeals for understanding and also attempts at persuasion.

The recipients' expectations and feelings about an adversary and its actions affect the likelihood of the recipient reacting in an escalatory fashion. Suppose, for example, both parties have mutual ties and friendly feelings. As shown in Figure 5.5, each starts out with initial friendliness toward the other. In this relationship, a hostile action by one side, even if responded to by hostility, will tend to move both parties toward greater friendliness. For example, if side A acts as hostile as P_o, B will increase its hostility and A will decrease its, since it is already at a higher level than is appropriate for the amount B has. The vector line shows that as a result they will move to P_1. After which they will *both* reduce their hostility. Some evidence consistent with this interpretation was cited in the preceding chapter. Naroll (1969) found that with higher levels of cultural exchange between rival nations, wars between them were less likely. Conversely, conflict parties with high initial hostility, sensitive to injuries from the other side, and who enjoy seeing the other side suffer, will tend to escalate conflict behavior (Valavanis, 1958).

The specific expectations each side has about the other's goals and about the other's conflict behavior have particular implications for escalation. For example, if side A expects no serious challenges from side B, the first signs of challenge will tend to be ignored and not treated seriously. Side B is likely to then increase the magnitude of its conflict behavior to gain attention. Such conduct may then be dismissed by side A as just "attention getting" and still not be treated seriously, further infuriating A. There are many variations of this pattern. For example, in response to the Women's Liberation movement, men have often conveyed a sense of ridicule. They may assert or imply that the protestors are simply sexually unsatisfied and need a "good man." Such defenses make it unnecessary and even impossible to understand what the other side is saying. Those put-downs are infuriating and help radicalize the protesting group.

Student objections, too, may be initially responded to with the dismissing notion that youth is idealistic, unrealistic, and a little wild. What students say, therefore, can be ignored because it will change when the students grow up. Elders may believe and even say, "I thought that way, too, when I was your age . . ." All such put-downs seem to require the protestor to raise the magnitude of conflict behavior. Persuasion as a mode of pursuing goals seem particularly ineffective until the other side takes the issue seriously. Not taking the protests seriously, however, does inhibit the escalation of conflict behavior by the recipient of the protests. At least initially, the behavior response may be benevolent and permissive, even if condescending.

Whether words and acts deter or invite escalation depends upon the interpretations made of those words and acts by the other side. Those interpretations rest partly upon expectations developed from past events. Thus, if one side has usually made concessions, the other side may expect them to continue and not believe a refusal coupled with a threat. The threat is not credible and does not deter (Ikle, 1971, p. 116).

Each side may also have specific expectations and standards about particular techniques of conflict behavior. We have already noted that some actions are not taken seriously by the other side and hence a conflict party escalates its mode of pursuing its goal. In addition, if the other side is outraged by an antagonist's conduct, a boundary may be crossed and the other side will feel free to escalate its tactics. There are also escalatory implications for violations of more specific expectations. Thus, if a conflict party, A, commits what B regards as an atrocity, B may consider A to be subhuman and hence justifiably subject to treatment which it in turn would regard as an atrocity. Soldiers who have witnessed enemy atrocities are more likely to be vindictive against the enemy (Stouffer, et al., 1949, vol. 2, p. 163).

Expectations about how to wage a conflict, of course, may inhibit escalation, so long as both sides adhere to the rules. Coercive forces, rather than being actually employed, may be tallied by both sides and the results accepted. This seems to be the case in some coups. Thus, a dissident faction tries to assemble sufficient military commanders to its side to make the other side vulnerable; when superiority is gained, the dissident faction may inform the incumbents. After careful negotiations and bargaining, the incumbents may recognize that they have lost and quietly yield and be allowed to depart (Gurr, 1970, pp. 271–72; Lieuwen, 1964).

Finally, we must also note that the mixture of ways used to reach an end affects escalation. As we have already indicated, each way of pursuing a goal, in actuality, is exercised in conjunction with other ways. Coercion is accompanied by some persuasive efforts and often even by rewards or the promise of rewards. The extent to which a particular coercive tactic, then is escalatory or de-escalatory depends partly on the entire mixture of ways being used.

Interestingly, as conflict behavior erupts and escalates, the prospects for an exchange relationship alters and in some ways is enhanced. The need for what the other side can give may increase and the ability of the other side to offer concessions or rewards may grow. For example, the very arousal and organization of a people in a previously neglected social category gives them desired resources. They acquire some power and merit so that their loyalty and respect are now valued. Thus, in the U.S., the growth of protest and liberation movements among blacks, students, women, and the poor has resulted in some courting of these groups by whites, faculty and administrators, men, and the wealthy respectively.

Issues. Matters of contention vary in their susceptibility for escalation and de-escalation. The more important is the issue in contention, the more likely is the conflict to escalate. Insofar as a party feels its vital interests are at stake, it will be willing to endure the other side's coercion and expend resources in trying to coerce the other side. For example, labor strikes about union recognition or about attempts to weaken the union are more likely to escalate to violence than are strikes about wages and hours (Oberschall, 1969).

The depth of the grievance may help to sustain conflict behavior and increase its magnitude once violence has erupted. Thus, although community variations in the condition of Negroes has not been found to be related to the outbreak of riots, the severity of riots has been. For example, Wanderer (1969) found that the percentage of nonwhites living in ten-year or older housing was highly correlated (.86) with the severity of riots.

In the preceding chapter we argued that in dissensual conflicts persuasion was more likely to be tried initially than in consensual ones. Now we suggest that once a conflict is being handled coercively or especially violently, then dissensual struggles generally have more potentiality for escalation than do consensual conflicts. In dissensual conflicts, the opposition is less likely to be considered equally human than in consensual ones. Dissensual conflicts seem more indivisible and therefore less able to be fractionated. Dissensual fights in which partisans proclaim exclusiveness relative to the opponent and which are coupled with an expandable domain are peculiarly subject to escalation, as in ideological control of territory. Thus, as one side gains more, a simple expansion of the domain sought increases the magnitude of the issue at stake. For example, when North Korean military forces pushed the South Korean and American forces under U.N. authority further and further south of the border at the 38th parallel, the American goal was presumably a return to that border. After the successful Inchon landing and the rapid movement northward, the 38th parallel was crossed and the troops continued to advance. Even suggestions of buffer zones below the Yalu river bordering China were ignored. "Appetites rose as the troops went forward" (Neustadt, 1960, p. 127; Paige, 1968).

The magnitude of the issue in contention underlies the evaluation of another side "over" or "under" reacting. It underlies the interpretation each side makes of the other and of its conflict behavior. It underlies the mixture of modes each can utilize, what persuasive efforts, what exchanges, and what magnitudes of coercion each can offer and sustain.

Issues also differ in the degree to which the aims are collective or aggregative. Insofar as they are collective, escalation is more likely because resistance to group reallocations seems more threatening than individual accommodations, even if numerous. Furthermore, collective goals usually require acknowledgment of change by the opponent.

In addition to the issue in contention, the full range of *possible* issues underlies the chances of escalation and de-escalation. Thus, the grievances which could arise between adversaries are the fuel for escalation. More generally, and more abstractly, the matrix of possible outcomes and the preferences of each side for every outcome helps determine the struggle's course. This is the overall payoff matrix. It underlies the shifting issues in contention and therefore the changes in conflict modes since the issue in contention strongly affects the choice of mode.

For example, the central issue in a conflict between a student organization and the administration may be the setting of dormitory hours. In addition there are underlying differences regarding other dormitory rights, classroom attendance, curriculum, tuition, dining halls, university investments, and faculty consultations. Depending upon how strongly each side feels about various degrees and ways of student participation in the management of such areas, the chances for escalation or de-escalation are different. That helps determine what concessions are promised and what exchanges are likely, as well as how high each side is ready to go in raising the level of conflict behavior.

The nature and magnitude of the incompatibility of the goals pursued by adversaries profoundly affects the course of a struggle. But each side's *perception* of the other's goals also affects escalation and de-escalation. The U.S. and the U.S.S.R. may each fear the expansionism of the other side and believe that the other must recognize its own nonexpansionist goals. Continuing hostility and mutual threats then would be likely. But if both governments really have goals which are limited, defensive, and to consolidate—not expand—then the struggle between them may continue with lower chances of escalatory use of coercion and violence. Gamson and Modigliani's (1971) systematic analysis of how each country actually responded to the other's foreign actions indicates that on the whole American and Soviet government leaders pursued limited, consolidationist aims.

Social Context. We discussed in the last chapter how the environment affects the selection of the conflict modes. We discussed how other parties, as possible allies and as possible models, affect the means chosen; we discussed how the social patterns and understandings within which the conflict parties operate affect the choice of mode; and, finally, we discussed the possible effects of technology and ecology. The factors and processes examined in analysing the choice of means also affect moving from one to another, of escalation and de-escalation. For example, the characteristics of the third parties who might become allies affect the likelihood of escalation as well as the initial choice of mode. At this point, then, we need add only a few additional specifications about the possible impact of the social context upon escalation or de-escalation.

We should recognize that third parties may be more or less attentive to particular adversaries and to the conflict behavior they are exhibiting. If third party inattention is sufficiently great, a conflict group may be successfully ignored even by the presumed opposition. For example, in 1948, when the World War II draft law was expiring, peacetime military conscription was about to be enacted for the first time in America's history. Protests, including the burning of draft cards, were held. Even burning draft cards were ignored and the protests de-escalated. Inattentiveness can also mean allowing conflict parties to fight it out without intervention. This limits the *scope* of conflict but it may permit higher and higher *levels* of conflict behavior as in civil wars or the suppression of rebellion. Modes and antagonists differ in visibility. Some modes are conducted secretly, as in negotiated exchanges and in general persuasion is a matter of relative disinterest to third parties. Some conflict parties are relatively ignored in the mass media; internationally some countries receive little international attention.

Visibility and attentiveness is dependent upon the means of communication available to the third parties. Currently we are particularly conscious of the possible role of television in conveying information about conflict events. The growth of the civil rights movement, and its success in getting voting rights and public accommodations legislation through Congress, is in part due to the support engendered by the spectacles on television of mass demonstrations and rallies and of the violence of the authorities in places like Birmingham, Alabama. This even set a model for possibly courting police violence (Walker, et al., 1968, pp. 287–331; Larsen, 1968; Baker and Ball, 1969). When the Chicago police charged repeatedly against the demonstrators during the 1968 Democratic Party convention, the demonstrators chanted, "The whole world is watching."

The events in Chicago in the summer of 1968, however, demonstrate that the consequences of visibility and attentiveness depends upon the standards, interests, and expectations of the third parties. Maybe the world was watching, but not with disapproval of what the police were doing. As a matter of fact, the American public generally thought the police did not use excessive force (Robinson, 1970; Gamson and Mc-Evoy, 1970).

The mass media are also often credited with feeding the flames of riots by giving them a great deal of attention. This increases participation in a given riot and hastens their spread from place to place. The media sometimes have played down such events to keep them from spreading. Mass media may well have such effects; we need to examine such possibilities carefully. We should keep in mind, however, that riots have spread quickly even before the era of mass media. Riots spread quickly, too, in East Germany in 1953 and in Poland in 1956.

The consequences of third parties noticing what a conflict party does depends upon the third parties' interests and expectations. In a rapidly escalating conflict, crossing a boundary of previously expected and acceptable behavior may provide the basis, or the excuse, for intervention and hence for escalation followed by de-escalation under the weight of the new balance of forces. For example, in September, 1970, Palestinian Arab groups were growing in international stature and vying for leadership in the struggle against Israel. Then the Popular Front for the Liberation of Palestine, one of the groups, hijacked four airplanes, blew up the planes after the passengers had been removed, and held the passengers as hostages. There was considerable outrage expressed by many nations. The Jordanian government, under King Hussein, had felt threatened by the Palestinian Arab groups on Jordanian territory. There had been some fighting between Jordanian troops and the Palestinian Arab groups. At this juncture, extensive open fighting broke out between the Jordanian army and the Palestinian Arab organizations. This was a major step in the suppression of these organizations in Jordan.

In chapter 4 we discussed how other parties constitute models or potential allies for the parties in conflict. But the discussion generally treated conflict groups as single entities. Yet, in the course of a struggle, subgroups within each party can also look for support and models from elsewhere. The general social atmosphere may lend support to one faction or another within conflict organizations. This helps determine the consequences of competition for leadership. For example, in the U.S. in the early cold war years and in the 1950s of McCarthyism, organization leaders were likely to be challenged internally by alternative leaders who were more "anti-Communist" and established leaders could successfully dismiss rivals for not being sufficiently "anti-Communist." This could be reflected in struggles over a variety of issues, such as civil liberties or militancy of demands within trade unions, political parties, and other organizations. Consequently, protesting groups would tend to be more ready to de-escalate than they would be if the temper of the times were different. On the other hand, conflict parties opposing protest groups might feel more able to escalate their demands and means of pursuing them. In the 1960s, internal challenges were more likely to have moved organizations toward a more militant direction and thus tended toward escalations, at least by protesting groups.

SUMMARY AND CONCLUSIONS

To conclude this chapter, I want to stress that the attributes of the conflict mode, the conflict units, the response of the other side, the issue in contention, and the social context all combine to determine the course of escalation or de-escalation. Furthermore, all the attributes have significance in the context of the parties' interaction over time. We shall discuss this sequential reciprocation as illustrated by two different kinds of cases: (1) efforts by dissidents to provoke escalation of conflict behavior in order to mobilize support, and (2) efforts at de-escalating the tension between the U.S. and the U.S.S.R. in 1963.

Independence and revolutionary movements have sometimes tried to create a revolutionary situation by provocation of the government. This strategy, for example, was used in Cyprus by Grivas (Purcell, 1969, p. 261ff). More recently, some of these efforts have been modeled on what allegedly happened in Cuba (Debray, 1967; de Gramont, 1970). A small guerilla band, with the leadership of Fidel Castro, operated from the rugged terrain of the Sierra Maestra mountains and raided small army units. The reprisals unleashed by Batista alienated more and more segments of Cuban society. Such defections strengthen the revolutionary movement as success seems more likely and as the movement's claims and interpretations seem to be confirmed by at least some segments of the opposition. Finally, even the army withdrew support and Batista fled. But similar efforts in Venezuela failed, as they did in Bolivia, even under the leadership of Che Guevara. Such failures are illuminating. In Venezuela, President Betancourt used very specific and limited countermeasures, waiting until there was public pressure to increase the countermeasures (Gude, 1969). The revolutionaries, instead of rallying support, found themselves isolated. The scope of the conflict behavior did not increase.

Clearly, making things worse for the people by provoking the government to harsh measures is an inadequate revolutionary program or course of action. Whether or not it even hastens the development of a revolutionary situation depends upon many other factors—the responsiveness of the government, the level of public discontent, and the degree of integration and mutual trust between the government and the masses. In the case of Bolivia, the conditions for a revolutionary movement, following the strategy attempted by Che Guevara, were not present. His small band remained isolated from popular support until they were destroyed by Bolivian military units.

In student uprisings, too, administrators may fail to be provoked. As the data from Morgan's (1970) study indicate, lower magnitude responses to demonstrations tend to prevent expansion of the conflict. We need to specify a variety of conditions in the extended interaction in order to explain why a low level of response is not interpreted as weakness and as an incitement for escalation in itself. The student sit-in at the University of Chicago is illustrative in this regard (Editors of the University of Chicago Magazine, 1969). On December 15, 1968, Marlene Dixon, assistant professor in the Department of Sociology and in the Committee of Human Development, was notified that her contract would not be renewed after it expired on September 30, 1969. A group of students demanded that Dr. Dixon be rehired and that students share equally in all future decisions in the hiring and firing of faculty. On January 19, 1969, the university vice-president and dean of faculties appointed a committee to review the case, including allegations that Dr. Dixon was not reappointed because she was a woman, a political radical, or approached sociology differently than others in the Department. Edward Levi, president of the university, released a statement from the academic deans emphasizing the desirability of regularly obtaining student views and having institutionalized channels for doing so, in accord with a policy announced over a year earlier. On January 21, the Council of the University Senate also warned that students engaged in disruptive acts are subject to disciplinary action.

On January 29, 444 students at a meeting voted for some form of militant action, 430 voted against it and 85 abstained. On the same day, President Levi issued a statement that any decision about rehiring Dr. Dixon would await the results of the investigating committee and that he did not endorse the principle of equal student power in decisions about hiring and rehiring faculty. The next day the students began to occupy the administration building. The university administration did not indicate any change in its position and tried to continue with its procedures for investigation and disciplinary action.

Note that the administration seemed to be responsive to the substance of some demands but also indicated an unyielding position on other matters. The students were not united in the goals nor the means to be used. On this issue, the faculty and administrators were probably more united than on other issues in university uprisings.

The sit-in lasted two weeks. On February 12, the investigating committee released its report recommending that Dr. Dixon's contract be extended for one year in the Committee of Human Development alone. At a press conference the same day, Marlene Dixon refused the contract extension. Meanwhile, students were being suspended for failing to appear before the Disciplinary Committee. Then, on February 14, the students voted to open or not open the university files; the affirmative did not have the two-thirds majority needed. They then voted to leave the building. Jeffrey Blum, one of the sit-in leaders, reportedly said, "We must admit to ourselves that we lost. There was no campus uproar over the failure to rehire Mrs. Dixon, nor was there any campus backing for our demand for amnesty for sit-inners" (Chicago American, February 15, 1969). They retained a platform urging the end to discrimination against women faculty, the displacement of residents from a largely black neighboring area, the addition of courses in the sociology of deprived groups, and the admission of more youth from working class origins. Individual hearings continued and as of April 8, 42 students had been expelled and 81 suspended.

Now we turn to a brief review of mutual reciprocity in the de-escalation of tension. We will consider the de-escalatory movement between the American and Soviet governments in 1963 (Etzioni, 1967). On June 10, President Kennedy made a conciliatory speech which provided a context for particular gestures. He announced the unilateral cessation of all nuclear tests in the atmosphere and stated they would not be resumed unless another country did. The Soviets published the speech in full and did not jam the Voice of America recording of the speech. On June 15, Premier Khrushchev spoke welcoming the Kennedy initiative and announced a halt to the production of strategic bombers. In the United Nations, on June 11, the Soviet Union ceased objecting to a Western-backed proposal to send observers to Yemen and the U.S. reciprocated by removing its objection to restoring full status to the Hungarian delegation, for the first time since 1956. The Soviet Union, on June 20, agreed to establish a direct communications line with the U.S., first proposed by the U.S. in 1962.

It should be recognized that these unilateral gestures probably had no substantive effect upon the balance of power nor altered the underlying bases of conflict between the U.S. and the U.S.S.R. But they could reduce tensions facilitating the recognition of common and complementary relations. Then, more formal negotiations regarding more substantive matters could be pursued. Indeed, multilateral negotiations on a test-ban agree-

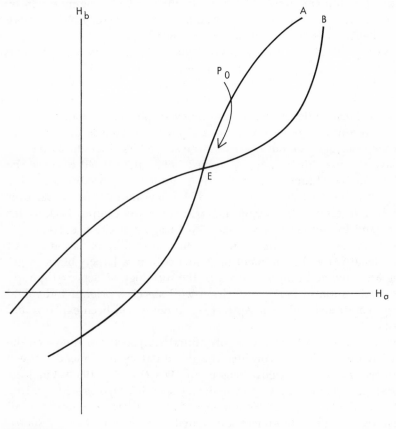

FIGURE 5.6

ment were renewed in July and on August 5, the agreement was signed.

Other symbolic gestures, expressions of hope for additional cooperative acts, and formal agreements followed. On October 9, President Kennedy approved the sale of $250 million worth of wheat to the U.S.S.R. On September 19, the Soviet government suggested banning orbiting weapons of mass destruction and an agreement in principle was announced on October 3 and embodied in a U.N. resolution passed on October 19. Spies were also exchanged in October. The movement, however, did not continue indefinitely. It almost completely stopped in late October and November.

How shall we interpret these events? It may be that the Cuban missile crisis of October, 1962 marked a point of hostility above the equilibrium point and these events merely marked the movement *from* a very hostile point, P_o, as shown in Figure 5.6. But the movement seems to have carried the two parties toward a lower level of mutual hostility than previously held. It may be that a new equilibrium was reached. The *joint* movement made it possible to reach a position which unilateral acts could not readily attain. Thus, let us return to the arms race dilemma discussed in chapter 1 and illustrated in table 1.4. In that case, it would be advantageous for A to increase its arms if B did *or* did not do so; similarly for B. Consequently they would both continue to increase their arms, although if they *both did not* they would both be better off. That movement requires communication and mutual trust. Perhaps the series of gestures made possible such a joint movement, as indicated in the dotted line of Figure 5.7.

The reaching of a new equilibrium point would indicate that one or both curves have shifted. Perhaps with the new understanding reached, initial hostility would be less and the reaction coefficient not as sharp. Such a shift is illustrated in Figure 5.8.

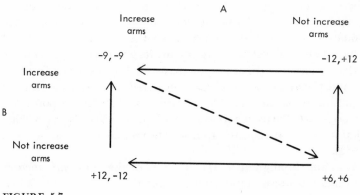

FIGURE 5.7

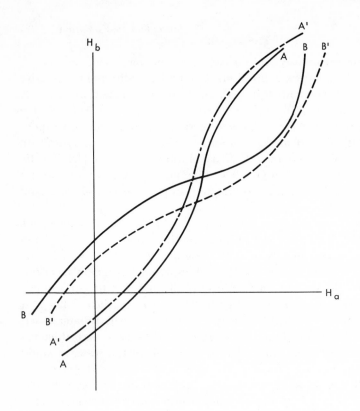

FIGURE 5.8

If a new equilibrium is reached, however, it generally reflects substantive changes in the underlying bases of the conflict. In this case,
several such changes may have been occurring. The solidarity of the two
blocs was weakening. This reduced the forces which might be available
against the other side and raised the costs of threatening it. Also, the
ideological fervor of each side may have been reduced when the mono-
lithic quality of communism and capitalism became patently absent. In
addition there were changes in the world systems. The growth of organizations and the increased role of noncommitted nations may have
tempered some of the cold war salience. Even the repeated handling of
crises may have helped develop a nascent institutionalization of conflict
regulation that reflected and became the basis for further acts of mutual
confidence. Additional factors might be suggested as causing a shift in
the underlying causes of the conflict. They are not needed to point out
that a shift occurred. Partisan recognition of such shifts also is needed
for de-escalation and that requires appropriate mutual response between
the adversaries.

The Gamson and Modigliani (1971) analysis of the cold war suggests
a somewhat different interpretation. For a short time prior to the Cuban

missile crisis, the Soviets under Khrushchev pursued more expansionist aims than previously; it was a period of heady Soviet actions. After the Cuban missile crisis the Soviet Union returned to its prior goals of consolidation rather than expansion.

In summary, once a conflict relationship erupts into coercive action, whether or not it escalates and how far it escalates, is dependent upon the underlying conditions *and* how the conflict parties perceive and respond to each other. The possible outcomes, the payoff matrices, indicate what concessions are feasible and attractive. In the next chapter we move on to discuss the actual outcomes of two parties pursuing conflicting goals.

BIBLIOGRAPHY

ARGYRIS, CHRIS, *Some Causes of Organizational Ineffectiveness within the Department of State* (Washington, D.C.: Center for International Systems Research, Department of State, 1967).

BAKER, ROBERT K. AND SANDRA J. BALL, *Mass Media and Violence* (Washington, D.C.: U.S. Government Printing Office, 1969).

BARTON, ALLEN H., "The Columbia Crisis: Campus, Vietnam, and the Ghetto," *The Public Opinion Quarterly*, 32 (Fall 1968), 333–51.

BELL, INGE POWELL, *CORE and the Strategy of Non-Violence* (New York: Random House, Inc., 1968).

BERKOWITZ, LEONARD, "The Frustration-Aggression Hypothesis Revisited" in Leonard Berkowitz (ed.), *Roots of Aggression* (New York: Atherton Press 1969), pp. 1–28.

BOULDING, KENNETH E., *Conflict and Defense* (New York: Harper and Brothers, 1962).

BRINK, WILLIAM AND LOUIS HARRIS, *Black and White* (New York: Simon and Schuster, Inc., 1969).

BROOKS, ROBIN, "Domestic Violence and America's Wars: An Historical Interpretation," in Hugh Davis Graham and Ted Robert Gurr (eds.), *Violence in America* (New York: Bantam Books, 1969), pp. 529–50.

BWY, DOUGLAS P., "Political Instability in Latin America: The Cross-Cultural Test of a Causal Model," *Latin American Research Review*, 3 (Spring 1968), 17–66.

COLEMAN, JAMES, *Community Conflict* (New York: The Free Press, 1957).

COSER, LEWIS A., *The Functions of Social Conflict* (New York: The Free Press, 1956).

DEBRAY, REGIS, *Revolution in the Revolution?* (New York: Grove Press, Inc., 1967).

DE GRAMONT, SANCHE, "How One Pleasant, Scholarly Young Man from Brazil Became a Kidnapping, Gun-Toting, Bombing Revolutionary," *The New York Times Magazine* (November 15, 1970), pp. 43–45, 136–53.

DEUTSCH, MORTON AND ROBERT M. KRAUSS, "The Effects of Threat upon Interpersonal Bargaining," *Journal of Abnormal and Social Psychology*, 61 (1960).

ECKSTEIN, HARRY (ed.), *Internal War: Problems and Approaches* (New York: The Free Press, 1966).

Editors of The University of Chicago Magazine, "The Sit-In: A Chronology," *The University of Chicago Magazine*, 61 (March/April 1969), 39–47.

ERSKINE, HAZEL, "The Polls: Demonstrations and Race Riots," *The Public Opinion Quarterly*, 31 (Winter 1967/1968), 655–77.

ETZIONI, AMITAI, "The Kennedy Experiment," *Western Political Quarterly*, 20 (June 1967), 361–80.

FANON, FRANTZ, *The Wretched of the Earth* (New York: Grove Press, Inc., 1966).

FISHER, ROGER, "Fractionating Conflict," in R. Fisher (ed.), *International Conflict and Behavioral Science* (New York: Basic Books, Inc., Publishers, 1964).

FLEXNER, ELEANOR, *Century of Struggle* (Cambridge, Mass.: Harvard University Press, 1959).

FRIEDMAN, EDWARD, "Problems in Dealing with an Irrational Power: America Declares War on China," pp. 207–52 in Edward Friedman and Mark Selden (eds.), *America's Asia: Dissenting Essays on Asian-American Relations* (New York: Random House, Inc., 1969).

GAMSON, WILLIAM A. AND JAMES MCEVOY, "Police Violence and Its Public Support," *The Annals*, 391 (September 1970), 97–110.

GAMSON, WILLIAM A. AND ANDRE MODIGLIANI, *Untangling the Cold War* (Boston: Little, Brown and Company, 1971).

GRODZINS, MORTON, *The Loyal and the Disloyal* (Chicago: The University of Chicago Press, 1956).

GROSS, FELIKS, *World Politics and Tension Areas* (New York: New York University Press, 1966).

GUDE, EDWARD W., "Batista and Betancourt: Alternative Responses to Violence," in Hugh Davis Graham and Ted Robert Gurr (eds.), *Violence in America* (New York: Bantam Books, 1969), pp. 731–48.

GURR, TED ROBERT, *Why Men Rebel* (Princeton, N.J.: Princeton University Press, 1970).

HAYKAL, HASSANAIN, "An Armed Clash with Israel Is Inevitable—Why?" in Walter Laqueur (ed.), *The Israel-Arab Reader*, rev. ed. (New York: Bantam Books, 1970), pp. 179–85. Originally published in Al Ahram, May 26, 1967.

HERMANN, CHARLES F., *Crises in Foreign Policy* (Indianapolis, Ind.: The Bobbs-Merrill Company, 1969).

HINCKLE, WARREN AND DAVID WELSH, "The Battles of Selma," in Walt Anderson (ed.), *The Age of Protest* (Pacific Palisades, Calif.: Goodyear Publishing Co., 1969), pp. 100–109.

HOLSTI, OLE R., "External Conflict and Internal Cohesion: The Sino-Soviet Case," in Jan F. Triska (ed.), *Communist Party-States* (New York: The Bobbs-Merrill Company, 1969), pp. 337–52.

———, "Crises, Stress, and Decision-Making," *International Social Science Journal*, 23, No. 1 (1971), 53–67.

————, RICHARD A. BRODY, AND ROBERT C. NORTH, "Measuring Affect and Action in International Reaction Models: Empirical Materials from the 1962 Cuban Crisis," *Journal of Peace Research*, Nos. 3–4 (1964), 170–89.

HOPMANN, P. T., "International Conflict and Cohesion in the Communist System," cited in R. C. North, J. F. Triska, R. A. Brody, and O. R. Holsti, *Stanford Studies in International Conflict and Integration, Progress Report*, 1966.

IKLE, FRED CHARLES, *Every War Must End* (New York: Columbia University Press, 1971).

KLINGBERG, FRANK L., "Predicting the Termination of War: Battle Casualties and Population Losses," *The Journal of Conflict Resolution*, 10 (June 1966), 129–71.

LANDECKER, WERNER S., "Status Congruence, Class Crystallization, and Social Cleavage," *Sociology and Social Research*, 54 (April 1970), 343–55.

LARSEN, OTTO N. (ed.), *Violence and the Mass Media* (New York: Harper & Row, Publishers, 1968).

LEWIN, KURT, *Resolving Social Conflicts* (New York: Harper & Brothers, 1948).

LIEUWEN, EDWIN, *Generals vs. Presidents: Neo-Militarism in Latin America* (New York: Frederick A. Praeger, Inc., 1964).

MCCARTNEY, ROY, "How War Came to Korea," in Norman Bartlett (ed.) *With the Australians in Korea* (Canberra: Australian War Memorial, 1954).

MCWORTER, GERALD A. AND ROBERT L. CRAIN, "Subcommunity Gladitorial Competition: Civil Rights Leadership as a Competitive Process," *Social Forces*, 46 (September 1967), 8–21.

MORGAN, WILLIAM R., "Faculty Mediation of Student War Protests," in Julian Foster and Durward Long (eds.), *Protest! Student Activism in America* (New York: William Morrow & Co., Inc., 1970), pp. 365–82.

MORISON, SAMUEL ELIOT, FREDERICK MERK, AND FRANK FREIDEL, *Dissent in Three American Wars* (Cambridge, Mass.: Harvard University Press, 1970).

NAROLL, RAOUL, "Deterrence in History," in Dean G. Pruitt and Richard C. Snyder (eds.), *Theory and Research on the Causes of War* (Englewood Cliffs, N.J.: Prentice-Hall, Inc., 1969), pp. 150–64.

NASSER, GAMAL ABDEL, "Speech at UAR Advanced Air Headquarters, May 25, 1967," in Walter Laqueur (ed.), *The Israel-Arab Reader*, rev. ed. (New York: Bantam Books, 1970), pp. 169–74.

National Advisory Commission on Civil Disorders (Kerner Commission), *Report of the National Commission on Civil Disorders* (New York: Bantam Books, 1968).

NEAR, HENRY (ed.), *The Seventh Day: Soldiers' Talk About the Six-Day War* (London: Penguin Books, Inc., 1971).

NEUSTADT, RICHARD, *Presidential Power* (New York: John Wiley & Sons, Inc., 1960). As cited in Edward Friedman, "Problems in Dealing with an Irrational Power: America Declares War on China," in Edward Friedman and Mark Selden (eds.), *America's Asia: Dissenting Essays on Asian-American Relations* (New York: Random House, Inc., 1969), p. 239.

OBERSCHALL, ANTHONY, "Group Violence: Some Hypotheses and Empirical Uniformities," paper presented at the meeting of the American Sociological Association, 1969.

PAIGE, GLENN, *The Korean Decision* (New York: The Free Press, 1968).

The President's Commission on Campus Unrest (Scranton Committee), *Campus Unrest* (Washington, D.C.: U.S. Government Printing Office, 1970).

PURCELL, HUGH D., *Cyprus* (New York: Frederick A. Praeger, Inc., 1969).

QUESTER, GEORGE H., "Wars Prolonged by Misunderstood Signals," *The Annals of the American Academy of Political and Social Science*, 392 (November 1970), 30–39.

RADER, DOTSON AND CRAIG ANDERSON, "Rebellion at Columbia," in Walt Anderson (ed.), *The Age of Protest* (Pacific Palisades, Calif.: Goodyear Publishing Company, 1969), pp. 67–72.

RAPOPORT, ANATOL, "Lewis F. Richardson's Mathematical Theory of War," *The Journal of Conflict Resolution*, 1 (September 1957), 249–304.

RICHARDSON, LEWIS F., *Statistics of Deadly Quarrels* (Pittsburgh: The Boxwood Press, 1960).

ROBINSON, JOHN P., "Public Reaction to Political Protest: Chicago 1968," *Public Opinion Quarterly*, 34 (Spring 1970), 1–9.

SAVIO, MARIO, "An End to History," in Seymour Martin Lipset and Sheldon S. Wolin (eds.), *The Berkeley Student Revolt* (Garden City, N.Y.: Anchor Books, 1965), pp. 216–19.

SCHELLING, THOMAS, *The Strategy of Conflict* (Cambridge, Mass.: Harvard University Press, 1960).

SHAPLEN, ROBERT, "Scarsdale's Battle of the Books," *Commentary*, 10 (December 1950), 530–40.

SHEEHAN, NEIL, et al., *The Pentagon Papers; As Published in the New York Times.* (New York: Bantam Books, Inc., 1971).

SHERWOOD, ROBERT E., *Roosevelt and Hopkins: An Intimate History* (New York: Harper and Brothers, 1948).

SINGER, J. DAVID AND SMALL, MELVIN, "Alliance Aggregation and the Onset of War, 1814–1945," in J. David Singer (ed.), *Quantitative International Politics* (New York: The Free Press, 1968).

SKJELSBAEK, KJELL AND J. DAVID SINGER, "Shared IGO Memberships and Dyadic War, 1865–1964," paper presented to Conference on the United Nations, Center for International Studies, 1971.

SMITH, ROBERT B., "Rebellion and Repression and the Vietnam War," *The Annals of the American Academy of Political and Social Science*, 391 (September 1970), 156–67.

STOUFFER, SAMUEL A., *Communism, Conformity, and Civil Liberties* (New York: Doubleday & Company, 1955).

———— et al., *The American Soldier: Combat and Its Aftermath*, Vol. 2 (Princeton, N.J.: Princeton University Press, 1949).

TANTER, RAYMOND, "Dimensions of Conflict Behavior Within and Between Nations, 1958–1960," *Journal of Conflict Resolution*, 10 (March 1966) 41–64.

THOMPSON, SIR ROBERT, *Defeating Communist Insurgency* (New York: Frederick A. Praeger Inc., 1966). As cited in Ted Robert Gurr, *Why Men Rebel* (Princeton, N.J.: Princeton University Press, 1970), p. 248.

TRAVIS, TOM ALLEN, "A Theoretical and Empirical Study of Communications

Relations in the NATO and Warsaw Interbloc and Intrabloc International Sub-Systems," unpublished Ph.D. dissertation, Department of Political Science, Syracuse University, 1970.

U.S. Strategic Bombing Survey, *The Effects of Strategic Bombing on German Morale*, 2 vols. (Washington, D.C.: U.S. Government Printing Office, 1946), and *The Effects of Strategic Bombing on Japanese Morale* (Washington, D.C.: U.S. Government Printing Office, 1947).

VALAVANIS, STEFAN, "The Resolution of Conflict when Utilities Interact," *The Journal of Conflict Resolution*, 2 (June 1958), 156–69.

WALKER, DANIEL, et al., *Rights in Conflict: A Report to the National Commission on the Causes and Prevention of Violence* (New York: Bantam Books, 1968).

WALTON, JENNIFER G., "Correlates of Coerciveness and Permissiveness of National Political Systems: A Cross-National Study," M.A. thesis, San Diego State College, June 1965. As cited in Ted Robert Gurr, *Why Men Rebel* (Princeton, N.J.: Princeton University Press, 1970), p. 250.

WANDERER, JULES J., "An Index of Riot Severity and Some Correlates." *American Journal of Sociology*, 74 (March 1969), 500–505.

WILENSKY, HAROLD L., *Organizational Intelligence: Knowledge and Policy in Government and Industry* (New York: Basic Books, Inc. Publishers, 1967).

WISE, DAVID AND THOMAS B. ROSS, *The U-2 Affair* (New York: Random House, Inc., 1962).

chapter six

Terminations and Outcomes

Every struggle ends. Of course the end is usually the beginning of a new conflict and other struggles continue concurrently. But each specific conflict terminates and has an outcome. In this chapter we will outline possible outcomes and how they are affected by terminating processes. Then we will analyze how various aspects of the struggle itself affects outcomes. We shall also point out some of the ways outcomes are affected by factors aside from the struggle. Finally, we shall examine a few specific outcomes and how they emerged.

The analysis of conflict termination has been particularly neglected in the study of social conflicts (Fox, 1970, Ikle, 1971, Carroll, 1970). Yet it obviously is an important matter. The concern in this chapter is upon the termination and immediate outcome of particular struggles. In the next chapter we examine longer run issues such as the consequences of a conflict and its outcome for each party, for their relations with each other, and for the system of which they are a part.

The first matter that confronts us in this chapter is how to decide that a conflict has ended. One consideration is how general or how specific to regard the conflict. In a sense, the divisions between social categories we have been using are permanent aspects of social life and objective conflicts between them never-ending. This discussion of termination is about specific fights. Even these, however, range broadly. The conflict between blacks and whites in America, for example, consists of innumerable struggles. They are in different social settings: neighborhoods, cities, states, or the nation; about various issues: school integration, housing, public accommodations, or jobs; and over different time periods: days, weeks, or years. There are no inherent boundaries to a conflict. The beginning and end of a conflict have arbitrary qualities. The next question is, who decides?

Terminating a conflict means that some people agree that it has ended. Either partisans or observers assert that it has ended. Partisan definitions of conflict termination may be explicit or implicit and may be asserted by only one side or agreed upon by both. There is usually a symbolically important event or an explicit agreement in order for both sides to agree that a conflict has ended (Coser, 1961). For example, the Constitution may be amended (as with women's suffrage), or an agreement between the adversaries may be signed (as in a labor-management agreement), or a capital city may be seized by rebels or by a foreign invader. Lacking such events, or simply not accepting their significance, one side may refuse to agree that the struggle has ended. Obviously this is generally the "defeated" side. Its continuance, or renewal of conflict behavior, generally forces the other side to do so also.

Explicitness and mutuality of agreement are not always associated with each other. A conflict may wither away and by mutual indifference be implicitly ended. On the other hand, even an explicit agreement between two adversaries terminating a dispute may be regarded by one side as an act committed under duress and not binding or segments of one side may not accept what their spokesman has done in their name and they therefore do not regard the struggle as ended.

Observers or analysts of social conflicts should take such partisan acts, definitions, and assertions into account in making their own decision about when a conflict has terminated. Nevertheless, a student of social conflict must choose criteria to define a conflict as terminated. When there are clear partisan definitions, it is useful and sensible to use them. Even when there are not, partisan cues may be significant. Thus we have seen how goals change in the course of a dispute. When the goals have changed very greatly, it may be useful to consider that a conflict has ended and a new one begun. For example, the emergence of significant groups with black separatist goals in the U.S. helps mark an end to the previous civil rights struggle.

Sometimes students of social conflict use arbitrary time periods to demarcate beginnings and endings. For example, we talk about the 1930s, the 1950s, or the 1960s as being periods of particular social conflicts, being guided by numerical conventions. Fixed time periods are also used because of the availability of data which aid assessment of changes induced by conflict behavior. This may seem utterly arbitrary, but most general struggles are continuous and demarcations must be somewhat arbitrary. Yet boundaries are needed in order to assess conflict outcomes.

History does not end. But that does not, and should not, stop us from writing histories. We must accept the often arbitrary demarcations of conflict terminations, but we should be explicit about the criteria used to mark the end of a conflict.

POSSIBLE OUTCOMES

Four basic types of outcomes can be distinguished: withdrawal, imposition by one side, compromise, and conversion. Any particular outcome may be a mixture of two or more types, but it will prove useful to first consider them separately.

Withdrawal. One side often initiates a fight by making demands and beginning to pursue its goals. A possible outcome is that the initiator simply withdraws its demands and the situation returns to the *status quo ante.* Of course, the situation cannot return to the identical one prior to the attempt to alter it. The attempt has effects upon each participant and their relationship. But the matter in contention may not be substantially altered. For example, university students may make demands and demonstrate in support of them. After a short time, with no progress toward the satisfaction of the demands, the attempt to attain them dissipates. For example, too, the status of West Berlin has been threatened several times only to return to the uneasy situation that prevailed before the threat.

A very different kind of withdrawal is also possible—the conflict parties break off relations with each other. This may occur when one party flees and ceases all or nearly all direct relations with its adversary. Religious groups fleeing persecution and moving to another country illustrate this outcome, viz., the Mennonites (Siegel, 1969). Even within a country, some people may engage in an "inner withdrawal." Thus, political dissidents, unable to make progress toward their goals and facing repression from overwhelming force, may become totally alienated from the regimes and express their dissent privately.

Imposition. Presumably the outcome each side desires is to impose its aims upon the other side. One side wins, the other loses. There is a victory and a defeat. Such outcomes occur but they are never pure. Some elements of compromise nearly always enter into an outcome. Even the unconditional surrender demands of the Allies against Japan in World War II were tempered at the very end by agreeing to allow the Emperor of Japan to retain his throne.

There is a more fundamental difficulty in assessing the degree to which a given outcome represents a victory for one side and a defeat for the other. Victory and defeat have meaning only relative to the goals both sides had. But goals change in the course of a conflict. They expand with gains and contrast with losses. Both sides may claim victories in terms of what they "really" wanted. Victory and defeat are participant terms; they are misleading as analytic terms. We shall consider outcomes in terms of the original aims of each participant. But even this is ambiguous since aims are often amorphous, gradually take specific shape and are not shared equally by all segments of a conflict group. This indicates an additional difficulty. The leadership or spokesmen for one side may change and with that change new goals may be asserted. For our present purposes this would mark the end of one conflict and the beginning of a new one. For example, when the Bolsheviks seized power in Russia, that marked the end of one fight between Germany and Russia and the beginning of a different one. Again, any resolution of all these difficulties has an arbitrary quality. What is important is to be explicit about the meaning of the terms and to use concepts which are most useful for the widest range of cases.

Often both sides agree about the signs of victory and defeat and that makes it easier to assess the outcome in terms of the adversaries' goals. This is most clearly the case when the issue is narrowly and dichotomously defined. For example, as in a strike for union recognition.

Compromise. Nearly all outcomes have some component of compromise. Compromise may refer to mutual concessions explicitly made by adversaries to terminate a conflict. It may also refer to an outcome which an analyst judges to be a mutual accommodation. In any case, neither party obtains all that it wants. Such compromises are even more ambiguous than ones explicitly made and recognized by partisans. Pervasive as compromise may be in outcomes, delimiting its terms in a specific termination is difficult. The matter is further complicated by the emergence of new demands and conflicts as previous ones lose salience.

It will be helpful to distinguish the major types of compromise. The most obvious kind is one in which the gap between the adversaries is bridged by splitting the difference. The parties each give something; in monetary bargaining the simple fifty-fifty split has salience and is likely to seem fair (Schelling, 1960). The other major kind of compromise is log-rolling. Each party gives something to the other side and receives some things which it wants in return. In other words, there is a trade-off in which each side forgoes something it wants and yet attains some of what it seeks.

Conversion. Finally, one side may come to agree with other side about what it seeks. It may be persuaded that their dissensual disagreement was in error. It is converted to the other side's faith. Or the consensual conflict is terminated as one side comes to agree that indeed what they both want ought properly belong to the other side. Conversion may also take the form of one or both sides acquiring values or beliefs which supersede the contentious goals. Thus both sides may come to devalue the ends sought and believe that other values which they now hold, and which are not in conflict, are more important. For example, after an extended struggle about religious differences, conflict parties may develop a norm of religious tolerance. In effect, both sides agree to disagree. They may even come to feel that pluralism is a desirable state. In industrial relations the expansion of fringe benefits instead of wage increases in another example.

It should be clear that conversion is often a part of compromise outcomes and even ones which are predominately imposition or withdrawal. For some contentious issues, conflict termination short of destroying one side requires some conversion, at least to the right of the other side to disagree. Conversion, of course, varies in degree and especially in its extent within each conflict party. The different modes of pursuing conflict all have some effect upon the convictions of each side. Persuasion is not the only way to bring about conversion. In the course of a struggle the contending parties perceive, if only dimly, the reality of what is happening. The resistance of an adversary, how members of the other side talk and work with each other, or the way they present themselves to third parties, all convey important information.

TERMINATION PROCESSES

The outcome of a specific conflict may be reached through a variety of courses. *How* the outcome is reached helps form it. In order to understand the ending of a conflict and its outcome we must consider the processes, implicit and explicit, which bring them about. As already indicated, a dispute may be implicitly terminated by participants or by observers. The course by which observers decide that a conflict has been terminated, when this is not recognized by the partisans, is of little interest here. For purposes of analysis, observers must sometimes call a conflict terminated and examine what the outcome is at that time. The considerations they use in deciding about terminations are relevant to the interpretation of findings regarding conflicts but do not tell us anything about the termination processes.

Participants themselves may implicitly terminate a struggle. Basically, what occurs is continuing de-escalation of conflict behavior. At a low enough level both sides may acknowledge that the status quo is the outcome of the conflict. Or one side may claim that the outcome has been attained and if the other side does not actively try to alter it, an implicit outcome has been reached. Even if the two sides do not interpret the situation in the same way, if they have ceased trying to change it or to alter the other side's views of it, then an implicit outcome has been reached. An implicit outcome, finally, may be reached without open acknowledgement from either side. The two sides simply cease conflict behavior in pursuit of their contrary goals.

Some kinds of outcomes can be attained by implicit acknowledgement and indeed may be more likely to be attained implicitly than explicitly. Thus a withdrawal to the *status quo ante* can be done more easily if not openly admitted. The contentious demand is simply dropped. The adversary, too, may facilitate this by allowing whatever face-saving is accomplished by silence. Conversion is also more likely to be attained implicitly than explicitly. If one side has changed its mind under the efforts of the other side, it may deny this to itself or in any case no open announcement is needed. The same is true for mutual conversions when a new shared value or norm which covers the previous conflict arises.

Implicit withdrawals to the *status quo ante* are most likely when one side seeks to attain a goal which is strongly countered by the adversary without fundamental escalation. That is, the adversary firmly and with enough power refuses to yield and its counter pressure and demands are contingent only upon the withdrawal of the initial conflicting goal. Implicit withdrawal is also possible if, after a conflicting behavior has been pursued, the conflict party seeking a change is so overwhelmed that it dissolves as an effective conflict group. Thus, revolutionary movements have spawned parties and groups who may even have mustered armed units and waged guerrilla warfare only, finally, to be dissolved. For example, the Hukbalahap movement in the Philippines was defeated by social-political reforms, in part conducted by the army. The secretary of defense, Ramon Magsaysay so effectively pursued a course of pressure and opportunities for the peasantry that the Hukbalahap movement began to split up and the leader himself surrendered to work with the government (Gross, 1966, pp. 162–86; Starner, 1961).

Conflict outcomes are often preceded by explicit negotiations. The negotiations are explicit insofar as the parties communicate symbolically with each other in seeking an agreement about an outcome which will be mutually accepted. Explicit negotiations may also, however, ratify an implicitly achieved outcome, even an imposed one. In the course of negotiations, some conversion is likely to occur; but the basic form of outcome is compromise *if an agreement is reached*. All negotiations need not and do not end in agreement. Coercive efforts to attain conflicting goals may be continued, renewed, initiated, or escalated if no agreement is reached. In such cases, negotiations are an episode in the course of a struggle. We now must consider what about the negotiating process itself increases the chances of reaching an agreement and the relative gains of each side in the agreed-upon outcome (Sawyer and Guetzkow, 1965).

Relative Gains.   First let us consider the factors in negotiation which affect the parties' positions in the agreed-upon outcome. This discussion will concentrate on consensual conflicts. The emphasis, then, is upon parties wanting more, or no less, of the same goal. As we have observed, no aim is unidimensional; hence there are almost certainly differing priorities regarding aspects of what might appear to be a single goal; consequently, trading is possible. Nevertheless, for the sake of simplicity, we will sometimes discuss negotiating as if there were a single dimension in dispute.

As Schelling (1960, pp. 21–52) has pointed out, although it might seem that the stronger and more skillful must win in negotiation, this is not necessarily so unless strength and skill are retroactively attributed to the winner. Power and many other factors are certainly important in producing the situation within which the parties are negotiating. They are also relevant to making an agreement, any agreement, desirable. But under certain conditions, weakness and even stupidity can help a party in the negotiating process. If an agreement is to be reached, one side must concede and the other side accept the concession. To induce the other side to accept, a negotiating party must convince the other side that it will not alter its position, that *it* will make no further concessions. If the other side is convinced, it believes that it must accept the terms or no agreement will be reached. A negotiating party which seems to be too ignorant or irresponsible to worry about longer-run interests may thus have a bargaining advantage over the party which considers longer-run interests and is responsive to the other side. Small groups of blacks and of students have sometimes adopted this tactic.

There are many ways in which negotiating parties try to commit themselves so that they induce the other side to believe it must accept these terms or fail to reach any agreement. One of the major techniques is by a public announcement which binds the party's reputation to a particular stand. Loudly proclaimed "nonnegotiable" demands are one form this may take. Such public announcements may be discounted by the other side; to what extent, depends upon the conventional understandings about such pronouncements. When both sides have taken fixed positions in public, reaching an agreement is made more difficult; but it is in each side's interest to stake out its position first. This way of making commitments is possible insofar as one side recognizes that the other negotiating party has a reputation to maintain with its constituency or third parties.

A negotiating party may also assume an unalterable position by entering the negotiations with binding instructions. The negotiating party then forces the other side to either accept the proferred terms or risk breaking up the negotiations without an agreement. In negotiations between the Soviet Union and the United States, Soviet intransigence was often attributed to the inability of the negotiators to deviate from strict instructions (Dennett and Johnson, 1951). Mosley (1951, p. 288) reports how he used the same technique in negotiating with the Russians in 1944 about the armistice terms for Bulgaria. The issue pertained to the payment of reparations; the U.S.S.R. opposed this in the case of Bulgaria. Mosley reports that he informally explained to the Soviet representatives that if this was not included a review by Congress might lead to an investigation and that he might be punished. The next day the Russians agreed to the inclusion of the disputed provision.

Related to assuming unalterable positions, the initial bargaining position can affect the relative gains or losses in the final outcome. If a negotiating party asks initially for much more than it would minimally accept, it will generally do better than if the initial demands are modest (Siegel and Fouraker, 1960). There is the risk that the opening bids be so unrealistically high that no agreement is reached (Bartos, 1970). Assuming that negotiations continue, there are a few reasons why high demands are advantageous. Suppose there are two parties, A and B and their minimal positions are Am and Bm, as shown in Figure 6.1. An agreement would be possible anywhere between Am and Bm. Now suppose A opens the negotiations by asking for Ai. B is likely to believe that A's minimal position is Apb and therefore agreement is possible only very close to its own minimal position, Bm. That is, B makes some judgment about what A will finally accept on the basis of A's initial demands. Furthermore, if there is pressure to reach an agreement, the more A has asked, the longer it would take to bargain it down to an acceptable position and therefore the more likely is B to settle for an agreement closer to Bm than Am (Cross, 1969). Furthermore, "splitting the difference" seems naturally fair and equitable and this gives an advantage to the side which makes a large opening bid. This brings us to another factor.

How far and in what way each side makes concessions also depends on possible "focal" points (Schelling, 1960). That is, some positions seem like natural stopping points or dividing lines and negotiating parties

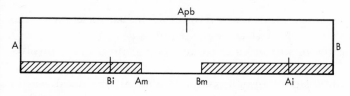

FIGURE 6.1

may move toward such positions as "natural," even if they might favor one side over the other. In international negotiations, natural borders such as rivers and mountains are examples of this. In many bargaining situations, a fifty-fifty division or "splitting the difference" seems like a naturally fair and equitable position. Therefore, it is a focal point, which is why, as we have noted, the side which initially makes a high demand has an advantage.

The cohesion of one or both adversaries also affects the terms offered for settlement and hence the outcome. If one side lacks cohesion, reaching a compromise is difficult; the outcome is more likely to be a victory or a defeat than if both sides are unified. In World War II, the anti-Fascist alliance held out for the unconditional surrender of the Axis partly in order to avoid allied recriminations about a separate peace or allied dissension regarding peace terms. In the more recent case of the Arab governments and Arab Palestinian organizations, disunity among them has contributed to their insistence upon total Israeli defeat; they could all agree upon that as desirable. Of course, the disarray that makes that an end also makes it difficult to achieve. It also makes it difficult to agree to any termination of the conflict.

Finally, the outcome may be more favorable to one side rather than another because one side may be able to use common values or standards to support its position more readily than can another. This is obviously true of dissensual conflicts where persuasion is particularly important. But even in consensual conflicts, the closeness of one side's goals to a shared value is helpful in negotiation. Presumably the aim of integration and equality between blacks and whites could be pursued in each specific case by calls to the basic American standards of equality (Myrdal, 1944). In conflicts between superordinates and subordinates, the subordinates often find that those in authority are armed with values and standards which support the basic relationship of the parties. Thus, in many disputes those with authority or who have had power longer are likely to find legal justifications for their positions while the protestors argue in terms of general moral precepts or in terms of raw power. For example the dominance of whites, of males, of colonial powers, or of university administrators is embedded in law and regulations. Consequently people who are dominated are likely to argue in terms of fundamental human rights.

Reaching Agreement. Now we turn to consider what variations in the negotiating process affect the chances of reaching any settlement. We will consider the degree of institutionalization, timing, third party involvement, and secrecy.

INSTITUTIONALIZATION. Insofar as the conflict is conducted within institutionalized procedures, the termination of a specific conflict will be explicit. One of the ways in which institutionalization significantly affects outcomes is by specifying who is involved in terminating a dispute. In highly institutionalized conflict relations with highly organized conflict parties there usually are special roles for interacting with the adversary. The occupants of those roles are the ones who usually engage in the direct negotiations to terminate a conflict. Sometimes the roles legitimate a wide latitude in the negotiation of an outcome. The existence of such roles increases the likelihood that a termination is explicitly reached.

In relatively undifferentiated conflict parties or in broad social movements there may be no clear role for negotiating with an adversary. Self-appointed or adversary-appointed spokesmen may try to negotiate a settlement, but such settlements may not bind the conflict parties. The actual outcome may be implicit rather than explicit. Sometimes conflict parties try to avoid any designation of leaders or spokesmen. In this way the rank and file believe they can participate more fully in the negotiations. This sometimes has occurred in student insurrections. In other cases there may not be enough organization to even refuse to designate leaders, viz. riots. In such circumstances the adversary may proffer some terms and these may be implicitly accepted.

Each side would like to choose the representative of the other side for negotiation. Indeed, sometimes the designation of the negotiating representative by a conflict party is contested by the other side. Even in institutionalized conflict relations and with highly organized conflict parties, one side may refuse to negotiate with a particular person from the other side. This has occurred in collective bargaining between trade unions and management and between governments.

Institutionalization may also give legitimacy to third party intervention in the form of mediation. Insofar as the partisans feel that the mediator is legitimate and they have in effect selected the mediator, his suggestions will be more readily accepted and therefore the chances of reaching an agreement will be enhanced.

Generally, insofar as the negotiations are institutionalized, the parties will have better information about each other and the meaning of each other's assertions and demands. Consequently, promises of future actions are more likely to be correctly understood by the other side. Similarly, the proper amount of discounting of the other side's demands are more likely to be made. Therefore the negotiations are more likely to be successfully concluded in agreement.

TIMING. Negotiations to explicitly terminate a conflict may occur at a wide range of times in the course of a struggle. At one extreme, negotiations may simply formalize what has already happened; they recognize an implicit outcome. At the other extreme, it is within the context of a

negotiating process that an outcome is arrived at with little conflict behavior prior to or aside from those efforts. In that case, both sides' coercive forces may be assessed and threatened and possible rewards in exchange for concessions tentatively proffered, but they may not actually
be exercised until a termination has been reached. Meanwhile, however,
persuasive efforts may be conducted vigorously. Negotiations at such an
early stage in the course of a struggle are typical in institutionalized conflicts.

Efforts to work out an explicit mutual recognition of a conflict termination may be unsuccessful. That is, parties try to reach a joint recognition of what the outcome of a struggle is, but they cannot. In that case,
the direct efforts may be ended and the conflict behavior continue, be
renewed, or escalated. Then, new efforts at reaching an explicit agreement may be made or an implicit ending finally occurs. The failure of
direct efforts may not be followed by any new conflict behavior. An implicit termination may be possible. Both parties may be willing at least
for a time to accept a given situation, if they do not have to openly admit
that they recognize and therefore acknowledge it.

Efforts to reach an explicit termination are often initiated after conflict behavior has been initiated and prior to a large anticipated escalation. Such negotiations are conducted with a threat hanging over the
negotiators and sometimes with tremendous time pressures. The sense
of tension has been recounted in reports of the Cuban missile crisis
negotiations. The mobilization of coercive forces takes on a dynamic of
its own; it cannot be sustained for long without being let loose. All this
burdens negotiators at the same time that the pressure for some kind of
agreement may be high. At such times there is the spectacle of round-the-
clock negotiations before a strike deadline or before the expiration of a
military ultimatum.

Lacking well developed conflict regulation, direct efforts to negotiate
a settlement without considerable agreement about what a mutually acceptable settlement would be are likely to fail. Insofar as conflict regulation is not institutionalized, the parties must be close to an implicit
termination in order to have an explicit one successfully achieved.

THIRD PARTY INVOLVEMENT.   At many points in this book we have
noted the possible roles third parties play in the course of a conflict.
They can play a crucial role in its termination too (Jackson, 1952). The
way they regard a situation can help determine whether or not an implicit termination becomes explicit. What is most interesting to us here,
however, are the variety of ways in which third parties can play a role
in formulating an explicit termination. Several possible roles of third
parties can usefully be distinguished. First, is the neutral go-between. A

third party serves as a messenger between adversaries who could not otherwise communicate with each other. Such indirect talks are useful when hostility is very high if an explicit accommodation is to be reached. This procedure was utilized, for example, when Ambassador Jarring, representing the United Nations, conveyed messages between Israel and Egypt.

The transmission of messages may be accompanied by interpretation and explanation. In a sense this involves conciliation. The third party may help penetrate emotional barriers of fear and hate which might otherwise perpetuate the conflict behavior. A mediator may be able to transmit meanings with less distortion than either party and thereby clear up misunderstandings. (Sometimes, of course, this can aggravate a conflict.)

Perhaps it is impossible, however, for any third party to be merely a transmitter of messages. Even such assistance betrays attention to the situation and also indicates that the status quo is not satisfactory. In this minimal sense, a third party introduces an additional element. Usually third parties assume a more active role and the potentiality of even more involvement affects the context within which the adversaries operate. During indirect negotiations the mediator may introduce the possibility of a compromise by reducing each side's asserted demand. For example, in a labor management dispute the union representative may tell the mediator that the workers will stay out until the fired worker, Joe Doakes, is rehired. The mediator conveys the message to the management representative that the union insists that "something be done" for Joe Doakes before they go back to work. In conducting direct negotiations, third parties may suggest possible formulations which neither side would have offered alone, viz., the compromise suggested by Collins to King and Lingo in Selma, Alabàma (Hinckle and Welsh, 1969), discussed in the preceding chapter.

A third party may be able to help bring about a termination by increasing the salience of a possible outcome. By suggesting a possible compromise, for example, he helps make it a focal point. The contending parties may then regard that outcome as having a particularly compelling quality. As Cross (1969, pp. 92–97) also points out, if either party offers a terminating compromise, the other side is likely to regard it as a negotiating bid and try to bargain further. Only a third party can present a compromise that both sides can regard as nonnegotiable.

A third party, then, introduces some new elements into the situation and this restructures the context within which the contending parties try to reach a settlement. The new context may affect the way each party sees its own and the other side's goals. Furthermore, with the active involvement of third party intermediaries, each side may alter its mode of pursuing its goal. The persuasive component often increases and even positive rewards are more likely to be proffered.

Finally, a third party may intervene more forcefully. In highly institutionalized relations, a third party may impose an outcome in the form of arbitration. In that case, the contending parties may agree, usually in advance, that a conflict which they cannot terminate themselves in direct negotiations will be settled by arbitration (Kellor, 1948). The third party then investigates and makes a recommendation which is binding upon the contending parties.

Even if the conflict relations are not highly regulated and institutionalized, insofar as the third party has overwhelming force, it may be able to impose a settlement against one or both parties. Less extremely, third party intervention can radically alter the balance of forces and hasten a termination. The third party may aid one of the contending parties or intimate that it will; if this is not countervailed by another party's aid to the other side, the side with third party support is likely to get more of what it seeks than does its adversary. The possible roles of third parties and the consequences for outcomes are many; we will consider their consequences for outcomes later in this chapter.

SECRECY.   Explicit agreements about the termination of a conflict may be reached more or less openly. It is possible for only a few spokesmen for each side to negotiate an agreement. Their constituencies may be kept in ignorance of the negotiations and even of the terms. It was against such practices that President Wilson raised the banner of open covenants openly arrived at. At the other extreme, the entire negotiating process is conducted in public with widespread participation of the constituencies of both sides. In between are various degrees of openness and secrecy. The circles involved in the negotiations vary in size and representativeness; the constituencies are more or less informed about the negotiations; and the constituencies have varying opportunities to ratify the agreements.

Secrecy in many ways makes it possible to reach agreements about terminations which openness would preclude. Particularly noteworthy is the flexibility in considering alternative outcomes which secrecy permits. Often, in the heat of battle, the constituencies have been mobilized to the point that concessions would seem traitorous. Or discussion of compromise seems to be an admission of weakness which if acknowledged would hasten the collapse of will to persevere in the struggle. Spokesmen for each side can conduct negotiations until a package of mutual concessions is constructed and present it as an entity which is acceptable to the opposing side. This may be accepted by the rank and file, while they would have refused support if the plan had been suggested only in part and only as a possibility for bargaining. Furthermore, negotiators with many items in dispute, often settle one at a time but regard none as completely and finally settled until all are agreed upon.

The secrecy of negotiations, nevertheless, leaves the leaders open to the suspicion of betrayal. In the extreme form of secrecy, when even the terms are not made public, their implementation is difficult indeed, unless the terms simply reflect an implicit accommodation. Consider the alleged agreement between the student leaders and the administrators of Columbia University in the 1968 rebellion (Rader and Anderson, 1969). President Kirk agreed not to build the gymnasium planned for Harlem's Morningside Park, to sever university ties with the Institute for Defense Analysis, to resign within a year for reasons of health, and, although refusing a general amnesty, he promised only reprimands. The student Steering Committee agreed not to seize additional buildings and, if a police raid became necessary, not to resist it. In this arrangement the Steering Committee would have held out to the bitter end for amnesty and the administration would not have yielded openly on this fundamental issue although agreeing on other issues. When the police made their raid, however, they used extreme violence on all the white-held buildings. This led to the closing down of classes and widespread support for the rebellious students. A termination was not reached; the conflict had escalated. The police were not party to any agreements. The agreement was not valid after the escalation; a new implicit accommodation had to be reached.

ASPECTS OF CONFLICT AFFECTING OUTCOME

The outcome of a conflict also depends upon many aspects of the conflict process prior to and underlying the termination processes. We shall consider particularly the goals of the contending parties, the way they pursue their aims, their relative power, and the role of third parties. We will consider how these attributes help determine what the conflict's outcome is. But the outcome is not determined by the struggle alone. Many other events are transpiring often quite independent of the efforts of the contending parties and their leaders. These other events and developments may largely determine the outcome. This possibility will be considered in the next section of this chapter.

Goals. The nature and the magnitude of the goals in contention very significantly affect a conflict's outcome. The relationship, however, is not a simple one. Thus, it is not true that the more a conflict party seeks, the more it gets of what it wants.

NATURE OF THE GOALS. In general, when the conflicting goals are consensual, the outcomes tend to be impositions by one side, compromise, or withdrawal to the *status quo ante*. When the aims constitute a dissensual conflict, the outcome tends to be either withdrawal in the sense of breaking relations or conversion. Conversion may take the form of tolerance of the differences rather than one side accepting the abhorrent views of its erstwhile adversary. For example, consider universities where students have won rights to have liquor and visitors in the dormitories. The increased freedom of university students in their living arrangements in part represents an outcome in which administrators are more tolerant of the variations in the way students may live. To some extent they have been converted to believe that students should have considerable control over their own lives.

Goals also differ in regard to the collective or aggregate nature of the benefits sought. When the aim is a collective one, when the members of the conflict party as an entity seek a particular benefit, the outcome is likely to be either imposition or withdrawal, but conversion and compromise are also possible. When the goals pertain more to the aggregate of individuals, compromise is likely, conversion in the form of tolerance, and withdrawal in the sense of returning to the *status quo ante*. Furthermore, aggregate goals are generally more readily attained than collective ones. The adversary need not as openly acknowledge what has happened and need not make as comprehensive concessions. For example, an improvement in opportunities for many blacks in the U.S. may be attained without immediately improving the collective status of blacks.

A more specific variation in goals is the degree to which what is sought is autonomy or domination, that is freedom from or control over the other side. In general, autonomy is easier to attain than control over others. This partly follows from two aspects of the relativity of power First, the effectiveness of power diminishes the more extended it is (Boulding, 1962, pp. 58–79). Second, the willingness to expend resources in exercising power and absorbing the pressure from the other side decreases as the goal diminishes in centrality. A group wishing to be free from control by an adversary generally would be exercising power closer to itself than to the other side. Seeking autonomy also generally means defending something which is more important to its seekers than is control by the other side to its opponent. This is the source of advantage that smaller countries have relative to powerful but distant adversaries. Even within a society, a group, particularly if it is relatively weak, has a better chance of attaining some autonomy than in gaining dominance over an adversary. Workers in a factory may gain some control over their own work activities through trade union power; effective worker control over the factory as an entity is more difficult.

MAGNITUDE OF THE GOALS. The last observations suggest that the very magnitude of the aims affect the chances of attaining them—the more a conflict party seeks to get, the more likely is it to fail to get it. The more it seeks, the more opposition it arouses from the other side. This line of reasoning can easily be reduced to absurdity: if you don't ask anything from the other side, the other side will give you what you ask for—nothing. The relationship between how much is sought and how much is actually gained, then, must be a little more complex.

One matter of importance is that the magnitude of an aim is largely defined by the response of the other side. Thus, some issues may be regarded as terribly significant—they take on symbolic importance, representing many other issues. For example, the termination of conflicts within organizations may be prolonged when the dissident faction demands amnesty for its protest actions. For those in authority granting amnesty seems like an abdication of their authority. The insistence upon punishing the leaders of a rebellion may be the basis for a new grievance and the continuation of the conflict behavior and even its escalation, as in the Columbia rebellion of 1968 (Cox Commission, 1968, pp. 182–83). On the other hand, the claim for amnesty may be insisted upon as an admission of error by the other side. As a leader of the Columbia students, Mark Rudd said, "We demanded an amnesty to all who participated in the demonstration. This would have forced the administration of Columbia to say we were right" (Rudd, 1968, p. 321).

When an issue takes on such symbolic significance, its final resolution does signal much about the outcome. Weighted with significance, the way it falls means victory for one side and defeat for the other. The point is, this need not be the case. An issue may not be regarded as important and then compromises are more likely and a certain amount of conversion may also occur. Even as crucial an issue as amnesty may be so treated. On the one hand, the authorities may regard the demonstrations, even if illegal activity was included, as simple protest and illegal action as resulting from contagion and collective behavior for which no individuals could be held responsible. On the other hand, the demonstrators may regard punishments as appropriate and their willingness to endure them as a further form of demonstrating the strength of their convictions. (Although a termination of the conflict usually includes ending the leaders' punishment.)

The magnitude of the issue in contention is not entirely a subjective matter, merely dependent upon the perspectives of the partisans. In general, goals which pertain to changing the rules under which conflicts are pursued are of greater magnitude than ones which seek to modify apportionments within the previous understandings. Thus, in labor-management relations a conflict over wages is more limited and of lesser magnitude than is one about union recognition or worker control of investment and marketing policies. In order to bring about changes of large magnitude, as in changing the rules governing the relationship, third party involvement in assistance to the conflict party seeking such changes is necessary. This is true in industrial relations when fundamental changes in labor-management regulations were made with the aid of the government; viz., the New Deal in the U.S., the introduction of codetermination in Germany (Kerr, 1954; McPherson, 1951; Potthoff, 1955), and of worker councils in Yugoslavia (Ward, 1957; Meier, 1956).

Closely related to the magnitude of conflict goals, as indicated by changing the rules rather than allotments within the rules, is the degree to which the basic relations between the contending parties is to be altered. In some struggles a conflict party may be seeking a fundamental restructuring of the relationship or a small modification. Since the structure of the relationship is part of a larger social system, any major restructuring also depends on the involvement of third parties. Basic changes in the relations between students and administrators, between the American and Soviet governments, or between white American segregationists and black American integrationists have depended in part upon the positions taken by third parties.

A different dimension of magnitude pertains to either the alteration or removal of personnel in the other side. That is, a conflict party may seek to make the other side more attentive and responsive or it may seek to displace and replace them. The "other side" may refer to an entire social unit or to its spokesmen. In the event that the other side is an entire unit, its removal means either genocide or withdrawal in the form of secession of relations. A genocidal outcome requires extraordinary power differences and intensity of feelings. A secession outcome requires the ability to move or sufficient indifference from the other side to accept the termination of relations. Such outcomes are rare in social conflicts. The displacement of the other side usually refers to a leadership segment of the opposing unit, not to the entire social unit which the leaders purport to represent. In that case the outcome may entail a simple exchange of incumbents and no alteration even in the basic relations between the conflict parties. That is, the ins may change places with the outs and not alter the meaning of being in and out. The success in such exchanges depends upon the rules by which the turnover is accomplished and the relative capacities and skills of each side according to those rules.

At the other end of this dimension, a conflict party may seek more attentiveness and responsiveness to its claims; this is generally more easily attained than the removal of the opposition. Gaining more responsiveness means an outcome which includes compromises or conversions. Withdrawal, in the sense that the conflict party drops its demands for change and returns to the *status quo ante*, is of course another possible outcome. Responsiveness, entailing as it does conversion or compromise, is appropriately sought by persuasion or reward, offering the other side something which it wants in addition to coercion. Poor capacities in these ways obviously lessen the chances of success. The application of inappropriate ways of pursuing the goals also lessens the chance of success. We must consider the ways used in pursuit of conflicting goals and the relative capacities in their application in order to account for the successful or unsuccessful attainment of the sought-for ends.

Modes. At several places in this book, we have pointed out the appropriateness of various means for different ends. We expect that one mode is more likely to achieve a given outcome than is another way. Thus, for conversion, persuasion seems appropriate; for imposition, coercion is necessary; for compromise, coercion combined with reward seems effective; and for withdrawal, coercion is usually necessary. But in any concrete conflict the goals are manifold and the ways used in pursuit of them mixed. Consequently a conflict party is unlikely to be able to pursue a comprehensive goal without doing some things which are inappropriate to some aspect of the sought-for end. This would be true even if the conflict party had all the resources for each mode and could select them only in terms of the likely effects upon the adversary, leaving aside its own predilections. This is one reason why outcomes are never what either side in a struggle anticipates at the outset.

To illustrate, in the late 1960s, university student demonstrations and nonviolent coercive actions were conducted to end military recruitment on campuses. The persuasive elements in the protests were often attended to, as well as the coercive. The outcome was often a compromise in the form of ending special privileges to military recruiters; they would have to share the same relatively inconspicuous locations as private recruiters using the student placement centers (Morgan, 1970). The ghetto riots of the 1960s while bringing some governmental attention to the plight and dissatisfactions of American blacks, probably did not increase the general social status of blacks as a category in the U.S. Thus for several decades a growing proportion of whites in America acknowledged that Negroes had as much native intelligence as whites (Schwartz, 1967; Sheatsley, 1966). But this movement showed some signs of possible disruption in the 1960s. In a series of surveys conducted in 1963, 1966, and 1967, whites were asked if they tended to agree or disagree with a variety of statements about Negroes. The proportion agreeing with derogatory statements about Negroes decreased slightly from 1963 to 1966 but then increased to above the 1963 level in 1967 (Erskine, 1967–1968, p. 666). See Table 6.1.

Aside from the appropriateness of the mode used in terms of the effect

TABLE 6.1 Proportion of American Whites Agreeing with Various Statements about American Negroes, 1963, 1966, 1967

Statement about Negroes compared to whites	1963	1966	1967
Negroes have less native intelligence	39	36	47
Negroes have less ambition	66	65	70
Negroes have looser morals	55	50	58

Source: Louis Harris and Associates national surveys as reported in Erskine, 1967–1968, p. 666.

upon the other side, conflict parties differ in the resources they have available for a given mode. Out of anger or desperation, conflict parties may resort to more coercive modes than they can sustain against a stronger adversary. This is the reason that so often violent uprisings against authorities result in many deaths among those conducting the uprisings and the demands are effectively withdrawn. Those in authority, in civil strife, are generally much more powerful and have much more access to violent and nonviolent means of coercion than are those who would rise against them domestically. Coercive action, even in the form of strikes, can be met with overwhelming force and set back the organizational efforts of the protesting groups. This has been the history of trade union efforts in the United States during the nineteenth century and even the beginning of the twentieth century (Taft and Ross, 1969). In this sense, violence is counterproductive—especially for the weaker party. In the longer run, however, the revelation of the other side's brutality and the creation of martyrs may help solidify the weaker party.

The escalation in the course of a social conflict may culminate in coercive means of such magnitude that third parties are outraged. The conflict party using coercion to finally triumph over the adversary may then find that third parties can effectively prevent it from attaining the desired outcome, although the adversary has been completely defeated in the struggle. Thus, in universities when police force was ultimately used to defeat student protest, very substantial concessions were made to the students. In universities at which as high magnitudes of coercion were not reached, the concessions often were less.

All other variables being equal, the more regulated the means of conflict employed, the more likely is the outcome to partake of some kind of compromise. Holsti (1966) analysed 77 major international conflicts between 1919 and 1939 and between 1945 and 1965. Using his categorizations of settlement attempts and outcomes it is possible to analyze the differences in outcomes associated with different settlement attempts. See Table 6.2. In 14 of the 77 conflicts there were no settlement attempts —the two sides battled it out; not surprisingly, the outcomes were con-

TABLE 6.2 Outcomes of International Conflicts, 1919–1965, by Settlement Attempts

Outcomes	Settlement Attempts		
	None	Bilateral only	Third party
Conquest, annexation	64	29	20
Forced submission, withdrawal, deterrence	36	36	14
Passive settlement	—	14	—
"Frozen" conflicts	—	—	6
Withdrawal-avoidance	—	7	14
Awards	—	—	23
Compromise	—	14	23
Totals percent	100	100	100
(N)	(14)	(14)	(49)

Source: Based upon data from Holsti, 1966.

quest or annexation (64 per cent of the conflicts) or forced submission, withdrawal, or deterrence (36 per cent of the conflicts). In the 14 conflicts in which there were only bilateral talks or effort at a settlement limited to the adversaries themselves, forced submission, withdrawal, or deterrence were particularly likely (36 per cent of the cases); conquest or annexation was another relatively frequent outcome (29 per cent of the cases); equally frequent were outcomes which entailed withdrawals, but relatively voluntary ones, passive settlements in which both sides begin to accept the new situation as legitimate or frozen ones in which both sides still had their incompatible goals, but did not pursue them. In 49 of the 77 conflicts there was third party intervention in the form of mediation, adjudication, involvement of international organizations, or multilateral conferences. In these cases, forced submission, withdrawal, or deterrence was relatively rare; conquest and annexation was also not very frequent. In 20 per cent there were voluntary withdrawals, passive understandings, or frozen outcomes. Compromise and awards were relatively common, 23 per cent each.

Power Differences. The major determinant of the outcome of a social conflict would seem to be the differences in power between the two parties. But several considerations limit the significance of this obviously important factor. First, in any concrete pursuit of conflicting goals, coercion is mixed with persuasion and rewards. Power differences are particularly relevant to coercion; in the case of persuasion and rewards, other resources determine their effectiveness. Thus, parties may differ in persuasive skills and this affects the outcome. Depending on the mode used in pursuing conflicting aims, such skills may help compensate for weaker power positions.

Second, power is always relative to the point of its application. Nearly all kinds of power dissipates as it is extended. A group defending itself against a distant antagonist need not have equal total forces to sustain itself against the antagonist. The nature of the forces, the intervening space, and the technologies involved all affect the rate at which power is dissipated. Guerrilla bands may be able to hold a small territory if the terrain is inhospitable to the adversary's superior forces (Gurr, 1970, pp. 262–63). In a small country which is covered by extensive means of ground transportation, a contemporary army can suppress dissident bands more readily than in an economically underdeveloped nation with rugged terrain; viz., the success of the Israeli armed forces against Arab Palestinian armed units trying to operate in Israeli-occupied Jordan.

Power is also relative to the issue in contention. This is true in a few senses. Power and coercion may be appropriate for some goals and not for others. Thus, if one side is seeking a conversion from the other side, power differences may be somewhat irrelevant. It should be obvious that love is not to be forced. Thus, a party usually says it is not seeking love, perhaps because that is unattainable by the methods it restricts itself to use.

Issues differ in significance to each side in a conflict. The more important a goal is to one side compared to the other, the more ready is it to absorb coercion from the other side and the more ready it is to expend its resources upon coercing the other side; this nullifies, to some extent, the other side's superior power. Very often the goal of autonomy is more vital to one side than is dominance of that side by the other. A group may be willing to make a proportionately greater sacrifice merely to sustain itself as a collective entity or to maintain some self-control over its members' lives than would another group to impose itself upon them. This is one reason why groups struggling for autonomy may be able to attain much of their goal even against what seems to be stronger forces.

This is related to the phenomena of the "strength of weakness" (Schelling, 1960, p. 22). A weak party may have few alternatives and this not only gives him the strength of desperation but has a compelling quality to his adversary when the terminating efforts are made. The stronger side may well recognize that the weaker has no retreat open to it and that makes its aims seem more invulnerable. A weaker party may ultimately defy the stronger to use its forces and inhibit it from doing so because of the unfairness of such conduct. This does presume normative constraints; but these may be held by the constituency of the stronger party's leaders and that constrains them even if the leaders' own norms were not constraining.

The significance of power differences in determining the outcome of a conflict, finally, is mitigated by the effectiveness with which each side organizes and applies its force. Herein lies the importance of strategy for applying coercion against a particular adversary. Herein, too, lies the importance of ideology in mobilizing one's own side and disorganizing the adversary. Analysts can develop measures of power difference which incorporate some indicators of effective application of force. Thus, Lammers (1969) studied strikes and mutinies; he rated the relative strength of the adversaries by assessing each side's degree of participation, degree of agreement among the leaders, and degree of clarity of strategy. He found that the greater the relative strength of the strikers the speedier and more completely did they attain their goals; the correlation was .51; for mutineers, the correlation was somewhat smaller, .43. Presumably in the case of mutinies other aspects of relative power were more important but unmeasured by the indicators used. This is suggested, too, by the relative significance of third party intervention, to be discussed later.

Despite these limitations and qualifications, power differences very significantly determine the outcome of conflicts. There is experimental evidence that the stronger party is more likely to win more bargaining sessions in relatively formal settings than in less formal ones (Morley and Stephenson, 1969). Presumably interpersonal factors can mitigate the full effects of having a stronger case.

In general we expect that the greater the power differences the more likely is the outcome to be (1) withdrawal in the sense that relations are terminated, or (2) domination, even to the point that the defeated party dissolves as an organized partisan. These may or may not be the sought-for goal of the stronger party. The totality of victory can alter the defeated in ways unforeseen by the victor. Thus, overwhelmingly powerful groups may so repress the defeated that they turn to religious or drug-aided ideologies which overtly are accommodative and passive but covertly hostile (Smelser, 1963, pp. 327ff). For example, Slotkin (1956) describes American Indian responses to the whites in the form of the peyote religion.

Extreme power differences almost invite domination and repression as an outcome once conflict behavior has escalated to intense forms. The victor may impose retributions and punishments which are not checked by the defeated and go beyond the presumed aims of the victor at the outset of the conflict.

Presumably, when the power differences are not extreme, the outcome is more likely to be in the form of compromise than of imposition. Conversion is also likely in the form of new common values and rules. The new norms tend to reflect the interests and concerns of both sides and they are shared. When the power differences are great, the imposed outcome may also yield conversions, but they are likely to be either one-sided or unshared. The defeated may come to accept the victor's values and norms or the defeated develop their own values and norms, not shared with the victor.

Jensen (1965) studied disarmament negotiations between the U.S. and

the U.S.S.R. between 1947 and 1960. He related the concessions and re-
tractions of concessions each side made to confidence in military capabilities and to popular confidence that war would be avoided. He concluded that concessions were most likely when there was slight lack of
confidence, when there was almost parity.

Third Parties. The fourth major set of factors which help determine
the outcome of a conflict is the active involvement of third parties.
Insofar as one side can garner support from previously uncommitted
groups, it has a better chance of gaining the outcome it seeks. The allies
increase its strength, persuasive resources, and capacity to reward the
other side. Before considering the ways in which third parties help determine the outcome of a conflict, we must acknowledge some of the
ambiguities about the distinction between active partisans and third
parties.

It must be recognized that the boundaries of partisan groups are not
sharp and the sides may disagree about where the boundaries are. Even
in international conflicts, ethnic or ideological ties may cross political
borders and be the basis of cleavage. Furthermore, the degree of involvement is multidimensional and infinitely graduated. The student of social
conflicts must decide about the boundaries for particular analytic purposes.

To illustrate, consider the many partisans in the conflicts pertaining
to Vietnam: the U.S. government, the North Vietnamese government,
the South Vietnamese government, the National Liberation Front, and
the U.S. "peace movement," to cite a few. In a sense the U.S. government
in the form of the Johnson Administration was "defeated." But who was
the adversary and who was the third party ally of the adversary? Did the
peace movement defeat the Johnson Administration with the assistance
of the North Vietnamese government and the National Liberation Front?
Or, did the peace movement aid the North Vietnamese government and
the National Liberation Front? This could well seem to be merely a
choice in perspective. A more substantive matter is raised by asking
whether the peace movement contributed at all to the defeat of the
Johnson Administration or actually helped sustain it by provoking counter movements to its demands. The defeat of the Johnson Administration, in that case, would be attributed to events in the international
sphere and particularly in South Vietnam, events which the spokesmen
in the peace movement accurately assessed but did not affect.

Such questions can hardly be answered in any particular conflict. I
raise them here to sensitize the reader to the complexities of the possible
role of third parties in a conflict. Rather than seek to assess the role of
different factors in determining a particular outcome, we wish to under-

stand the major processes and tendencies in terminating conflicts and shaping outcomes. We now turn to those more general tendencies.

The involvement of third parties as allies is necessary to attain certain kinds of outcomes. Leaving aside the relativity of power to the issue in contention, if power differences are great, the weaker can impose its aims or attain a compromise only if strong third parties become allies. For example, Lammers, (1969) in his study of strikes and mutinies, found that intervention was correlated with outcome; outcome was measured by the speed and degree to which the aided party, mutineers and strikers, attained their ends. In the case of mutinies, the correlation between intervention and realization of goals was high, .67; it was much lower in the case of strikes, .18. Without outside intervention, mutineers have little chance of winning. For most of the issues about which workers strike, outside intervention is not necessary for the union to attain its aims. But workers cannot attain goals of large magnitude, without third party alliances. Thus, the major shifts in worker-management relations, as occurred in general union recognition or worker participation in management, needed third party assistance. This was the case in the U.S. with the New Deal of the 1930s and with the Communist party in Yugoslavia in the establishment of worker control in Yugoslav factories after World War II.

The importance of third party intervention in determining the outcome of a conflict makes it desirable to understand what affects the choices of possible allies. Each adversary tries to win over third parties to its own side. Third parties make their choices in terms of their own assessments of their relations with both sides and their own preferences regarding possible outcomes with and without their intervention.

Answers to questions about the choices of allies can draw from the burgeoning theoretical and empirical studies of coalitions and alliances (Groennings, Kelley, and Leiserson, 1970; Riker, 1962; Friedman, Bladen, and Rosen, 1970). It is impossible to summarize here all the ideas and findings from these studies. We will select those which are particularly relevant to our present concerns. Coalition theory usually begins with parties who could form any possible coalition. In the present context, there are contending adversaries who are not potential coalition partners. Nevertheless, three major sets of considerations affect the parties' choices in forming coalitions at the beginning or at the end of a conflict: (1) the distribution of power resources among the contending parties and possible allies, (2) the preferences of each party for alternative outcomes, and (3) the particular ties between the parties and the context of the outcome.

A primary focus of attention in coalition theory and studies is the distribution of power among the parties. How much does each party have and how much is needed to win? Let us consider three parties, A, B, and C; suppose A is stronger than B and B is equal to C but B and C together are stronger than A. The theories of Caplow (1968) and Gamson (1961a and 1961b) both predict that BC would be the most likely coalition. Hence, if A and B were adversaries, C would join B; if A and C were adversaries, then B would join C; and if B and C were adversaries, it is indeterminate whether A would join B or C. The reasoning is as follows: weaker parties would ally themselves if they can win, because each will benefit more than each would if allied with a much stronger party. This makes the weaker party attractive as an ally, if his contribution is sufficient to help form a winning coalition. Experimental evidence is consistent with this reasoning (Chertkoff, 1970). Thus, a strong university administration and a weak faculty group makes a faculty-student alliance more likely than if the faculty were at least as strong as the administration. For example, the weakness of the faculty group at Columbia University contributed to the isolation of the administration and an outcome which lessened administration authority (Cox Commission, 1968).

The second set of considerations pertains to the substance of the issue in contention and the preferences of each party for possible outcomes. This may be conceptualized as the pay-offs in coalition theory wherein the winning coalition divides the spoils of victory. In that case we presume that the value of the spoils is the same for all parties. In simple consensual conflicts this may be true in regard to power or material benefits. But, in concrete actual conflicts, possible outcomes have different and changing values to the parties. For example, the women's suffrage movement was able to obtain more allies among males after World War I by arguing in terms of fairness and justice and pointing to the contribution women made to the war effort (Flexner, 1959). For those males who allied themselves in the cause, many supported women's right to vote at least partly because they believed it was right, and not merely expedient in terms of political power calculations. Or, consider support for increasing the right for legal abortions. Feminist groups have been urging the legalization of abortion. Although until the mid-1960s there was almost universal opposition to extending the grounds for legal abortions, support for such extensions was slightly greater among men than women, according to national surveys (Blake, 1971). Moreover, the segment of the population most likely to support legalized abortion are college-educated non-Catholic men. As Blake points out, upper-class men have little to lose and much to gain by easing legal restrictions against abortion. They are satisfied with small families, their sexual freedom is not curtailed, and they suffer no risks; on the other hand, women (and less advantaged persons generally) derive their greatest rewards from their families and therefore norms which seem to uphold the institution would be supported.

Thirdly, particular ties between each party and its possible allies and the general context of the conflict strongly affect which side a third party would tend to choose. All else being equal, a third party would tend to ally itself with the partisan group with which it is already most friendly or least hostile. This is analogous, then, to "balance theory" (Taylor, 1970, pp. 288–93). In specific conflicts this means that ideological commonalities, interpersonal friendships, general cooperative relations in other contexts, all may help determine or dictate alliances. For example, the various liberation groups of the 1960s tend to ally themselves together and constitute a movement.

The ties may be more indirect and closely related to the development of preferences which bring third parties closer to one or the other side in contention. Thus, Wences and Abramson (1970) found that University of Connecticut faculty members, by means of longer residence and common interests with the local community, tended to oppose the promotion of dissent and not oppose on-campus military recruiting, compared to newly arrived faculty. Presumably, newly arrived faculty, then, would tend to ally themselves with student dissidents more than would faculty with longer local residence.

The context within which the parties view the conflict also affects the coalitions formed. In part, this is true because the context indicates other possible ties. Thus if the conflict is among parties with a common interest against an external power, an alliance between a weak and a strong partner is likely, but if the conflict is among the parties themselves, the two weaker groups will join together (Chertkoff, 1966; 1970). We may refer back to the earlier illustration. If A is stronger than B, B equals C, and B and C together are stronger than A. The coalition of BC is most likely. But if there is an external threat, then in a conflict between A and C, B might well join A rather than C in order to form a stronger front against the external adversary. This may be a component of an explanation of faculty siding with administration against the students when the university is also threatened externally.

Third parties are not merely potential and then actual partisans. Their intervention and active involvement is much more complex than simply choosing sides. Their intervention changes the parameters of the conflict and the possible payoffs for all parties. As the previous discussion indicated, third parties have their own interests and this affects their conduct in any given conflict. If the third party is sufficiently powerful relative to the contestants, it may be able to impose its terms upon the contending parties. The outcome of the 1956 war between

Egypt and Israel illustrates this. The withdrawal of Israeli forces from Sinai and Gaza and the stationing of United Nations forces along the cease fire line and at Sharm el Sheikh was the result largely of U.S. and U.N. pressure, persuasion, and inducements (Campbell, 1960, pp. 108–20).

NONCONFLICT DETERMINANTS OF OUTCOME

It might seem reasonable to suppose that the outcome of a conflict is determined by the struggle itself. But the relations between any two groups are affected by many factors and processes which exist before, during, and after any specific conflict. The outcome to a conflict is affected by other factors than those we have analyzed in accounting for a social conflict's trajectory. We shall review only a few here: the general level of resources, the alternatives available, and the social context.

Resources.   Many particular outcomes depend upon the availability of resources for their implementation. Without needed preconditions certain outcomes cannot be attained and maintained. Once those preconditions exist, goals which might otherwise be conflicting may be attained with little controversy and no nonlegitimate conflict behavior. For example, Cutright (1965) studied the introduction of social security programs in 76 nations. He found that the level of social security programs was very highly related to level of economic development (.90). Political representativeness also had some effect, particularly at the highest economic stratum; furthermore, politically non–self-governing countries lagged in the establishment of social security programs. Cutright concludes that despite great differences in ideology and political organization, actual activities of a government in the social security field are closely related to the complexity of the social organization.

Alternatives.   The outcome of any specific struggle is affected by the alternatives persons on each side have, as well as by collective efforts of each side to change the other. This is particularly the case when the conflicting goals pertain to the members of the conflict parties as aggregates. Thus, changes in the general employment rate, in occupational distribution, or in technology, have had profound effects upon the relative income, status, and power of American workers and managers, of blacks and whites, and of women and men. For example, the growing participation of women in the labor force is in part due to changes in occupational distribution—the increased proportion of white collar workers. Large short term variations have been due to major shifts in the availability of men for employment. For example, during World War II, women's participation rose rapidly only to fall precipitously at the end of the war. Similarly, the proportion of women making up the college classes rose rapidly during the war, as men left and as the colleges' need for paying students also grew (Millett, 1970, p. 76).

Social Context. Any specific conflicting relations between parties are embedded in a larger set of social relations. These may have the effect of interfering with the attainment of particular goals. Within a given social context, certain sets of goals are inconsistent. For example, there are incompatible components in the aims of racial integration and black separatism. For example, too, it is difficult for women to play all the same occupational roles as men while the nuclear family and the division of labor within it is structured so differently for men and women (Millett, 1970, p. 158). Similarly, there are contradictory implications between workers as subordinate employees and as a constituency electing or otherwise directing higher management (Strauss and Rosenstein, 1970; Kolaja, 1966).

All this means that there are limits to attaining any particular goal. It may not be attainable without reordering other aspects of the social context. In some cases such reordering may have to be massive and fundamental. Failing to make such changes, the specific goal may not be achieved regardless of efforts. Of course, there may be a variety of partial attainments and success among some segments of a population for certain periods of time. The point is that the outcome of any specific struggle is constrained by a variety of interrelations between roles and social patterns. It is not determined by the contending parties within the confines of their struggle as they define it.

ILLUSTRATIVE OUTCOMES

Many of the points discussed in this chapter can be illustrated by examining outcomes in the major conflicts we have been considering throughout the book. We will examine outcomes in the conflicts between workers and managers, blacks and whites, men and women, the U.S. and the U.S.S.R., and Israel and the neighboring Arab countries. We will not focus upon the outcomes to limited specific struggles; rather, we will look at some information about changes in the relative position of contending groups and discuss the variety of forces which resulted in those outcomes.

Workers–Managers. We will consider a few changes in the position of workers relative to managers as aggregates and as collectivities. We will also consider evidence pertaining to the possible role of labor militancy and trade union activity as a factor in the changes noted.

WORKERS AS AN AGGREGATE. One aspect of changes in the position of workers as an aggregate is the extent to which they leave it and enter the superordinate group. Mobility into the managerial stratum is not an avowed major goal of trade unions or of labor groups generally. Such social aims for the society as a whole seem to presume more ideological goals than the American workers have shown. Nevertheless, the wish for equality of opportunity, generally voiced in American society, does exist among workers and their leaders. Improvements in the relative position of workers presumably should ease their mobility out of the stratum, even if the improvements might reduce the pressure to seek movement out of the stratum. In any case, there is evidence that over the last three generations before 1950, the business elite has been increasingly drawn from the worker stratum; although even in 1950, only 15 percent of the business elite had fathers who were manual workers (Warner and Abegglen, 1955, p. 66; Keller, 1963, p. 307). Presumably the general increase in the standards of life of workers makes more of the children available for recruitment into the managerial stratum. Whether or not the trade union efforts contributed to that general increase of the workers' conditions is another question.

Another issue is related and also pertains to the diversity and ambiguity of trade union goals. That is, should and do trade union efforts redound to the benefit of all workers or only union members? It might be argued that this is a false question: whatever helps one helps the other. Undoubtedly there is a positive relationship between the two, but the relationship is not always perfect. Part of the issue here is the extent of unionization. Given the degree of unionization in different industries, trade unions have had little impact upon the relative inequality of wages among all workers—about 6 percent. This is the net effect of increased inequality among industries and decreased inequality within industries (Lewis, 1963, pp. 292–95).

WORKERS AS A COLLECTIVITY. The primary goals of trade unions have been to improve their members' working conditions and to raise their wages. Undoubtedly, unions have led to improved working conditions in several ways. First, security against arbitrary firing and protection against harassment by supervisory personnel has been secured. Through the union workers have some group control over the pace of work and the organization of work activities. The extent of such control varies by industry and trade union; but the union effort played an important role in introducing such autonomy and promoting its extension so that it now exists to some extent even in factories which are not unionized.

The impact of unions upon the wages of union members has been extensively studied by economists (Levinson, 1951; Lewis, 1963; James and James, 1964). On the whole, studies of particular industries and of the American economy as a whole indicate that unionized workers earn higher wages than nonunionized workers. But the differences vary considerably, depending upon a number of conditions. As Lewis (1963,

p. 194) concludes, in the early 1930s, unionism may have raised the relative wages of union workers by more than 23 percent. But unionism had little effect during the inflation following World War II, while more recently it may have raised the relative wages of union labor by about 7 to 11 percent. Market forces as well as conflict behavior are relevant for understanding such differences.

Although manual workers are not organized in conflict groups in the form of trade unions, there has been a general increase in the material well being of workers in an absolute sense. Trade union activity has helped the development of worker autonomy within the workplace. Such changes in the condition of workers might be reflected in a changing status of manual workers in general. There is some evidence of a small change of this sort. Hodge, Siegel, and Rossi (1966) compared the prestige of many occupations assessed in 1947 and 1963. They found that blue collar work in general and particularly dead-end jobs had increased in general prestige more than had white collar work.

Given the modest goals of most trade unions, they have made some progress toward their realization, if assessed over a period of a few decades. More fundamental changes in the structure of the economy, the role of workers in it, and income differentials between workers and managers, were not sought by most trade unions and did not occur.

University Students–Administrators.   College and university-based student conflicts of the 1960s were largely directed at collective goals. While students have been engaged in conflicts about community, national and international issues, we will restrict our analysis to outcomes of struggles within colleges and universities. Some conflicts were about the role of the university in national and neighborhood affairs. For example, university investment policies and research activities were disputed as was university expansion displacing poor people in the surrounding area. Some issues pertained to academic matters such as the relevance or irrelevance of courses and study programs and the mode of teaching and grading. Another set of issues pertained to living conditions on college and university campuses, for example, regarding dormitory rules.

By the end of the 1960s, significant changes in these areas have occurred on campuses throughout the country. In dormitories, rules regarding hours for checking in, the right to have visitors of the opposite sex in the room, and the drinking of alcohol have been broadened or eliminated. Informally there is more permissiveness of rule violations (Young, 1972). There have also been significant changes in the curriculum and even grading procedures. Thus, special programs in black studies and new courses on women in society and on environmental pollution have been added to the curriculum on many campuses. Flexibility in the requirements for graduation has also increased, allowing students more course alternatives. In addition, in some schools, work done outside of the classroom in an intern capacity, is allowed credit and courses given in whole or in part under student leadership also are given academic credit. Overall, too, there has been an inflation of grades; "A" and "B" are more often received now. Finally, schools have increasingly found alternatives to the simple grading of each student in each course. One alternative has been for students to choose to take a course on a pass or fail basis. By the end of the 1970–1971 academic year, about three-fourths of the institutions of higher learning utilized the pass-fail as an option to some degree (*New York Times*, June 7, 1971).

Student claims about the direction of institutional policies in the neighborhood and nationally have not been so clearly incorporated in outcomes. Yet, the general direction of change has been that urged by student protestors. Several institutions of higher learning had research affiliated organizations which engaged in research under contract with the armed services; some of these affiliations were terminated. The recruitment activities of the armed services were often made to conform to the same procedures as recruitment by private companies.

Fundamentally, students have gained a more direct voice in the management of college and university affairs, particularly as it pertains to internal affairs. Thus, responses to a questionnaire mailed in September, 1969, indicated that students participated on the Board of Trustees of 20 percent of the institutions, 3 percent on a voting basis. In 58 percent of the institutions students participated in faculty curriculum committees, in 46 percent of the institutions as voting members (McGrath, 1970, p. 170). In only 5 percent of the schools, however, did students have any participation on committees pertaining to faculty selection, promotion, and tenure.

These changes were certainly partly a result of the student protests of the 1960s. In many institutions, student demonstrations sought to coerce a few of these changes. In many other institutions changes were introduced without widespread coercive action, indeed without much student demand, but in anticipation of possible demands. Perhaps administrative and faculty fears of student coercive actions hastened concessions not yet demanded or even widely considered by the bulk of students.

It would be an error, however, to regard all these changes as the product of a simple conflict between students and administrators and faculty in which coercion was the sole or even dominant way of changing the other side's position. First of all, in some degree the changes reflect widely shared ideas in the society, ideas which the students had helped formulate but which they derived their thinking from also. Changed social conventions about prescribing and proscribing personal conduct, then, would encourage students to think they should have more autonomy in their private lives and faculty and administrators to believe so also.

Undoubtedly, too, considerable mutual persuasion was attempted and some of it succeeded. Heightened interaction may have reduced dissensus.

Some of these changes also reflect nonconflicting forces. Shifts in the general level of the economy and in the population of students has fostered changes in the curriculum in a kind of market response. That is, faculty and administrators, taking into account student interests, shift course offerings and ways of teaching and grading to maintain enrollment.

It may be useful to compare, even briefly, these outcomes with those in European universities. At least in many universities in many European countries, even more radical transformations have occurred so that students have more power relative to faculty than is true in the U.S. In part, this may be the consequence of more radical demands arising from previously more oppressive faculty-student relations. The power of the professor over students and junior faculty was great. In addition, the greater pervasiveness of Marxist thought among university students may have fostered more radical student goals. Furthermore, the professors had power over academic affairs which in America often are in the control of administrators. The extra-curricular supervision of American college students has fostered a large administrative component. When American students sought changes, they more directly confronted the administrators; the faculty at times could mediate and gain power at the expense of the administration. In European universities, clearer separation of responsibilities and a reduced administrative component meant that students could and would make direct claims against the faculty or senior professors. A gain in student autonomy and academic power would then come at the expense of the professors. Nevertheless, some universities and some institutes within the universities have changed little and all remain in great flux.

Blacks–Whites. American racial conflicts in the 1960s have been basically consensual and about both collective and aggregative goals. We should consider some outcomes of consensual struggles and of dissensual conflicts as well. Let us begin by considering the data on the income of Negroes relative to whites. The U.S. Bureau of the Census (1971) provides a yearly series from 1950 to 1970 of the median family income of Negro and other races as a percentage of the median white family income. From 1950 to 1965, nonwhites had median family incomes which ranged from 57 to 51 percent of white incomes. During this period the percentages fluctuated with no discernible pattern (the highest point was in 1952 and the lowest in 1958). But after 1965 there was a small but steady increase; in 1965, nonwhites had 55 percent of white family income, in 1966, 60 percent, in 1967, 62 percent, 63 percent in 1968 and 1969 and 64 percent in 1970.

This increase in income of nonwhites cannot be attributed to any decrease in unemployment of nonwhites: during the entire two decades, unemployment of nonwhites was much higher than of whites but fluctuated with no particular pattern. During the 1960–1970 decade, however, there was a shift in the occupational distribution of Negroes. They increased their representation in nonmanual occupations and in higher manual occupations and decreased their overrepresentation in the laborer and other manual and service occupations.

Changes in status and power of blacks pertain more to collective than to aggregative goals. One indicator of the status of blacks is the opinion of whites. A minimal status is that whites accord the same rights to blacks as whites. That is, they think it is right for blacks to have equal civil rights. Answers to questions repeated in national surveys conducted in 1964, 1968, and 1970 provide some information in this regard (Campbell, 1971). The percentage of whites saying that Negroes have a right to live wherever they can afford to rose from 53 percent in 1964 to 65 percent in 1968 and 67 percent in 1970.

Increasing acknowledgement of the rights of blacks cannot be seen as simply a response to the civil rights movement and the protests by blacks in the form of riots and other forceful demonstrations. For one thing, there had been a constantly growing recognition of the legitimacy of the claims of blacks from as early as survey data on this point are available (Schwartz, 1967). Furthermore, there is evidence that the support for governmental intervention to gain equal rights for Negroes may have declined in the face of the most coercive actions. For example, the percentage of whites who said the government in Washington should see to it that white and Negro children are allowed to go to the same schools declined from 38 percent in 1964 to 33 percent in 1968 and rose to 41 percent in 1970 (Campbell, 1971, p. 130).

The political power of blacks as a collectivity in American society is still much less than their proportion in the population. Nevertheless, the last decade has seen important gains in the collective power of blacks, particularly at the community and city level. The changes are particularly noteworthy in the South. This reflects the changes in voting rights after the passage of the federal voting rights bill and the registration efforts of many organizations.

Growing numbers of blacks in urban centers and no easing of residential segregation (Farley and Taeuber, 1968) provide one base for dissensus. The polarization of society between blacks and whites foreseen by the Kerner Commission could be the consequence of black efforts toward equality and the failure to realize those aims. Actually, there is no clear evidence that this is occurring. Rather, there has been a growing acceptance of the rights of blacks. There seems to have been no dramatic change in feelings between the races even during the most intense periods of conflict behavior. It is discernible, however, that general feelings of approval of whites by blacks and of blacks by whites decreased slightly between 1968 and 1970 (Campbell, 1971, Table 7.12). Nevertheless direct personal interaction between the races has not decreased and at the level of friends has even increased.

This mixture of evidence is what one should expect between categories and organizations which are still in the course of great change. We cannot expect that all aspects of a struggle affect outcomes in the same direction. We must also ask about the possible effects of different modes of pursuing conflicting goals. Some of the changes in the 1960s seem to have involved conversion of whites. There may even be the emergence or reemergence of pluralist values which acknowledge the propriety of ethnic groups exhibiting more autonomy. The emergence of such views is one way in which differences can be accepted without dissensual conflict and yet which reduce consensual conflicts. This is similar to norms of tolerance in religious conflicts.

Females–Males. The conflict between men and women has involved only a small percentage of each group in overt partisan activities. But the struggle has also been conducted at a more individual level within places of work and study and in the home. The aims, from the perspective of the challenging group, women, have been largely consensual, and perhaps more for aggregate goals than collective ones. We shall begin then, with a consideration of aggregate outcomes and review the findings regarding occupational, educational, and income distribution of women compared to men.

On the whole, the data do not indicate greater equality in these matters from 1940 to the mid-1960s (Knudsen, 1969). A slightly smaller percentage of employed women are private household workers or operative and kindred workers and more of them are clerical and kindred workers. But this reflects a changing occupational distribution rather than an upgrading of employment of women relative to men. Thus women actually constitute a large proportion of private household workers and of operative and kindred workers in the mid-1960s than in 1940. The shift has been to lower white collar work, not to professional, and technical work. Women constituted 53.9 percent of the clerical and kindred workers in 1940 and 71.3 percent in 1966; but they constituted 41.6 percent of professional and technical workers in 1940 and 37.9 percent in 1966. The earnings of full-time employed women also have not increased relative to men; indeed between 1939 and 1966, women earned a smaller percentage of the median income of men in nearly

TABLE 6.3 Percentage of Bachelors or First Professional Degree Awarded to Women by Year

1900	1930	1940	1950	1960	1965
19.1	39.9	41.3	23.9	35.3	40.7

Source: Epstein, 1970, pp. 57–58.

every occupational category. For example, among clerical workers in 1939 the female median income was 78.5 percent of the male median income; in 1966 it was only 66.5.

Women's attainment of higher education compared to men also fell after World War II, but it has been rising relative to men so that by the mid-1960s it had reached the level of 1940. As seen in Table 6.3, even in 1965, of all the bachelors or first professional degrees granted, women received 40.7 percent. As noted in chapter 2, the proportion of higher degrees awarded to women is much less.

The collective status of women has changed over the last several decades in some regards. The general acceptance of the propriety of women holding public office and of working for pay outside the home has risen. For example, one similarly worded question has been asked in national surveys several times: "If your party nominated a woman for president, would you vote for her if she were qualified for the job?" As shown in Table 6.4, the percentage of men who said they would was very small in the 1930s and mid-1940s; it rose during the 1950s; and then rose again in the mid-1960s. Among women, however, there also was a significant increase in the 1950s, but not in the mid-1960s.

On the whole, changes at the aggregate level in occupational and income have not shown any regular increase for women relative to men; indeed from the high points reached in the early 1940s, there has been

TABLE 6.4 Percentage of Men and Women Who Would Vote for a Woman for President by Year

	Women	Men
1937	27	40
1945	29	37
1949	45	51
1955	47	57
1963	58	51
1967	61	53
1969	58	49

Source: Gallup Polls cited in Erskine, 1971, p. 278.

a decline in many ways. This decline is part of the feminine mystique (Friedan, 1963). Many of the changes in women's role in the labor market and in the home are related to the societal context within which men and women have lived: for example, a depression and a world war. Some of these shifts in women's aggregate and collective status may have been a source of the sense of grievance which was the beginning of the Women's Liberation movement. At this point in this book, however, we wish to consider what discernible outcome there is to the struggle thus far.

There are a few indications that the declining position of women in occupations held and income earned may have leveled off since the mid-1960s. The percentage of the professional and technical workers who are women stopped declining and by 1970 was almost as high as it was in 1940. In 1970, 40.1 percent of the professional and technical workers were women (U.S. Bureau of the Census, 1971, p. 110). But the median income of women relative to men actually decreased in some occupational strata and only slightly increased in others, but not to the higher proportions previously reached.

A dramatic shift seems to have occurred in another sphere. One issue which has been pursued by several groups within the women's movement has been the reduction or removal of restrictions regarding abortion. Phrased most forcefully, this has been sometimes put in terms of a woman's right to control her own body. Until the mid-1960s there had been almost total popular opposition to liberalization of abortion policies (Blake, 1971). But, the proportion of the population opposed to more liberal abortion policies has declined from 91 percent in 1965 to 85 percent in 1968, 79 percent in 1969, and less than 50 percent in 1971 (*New York Times*, Oct. 28, 1971).

Certainly, such changes cannot be attributed solely to the conflict behavior of groups within the women's movement. A variety of other forces are affecting the relative position of women and men and even the degree of dissensus between them. Nevertheless, it is also probable that the persuasive and coercive efforts of women's groups have affected the views many men have of women and reduced the degree of outright discrimination in public accommodations, employment, and legal rights (Rossi, 1970). For example, the Civil Rights Act of 1964 prohibits discrimination based upon sex by employers of 25 or more employees.

Assessment of the outcome of efforts of women's rights groups is difficult because the current struggle has been pursued for less than half a decade. Furthermore, changes in the place of women in society are circumscribed by the extensive interrelations among many social institutions within which sexual role differentiation is embedded. Recognition of this is one of the bases for the radicalization of some feminist organizations.

International. It is absurd to assess the outcome of the struggles between the U.S. and the U.S.S.R. and between Israel and its neighbors in a few paragraphs. Yet some consideration of the outcomes is necessary. In the case of the U.S. and the U.S.S.R., at least, there has been a somewhat delimited conflict: the Cold War. However one would characterize the present relations between America and Russia, it is different from the 1950s. Assuming the present situation to be the outcome of the Cold War begun after World War II, we can consider a few aspects of the struggle's outcome. First, there probably has been a lessening of dissensual conflict as both sides have become more tolerant of the other's ideology and less insistent in making universal claims for their ideologies. This is probably particularly true for the Russians who have increasingly (although not always consistently) recognized that there are many roads to socialism. At the same time there has been generally increasing equality in collective power, status, and material well being.

These changes have not been primarily the result of the efforts of each side directed at each other. Rather, they have been the result of developments within each country and changes in the world system of which they are parts. Thus, the development of independent Communist governments, such as those in Yugoslavia and China, have not been determined by either the U.S.S.R. nor the U.S. Furthermore, the increasing role of many other countries in the world system reduces the predominance of the U.S. and of the U.S.S.R. These other countries include the developed countries which were allies and enemies of Russia and America during World War II. In addition, the emergence of the many newly independent and economically underdeveloped nations helped modify the view of the relations between the U.S. and the U.S.S.R. as a simple zero-sum conflict relationship.

Of course, the conflict efforts, even coercive and violent ones, of each party against the other are not irrelevant to the outcome. First, it might be argued that each side successfully deterred the other from using large-scale violence against the other. Insofar as deterrence worked it was because neither side pressed claims against the other which the other side considered warranted the use of large-scale violence. Neither side sought to destroy the other; neither was expansionist; rather both sought to consolidate and secure their world positions (Gamson and Modigliani, 1971; Ulam, 1971).

As regards the Israeli-Arab struggle, there is no mutually recognized outcome nor does one seem much closer now than it did in the 1950s. There have been, of course, three wars and much violence between the wars. Some specific gains were attained by Israel by each war: in 1948, independence; in 1956, the opening of the Gulf of Aqabah and passage to the port of Eilat; and in 1967, the occupation of the land to the west of the Jordan River, the Sinai, the Golan Heights, and the Gaza strip. Although Israel has thwarted its adversaries' aims and has maintained itself, it has not attained its own aim of gaining Arab acceptance of that.

There has been no alteration of goals which would yield a mutually acceptable agreement. The outcome that does exist is largely the resultant of mutual coercion. We should note, however, that the coercion each side has exercised is not simply the result of each side's military strength. The various partisans of the Middle East conflict have governmental and nongovernmental allies, based on religion, ethnicity, ideology, and balance of power calculations. Moreover, developments within each society affect the coercive efforts each can mount. As the figures in Table 2.4 show, Israel has developed economically at a much higher rate than the countries surrounding it. The power, status, and material well-being of Israel relative to its Arab neighbors has increased as a result of factors and processes aside from the conflict between the Israeli and Arab governments.

SUMMARY AND CONCLUSIONS

The indications of change in the relative position of different social units in conflict are not meant to represent a complete assessment of the outcome of a struggle. Indeed, the analyses in the preceding chapters have focused upon more circumscribed struggles than decade-long confrontations between entire social categories. What is intended, however, is to point to some changes and nonchanges and to point out ways in which the conflicting efforts of the contending parties have affected both. A comprehensive assessment would require another book for each case.

Even this cursory review of changes helps illuminate a few important implications. First, no one side determines the outcome of any conflict. As any group pursues its aims, they are modified in interaction. In unforeseen ways, pursuing one goal modifies the adversary and the group itself. The outcome embodies new elements unanticipated by either side. In ongoing social relations, these new elements often entail mutual recognition of the other side's claims.

Second, within any struggle, coercion is only one of the ways which are used to accomplish any changes. Persuasion and reward are inevitably intertwined and hence help shape the outcome. Coercion is particularly relevant to the power component of outcomes and especially to collective goals regarding power. There is another implication, related to these two: collective autonomy is more readily attained than a change in relative domination between major social categories.

Finally, it is important to keep in mind that the efforts of contending parties in pursuit of their goals do not themselves determine outcomes. Many other social forces and processes help shape them. There are non-conflicting aspects of the relations between contending parties which also affect their new relations as well as their old ones. Furthermore, contending parties are part of a larger social environment of other units and relations. Those, too, are important shapers of all outcomes.

In this chapter we have focussed our attention upon the termination and immediate outcome of social conflicts. We have been concerned especially with the outcomes relative to the goals of the contending parties. In the next chapter we turn to consider the longer-run consequences of struggles. This will require consideration, too, of unintended consequences.

BIBLIOGRAPHY

BARTOS, OTOMAR J., "Determinants and Consequences of Toughness," in Paul G. Swingle (ed.), *The Structure and Conflict* (New York: Academic Press Inc., 1970), pp. 45–68.

BLAKE, JUDITH, "Abortion and Public Opinion: the 1960–1970 Decade," *Science,* 171 (February 1971), 540–49.

BOULDING, KENNETH E., *Conflict and Defense* (New York: Harper and Brothers, 1962).

CAMPBELL, ANGUS, *White Attitudes toward Black People* (Ann Arbor: Institute for Social Research, University of Michigan, 1971).

CAMPBELL, JOHN C., *Defense of the Middle East*, rev. ed. (New York: Frederick A. Praeger, Inc. 1960).

CAPLOW, THEODORE, *Two Against One: Coalitions in Triads* (Englewood Cliffs, N.J.: Prentice-Hall, Inc., 1968).

CARROLL, BERENICE A., "War Termination and Conflict Theory: Value Premises, Theories and Policies," *The Annals of the American Academy of Political and Social Science*, 392 (November 1970), 14–29.

CHERTKOFF, JEROME M., "The Effects of Probability of Future Success on Coalition Formation," *Journal of Experimental Social Psychology*, 2 (1966), 265–77.

————, "Sociopsychological Theories and Research on Coalition Formation," in S. Groennings, E. W. Kelley, and M. Leiserson (eds.), *The Study of Coalition Behavior* (New York: Holt, Rinehart, & Winston, Inc., 1970), pp. 297–322.

COSER, LEWIS A., "The Termination of Conflict," *The Journal of Conflict Resolution*, 5 (December 1961), 347–53.

The Cox Commission, *Crisis at Columbia: Report of the Fact-Finding Commission Appointed to Investigate the Disturbances at Columbia University in April and May 1968* (New York: Vintage Books, 1968).

CROSS, JOHN G., *The Economics of Bargaining* (New York: Basic Books, Inc., Publishers, 1969).

CUTRIGHT, PHILLIPS, "Political Structure, Economic Development, and National Security Programs," *The American Journal of Sociology*, 70 (March 1965), 537–50.

DENNETT, RAYMOND AND JOSEPH E. JOHNSON (eds.), *Negotiating with the Russians* (Boston: World Peace Foundation, 1951).

EPSTEIN, CYNTHIA FUCHS, *Woman's Place: Options and Limits in Professional Careers* (Berkeley: University of California Press, 1970).

ERSKINE, HAZEL, "The Polls: Demonstrations and Race Riots," *The Public Opinion Quarterly*, 31 (Winter 1967/1968), 655–77.

———, "The Polls: Women's Role," *Public Opinion Quarterly*, 35 (Summer 1971), 275–90.

FARLEY, REYNOLDS AND KARL E. TAEUBER, "Population Trends and Residential Segregation since 1960," *Science*, 159 (March 1, 1968), 953–56.

FLEXNER, ELEANOR, *Century of Struggle* (Cambridge, Mass.: Harvard University Press, 1959).

FOX, WILLIAM T. R., "The Causes of Peace and Conditions of War," *The Annals of the American Academy of Political and Social Science*, 392 (November 1970), 1–13.

FRIEDAN, BETTY, *The Feminine Mystique* (New York: W. W. Norton & Company, Inc., 1963).

FRIEDMAN, JULIAN R., CHRISTOPHER BLADEN, AND STEVEN ROSEN (eds.), *Alliance in International Politics* (Boston: Allyn & Bacon, Inc., 1970).

GAMSON, WILLIAM A., "Experimental Test of a Theory of Coalition Formation," *American Sociological Review*, 26 (August 1961a), 565–73.

———, "A Theory of Coalition Formation," *American Sociological Review*, 26 (June 1961b), 373–82.

GAMSON, WILLIAM A. AND ANDRE MODIGLIANI, *Untangling the Cold War.* (Boston: Little, Brown and Company, 1971).

GROENNINGS, SVEN, E. W. KELLEY, AND MICHAEL LEISERSON (eds.), *The Study of Coalition Behavior: Theoretical Perspectives and Cases from Four Continents* (New York: Holt, Rinehart & Winston, Inc., 1970).

GROSS, FELIKS, *World Politics and Tension Areas* (New York: New York University Press, 1966).

GURR, TED ROBERT, *Why Men Rebel* (Princeton, N.J.: Princeton University Press, 1970).

HINCKLE, WARREN AND DAVID WELSH, "The Battles of Selma," in Walt Anderson (ed.), *The Age of Protest* (Pacific Palisades, Calif.: Goodyear Publishing Company, 1969), pp. 100–109.

HODGE, ROBERT W., PAUL M. SIEGEL AND PETER H. ROSSI, "Occupational Prestige in the United States: 1925–1963," in R. Bendix and S. M. Lipset (eds.), *Class Status and Power* (New York: The Free Press, 1966), pp. 322–34.

HOLSTI, K. J., "Resolving International Conflicts: A Taxonomy of Behavior and Some Figures," *Journal of Conflict Resolution*, 10 (September 1966), 272–96.

IKLE, FRED CHARLES, *Every War Must End* (New York: Columbia University Press, 1971).

JACKSON, ELMORE, *Meeting of Minds: A Way of Peace through Mediation* (New York: McGraw-Hill Book Company, 1952).

JAMES, RALPH AND ESTELLE JAMES, "Hoffa's Impact on Teamster Wages," *Industrial Relations*, 4 (October 1964), 60–76.

JENSEN, LLOYD, "Military Capabilities and Bargaining Behavior," *The Journal of Conflict Resolution*, 9 (June 1965), 155–63.

KELLER, SUZANNE, *Beyond the Ruling Class* (New York: Random House, Inc., 1963).

KELLOR, FRANCES, *American Arbitration: Its History, Functions and Achievements* (New York: Harper and Brothers, 1948).

KERR, CLARK, "The Trade Union Movement and the Redistribution of Power in Postwar Germany," *The Quarterly Journal of Economics*, 68 (November 1954), 535–64.

KNUDSEN, DEAN D., "The Declining Status of Women: Popular Myths and the Failure of Functionalist Thought," *Social Forces*, 48 (December 1969), 183–93.

KOLAJA, JERI, *Workers' Councils: The Yugoslav Experience* (New York: Frederick A. Praeger, Inc., 1966).

LAMMERS, CORNELIUS J., "Strikes and Mutinies: A Comparative Study of Organizational Conflicts Between Rulers and Ruled," *Administrative Quarterly*, 14 (December 1969), 558–72.

LEVINSON, HAROLD M., "Unionism, Wage Trends, and Income Distribution, 1914–1947," *Michigan Business Studies*, 10, No. 1 (Ann Arbor: Bureau of Business Research, Graduate School of Business, University of Michigan, 1951).

LEWIS, H. GREGG, *Unionism and Relative Wages in the United States* (Chicago: University of Chicago Press, 1963).

McGRATH, EARL J., *Should Students Share the Power?* (Philadelphia: Temple University Press, 1970).

McPHERSON, WILLIAM H., "Codetermination: Germany's Move toward a New Economy," *Industrial and Labor Relations Review*, 5 (October 1951), 20–32.

MEIER, VIKTOR, *Das Neue Jugoslawische Wirtschafts-system* (Zurich: Polygraphischer Verlag, 1956).

MILLETT, KATE, *Sexual Politics* (Garden City, N.Y.: Doubleday & Company, Inc., 1970).

MORGAN, WILLIAM R., "Faculty Mediation of Student War Protests," in Julian Foster and Durward Long (eds.), *Protest! Student Activism in America* (New York: William Morrow & Co., Inc., 1970), pp. 365–82.

MORLEY, IAN E. AND GEOFFREY M. STEPHENSON, "Interpersonal and Inter-Party Exchange: A Laboratory Simulation of an Industrial Negotiation at the Plant Level," *British Journal of Psychology*, 60, No. 4 (1969), 543–45.

MOSLEY, PHILIP E., "Some Soviet Techniques of Negotiation," pp. 271–303 in Raymond Dennett and Joseph E. Johnson (eds.), *Negotiating with the Russians* (Boston: World Peace Foundation, 1951).

MYRDAL, GUNNAR, *An American Dilemma* (New York: Harper and Brothers, 1944).

POTTHOFF, ERICH, "Zur Geschichte der Montan-Mitbestimmung," *Gewerkschaftlichen Monatshefte*, Nos. 3, 4, and 5 (1955).

RADER, DOTSON AND CRAIG ANDERSON, "Rebellion at Columbia," in Walt Anderson (ed.), *The Age of Protest* (Pacific Palisades, Calif.: Goodyear Publishing Company, 1969), pp. 67–72.

RIKER, WILLIAM H., *The Theory of Political Coalitions* (New Haven, Conn.: Yale University Press, 1962).

ROSSI, ALICE S., "Women—Terms of Liberation," *Dissent* (November-December 1970), 531–41.

RUDD, MARK, "We Want Revolution," *Saturday Evening Post,* as reprinted in William Lutz and Harry Brent (eds.), *On Revolution* (Cambridge, Mass.: Winthrop Publishers, 1968), pp. 319–22.

SAWYER, JACK AND HAROLD GUETZKOW, "Bargaining and Negotiation in International Relations," in Herbert C. Kelman (ed.), *International Behavior* (New York: Holt, Rinehart & Winston, Inc., 1965), pp. 466–520.

SCHELLING, THOMAS C., *The Strategy of Conflict* (Cambridge, Mass.: Harvard University Press, 1960).

SCHWARTZ, MILDRED, *Trends in White Attitudes toward Negroes* (Chicago: National Opinion Research Center, 1967).

SHEATSLEY, PAUL B., "White Attitudes Toward the Negro," *Daedalus,* 95 (Winter 1966), 217–38.

SIEGEL, BERNARD J., "Defensive Cultural Adaptation," in Hugh Davis Graham and Ted Robert Gurr (eds.), *Violence in America* (New York: Bantam Books, 1969), pp. 764–87.

SIEGEL, SIDNEY AND LAWRENCE FOURAKER, *Bargaining and Group Decision-Making* (New York: McGraw-Hill Book Company, 1960).

SMELSER, NEIL J., *Theory of Collective Behavior* (New York: The Free Press, 1963).

SLOTKIN, JAMES S., *The Peyote Religion: A Study in Indian-White Relations* (New York: The Free Press, 1956).

STARNER, FRANCES LUCILLE, *Magsaysay and the Philippine Peasantry* (Berkeley: University of California Press, 1961).

STRAUSS, GEORGE AND ELIEZER ROSENSTEIN, "Workers' Participation: A Critical View," *Industrial Relations,* 9 (February 1970), 197–214.

TAFT, PHILIP AND PHILIP ROSS, "American Labor Violence: Its Causes, Character, and Outcome," pp. 281–395 in Hugh Davis Graham and Ted Robert Gurr (eds.), *Violence in America* (New York: Bantam Books, 1969).

TAYLOR, HOWARD F., *Balance in Small Groups* (New York: Van Nostrand Reinhold, 1970).

ULAM, ADAM B., *The Rivals: America and Russia Since World War II* (New York: The Viking Press, 1971).

U.S. Bureau of the Census, *Current Population Reports,* Series P-60, No. 80, "Income in 1970 of Families and Persons in the United States," (Washington, D.C.: U.S. Government Printing Office, 1971).

————, *Statistical Abstract of the United States: 1971,* 92nd ed. (Washington, D.C.: U.S. Government Printing Office, 1971).

WARD, BENJAMIN, "Worker's Management in Yugoslavia," *The Journal of Political Economy,* 65 (October 1957), 373–86.

WARNER, W. LLOYD AND JAMES C. ABEGGLEN, *Occupational Mobility in American Business and Industry, 1928–1952* (Minneapolis: University of Minnesota Press, 1955).

WENCES, ROSALIO AND HAROLD J. ABRAMSON, "Faculty Opinion on the Issues of Job Placement and Dissent in the University," *Social Problems,* 18 (Summer 1970), 27–38.

YOUNG, ESTHER N., "Sources of Campus Control Agents' Orientations Toward Drug Use," unpublished Ph.D. dissertation, Department of Sociology, Syracuse University, 1972.

chapter seven

Consequences
of Social Conflicts

Having mentioned several times that the development of conflicts are never completely anticipated by either side in a struggle, we must finally turn our attention to the unintended consequences of social conflicts. In this chapter we will examine the long-run and indirect consequences of specific social conflicts. It should be noted that I am using the term consequences, not functions. The point is that I do not want to imply that the consequences of a social conflict account for or explain the prior emergence of persistence of a particular conflict or of conflicts in general. Nor do I want to imply that conflicts arise and persist for the survival or equilibrium of a larger social entity. We will examine the manifold consequences of particular struggles. Of course, partisans may foresee some indirect effects of particular conflicts and this affects their choices of goals and ways of pursuing them.

We will examine the consequences of social conflicts upon: (1) each party to the conflict; (2) the relation of a conflict party to a third party; (3) the relations between the struggling parties; and (4) the system of which the adversaries are a part. We will focus upon two sources of consequences: the means used in the struggle and the outcome of the struggle.

One general issue is involved in several aspects of this discussion: the interdependence of different social conflicts. Each party to a struggle has constituent parts which themselves may be in conflict. Each pair of adversaries may, in a larger context be allies against another adversary. We must address ourselves to these complexities. Of special interest in this context is the possibility that external conflict causes internal dissension and division. There is even the possibility that internal discord *produces* conflicts with external third parties or that domestic conflict *inhibits* external struggles. In assessing and specifying such possibilities we will apply the concepts and propositions developed thus far.

CONSEQUENCES WITHIN PARTISAN GROUP

We begin analysing the consequences of social conflicts by considering their effects upon the adversaries themselves. We will consider the effects of the mode used and of the outcome achieved.

Consequences of the Mode. How a party pursues its goals affects the conflict group itself as well as its adversary. It has effects upon the group's feelings and evaluations of itself; it affects the culture and social organization of the group, and may affect the technology and general level of material well being. These effects also have consequences for the emergence and expression of internal conflicts. This is the major possible kind of consequence we wish to consider: whether or not external conflict produces internal solidarity and the lessening of discord.

STRUCTURE AND CULTURE. One consequence of a struggle is increased innovation, at least in the means used in conducting the conflict. This is most obvious in the case of weapons technology in wartime. Allocating more resources to the development of means of coercing the other side speeds the development of new techniques. This is also true of the development of techniques of persuasion, as in psychological warfare. In domestic struggles, too, innovation in the methods of waging the struggle increases in the course of a conflict.

The impact of manifest conflict and the coercive pursuit of goals is also notable upon the differentiation of each conflict unit. It has been asserted that societies at war become more centralized in power. Simmel (1955, pp. 87–89), for example, has argued that war tends to promote the concentration of power in the highest levels of government. There is systematic evidence consistent with his idea. Cutright (1963) studied the degree of political development or democracy in nations of the world between 1940 and 1961. Political development or democracy was measured by the number of years there was a parliament with more than one significant party and the number of years with an elected executive; let us assume that politically developed countries are less centralized. He found among countries of the Western Hemisphere and Europe that only 31 percent of the countries which has been invaded during war revealed political development gains while 76 percent of the countries whose territory had not been invaded in war showed such gains. Naroll (1969) studied pairs of conspicuous states of several major world civilizations. He found wars somewhat correlated with political centralization. It is also possible, of course, that more centralized states were more war prone. Ethnographic evidence from studies of preindustrial societies yield ambiguous results (Otterbein, 1968; Abrahamson, 1969). Certainly external conflict is only one among many other determinants of the level of political centralization.

Within a society, groups regularly engaged in conflict behavior might also be expected to be hierarchically controlled. But struggles with adversaries also can require constituency support and therefore widespread participation. Struggles also can bring defeats and adversity which would promote dissension and hence weaken oligarchic control (Barbash, 1967, p. 98). The various possible consequences of conflict may be the reason that Tannenbaum and Kahn (1957), in a study of four local unions, found no relationship between the amount of union-management conflict and the hierarchical distribution of power.

Conflict per se does not determine the degree of centralized control within the contending parties. Whether or not struggling contributes to centralization depends upon the characteristics of the conflicts: for example, their degree of regulation, the nature of the adversary, and the relative power of the parties. Thus, a group engaged in a struggle with a much stronger adversary and seeking large changes tends to develop an ideology and strategy of conflict behavior which require great membership commitment. Such organizations also tend to develop centralized control and obedience (Coser, 1956, p. 103). Revolutionary groups such as those in Czarist Russia are illustrative (Nahirny, 1962; Selznick, 1952).

The point is that the commitment and the allocation of resources in accord with the way in which a conflict is pursued has lasting implications (Russett, 1969). Herein lies one of the fundamental tragedies of social conflicts. In struggling for a particular end the means used can preclude the attainment of the sought-for goals. Thus:

> the types of personalities, as well as the forms of organization
> that usually emerge in a violent revolutionary struggle . . . are
> those which undercut the humanistic hopes of such endeavors
> (Oppenheimer, 1969, p. 71).

Violence and the suppression of internal dissent inhibit popular participation even after "victory."

The means used in a struggle have enduring consequences for the self-conceptions of the users. This is, indeed, part of the argument some people make to justify coercive action and even violence (Fanon, 1966). By such actions oppressed persons prove themselves to themselves. For example, some persons have contended that American black men will achieve a greater sense of manliness by acting with courage and bravado.

Of course, asserting one's claims for equality need not be done violently in order to demonstrate male or human liberation. In any case, clearly, the kinds of experiences which people have in the course of a conflict affect their views of themselves and of the world. It behooves us to examine what evidence there is about such possible effects.

In a series of national public opinion surveys conducted in 1964, 1968, and 1970, a cross section of blacks and whites were asked to say where they would put various groups on a "feeling scale," ranging from zero (very unfavorable) to 100 (very favorable) (Campbell, 1971, p. 141). In 1964 about half of the whites reported they were very favorable to whites and this declined to 39 percent in 1968 and 30 percent in 1970. A higher proportion of blacks were very favorable toward blacks and this proportion did not decline over this period; nor, however, did it rise (the percentage saying they felt very favorable was 65, 65, and 63 in 1964, 1968, and 1970 respectively.). Obviously, the interracial conflict behavior is not the sole determinant of such assessments. But it probably contributed to the decline in white regard for whites while it may have raised self-regard for some blacks and lowered it for others. A struggle and how it is waged has many consequences and the meaning depends upon the interpretations and expectations people make as the struggle proceeds.

It is important to study even longer-run effects. Major conflicts can have a particularly strong impact upon the age group which reaches political maturity in the midst of it. This derives from the idea of political generations (Mannheim, 1952; Heberle, 1951, pp. 120–27). The conditions of social life, the salient issues, and the means used in settling them have enduring consequences. Thus the American depression generation is relatively more class conscious than other generations (Leggett, 1968, pp. 90–91). A detailed analysis of generational experiences upon foreign policy views was made by Cutler (1970) using survey data from 1946, 1951, 1956, 1961, and 1966. The data indicate that views of foreign policy do vary with different age cohorts. Thus, the salience of foreign policy issues has tended to increase with each age cohort and is particularly high among persons who became 18 years old between 1914 and 1918 and between 1934 and 1938. Advocacy of war in dealing with international crises is particularly low for two age cohorts: those who became 18 between 1919 and 1923 and between 1924 and 1928; the World War I and World War II cohorts seem particularly likely to advocate war.

INTERNAL CONFLICTS. External conflict might be expected to lead to the submergence of internal conflicts; in the face of a common enemy, internal differences become less salient. On the other hand, it might be expected that external conflicts aggravate internal divisions and induce more open expression of internal discord. Evidence of both tendencies can be cited. Rather than try to resolve this issue by asserting that external conflict induces or inhibits internal conflict, we need to specify the conditions under which each happens. Both may be occurring at the same time but with varying strength and for different segments of the population. In order to specify the effects of external struggles upon internal conflicts, we should be able to apply the mode of analysis already presented. We will look at the ways in which external conflicts affect the bases for conflict, the emergence of conflict awareness, and the ways in which struggles are conducted.

External conflict increases the bases for internal conflict in several ways. Generally, insofar as sacrifices are made to sustain coercive behavior against an adversary, a basis for conflict grows. Sacrificing to exert coercion means that the people have less of what they want than they previously had. Furthermore, the deprivations are productive of conflict insofar as there are inequities in the deprivations among the members of a conflict unit.

Conflict behavior, however, need not entail only sacrifices from constituent members. We saw in chapter 4 that some conflict modes are themselves gratifying to some people. Aside from such considerations, the mobilization of persons for a struggle gives importance to everyone who is being mobilized. People who had been relatively marginal or relatively unimportant are now accorded more status and more equal access to other limited resources. For example, in World War I and II, American blacks and women radically improved their relative position in the labor market. They entered occupations which had been previously closed to them. Such improvement, it is true, may be seen as a relative deprivation by whites and by men. The invasion of preserves of superiority may be resented. This might have played a role in antiblack riots such as the 1943 Detroit riot (Brown, 1944).

The previously noted possibility that conflict increases centralization of power may also be a source of deprivation and hence of dissent. Insistence upon unity and support for the struggle against an adversary may impose severe burdens upon significant groups.

External conflict may also markedly affect the emergence of internal social conflicts. Participation in an external struggle may give partisans an increased sense of their own rights and ability to attain them. Fighting one battle may give them the confidence to fight another. Veterans of wars may reenter civilian society with more militancy than they had prior to combat. At the officer level this may encourage coups and at the rank-and-file level, increased militancy in defense of old claims.

The other basic way an external conflict may affect the emergence of internal disputes is by reducing the salience of internal dissension. Engaging in a common popular purpose submerges internal discord. For example, there is some evidence that during civil rights campaigns aggressive crimes by Negroes decreased (Solomon, et al., 1965). This can happen by absorbing energy and attention or by seeming to provide alternative ways of attaining sought-for ends. It can also happen by placing internal divisions within the context of a common enemy. When the major basis for solidarity is a common enemy, then hostility toward that foe will strengthen solidarity. Thus, military alliances have lessened internal dissension as the conflict with the adversary increases. This seems to be the case for NATO solidarity and Soviet-Chinese solidarity (Travis, 1970; Holsti, 1969; Hopmann, 1967). Of course this is true relative to the deprivations which hostility and coercion from the adversary may engender. External pressure places strains upon internal solidarity. But collectivities organized in order to confront an adversary tend to show decreased solidarity when the threat from the external adversary is lessened.

The balance between deprivation and presumed purpose helps explain the different internal consequences of limited and unlimited war. Smith (1971) analysed domestic responses to World War II, the Korean War and the Vietnam War. He studied changes in public attitudes about support for each war, changes in evasive draft behavior, and changes in protests and repression during each war. He found that during both the Korean War and the Vietnam War, but not during World War II, there was increasing dissaffection and dissent. In the Korean War dissatisfaction and delegitimation contributed to the support of McCarthyism, conservatism, and repression of Communist and allegedly Communist dissent. In the Vietnam War, the dissatisfaction supported violent and nonviolent demonstrations in opposition to the war.

Let us see if we can interpret these findings in terms of the ideas discussed in this book. First, the general mobilization of a total war, although entailing deprivations, is generally more equally deprivational than a limited war. Thus, in the U.S. there was a decrease in income inequality during World War II, but no appreciable decline during the Korean War (Budd, 1967). Secondly, the limited character of a war and the limited nature of its goals are less able to supersede domestic differences. That is, insofar as the struggle seems to be about issues which are not threatening to the collectivity and its members, then it does not reduce the salience and awareness of internal struggles. Neither the Vietnam nor the Korean War was viewed as involving the same threat to the nation that World War II was seen to have. The Korean War, however, was generally viewed as more justified and morally correct than the Vietnam and this may account for the differences in the degree and direction of disaffection, dissent, and protest between the two wars (Smith, 1971).

Finally, it so happens that the conduct of the limited wars was not generally viewed as successful as was the course of World War II. Of course, failure is reason enough to punish leaders and withdraw support. But in terms of the analysis we have been making, failure has other implications for internal conflict. The leaders and authorities generally are perceived as less competent. The chances of successfully challenging them is therefore augmented. In other words, failure is a source of grievance, does not compensate for deprivations, and invites the assertion of previously submerged grievances against authorities.

External conflict affects how internal conflicts are pursued as well as their bases and emergence. Often there is an attempt to stifle or suppress overt conflict behavior which might interfere with the pursuit of the collectivities' external conflict. For example, during World War II, trade unions were induced by the federal government to pledge not to strike. Nevertheless, strikes increased with each year of the war except 1942. Presumably, the relative power of workers was greater in this tight labor market. This would be an inducement to strike, as noted in chapter 4. Nevertheless, the great wave of strikes immediately after the war indicated that some stifling of labor disputes may have been accomplished. The upsurge after the war may also have reflected efforts to redress grievances by employers who felt they had been in weaker bargaining position. At the same time the inflation of the postwar period was another inducement for strikes.

The way in which external conflict affects internal conflicts, then, might be expected to differ with the preexisting discord and the character of the unit. In the case of nation-states, the political organization of the state should significantly affect the degree and nature of any relationship between foreign and domestic conflict behavior. This is the case. Wilkenfeld (1969) reanalyzed Tanter and Rummel's (Tanter, 1966) data on internal and external conflict behavior in 83 nations between 1955–1957. Two dimensions of internal conflict were distinguished: turmoil (riots, demonstrations, general strikes, assassinations, and government crises) and internal war (revolutions, purges, guerilla warfare, and number killed in all domestic violence). Three dimensions of external conflict were distinguished: diplomatic (number of ambassadors and other officials expelled or recalled), belligerent (number of antiforeign demonstrations and number of countries with which diplomatic relations were severed), and war (military clashes, number of wars, mobilizations, and people killed in foreign conflict behavior).

Wilkenfeld examined the relationship between external conflict and internal conflict in countries with three kinds of regimes: personalist, centrist, and polyarchic. Personalist regimes are dictatorial but less centralized than the centrist regimes; they are primarily Latin American countries. The centrist regimes are centralized dictatorships; half are socialist and some are Middle Eastern. The polyarchic regimes are in economically developed Western nations. Wilkenfeld reports the relationship between external conflict in one year with internal conflict one year later, and two years later. In countries with personalist regimes he found that diplomatic conflict behavior was somewhat related (.26) to internal turmoil a year later, belligerency was related to internal war one year and two years later (.37 and .29 respectively). War was related, two years later, to both turmoil and internal war (.17 and .15 respectively). Presumably personalist regimes are generally neither able to suppress internal dissension nor conduct popularly supported external conflict.

In countries with centrist regimes external conflict behavior is not related at all to subsequent domestic turmoil nor with internal war. Presumably centrist regimes are able to control whatever dissension external conflict might induce. In polyarchic societies, there is a small relationship between diplomatic conflict behavior and internal turmoil one and two years later (.21 and .19, respectively); there are also positive relations, although even smaller, between belligerency and war and subsequent internal turmoil. But, there is no statistically significant relationship between external conflict and internal war; there is some indication of a negative relationship: diplomacy and belligerency are negatively related to internal war two years later ($-.15$ and $-.11$). Presumably polyarchic regimes may permit the expression of dissent about external policies and about other issues; but this does not escalate to internal war. Indeed, for legitimate regimes waging relatively popular foreign conflict behavior, the chances of internal war may be reduced.

On the whole, in the contemporary world, the relative significance of internal conflict issues and the strains which result for conducting external conflict behavior are such that external conflict behavior is slightly *positively* related to conflict behavior (Tanter, 1966). Foreign provocative ventures generally would *not* lessen internal discord. But the major point is another one. Whether external conflict behavior makes internal struggles more or less likely and severe depends on three kinds of possible effects. First, external conflicts may increase or decrease the underlying bases for conflicts within an adversary group. This varies, for example, with the equity with which the costs of waging a struggle are borne. Second, external conflicts may make potential internal conflicts more or less visible to domestic partisans. This varies with the nature of the goals in the external struggle and also with how the adversary defines the struggle and its antagonist. Finally, external conflicts may tend to induce or inhibit the use of coercion in waging conflicts. People learn from their experiences with external struggles and apply what they think they learned to their pursuit of conflicting goals within their own partisan side. Furthermore, leaders of a conflict group may be more or less permissive about the coercive expression of dissent while a fight is on. Ultimately, whether an external fight increases or reduces internal conflict behavior depends upon the balancing of all these kinds of effects.

Consequences of the Outcome.   The way a struggle is ended, as well as how it is pursued, has consequences for conflict parties. Let us consider how the outcome of a struggle affects a party's future aims, capacity to pursue them, and internal conflicts.

FUTURE GOALS.   The aspect of an outcome which importantly affects the nature of future aims is the conflict party's view of the outcome as a victory or a defeat. To oversimplify somewhat, a conflict party's goals may be extended or contracted. Victory may result in the expansion of aims or in the cessation of other demands. On the other hand, defeat may result in the abandonment of previous goals or their further expansion. For example, the victory of women's suffrage was more of a culmination than a stimulus for the women's movement of the time. The victory of the civil rights movement in gaining the passage of legislation making voting for blacks in the South more equitable was more a stimulus for further demands than a culmination. Defeat of Japan after World War II did result in the abandonment of its previous imperial goals but the defeat of France in 1870 did not make it relinquish its claim to lost territories.

Whether an outcome, regarded as victory or defeat, results in expanding or contracting aims depends upon how the outcome has altered the conditions which determine a unit's aims. The outcome may change the unit in ways which markedly affect its formulation of goals. Particularly important are changes in the collective identity of the conflict group, changes in the magnitude of the group's grievance, and changes in the belief that the grievance can be redressed. The content of the group's ideology and the specific terms of the outcome strongly affect the character of its future goals.

For example, a defeat which seems irreversible would lead to the abandonment of former aims. The belief that the grievances cannot be redressed may follow from experiencing a clear and crushing defeat. Clarity is aided by institutionalization, otherwise the coercive force must appear to be totally overwhelming. It is not the mere defeat that makes this clear, but the entire outcome and its context that underlie the recognition of irreversibility. Germany and Japan abandoned former goals after World War II because the changed position of those countries within the international system made the goals clearly seem impossible. Thus, too, in the case of the trade union movement, management's acceptance of employee rights to form trade unions and bargain collectively reflects the consequences of the outcome of a long struggle. That outcome includes legislative (and therefore governmental) support for collective bargaining and the power of employees organized in trade unions.

It should be recognized that a defeat in itself is often an additional grievance and the outcome the source of additional grievances. For example, the shame of defeat seems to require another battle and a victory in order to vindicate honor and self respect. This is the case for example among some Arab conflict groups vis-a-vis Israel (Peretz, 1970; Harkabi, 1970). In addition, the loss of territory or other resources may be part of the outcome. For example, Finland joined with Hitler's Germany to regain territory lost to the Soviet Union in the 1940 war between Finland and the Soviet Union. In ending World War II the Soviet Union obtained portions of Finnish territory. The Finnish leader, Urbo Kekkonen, however, told the Finnish people: "We must own our defeat to be final. The superior force of the Soviet Union is absolute and continuing; to harbor revanchist thoughts or indulge in open or secret scheming to regain lost territory means the destruction of our people" (Reston, 1970).

Although new grievances may be added with defeat, changes in the social structure and the character of the collective identity may insulate or diminish the grievances. The defeat is attributable to the now dismissed leaders; they bear the shame of defeat. Or the dominant group or class within a conflict organization is overthrown and the support for the former goals is not continued by the newly dominant group. Therefore victors sometimes try to alter the social structure of their defeated adversary. For example, efforts to democratize Japan and Germany after World War II by breaking the power of the military, large landlords, and industrialists presumed this strategy.

Conversions sometimes related to such structural changes also may lead to fundamental alterations in aims. For example, business managers may become convinced that trade unions are in their own best interests by reducing labor turnover and further legitimating the distinctive managerial role.

Even a great victory may be the incentive for an expansion of goals. The fruits of victory often seem disappointing. Having gained the long sought-for end, it does not yield the anticipated pleasures. In that case, aims may be extended. The partisans realize that they had set their goals too modestly. For example, in a newly independent nation the leaders may find many problems remaining and believe that political sovereignty is not enough; economic liberation from neocolonialism becomes a new goal.

CAPACITY TO PURSUE GOALS. As we have already suggested, a major component of a conflict group's expansion or contraction of aims is its belief in its ability to redress the grievances it has. That belief is largely dependent upon its capacities relative to particular adversaries. We must consider how outcomes affect the capacities of contending parties for waging future struggles.

Victory should strengthen a conflict group for new struggles and defeats weaken it. Victory, especially immediately afterwards, increases the commitment of marginal members to the conflict group; collective solidarity is increased and sense of confidence strengthened. For example, following the Israeli victory in the Six-Day War of 1967, Jewish support from other countries grew. Contributions, immigration and emotional involvement grew (Vocse, 1971). Victory may also mean the creation of an increasingly effective organization for the waging of conflict and hence the search for new goals to which the capacity can be directed.

But victory does not always strengthen a group for new fights. We must also consider how victory may weaken the capacity to pursue additional struggles. First, victory may entail burdens and costs which drain energy and other resources, making them unavailable for conflict. This can be variously exemplified. Student victories in gaining participation in the governance of universities then require searching for representatives, discussing positions, and attending what often seems like interminable committee and general meetings. Victory in international wars also may entail burdens of administering the gains which may not be fully compensated for by what is taken from the vanquished or what is made available for exploitation by the outcome.

A victorious outcome may weaken the capacity to wage future conflicts in more indirect ways. Fundamentally, the sense of grievance may be lessened by victory and therefore the drive for further pursuit of a conflicting goal reduced. In other words, if you get what you fought for, you do not need to fight on. Victory may even result in the lessening of collective solidarity, in the long run. This is particularly the case for consensual conflicts about aggregative goals. Thus, an ethnic group, having struggled for equal opportunities for its members may find that with equality members have lost some of their solidarity and sense of collective identity. In the U.S. successful assimilation of ethnic groups has meant such losses of identity. This need not be permanent and indeed through confrontation with other groups on ethnic lines we are witnessing a resurgence of collective identities on the basis of ethnicity.

Of course, victory always brings some disappointment, even bitterness. What was anticipated in the storm of a struggle must be purer and better than the ambiguous and complex reality of even a victorious outcome. Revolutionary leaders can look back with fondness upon the purity of the struggle compared to the drabness and complexity of governing. For all participants in an intense struggle, great hopes inevitably are not all fulfilled.

INTERNAL CONFLICTS.   Outcomes as well as the conduct of a struggle may affect the emergence of conflicts within one of the units. First, any conflict group is diverse enough that a particular outcome will benefit some members more than others and perhaps at the expense of others. For example, a collective bargaining agreement which gives all workers a fixed sum increase will improve the relative position of the lower-paid workers while an across-the-board percentage increase will benefit the higher-paid workers relative to those who already earn less. Either strategy pursued long or in an extreme form would create internal dissension and the aggrieved category might come increasingly to oppose the union leadership and that portion of the members which support it. Thus, too, racial integration may adversely affect those blacks who had a protected occupational niche within a segregated labor market. For example, public school integration in the South threatened the jobs of black teachers in predominantly black schools when universalistic evaluations of credentials were used. Of course, this indicates that other outcomes could be imagined which would not be divisive to the black community. The attainment of such outcomes from the adversary, however, may be more difficult.

Victory, as we have noted, may itself arouse internal dissension when the hopes raised in the struggle are not realized upon gaining the prized outcome. Revolutions, national liberation, participation in governance, or equality of access to previously closed occupations or institutions may seem disappointing in the cold dawn of their attainment. Dissension and revolt, at least against the leaders, would be one possible response. Systematic empirical data is lacking, however, on the extent to which conflicts are more likely after a victory than when the adversary was still engaged in conflict behavior.

Even without systematic data, it seems safe to suggest that defeat is more productive of internal discord than is victory. Not only does the defeated party suffer increased grievances, but the leaders are likely to be viewed as incompetent. Attacks against the particular leaders and sometimes of the stratum from which they come are likely after a defeat. The protests in the case of national societies may take the form of coups or of social revolutions. The Egyptian army officers who overthrew King Faruq in 1952 were at least partly reacting to the defeat suffered in the 1948 war with Israel (Walz, 1966, p. 79). Trade union leaders who fail to win benefits desired by their constituency are likely to face factional disputes and challenges to their leadership (Weir, 1970).

CONSEQUENCES FOR CONFLICTS WITH THIRD PARTIES

Conflicts between two parties also have effects upon each side's relations with third parties. Heretofore we considered third parties largely in terms of their possible intervention in an on-going social conflict. Now we wish to add the question: will a party which is engaged in a struggle be more or less likely to engage another group in another struggle? We shall consider the arguments for answering the question each way and then try to reconcile the answers.

The discussion will be limited to the ways in which internal conflicts may affect the emergence of external ones. We will not consider how each side in a conflict may be more or less likely to become embroiled in a struggle with third parties simply because it is in a struggle. We have already examined some aspects of this in the earlier discussions about the possible intervention of third parties, polarization, and coalition formation. All that needs to be added here are grounds for a conflict party to attack a third party. As already suggested, conflict parties would be expected to avoid involving third parties as allies of their adversaries. Nevertheless, sometimes a conflict party may attack a third party in order to more effectively combat its main adversary. A prototype of this is the attack of Imperial Germany against Belgium in order to fight France.

This discussion also excludes the consequences of the outcome of conflicts. The outcome's implications for conflicts with third parties are stated in earlier chapters of the book, once we read outcome to mean unit conditions which affect conflict awareness and pursuit. Now we discuss possible effects of the conflict when it is direct and coercive.

Possible Effects. There are a few major reasons why internal dissension may induce external conflicts. One idea is that leaders of a collectivity, challenged by elements of their constituency or seeing a strife-ridden constituency, would provoke or otherwise become entangled with an external enemy in order to rally support and achieve collective solidarity. From what we saw earlier, it is not at all certain that external conflict mitigates internal conflict; but perhaps leaders believe that this would happen and so use external adventures to get support from their constituency.

Internal disorders can result in external conflict by embroiling a third party in hostile actions with one or both contending parties. Thus, foreigners and their goods may be hurt, damaged, or threatened by a segment of another country and so entangle the remainder of the group to which the foreigner belongs. For example, in international conflicts, disorders or threats to corporate investments may bring intervention to protect citizens and their goods. Internal factional disputes may also mean that a group is neglected by its purported representative; consequently, it seeks its own redress of grievances against a third party. For example, a trade union group may feel that the union leaders are insufficiently assertive and it acts independently against the management, by wildcat strikes.

It is also conceivable that internal conflicts stimulate feelings of hostility which are generalized and third parties become targets for aggression. This, of course, is one kind of "unrealistic" conflict. Finally, it is possible that internal dissension so weakens a group that it is vulnerable to attack and therefore "invites" conflict.

On the other hand there are reasons to suppose that internal dissension inhibits the emergence of external conflicts and engaging in conflict behavior. First, internal struggles may so weaken a potential conflict group that it avoids confrontations with other groups. Second, internal dissension absorbs energies and resources with coercive efforts against third parties. For example, a nation-state which is plagued by claims for more goods and services by generally submerged groups may find that foreign wars draw resources away from home. Finally, internal dissension reduces collective solidarity and support for collective goals against any adversary.

Specification. The effects of internal dissension depend on the nature of the conflict unit, the degree of internal dissension, the state of relations with third parties, and the level of conflict behavior toward the third party being considered.

In order to wage vigorous external conflict involving organized collective violence, as in wars, the conflict unit must have at least minimal solidarity and internal order. There is a variety of evidence consistent with this idea (Broch and Galtung, 1966; LeVine, 1965). Wilkenfeld's (1969) analysis of internal and external conflict also gives evidence consistent with this interpretation. He found that in countries with personalist regimes, but not with centrist nor polyarchic regimes, internal warfare was inversely related with external war one and two years later, $-.15$ and $-.30$ respectively. Internal war, however, was positively related to belligerence (antiforeign demonstrations and severance of diplomatic relations) one and two years later, .28 and .29, respectively. Presumably in countries which are relatively weak, internal disorders may stimulate leaders to act belligerently, but not to the point of entering into military clashes and wars.

In countries with polyarchic regimes, internal war is not related to belligerence nor external war. Perhaps internal war stimulates and inhibits external conflict behavior depending on additional considerations. Turmoil, however, is positively related to belligerence one year later (.19) and to war two years later (.32). It is possible that leaders in such regimes are willing to try to use external conflict to counter internal dissension.

In countries with centrist regimes turmoil was also related to belligerence a year later (.28). But more strikingly, internal war was related to external war one and two years later (.32 and .43 respectively). In such regimes it may be that leaders become involved in external wars following internal dissension as a result of the regime's own provocation. It may also be that internal war invites external intervention, particularly in such societies. Furthermore, it is possible that internal war which is successful for the revolutionaries installs a more ideologically crusading regime and a more activist foreign policy.

In all these cases we are considering struggles which are hardly regulated. In more institutionalized conflict relationships, between parties organized for conflict, dissension within one of the parties stimulates more aggressive conduct if it is not so great as to weaken the party. Thus trade union factionalism generally does not lessen union militancy toward management (Seidman, London, Karsh, and Tagliacozzo, 1958). Indeed, union factionalism may lead to more external conflict than would be the case with more quiescent memberships (Ross and Irwin, 1951). We have previously noted some similar evidence indicting the same pattern within the civil rights movement (McWorter and Crain, 1967).

CONSEQUENCES FOR RELATIONS
BETWEEN PARTIES

Now we consider one of the fundamental issues about any struggle: how does it affect future relations between the contending parties? We are now asking about the consequences of how a conflict is pursued and of its outcome upon the continuing relations between the previous adversaries.

Consequences of the Mode. How each side tries to reach its goals affects the feelings the adversaries have toward each other. The exchange of violence in itself tends to embitter relations. This is particularly likely if the violence exceeds the conventional understandings of what is appropriate. Such feelings make a stable outcome less likely. An outcome attained in large part through persuasion is more likely to be stable. Outcomes reached through explicit terminating processes and which are mutually and openly agreed upon, tend to be more stable than outcomes which are only implicit.

The way in which a struggle is waged also affects how the parties will fight each other in the future. Whatever has happened becomes a precedent for its repetition. Having used violence once, it is easier to use it again toward each other. For example, Israel and Egypt are freer to resort to military violence against each other because they have done so in the past.

This is not to say that extreme coercion, if victorious, cannot so crush one side that the defeated one does not venture to contest the victor. When dealing with major social categories, however, even overwhelming defeats succeed only in demolishing particular organizations engaged in the conflict; new organizations emerge again. Thus, the American Railway Union led by Eugene Debs may have been crushed after the Pullman

Strike of 1894, but railroad workers and workers generally went on to organize again and eventually win political support to secure many of the goals they sought (Lindsey, 1942).

The means used at one time may be a lesson about what is to be avoided as well as a precedent for the future. Which it is depends on the assessment the parties make about the results of the mode used. This is discussed later in the chapter.

Consequences of the Outcome. The outcome of every struggle is the basis for a new one. Whether that new one emerges into awareness, what the magnitude of the issues in contention may be, and the means used in the conflict, however, vary with the outcome. We will limit our observations here only to the emergence of a new struggle. In other words, we are concerned particularly with the stability or endurance of the outcome. We ask: what about the outcome makes it more or less likely to remain as it is?

BASES FOR CONFLICT. In the case of dissensual conflicts, outcomes which entail conversion may mean the disappearance of the bases for a perpetuation or renewal of the struggle. Thus, if the bases for conflict had been one side's insistence that the other hold "right" ideas (namely its own), then if the other side conforms, the conflict has vanished. Similarly, if the side making claims upon the other is converted to the belief that the other side's beliefs are equally valid, or anyway valid for *them*, again the basis for dissensual conflict has gone.

In the case of consensual conflicts outcomes may reduce the bases of conflict by reducing the disparities in what is valued. An outcome, however, may also entail the loss of what is valued by one side and its receipt by the other. A victor, indeed, is likely to impose terms of settlement which make the defeated, at least initially, worse off than it had been earlier. Presumably that is an unstable outcome. The seeds of a new struggle are thus planted. Whether or not a fight breaks out, however, depends on the conditions which are relevant to the emergence of a struggle.

EMERGENCE OF CONFLICT. One way in which an outcome affects the likelihood that a new struggle will erupt is that conditions are created which affect the sense of grievance and the belief that something can be done about it. We meet again with contradictory implications of the same event. The imposition of severe losses in status, power, or material resources is the basis of a grievance and a motive for instituting a struggle, but it also reduces the chances of redressing the grievance and therefore reduces the likelihood of entering a fight.

A reason that imposition of severe sanctions is conducive to later strife is that the imposition of losses gradually dissipates, leaving the side which suffered losses with increasing ability to redress old grievances.

Or, if the conditions imposed lead to continuing deterioration, then struggles can occur from desperation. As Keynes (1920, p. 249) wrote of the implications of the harsh terms of the treaty of Versailles, "An inefficient, unemployed, disorganized Europe faces us, torn by internal strife and international hate, fighting, starving, pillaging, and lying."

Making changes which produce a basic grievance from the other side must be compensated by other gains or involve sufficient reordering of strength, that conflictful redress is viewed as impossible. Otherwise the losses and resulting grievance is the basis for a new struggle. This is reason for counterrevolutions. Half-won revolutions face efforts to restore the status quo ante. As a revolutionary group attempts to smash the bases of strength of its adversary, it increases their grievance. Considering only the stability of an outcome, the revolutionary group must balance the grievance it is creating, the effective power to overwhelm efforts to redress the grievances, and compensating gains to the aggrieved party in order to sustain the outcome.

Outcomes which introduce *major* changes in only *limited* spheres of the relations between adversary parties are likely to be turned back. Thus, black liberation after the American Civil War established legal rights for blacks but without effective economic and political power equal to those rights, they were lost in practice as voting was restricted and Jim Crow laws were imposed by whites (Woodward, 1957).

On the other hand, outcomes involving changes in only limited spheres may provide the bases for further changes which can occur without conflict behavior. This is more often true of aggregate goals. For example, blacks gaining more equal access to educational facilities in the 1950s are then more likely to enter occupations from which they had been barred by lack of credentials and by discrimination. Even the continuing discrimination, in the aggregate, is likely to be less effective. A changing occupational distribution of blacks then opens up other opportunities to use economic and political pressure, individually and collectively.

CONSEQUENCES FOR THE
SOCIAL CONTEXT

In addition to consequences for each adversary, for relations between them, and for third parties, struggles affect the entire system of which the adversaries are a part. The prevailing expectations, the basic rules for collective decision making, the relative position of major social groups, and nearly every other characteristic of any social system is markedly affected by struggles between component social groups. How the struggle is pursued and its outcome affects the social context within which the parties continue to exist. Conflicts are of primary significance in social change *of* and *within* a system (Coser, 1967, pp. 17–35; Marx, 1910; Dewey, 1930).

Consequences of the Mode. The mode used in a struggle may affect the larger social system by establishing precedents for future struggles. Violence in one fight often makes it more likely in another, even among different partisans in the same system. We noted the pertinence of models in the choice of means to pursue conflicting objectives, in chapter 4. Thus, in the U.S. in the 1960s, demonstrations and nonviolent civil disobedience became ways of pursuing objectives that a variety of conflict groups adopted.

But the modes used do not necessarily result in their continual repetition. Some modes can serve as negative as well as positive models. Having seen the losses suffered by the use of a particular mode, its use may be shunned by others. Thus, following World War I, the revulsion with war and militarism seemed to affect many sectors of the French, English and German populations as well as their governmental leaders. Following World War II there was a turning away from militarism, especially in the defeated countries of Germany and Japan. Many Germans, for example, were sufficiently disgusted with war and nationalism to look for its avoidance by lessening national sovereignty within a united Europe.

One kind of evidence of such turning away from war as a result of experiencing it might be found in survey data. Earlier, we noted that reanalysis of public opinion surveys conducted in the U.S. could be examined to discover if there were any generational effects. People who were young adults in World War I or in World War II showed no tendency to be pacifist compared to other generations; rather, they were more likely to advocate war (Cutler, 1970). Furthermore, this is not inconsistent with the evidence of a cycle in international violence. Denton and Phillips (1968) found evidence of an upswing in the level of violence about every 25 years. Perhaps the decision makers involved in a war particularly wish to avoid a recurrence and know better how to do so. The next generation of leaders are more ready to see war as a possible means, perhaps even romantizing it in retrospect, or are more prone to blunder into violence.

Obviously we need to know much more about the extent to which experience with a particular means, such as violence, establishes a precedent for its recurrence or a warning of what is to be avoided. The consequences of the mode are in some ways inseparable from the consequences of the outcome. The disgust with war, for example, may be greatest among those who failed most in getting what they sought from the war.

The long run effects of the mode, then, are related to the meaning and interpretation given to it. A particular effort is interpreted as having been a success or a failure and may have considerable consequences as a prevailing metaphor. For example, the way in which the English and French government leaders dealt with Hitler and the Nazis between 1933 and 1939 was generally regarded as appeasement and a disastrous failure. The metaphor of such appeasement dominated thinking about Hitler's Germany. The metaphor then played a role in the emergence of the Cold War between the U.S. and the U.S.S.R. It persisted and helps account for U.S. intervention in Vietnam, when the choice was viewed simply as between appeasement or military resolve (Hoopes, 1969, pp. 7–16). It played a role in English and French dealings with Nasser leading to the 1956 Suez attack. Other metaphors might have been constructed. For example, the need for collective solidarity and alliances even with lesser evils (e.g., the Soviet Union). Or for example, early recognition of the rights of others (e.g., German claims prior to the rise of Nazism). Or, for example, the value of gaining time by allowing the adversary to prove his unlimited aggressive aims (the war against Nazism was more popular and perhaps more successful than an early attack upon Germany might otherwise have been). These rival interpretations enjoy little credence. A particular interpretation of past events often dominates over alternative interpretations and then affects the interpretation of current and oncoming events. Imposing a simple analysis of a specific past case to a current one will inevitably produce errors.

The dominant interpretation of some events usually differs among the partisans. Blacks and whites tend to differ about the meaning and success of the urban riots in the 1960s. Students and administrators have their distinctive as well as shared ideas about the causes and consequences of particular conflict modes. These ideas and interpretations, as well as the events themselves, affect the working of the larger social system.

Consequences of the Outcome. The outcome of a particular struggle or a series of struggles may alter relations and rules for reaching collective decisions in the social system at large. For example, when workers through collective bargaining and political action win representation in the management of industrial enterprises, the governance of the factories has been changed. It is also likely that the role of workers in the larger society has been changed and it may even be that the rules governing other formerly less powerful groups will also be altered. Even without gaining managerial representation, the increased power of workers relative to managers has meant that they and their trade unions have more political power in the city and state governments and in the federal government as well.

The outcomes of social conflicts may have long run indirect consequences. For example, if workers can increase their wages they increase labor costs to the employer and this is a strong incentive for the employer to use labor more efficiently. Indeed, it is an incentive to replace labor by machinery. Labor leaders and economists have argued that unions contribute to the general economy by acting in ways which pressure management to introduce technical improvements and increase capital investments (Sufrin, 1951; Coser, 1967; Melman, 1956).

SUMMARY AND CONCLUSIONS

We have seen how both the way in which a struggle is conducted and its outcome have consequences for each party to the fight, the future relations of the contending parties, third parties, and the entire system of which they are a part. We have especially discussed the relationship between one struggle and other possible ones. We have seen that external conflict may both increase and decrease internal conflict behavior. The consequences depend upon the characteristics of the external struggle and how they affect the bases of conflict within the group, the awareness of the conflict, and its pursuit by coercive means.

Conflicts are important stimulators of social change. But, just as conflict behavior does not alone determine the outcome of a struggle, so do struggles not alone determine the degree or course of social change. Competition, cooperation, and many other social processes underlie social change. But conflicts are essential in changes pertaining to the reallocation of power and rules about how collective decisions are made.

BIBLIOGRAPHY

ABRAHAMSON, MARK, "Correlates of Political Complexity," *American Sociological Review*, 34 (October 1969), 690–701.

BARBASH, JACK, *American Unions: Structure, Government, and Politics* (New York: Random House, Inc., 1967).

BROCH, TOM AND JOHAN GALTUNG, "Belligerence Among the Primitives," *Journal of Peace Research*, 1 (1966), 33–45.

BROWN, E., *Why Race Riots? Lessons from Detroit* (New York: Public Affairs Committee, Public Affairs Pamphlet No. 87, 1944).

BUDD, EDWARD C., "An Introduction to a Current Issue of Public Policy," in Edward C. Budd (ed.), *Inequality and Poverty* (New York: W. W. Norton & Company, Inc., 1967), pp. x–xix.

CAMPBELL, ANGUS, *White Attitudes toward Black People* (Ann Arbor: Institute for Social Research, University of Michigan, 1971).

COSER, LEWIS A., *The Functions of Social Conflict* (New York: The Free Press, 1956).

————, *Continuities in the Study of Social Conflict* (New York: The Free Press, 1967).

CUTLER, NEAL E., "Generational Succession as a Source of Foreign Policy Attitudes," *Journal of Peace Research*, 1 (1970), 33–47.

CUTRIGHT, PHILLIPS, "National Political Development," in N. W. Polsby, R. A. Dentler, and P. A. Smith (eds.), *Politics and Social Life* (Boston: Houghton Mifflin Company, 1963), pp. 569–82.

DENTON, FRANK H. AND WARREN PHILLIPS, "Some Patterns in the History of Violence," *The Journal of Conflict Resolution*, 12 (June 1968), 182–95.

DEWEY, JOHN, *Human Nature and Conduct* (New York: Modern Library, Inc., 1930).

FANON, FRANTZ, *The Wretched of the Earth* (New York: Grove Press, Inc., 1966).

HARKABI, Y., "Al Fatah's Doctrine," in Walter Laquer (ed.), *The Israel-Arab Reader*, revised edition (New York: Bantam Books, 1970), 390–406. Originally published in December, 1968.

HEBERLE, RUDOLF, *Social Movements* (New York: Appleton-Century-Crofts, Inc., 1951).

HOLSTI, OLE R., "External Conflict and Internal Cohesion: The Sino-Soviet Case," in Jan F. Triska (ed.), *Communist Party-States* (New York: Bobbs-Merrill Co., Inc., 1969), pp. 337–52.

HOOPES, TOWNSEND, *The Limits of Intervention* (New York: David McKay Co., Inc., 1969).

HOPMANN, P. T., "International Conflict and Cohesion in the Communist System," *International Studies Quarterly*, 11 (September 1967), 212–36.

KEYNES, JOHN MAYNARD, *The Economic Consequences of the Peace* (New York: Harcourt, Brace and Howe, 1920).

LEGGETT, JOHN C., *Class, Race, and Labor* (New York: Oxford University Press, Inc., 1968).

LEVINE, ROBERT A., "Socialization, Social Structure, and Intersocietal Images," in Herbert C. Kelman (ed.), *International Behavior* (New York: Holt, Rinehart and Winston, Inc., 1965), 45–69.

LINDSEY, ALMONT, *The Pullman Strike* (Chicago: The University of Chicago Press, 1942).

McWORTER, GERALD A. AND ROBERT L. CRAIN, "Subcommunity Gladitorial Competition: Civil Rights Leadership as a Competitive Process," *Social Forces*, 46 (September 1967), 8–21.

MANNHEIM, KARL, "The Sociological Problem of Generations," in Paul Kecskemeti (ed.), *Essays on the Sociology of Knowledge* (New York: Oxford University Press, 1952), pp. 276–322. Originally published in 1928.

MARX, KARL, *The Poverty of Philosophy* (Chicago: Charles H. Kerr, 1910). Originally published in 1847.

MELMAN, SEYMOUR, *Dynamic Factors in Industrial Productivity* (Oxford: Blackwell, 1956).

NAROLL, RAOUL, "Deterrence in History," in Dean G. Pruitt and Richard C. Snyder (eds.), *Theory and Research on the Causes of War* (Englewood Cliffs, N.J.: Prentice-Hall, Inc., 1969), pp. 150–64.

NAHIRNY, VLADIMIR, "Some Observations on Ideological Groups," *American Journal of Sociology*, 67 (January 1962), 397–405.

OPPENHEIMER, MARTIN, *The Urban Guerrilla* (Chicago: Quadrangle Books, 1969).

OTTERBEIN, KEITH F., "Internal War: A Cross-Cultural Study," *American Anthropologist*, 70 (April 1968), 277–89.

PERETZ, DON, "Palestine's Arabs," *Transaction*, 7 (August 1970), 43–49.

RESTON, JAMES, "The New Political Pragmatism," *The New York Times* (December 11, 1970).

ROSS, ARTHUR M. AND DONALD IRWIN, "Strike Experience in Five Countries, 1927–1947: An Interpretation," *Industrial and Labor Relations Review*, 4 (April 1951), 323–42.

RUSSETT, BRUCE M., "Who Pays for Defense," *American Political Science Review*, 63 (June 1969), 412–26.

SEIDMAN, JOEL, AND JACK LONDON, BERNARD KARSH, AND DAISY L. TAGLIACOZZO, *The Worker Views His Union* (Chicago: The University of Chicago Press, 1958).

SELZNICK, PHILIP, *The Organizational Weapon* (New York: McGraw-Hill Book Company, 1952).

SIMMEL, GEORG, *Conflict*, translated by K. H. Wolff (New York: The Free Press, 1955); and *The Web of Group-Affiliations*, translated by R. Bendix. (New York: The Free Press, 1955). Originally published in 1908 and 1922, respectively.

SOLOMON, F., et al., "Civil Rights Activity and Reduction in Crime Among Negroes," *Archives of General Psychiatry*, 12 (March 1965), 227–36.

SMITH, ROBERT B., *Some Effects of Limited War*, unpublished manuscript, 1971.

SUFRIN, SIDNEY C., *Union Wages and Labor's Earnings*, (Syracuse: Syracuse University Press, 1951).

TANNENBAUM, ARNOLD S. AND KAHN, ROBERT L., "Organizational Control Structure," *Human Relations*, 10, No. 2 (1957), 127–40.

TANTER, RAYMOND, "Dimensions of Conflict Behavior Within and Between Nations, 1958–1960," *Journal of Conflict Resolution*, 10 (March 1966), 41–64.

TRAVIS, TOM ALLEN, "A Theoretical and Empirical Study of Communications Relations in the NATO and Warsaw Inter-bloc and Intrabloc International Sub-Systems," unpublished Ph.D. dissertation, Department of Political Science, Syracuse University, 1970.

VOCSE, TRUDIE, "24 Years in the Life of Lyuba Bershadskaya," *The New York Times Magazine* (March 14, 1971), p. 88.

WALZ, JAY, *The Middle East* (New York: Atheneum Publishers. 1966).

WEIR, STANLEY, "U.S.A.: The Labor Revolt," in Maurice Zeitlin (ed.), *American Society, Inc.* (Chicago: Markham Publishing Co., 1970), pp. 466–501.

WILKENFELD, JONATHAN, "Some Further Findings Regarding the Domestic and Foreign Conflict Behavior of Nations," *Journal of Peace Research*, 2 (1969), 147–56.

WOODWARD, C. VANN, *The Strange Career of Jim Crow*, rev. ed. (New York: Oxford University Press, 1957).

chapter eight

Essentials,
Settings, and Implications

We have traced one full cycle of any specific social conflict: from underlying conditions to its emergence, from the choice of the way to conduct the conflict, to its escalation, de-escalation, termination and outcome, and finally to the longer-run and indirect consequences of all that went on before. Now we can review the model of social conflicts as it was developed. We can present the interplay of stages and its recursive nature more fully now that the whole possible sequence is before us. We will discuss, too, the peculiarities of social conflicts in different settings. We can also point out the special features of the approach presented here and consider the relevance of the theoretical approach for different kinds of conflict as well as for social conflicts in general. Finally, some policy implications which derive from this analysis will be noted.

THE MODEL

This book has been about specific conflicts, about struggles, fights, strikes, campaigns, and wars. We have analyzed them in terms of a series of stages or steps. In a way, this may seem obvious. That does not make it true, nor does it make it false. Other persons must use other evidence than that selected here to test the ideas. The ideas cannot be tested unless they are presented in a refutable form. The whole framework cannot be phrased in neat propositions which might be proven wrong. The approach is too general. But two things can be done. First, the ideas can be stated clearly and precisely in an interrelated manner. Second, the peculiarities of the approach can be stressed so that the alternative approaches are salient enough to be compared with the approach taken here.

Summary Outline.   In this approach, social conflicts are seen as moving through a series of stages. Not every struggle goes through every stage. But each stage significantly depends upon an earlier one. Nevertheless later stages affect what is analytically prior. This recursive quality occurs through feedback and anticipations of later stages. Finally, specific struggles never revert to prior conditions exactly as they were. One struggle generally leads to another in an on-going spiral of conflicts. In this summary, then, we will review the stages of a social conflict, their recursive character, and their spiral continuity.

STAGES.   A full cycle in a social conflict consists of five stages. First, is the objective or underlying social conflict relationship. Second, when two or more parties believe they have incompatible goals a social conflict has emerged. Third, there is the initial way in which the adversaries pursue their contradictory aims. Fourth, the intensity and scope of the struggle escalates and de-escalates and then finally, the struggle comes to some kind of end and there is an outcome.

In discussing the bases of social conflicts we distinguished two fundamental kinds of objective conflicts: consensual and dissensual ones. In consensual conflicts, potential adversaries agree about what is valued and are so located that each believes that it cannot attain more of what is valued except at the expense of the other side. In dissensual conflicts, potential adversaries differ about what is desired or how to attain desired positions and find such differences objectionable. Note that these objective conflicts are between categories of people, not within the minds of all people in a social system. In other words, we are concerned here with the bases for group conflicts, not the strains or role conflicts arising from cultural inconsistencies. It should also be kept in mind that the relations between any pair of possible adversaries need not (and indeed never are) purely conflicting. Objective common and complementary relations may also be discerned.

A social conflict emerges when adversaries define goals which are opposed by the other side. These aims are based upon some collective identity and sense of grievance. These depend upon the underlying relations which constitute the objective social conflict. Only some of these become actualized. Whether or not the conflict emerges depends on characteristics of the social units involved, the relations between them, and their social environment.

Once the adversaries are in conflict, they select some way of contending with each other. Three fundamental ways of inducing the other side to yield what is desired were distinguished: coercion, persuasion, and reward. One conventional meaning of conflict requires that coercion, especially nonlegitimate coercion, be used in pursuit of the incompatible goals. According to the approach taken here, conflict is defined to exist, aside from how it is conducted. Furthermore, attention is directed at noncoercive ways of pursuing conflicting aims. This is possible because in any concrete struggle, the parties actually have common and complementary relations as well as conflicting ones. We analysed how the mode used is affected by the issue in contention, the characteristics of the adversaries, the relations between them, and their social environment.

Once either side has begun to pursue its goal in opposition to an adversary, the struggle between them usually escalates before the fight ends. Escalation means increased magnitudes of conflict behavior either in scope or in the way in which the struggle is conducted. But conflict behavior also may de-escalate. De-escalation usually precedes conflict termination. In an extended struggle, escalation and de-escalation can recur again and again. Movements toward escalation and de-escalation proceed through processes internal to each adversary and ones which pertain to their relations. Whether the processes result in escalation or de-escalation depends on the mode of conflict, characteristics of the adversaries, the response of the other side, the issue in contention, and the general context of the conflict parties. What is particularly important to recognize is that escalation is not inevitable and endless. Furthermore, the processes that result in escalation are dependent on certain conditions or inputs; other conditions or inputs would halt or reverse the escalatory movement.

The processes of escalation and de-escalation bring combatants to the termination stage. Termination may be implicit or explicit; if explicit, it may differ in the particular rules governing the terminating processes and in their degree of institutionalization.

After termination the last stage is reached: the conflict's outcome. We distinguished four major pure types of outcomes: withdrawal, imposition, compromise, and conversion. In any specific conflict outcome, these various types will be combined. It is important to keep in mind that the outcome of a conflict is rarely if ever the simple imposition of one side's goal upon its adversary.

Perhaps it needs to be reiterated: a particular struggle may end and the objective conflict remains, changed only a little. Furthermore, the outcome may be the starting ground for a new conflict while many other struggles between the adversaries continue. Nevertheless, it is necessary to consider how specific fights end and what the result is at that time and consequently. The partisans often make such assessments and therefore we must understand where the partisans think they are at. As analysts, we must make such assessments even if the partisans do not. Such assessments help us understand what has happened, what is happening, and what is likely to happen.

RECURSIONS. The discussion of stages and the general approach might be viewed as one in which conflicts flow like a stream through a number of locks, waterfalls, and pumping stations. The image of such a stream may be helpful, but it can be terribly misleading. It is necessary to consider the many ways in which the stages are interconnected and how "later" stages may affect "earlier" ones. One possibility, of course, is that each struggle is part of some larger one and each one is accompanied by several others. In that case, two adversaries in a dispute may be at a particular point in that struggle, but located at other points in other fights. Yet, where they are in other fights must affect the developments of each struggle.

Our consideration of how later stages affect earlier ones, however, is largely confined to a single conflict, regardless of how it is delimited. Such apparent reversals of sequences or backward flow of influence may occur in two ways: by feedbacks and by anticipation. Let us see how each operates between various stages. The links are diagrammed in figure 8.1, a more complicated version of the figure presented in chapter 1. First let us consider how the mode selected to pursue a goal may affect the awareness of conflict. One way is by anticipation. For example, the conflict mode members of one side think they will be able to use affects the formulation of their goals. Collective identity and the sense of grievance will be affected by the kind of behavior they expect to use in trying to attain their ends. In addition, the actual choice of mode affects the members' sense of grievance and identity by feedback processes. That is, having certain experiences in the initial choice of mode then effects the sense of identity, grievances, and formulation of aims. For example, people who demonstrate for the first time and experience physical violence from police are likely to feel more solidarity with their fellow demonstrators. Of course, continued escalation of such confrontations may frighten away some demonstrators unless the aims increase in importance to make the losses acceptable.

Similarly, the escalation or de-escalation of conflict behavior affects the initial selection of the mode. Expecting that the use of a particular conflict mode will lead to much escalation may inhibit its utilization. Anticipation of the outcome certainly affects the initial choice of the way to pursue a goal and influences the escalatory and de-escalatory movement. Anticipation of the outcome even affects the very emergence of a conflict. As we noted, insofar as members of a group believe they can redress their grievances, everything else being equal, they will try to do so. Undoubtedly, anticipations do not as strongly affect the formulation of

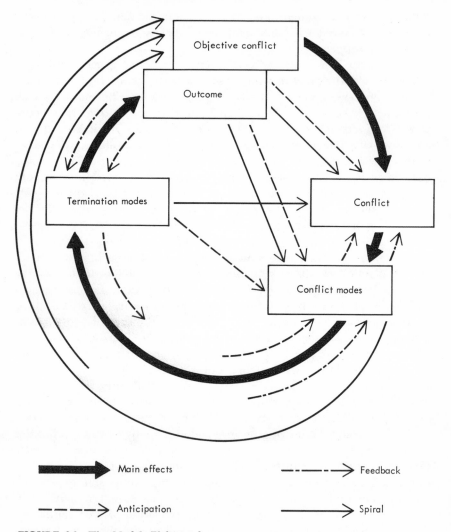

FIGURE 8.1 The Model, Elaborated.

goals, the choice of ways to pursue them, or the degree of conflict escalation, compared to more contemporaneous factors. The anticipated future is more easily distorted to be consistent with current circumstances than are current circumstances vulnerable to reinterpretation in the light of expectations of the future. Of course, this is not unreasonable: the future is even more uncertain than the ambiguous present.

SPIRALS. The outcome of every conflict is the possible basis for another struggle. But no struggle returns to exactly the same condition which existed before the struggle began. In this sense conflicts are continuous and even when they make a full cycle of stages and then begin again, they do so at a somewhat different level. See figure 8.2. First, an outcome, even in the case of a withdrawal of demands, does not signal a perfect return to the conditions prior to the assertion of the demands. A failed effort provides information and alters expectations of all parties to the struggle.

In the preceding chapter we discussed the variety of ways in which the outcome of a conflict and how it was pursued have long-run consequences. We saw how they affect the relations between the adversaries and the possible emergence of a new struggle. Such spiral effects are also included in Figure 8.1. Thus the outcome of a struggle has implications for the collective identity of the adversaries, their sense of grievance, and the formulation of new aims. For example, an outcome which yields a conflict group many of its goals may increase its hopes for further benefits and strengthen support for new conflict-behavior efforts. Furthermore, how a conflict came out has implications for *how* another one is likely to be pursued. The conflict group has strengthened or weakened confidence in the mode it used depending upon the outcome of its use, as the group interprets the mode's effects.

In an important sense the emergence of a new struggle helps explain what the previous one was really about. That is, if the adversaries define their goals relevantly to the major objective conflicts, outcomes may alter the conditions underlying conflict in ways which significantly reduce the probability or intensity of new struggles. For example, the increased job control and security won by trade unions has modified the objective conflict between labor and management. Some issues persist, for example, regarding wages and fringe benefits. Other issues may even become more salient, for example the dissatisfaction with work activities which lack inherent meaning and gratification.

On the other hand, some outcomes seem to be the realization of what had been sought; but upon attainment seem unsatisfactory. Then a quite different set of aims are formulated and a new struggle ensues. Such sequences indicate that the previous struggle had been "unrealistic." A partisan group may then be revealed to have been attacking a scapegoat. In a fundamental sense our assessment of whether a fight is realistic or not depends upon the consequences of the outcome of the fight. Depending upon how the adversaries then relate to each other we can better judge the appropriateness of their aims and their means of pursuing them.

Unrealistic conflict has two major dimensions. What the parties are apparently struggling about is not what "really" divides them and the level of conflict behavior is more extreme than is warranted by the sought-for goals. In the former case, one or both sides may be misin-

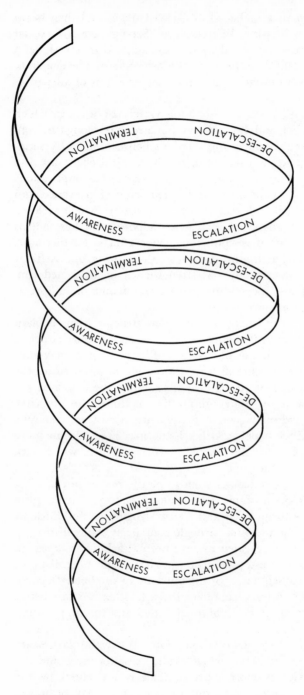

FIGURE 8.2

formed, misled, or otherwise inaccurate in their assessments of what divides them. In the latter case it is often a matter of conflict behavior escalating in a mutual interaction of fear, injury, and animosity. In both cases, accurate assessments can be most readily made after the consequences of a struggle are discernible.

Emphases in the Model. Sound and convincing as this model may seem, its value can be estimated only relative to alternative models. It is important to stress the peculiarities of this approach compared to other possible approaches. Five aspects of the approach taken here deserve particular attention: the rationality of conflict, the mixed character of any particular struggle, the importance of interaction, the significance of third parties, and the variety of means by which conflicts may be conducted.

RATIONALITY. Rationality is an elusive concept. A reader may judge the approach taken here as one which emphasizes rationality in a variety of ways. Without attempting a discourse on the topic, we should consider some meanings of rationality and in what sense this model embodies an analysis of conflicts as rational activities.

First, the approach taken here does stress that the partisans think they are rational. Indeed, as analysts, we must pay attention to what the partisans think they are fighting about. That affects how they pursue their goals and how the conflict will be terminated. If we become too subtle and devious in our interpretations, we can err seriously in understanding the development of a struggle. At the subjective level for each side, then, the partisans try to be reasonable. They try to calculate costs and benefits and therefore try to interpret and justify their actions so they are consistent with their avowed purposes.

But each party trying to be rational does not make for a rational outcome. That is, none of the parties may be really getting what it most prefers. An observer may judge the parties are not pursuing policies which make their goals more likely to be reached. This may occur because of two fundamental reasons. First, the development of a struggle depends on interaction. Neither side determines the course of a fight. Secondly, parties may be misinformed and lack crucial information. Therefore they do not pursue their self-interest in what the analyst would judge to be a rational way. Such partisan misjudgments, furthermore, may well be the consequence of emotions, of fears, hates, and loves. This does not gainsay, however, that the partisans are trying to make as good judgments as they can within the limits of their abilities. Nor does all this deny the possibility of analyzing how emotions play a role in defining goals and ways of pursuing them. Such analysis, of course, should be conducted in a logical and rational manner.

This brings us to another way in which this model emphasizes what might be called the rationality of social conflicts. On the whole, we are asserting that fights are about something. Conflict awareness, by definition, involves incompatible goals. But more than that, the notion of objective conflict presumes that there are bases for struggles even before partisans may be aware of it. If we as observers could make such assessments accurately, we would have a powerful predictive capacity. The framework for analysis presented in this book should increase the likelihood of successful predictions, but it is not sufficiently detailed to readily yield the innumerable predictions anyone might wish to make.

In this approach, then, there is a presumption that objective grounds of conflict underlie an emerging struggle. Such underlying conflicts continue to be pertinent when we want to understand the course of a fight and its termination and outcome.

The term rational is loaded with too many connotations and implications for easy communication. The main points of this discussion may be better summarized without using the word rational. We presume that an observer can make sense of the course of a social conflict. In doing so, it is helpful to consider that partisans are trying to be reasonable and even calculative in what they are doing. In trying to explain the course of a conflict, an observer should also take into account the conditions which each party faces and which then affect how the partisans feel, think, and act. In this way, we may understand how adversaries each reasonably seeking particular goals may individually or jointly find themselves in situations they would wish to avoid.

MIXED CHARACTER OF CONFLICTS. Any specific social conflict is not purely conflicting. The problem is that the word conflict is being used in two different senses. In one sense we refer to a struggle, fight, confrontation, or other opposition between adversaries with what they believe to be incompatible goals. In the other we refer to a quality or aspect of a social relationship. In other words, the relations between any two groups have conflicting, cooperative, accommodative, and many other qualities. We may abstract from that totality those aspects which are conflicting. We may also abstract a sequence of events which are regarded by the groups as a struggle or fight. In this book specific social conflicts refer to those sequences of events we call struggles, fights, wars, strikes, or demonstrations. Such sequences of events are between groups which have a whole range of relations, not all of which are purely conflicting. For example, during the extended student occupation of the University of Chicago administration building, some students slipped out, attended class, and returned to continue the sit-in.

INTERACTION BETWEEN THE ADVERSARIES. The emergence, development, and termination of a struggle are not determined by the internal characteristics of a conflict unit. They depend predominantly on the interaction between the adversaries. Neither party can alone determine the course of a social conflict. This is one reason why, even if each party tries to be rational, the outcome for the two of them may be undesired by both. We saw how this could be the case for an arms race, as discussed in chapter 1 and diagrammed in Figure 1.4. Each country, acting reasonably to prevent being at a military disadvantage to the other, increases its arms. Consequently, they are both worse off than if they agreed to limit arms. This is true, granted the relative values of the cells in the payoff matrix of Figure 1.3.

The importance of interaction in determining the development of a social conflict may be seen, too, in the way each party even helps determine the identity of the other. The shape and character of any adversary always is somewhat problematic. Even in international conflicts, the governments cannot be certain who their constituency is. The opponent helps shape that, as in the case of the Nazi-Soviet war.

The interactional character of conflicts also helps provide a means by which third party and contextual influences affect the course of a struggle. Each side is exposed to many aspects of the larger social context to which the other is exposed. Consequently, just as one side may model itself upon counterparts to act in a particular way, its adversary may expect such actions because it can also see how its adversary's counterparts are acting. This helps account for the sudden convergences in conflict modes. For example, when university students are demonstrating, the students at a given university may think it is appropriate that they, too, demonstrate. Furthermore, the administrators at that same university may even expect that "their" students will demonstrate. Such shared expectations may increase the probability of the event occurring.

THIRD PARTY EFFECTS. Despite the emphasis upon the interactional character of social conflicts, we are also stressing that the interaction occurs within a social context. That context importantly includes other parties who are an audience, potential allies, adversaries, judges of the means and ends of the parties to the conflict, and potential beneficiaries of the losses suffered by both parties in the fight.

In one sense or another, then, third parties cannot be neutral or without influence upon the course of a conflict. The very expression of disinterest communicates a judgment of the issues at stake and the acceptance of the likely outcome. More generally, third parties help define the terms by which adversaries define who they are, what they are striving for, how they should pursue their goals, and their expectations about the likely outcomes.

ALTERNATIVE MEANS. Finally, a peculiarity of the approach taken here is the attention given to non-coercive conflict modes. We have argued that persuasion and even rewards may be used to pursue aims in a particular struggle. This is related to the presumption that no struggle is purely conflicting. Furthermore, we have stressed that the conflict modes may vary in their degree of regulation and institutionalization. This, however, is more generally noted in writings about social conflicts.

SETTINGS FOR SOCIAL CONFLICTS

At the outset, we said that we wanted to analyze all kinds of social conflicts. We argued for the advisability of avoiding conventional distinctions among types of disputes. Rather, we outlined several dimensions of conflicting relations and of conflict units. It was then possible to consider what were the significant aspects of the differences and similarities among particular struggles.

In this concluding chapter, it seems advisable to explicitly consider the implications of various settings within which conflicts occur. Now we will utilize conventional categories such as international conflict, organizational conflict, community conflict, and class conflict. The attention is directed to the implications of struggles in settings as various as the world of nation-states, organizations, communities, and societies.

Community. The community as a setting for social conflicts refers to any territorially limited, relatively dense, residential area. Thus, cities, towns, villages are all communities. This list also suggests that the term should be restricted to territories with some kind of governmental structure and thus exclude neighborhoods within a city or town. Community conflict conventionally refers to disagreements in which partisans contend with each other using means which exceed the usual and legitimate ones (Coleman, 1957). We shall continue to use the definitions of social conflicts developed in this book, but the conventional meanings of community conflicts indicate some of the peculiarities of this setting for struggles.

PECULIARITIES. We shall first discuss what are the particularly important characteristics of communities that are relevant for social conflicts. Then we will consider their implications for the spiral of conflicts. Four dimensions of each setting will be examined: the nature of the social relations within it, the degree of organization of the whole system, the rules about conflict within the system, and the autonomy of the system.

Within communities people interact with each other in multiple roles, compared, for example, with the segmental and specialized role relations of members of most organizations. In addition, interactions are extensive, crosscutting, and involve large components of nonconflicting relationships.

Communities generally have some degree of organization and differentiation relevant to the handling of conflicts: more than in the world as a system of nation-states, more than in many organizations, but less than in most societies. The rules for conflict regulation usually restrict the means to nonviolent ones and to nonphysical coercion; there are usually even limits to verbal abuse. Communities, like organizations and unlike societies, have relatively little autonomy. Consequently, the social environment within which they exist can have important consequences for the course of social conflicts.

IMPLICATIONS. These particular features of communities have implications for each stage of community conflicts. The underlying bases for conflicts are innumerable, but none is inherently salient. The multiple crosscutting relations and the availability of means for reaching collective decisions tends to keep most conflicts only potential.

This makes problematic the emergence of struggles and the mobilization of partisans. Changes in relative numbers or power of particular categories of community members are often related to the emergence of community conflicts. Thus, a rapid immigration of young urban families into a village-becoming-a-suburb may require readjustments that the old decision-making mechanisms are unable to construct without high levels of controversy which the citizens regard as conflict behavior. Furthermore, the existence of differentiated structures for collective decision making, as in the form of governments, often makes the governmental leaders the targets for one side in the conflict. The struggle then may take on the form of a challenge to the authorities. It is also worth noting that the lack of autonomy of communities means that conflict awareness may be speeded and conveyed among communities by society-wide leaders, ideologues, agitators and others representing a segment of people in many communities.

The conflict modes used are generally nonviolent and even if coercive, have high admixtures of persuasion and reward. This is partly because there are collective decision-making structures and institutionalized rules for handling conflict. This constrains the means used and inhibits escalation. Moreover, the lack of community autonomy means that superordinate collective decision-making structures and possible third party intervention further inhibits and often enforce limits to escalation.

Organizations. Organizations as settings for social conflicts refers to large formal organizations such as armies, prisons, industrial plants, government agencies, universities, professional associations, and churches. There is specialized literature on each of these kinds of organizations and also some attempts to analyse organizations comprehensively (Blau and Scott, 1962; Etzioni, 1961; Caplow, 1964).

PECULIARITIES. As in the case of communities, we will briefly note some of the characteristics of organizations which have implications for the course of social conflicts. First, social relations within organizations are generally more segmental than within communities. That is, persons relate to each other predominantly in terms of their organizational roles. It is true that some organizations entail extensive involvement of members and relations covering a wide sphere of activities. But as these become extensive the organization merges or turns into communities or societies (Diamond, 1958). Even with segmental relations, there is often mutual dependence of categories of members. Such complementary and common interests which may exist, however, should not lead to any assumption or proof-by-definition that organizations have common purposes shared by all members.

Organizations vary in the degree to which there is differentiation and structures for collective decision-making. All organizations have such structures even if they are informal and minimal. Frequently the basic form this takes is hierarchal: decisions are made by those with higher authority. This authority may be more or less clearly delegated by a larger constituency of owners, contributors, or citizens, or even by the totality of members.

Organizations often lack any rules for handling conflicts aside from the procedures for reaching collective decisions. There may be appeal procedures for individual members (Scott, 1965). There may be some institutionalized conflict regulation mechanism, as in collective bargaining. But many organizations lack any devices for handling group conflict internal to the organization.

Finally, organizations have relatively little autonomy. Not only are member relations segmental but the members conduct only a portion of their lives within that setting. The organizations are generally very dependent upon the social environment. Usually any given organization is not the sole alternative for its members. People can look for other organizations in which to conduct their affairs.

IMPLICATIONS.   There are several implications for objective conflicts of these organizational peculiarities. On the one hand the segmental character of relations and the hierarchical nature of decision making produces relatively discernible objective conflicts. Demarcations are simpler than where multiple and crosscutting relations predominate. On the other hand the existence of alternatives may make possible a variety of self-selection and turnover patterns that tend to reduce potential conflicts. Thus, persons are recruited into, and remain within, particular organizations to some extent only insofar as they accept the terms of membership. For example, ideologically oriented voluntary organizations, obviously, will tend to select and be selected by similarly minded persons.

When it comes to emergent conflict the existence of clear categories makes lines of cleavage relatively salient. Collective identity is more easily developed. In general mobilization is less problematic than within communities. Given the common hierarchical structure, opposition is often directed across that line of cleavage, as in the frequent case of subordinates seeking redress of grievances against their superordinates. Struggles often take the form, then, of challenges to those in authority.

Given the power differences and the usual modes of reaching collective decisions, objective conflicts often do not become actualized. If they do, the mode used will often involve persuasion (appeal to the organizational charter and rules of fairness). The interdependence also means that exchange of rewards or bargaining is likely. This may be done collectively or individually (and hence on an aggregate basis). Furthermore, individuals can act on a private basis by withdrawing from the organization, insofar as there are reasonable alternatives. Such aggregate rather than collective actions are another way of inducing change and redressing grievances, aside from the use of group conflict (Scott, et al., 1963).

When alternatives are limited and the grievances severe, then the absence of institutionalized regulations regarding group conflict may mean the occasional eruption of high levels of coercion. For example, consider prison riots and naval mutinies. Yet, there are limits to the escalation of violence which are set by the more encompassing societal agencies and organizations.

Society.   Given the lack of autonomy of both communities and organizations, the society often appears to be the ultimate setting of most social conflicts. Struggles within organizations or within communities cannot be understood and their outcomes explained without recourse to third parties and the social environment generally. This is less true for society-wide conflicts based upon general cleavages such as race, sex, age, ideology, religion, and class.

PECULIARITIES.   First, societies, like communities, are settings in which people are implicated in multiple relations with each other. Crosscutting bonds and cleavages are inevitable. But, categories of people are large enough that such relationships are not interpersonally enacted. They depend upon intermediaries, impersonal communications, and symbolic identifications (Blau, 1964).

Societies generally have the most elaborated collective decision-making structures among the settings we are discussing. These structures are typically the governmental ones. A government claiming sovereignty over the society is a predominant condition. Within each society there are generally elaborate institutionalized rules about conflict. Finally, societies are relatively autonomous. The bulk of interactions are conducted within each society and governments act to preserve societal boundaries. Nevertheless societies are not completely autonomous: there are extensive movements of people, goods, and ideas across societal boundaries (Angell, 1969; Kriesberg, 1968).

IMPLICATIONS. The diversity of persons and the multiplicity of activities conducted within societies means that objective conflicts are infinite. The predominance of major institutions helps determine which are particularly salient. Generally the existence of government makes relative political power a fundamental cleavage. Furthermore, the considerable autonomy of societies makes struggles among component parts seem more like zero-sum contests: the separateness of a society implies that allocations of what is valued must be made within the confines of the society.

The numbers of persons within various categories are sufficiently large to make possible a sense of collective power and solidarity. This also helps provide a basis for the differentiation and the history needed to develop ideologies which help make conflicts emerge from underlying conditions. Governments, either as arbitrators or as direct partisans, are likely to be the focus of conflicting aims. On the other hand, some of the peculiarities of societies makes conflict less likely than is true of other settings. The autonomy and existence of other societies, who may be rivals or adversaries, and the often long socialization and indoctrination in societal identification, all contribute to some sense of common interest with others in the society. In addition, the elaboration of rules for handling conflict may reduce struggles so they appear to be games rather than fights.

For similar reasons, persuasion and the trading of rewards are possible and likely modes of conducting struggles. The existence of collective decision-making structures and the institutionalization of rules about conflict behavior generally limits escalation and helps restrict the level of coercion. Nevertheless, if the issue is one that does not readily fit into the extant understandings, fights may assume much less limited dimensions. This is particularly likely to be the case on moral issues. The relative autonomy of societies leaves the possible escalation open-ended. Outside intervention cannot readily impose a settlement. If it does not occur, the domestic adversaries may be free to fight it out; that is, escalation may occur until one side is fundamentally defeated. If intervention does occur, it is likely to be partisan and itself be the source of additional escalation.

The World. The setting for international conflicts is the world. The world can be the setting for other kinds of conflict as well: religious, racial, and ideological. Although the whole world is rarely involved in a particular conflict, this potentiality exists and we will briefly consider the whole earth as a context within which struggles are waged.

PECULIARITIES. First, the world as a whole is not highly integrated. Neither governments nor societies nor crosscutting identities or associations are world-wide in scope. Societies and cultures are diverse and much interaction occurs within rather than across their boundaries.

There is little institutionalized collective decision-making structure at the world level, even if some rudimentary procedures do exist (Aron, 1966; Morgenthau, 1962). Governments presume sovereignty and mutually support this conception. The rules for regulated conflict are not highly institutionalized, even when and where they exist (Kaplan and Katzenbach, 1961). Supranational structures where they exist are regional or restricted in spheres of activity (Etzioni, 1965; Haas, 1964; Kriesberg, 1960).

To speak of the autonomy of the world raises supernatural and other-worldly prospects. We shall leave those aside. The world then is completely autonomous, but most struggles within it are conducted in a portion of it and that part, we are stressing, is not fixed. It may expand to involve the rest of the world.

IMPLICATIONS.   Major objective conflicts may be less numerous on a world basis than in other settings. The lack of integration and of organized collective decision-making structures means that many of the things groups value and wish for cannot be given by others. But the central identification with nation-states within a system without highly institutionalized collective decision-making structures makes differences in inherently scarce resources saliently conflicting. It also means that mobilization of the constituency is taken for granted; yet this cannot be done completely (Kriesberg, 1956).

Within the contemporary world system, national governments are likely to view others as allies or as adversaries. Adversaries confront each other at least defensively and with fear. The prospect of efforts at aggrandizement by one or another side seems omnipresent.

The lack of integration and cultural diversity limits the use of persuasion as a way to pursue conflicting goals. The minimal integration also reduces the possibility of exchanging rewards in trade-offs. These conditions and the lack of institutionalized ways of reaching joint decisions makes coercion seem essential in the pursuit of conflicting aims. The lack of rules for regulating conflict behavior and the autonomy of the system makes violence and the escalation of violence likely. What makes such circumstances additionally frightening and frightful is the immense power of contemporary weapons.

POLICY IMPLICATIONS

In a book about social conflicts, I feel it is incumbent upon me to make some observations about the policy implications of the approach taken and the analyses made in the book. It may be helpful in this regard to state explicitly the general orientation underlying the analysis which has been made. Social life is viewed as a constantly changing resultant of a complex interplay of many social processes. People construct their own worlds. They strive and contend as individuals, groups, movements, classes and societies. In most relations they cooperate, exchange, accommodate, assimilate and conflict with each other. This welter is not without order and some stability. But it is an order that is not controlled or even fully predictable by any of the participants.

The analysis made in this book is intended to account for how people act in conflicts. It does not purport to state normative laws asserting how people should act nor "natural" laws asserting that their actions are determined. Presumably a fuller and more accurate understanding of how processes interact and how conditions result in particular consequences can affect the courses of conduct people follow. Adversaries may act as if they forget what they are fighting for (Ikle, 1971). But the approach taken here attempts to explain this. Partisans are not willfully unreasonable. They follow courses which seem best among the alternatives they believe available. Consider the use of violence. It often seems counterproductive and very costly to other values, for what is gained. It is frequently resorted to out of a sense of desperation. I assume that a more accurate and comprehensive view of social conflicts, by the partisans, will make their actions even in retrospect, appear more reasonable, rational, and efficient, than they otherwise would be.

One other aspect of the general view assumed in this book should be noted. Although the book is about social conflicts, I do not wish to imply that conflict is the paramount social process nor that specific conflicts are the only way in which change occurs or more equity is attained. First of all, many kinds of grievances are not amenable to solution by any conflict behavior; they are part of the human condition, at least under existing circumstances. Thus, natural disasters, many illnesses, ultimately death cannot be prevented—but their costs and probabilities may be variously distributed. Social life and equity may be improved in many ways aside from conflict. Cooperation among persons and the cumulative developments of material goods and of ideas may profoundly affect the human condition.

The perspective taken in this analysis has several general and specific implications for people in conflict relationships. A few will be singled out. In general it follows from what has been presented that people should not deny the existence of conflicts or seek to end them all. Such efforts in effect are often refusals to recognize the interests of other groups. Objective conflicts are omnipresent. If they are not manifest it may be out of hopelessness of the aggrieved party rather than the irrelevance of conflict. On the other hand, seekers after justice should not believe that conflict behavior is the only way to attain what they seek.

Even if conflict behavior is undertaken, the alternatives to coercion should be considered. Even if coercion is applied, the addition of persuasion and possible rewards should also be considered. Some combinations may be more effective for particular aims than the simple exercise of coercion or of violence.

There is another important reason to carefully consider the choice of means to pursue conflicting goals, the course of a struggle and of its outcome is problematic and in fact is ultimately unpredictable. Therefore, it is risking much to justify harsh means by pointing to some to-be-attained end. Since the final outcome and indirect consequences are unknown, at least the way chosen in trying to reach a goal should be minimally harmful.

Although the outcome of a struggle may be unknown, it is important for the partisans to consider what are the likely outcomes and indeed that there will be one. Keeping in mind that fights end and then there still is a future to be lived, should make partisans more sensible throughout the course of a struggle. Throughout a fight, partisans should keep in mind the broad spectrum of possible consequences presented here, the variety of possible outcomes, and of alternative ways in which they may be attained. In considering outcomes and consequences partisans should assess those they do not want as well as the desired ones. Thus, giving attention to unsatisfactory consequences would also suggest ways which might minimize those consequences without reducing the desired consequences.

In formulating goals for fights it is well to seek ones which are attainable. (Perhaps also limit them to those which are attainable by acceptable means.) Partisans should keep in mind that there is a fundamental relationship between the means and the ends. Thus, deterrence is effective if the demands are not too severe. The more stringent are the goals as far as the adversary is concerned, the more coercion may be necessary to attain them. This is one reason that autonomy from others is a more attainable aim than domination over others.

Generally, considering the interactional nature of social conflicts it is wise to take the role of the other side as the struggle develops. Sometimes failure to do so, perhaps out of passion, may enable one side to pursue its aim further than it might otherwise do. Taking the role of the adversary may temper ruthlessness and even faith and conviction in one's own goals. But, usually and in the long run, taking into account how the other side views a struggle will decrease the chances of mistakes and disasters. The outcome will be more stable. And from the perspective of the larger system of which the partisans are constituent parts, benefits are more likely to be maximized.

Means and ends which have as consequences the furthering of conflict regulation and its institutionalization should be considered especially attractive. Since partisans are members of a larger system of relations and since other fights will occur after each is settled, conflict regulation is important in the long run for all participants. The form and content of the rules regulating conflict, it should not be forgotten, are not simply neutral to the sides in contention. Increased equity as well as institutionalization of conflict regulations should be sought.

Peace and universal solidarity may be wished for but they are unattainable. People will strive collectively against each other. Such contentions are not without benefits to one side nor even to both sides in the long run. Nor, however, are they without costs and often great pain and anguish, and too frequently much death. We cannot escape the inherent strife of social life, but human knowledge and wisdom can help reduce its pain and increase its benefits. Let us try to contribute to such knowledge and wisdom. Let us try to act in accord with them.

BIBLIOGRAPHY

ANGELL, ROBERT C., *Peace on the March: Transnational Participation* (New York: van Nostrand Reinhold, 1969).

ARON, RAYMOND, *Peace and War* (Garden City: Doubleday & Company, Inc., 1966).

BLAU, PETER M., *Exchange and Power in Social Life* (New York: John Wiley & Sons, Inc., 1964).

BLAU, PETER M. AND W. RICHARD SCOTT, *Formal Organizations: A Comparative Approach* (San Francisco: Chandler Publishing Company, 1962).

CAPLOW, THEODORE, *Principles of Organization* (New York: Harcourt, Brace & World, Inc., 1964).

COLEMAN, JAMES, *Community Conflict* (New York: The Free Press, 1957).

DIAMOND, SIGMUND, "From Organization to Society," *American Journal of Sociology*, 63 (March 1958), 457–75.

ETZIONI, AMITAI, *A Comparative Analysis of Complex Organizations* (New York: The Free Press, 1961).

————, *Political Unification* (New York: Holt, Rinehart & Winston, Inc., 1965).

HAAS, ERNST B., *Beyond the Nation-State: Functionalism and International Organization* (Stanford, Calif.: Stanford University Press, 1965).

IKLE, FRED CHARLES, *Every War Must End* (New York: Columbia University Press, 1971).

KAPLAN, MORTON A. AND NICHOLAS DEB. KATZENBACH, *The Political Foundations of International Law* (New York: John Wiley and Sons, Inc., 1961).

KRIESBERG, LOUIS, "National Security and Conduct in the Steel Gray Market," *Social Forces*, 34 (March 1956), 268–77.

————, "German Leaders and the Schuman Plan," *Social Science*, 35 (April 1960), 114–21.

————, "U.S. and U.S.S.R. Participation in International Non-Governmental Organizations," in L. Kriesberg (ed.), *Social Processes in International Relations* (New York: John Wiley & Sons, Inc., 1968), pp. 466–85.

MORGENTHAU, HANS, *Politics Among Nations*, 3rd ed. (New York: Alfred A. Knopf, Inc., 1962).

SCOTT, W. H., ENID MUMFORD, L. C. McGIVERING, AND J. M. KIRKBY, *Coal and Conflict: A Study of Industrial Relations at Collieries* (Liverpool: Liverpool University Press, 1963).

SCOTT, WILLIAM G., *The Management of Conflict: Appeal Systems in Organizations* (Homewood, Ill.: Richard D. Irwin, Inc., and The Dorsey Press, 1965).

Author Index

Subject Index